The Turn to Gruesomeness
in American Horror
Films, 1931–1936

ALSO BY JON TOWLSON

Subversive Horror Cinema: Countercultural Messages of Films from Frankenstein *to the Present*
(McFarland, 2014)

The Turn to Gruesomeness in American Horror Films, 1931–1936

Jon Towlson

McFarland & Company, Inc., Publishers
Jefferson, North Carolina

LIBRARY OF CONGRESS CATALOGUING-IN-PUBLICATION DATA

Names: Towlson, Jon, 1967– author.
Title: The turn to gruesomeness in American horror films, 1931–1936 / Jon Towlson.
Description: Jefferson, North Carolina : McFarland & Company, Inc., Publishers, 2016 | Includes bibliographical references and index.
Identifiers: LCCN 2016037223 | ISBN 9780786494743 (softcover : acid free paper) ∞
Subjects: LCSH: Horror films—United States—History and criticism. | Motion pictures—United States—History—20th century.
Classification: LCC PN1995.9.H6 T695 2016 | DDC 791.43/6164—dc23
LC record available at https://lccn.loc.gov/2016037223

BRITISH LIBRARY CATALOGUING DATA ARE AVAILABLE

ISBN (print) 978-0-7864-9474-3
ISBN (ebook) 978-1-4766-2639-0

© 2016 Jon Towlson. All rights reserved

No part of this book may be reproduced or transmitted in any form or by any means, electronic or mechanical, including photocopying or recording, or by any information storage and retrieval system, without permission in writing from the publisher.

Front cover: Bela Lugosi and Arlene Francis in *Murders in the Rue Morgue*, 1932 (Universal Pictures/Photofest)

Printed in the United States of America

*McFarland & Company, Inc., Publishers
Box 611, Jefferson, North Carolina 28640
www.mcfarlandpub.com*

For Donato Totaro,
who inspired this book.

Table of Contents

Preface	1
Introduction: "Misery likes reality for company"	5
1. "Nightmare pictures": Thirties Horror and the Hollywood Film Industry	17
2. "Five reels of transgression followed by one reel of retribution": Thirties Horror and the Studios	39
3. "Brutality, horror and gruesomeness": Thirties Horror and the Hays Office	141
4. "Why should Cecil B. De Mille have a monopoly on torture and cruelty?" Thirties Horror and the Filmmaker	164
5. "A secure universe"? Thirties Horror and the Critics	184
Afterword	203
Chapter Notes	207
Bibliography	224
Index	227

Preface

Our understanding of thirties horror has changed somewhat in recent years. Until not long ago we had forgotten—or were not fully aware of—how shockingly graphic the early thirties horror films actually were. Only in the age of the DVD have we been able to view these films in uncensored versions, and become aware of previously censored and deleted scenes, changed and tacked-on endings, reshoots and added scenes that changed or diluted the original versions of classic horror films and gave previous generations of horror fans and critics the impression that the thirties horror film was safer and more reassuring to audiences than it actually was. Film historians and fans (thanks partly to a raised awareness of pre–Code Hollywood cinema) are now beginning to separate their nostalgia for Universal's family-friendly "monster rally" horror films of the forties from their growing appreciation of the gruesome and brutal nature of the thirties cycle. Certainly the term "gruesomeness" is one that crops up again and again in the censor reports, film reviews, marketing and publicity materials produced by the studios (which routinely played up the sensationalist aspects of the films, including their gruesomeness) and industry journals of the 1930s; it is arguably *the* defining characteristic of thirties horror, and undoubtedly key to its popularity with audiences of the time.

The infamous scene in *Murders in the Rue Morgue* (1932) where Lugosi strings up a prostitute on a cross while he takes samples of her "rotten blood," might, for example, be seen as a precursor of torture porn; it is certainly strikingly similar, in the way it is staged, to an equally infamous scene in *The Texas Chain Saw Massacre* (1974) in which Leatherface (Gunnar Hansen) carves up a body, while another victim dangles from the meat hook behind him. Both are shocking examples of Grand Guignol. This raises the question: *Is the thirties horror film more akin to graphic modern horror than is often thought?*

However, many critics have in the past drawn sharp distinctions between the classic (1930s–1940s) and modern (1960s–present) horror film, claiming that whereas the former seeks to reaffirm the status quo (the classic horror film inevitably ends with the monster destroyed and normality restored), the modern apocalyptic horror film (from *Psycho* [1960] onward) is, by contrast, open-ended, nihilistic, paranoid, and subversive. But, despite their restorative endings, horror films of the thirties—with their social outcast monsters, mad scientists, torture chamber imagery, libidinous maniacal killers and often overt sadism—posed considerable challenges to censors and audiences. Moreover, by closely examining the so-called restorative endings of films like *The Black Cat* (1934), *The Raven* (1935) and *Mad Love* (1935), these endings can be revealed as tacked-on, formulaic (usually as a sop to the Production Code and state censors) and unconvincing, running counter to the main body of the films: they simply don't "fit." In some cases (*Frankenstein* [1931]), *Freaks* [1932]) endings were changed after preview screenings in order to provide audiences with closure and reassurance where none had previously existed.

So How Safe and Reassuring Were the Thirties Films Really?

To explore such questions is the intention of this book. *The Turn to Gruesomeness in American Horror Films, 1931–1936* challenges the critical opinion that classic horror is inherently conservative as defined by endings which restore normative order; instead it argues that the essential characteristics of thirties horror are its gruesomeness and brutality, and that happy endings in the thirties cycle are almost entirely lacking conviction. In order to do this it looks first at how the genre was formulated in the thirties and examines the evolution of the classic horror film from various perspectives.

Chapter 1, "'Nightmare pictures,'" charts the emergence of the thirties cycle in an industrial context, showing how various socio-economic stresses during the Great Depression, censorship controversy over sex and crime films, declining audiences and growing opposition to unfair business practices, formed a backdrop of rupture and contradiction during horror's first golden age. This chapter draws on trade journals of the day to track the cycle from *Dracula* (1931) and *Frankenstein* (1931) to its becoming a firmly established niche product by the mid-thirties. At the same time, the trade journals also report on the growing concerns about this "gruesome" cycle by state censors, church groups and exhibitor organizations. This chapter thus attempts to contextualize the emergence of horror in light of the politics of the industry of the time, and how these factors almost led to the cycle being killed off in 1932 before jungle movies revived the horror cycle at the box office with the extraordinary success of *King Kong* (1933); thereafter the genre continued to thrive on sadism despite moving away from its gothic roots.

Chapter 2 goes on to show how cash-strapped studios pushed for increasingly gruesome and sensational screen content to attract audiences, while simultaneously placating the Hays Office with moral endings, and how, in conjunction, the production practices pioneered by Irving Thalberg—such as audience previews and retakes—also helped shape the form of the thirties cycle as we know it. Critics of the genre at the time called such studio tactics "five reels of transgression followed by one reel of retribution" (the title given to this chapter). This chapter thus takes the studio perspective on the burgeoning horror cycle, from Universal's initial appropriation of the genre, to other studios' adoption of it.

In their bid to attract audiences through sensational content, studios often flouted the Production Code; however, horror pictures (in contrast with sex pictures and underworld crime movies) were of only mild concern to the Hays Office at the start. Later, though, the rigid enforcement of the Production Code under Joseph Breen saw horror increasingly censored in terms of its gruesomeness and brutality to the point where, by 1936, the Code had an overbearing influence on actual story content and plot construction—as can be seen in *Dracula's Daughter, The Walking Dead* and *The Devil Doll* (all 1936)—effectively emasculating the genre. Chapter 3, "'Brutality, horror and gruesomeness,'" thus documents from the censors' perspective the changing ways in which the Hays Office responded to gruesomeness in the thirties cycle, from relatively light interference in the early days to heavily influencing the allowable level of gruesomeness after July 1934. It charts an arc of trajectory from *Dracula* to *The Devil Doll* and discusses the implications of reissues of pre-Code horror films also being cut after 1934 (these cut versions became the official distributed ones, influencing how audiences and critics in the 1950s, 1960s and 1970s perceived classic horror).

Chapter 4, "'Why should Cecil B. DeMille have a monopoly on torture and cruelty?,'" further explores links between producer, audience and censor to examine how screenwriters and directors deployed gruesomeness and brutality in the mise-en-scène through special make-up effects and the use of shadow play. The chapter explores the ways in which sound was used to heighten realism, and how filmmakers used off-screen space as one of several cinematic strategies to circumvent objections to gruesomeness raised by the Hays Office and state censors. The arguably transgressive qualities of the thirties cycle culminated in an unproduced version of *Dracula's Daughter* which was vetoed by the Production Code Administration as "utterly impossible for approval under the Production Code," and in *Mad Love*, a film described by one industry journal (*Motion Picture Herald*, July 6, 1935) as "the type of picture that brought about censorship."

It is hoped that by bringing together these four perspectives of industry, studio, censorship and production practices, this study will highlight gruesomeness as a primary characteristic of the thirties horror film, equal to the happy ending as a key signifier of the cycle. Chapter 5, "'A secure universe'?," discusses how and why many past critics have misread the thirties cycle. My contention is that—up until relatively recently—critical appraisal of thirties horror has been based on this misperception of what thirties horror actually "is." There are several reasons for this confusion: a number of key films (such as *Mystery of the Wax Museum* [1933], *Dr. Jekyll and Mr. Hyde* [1931], *The Old Dark House* [1932]) remained unavailable or lost for many years; TV revivals such as *Shock Theater* in the late fifties, where the Monster Kid generation first saw many of these films, mixed the thirties and forties films in their programming, encouraging a lumping together of the two cycles; and those pre-Code thirties films that were shown on TV and in cinema revivals were often PCA-cut reissues shorn of their more shocking scenes. These factors combined led to an incomplete picture of the thirties cycle in the minds of viewers, and formed the basis of much of the critical opinion that followed. The graphic explicitness of the thirties horror film was underplayed and the happy ending overemphasized, creating an impression of tameness.

This misperception, I believe, was followed through by academics in their arguing that the classic horror film (in comparison to the modern or postmodern horror film) is—based largely on the ending in which "normative order is restored"—inherently conservative or reactionary (Wood, "The American Nightmare"; Tudor, *Monsters and Mad Scientists*; Pinedo, *Recreational Terror*), or at best (and probably more accurately) a site of "ideological contradiction and negotiation" (Berenstein, *Attack of the Leading Ladies*). Only more recently have scholars begun to question the nature of the restorative ending in thirties horror films and its significance within the cycle (e.g., Hutchings, *The Horror Film*).

Therefore redefining the thirties horror film in light of its gruesomeness and its *perfunctory* restorative ending (which, as I hope to demonstrate, was more often than not simply a means by which censorship could be avoided by providing "compensating moral values" for the sensational content that preceded; therefore how much ideological significance can be attached to it?) questions the general conception of thirties horror, and will, I hope, pave the way for future re-evaluation of classic horror cinema.

I am grateful to a number of individuals, organizations and businesses who have helped me in the research of this book: Jenny Romero, Marisa Duron and staff at the Margaret Herrick Library, AMPAS; Ned Comstock and Sandra M. Garcia-Myers at the USC Archives of the Cinematic Arts; Julianna Jenkins and staff at the UCLA Library of Performing Arts Special Collections; staff at the BFI Reuben Library, Southbank; staff at the University of Hull's Brynmor Jones Library; and staff at the Nottingham City Library. For their help in sourcing photographs and publicity materials, I thank Ron and Margaret Borst at Hollywood Movie Posters; the late Eric Caidin and staff at Hollywood Book and Poster Company; and Mike Hawks and staff at Larry Edmunds Bookshop.

I'd like to thank—for their general support and encouragement during the writing of this book—James Aston; John Atkinson; the Classic Horror Film Board; David Colton; Amy M. Davis; Jeff Lieberman; Joseph Maddrey; Elizabeth McCarthy; Xavier Mendik; Wes Moynihan; Bernice M. Murphy; Emma Philipson; David Pirie; Gary Don Rhodes; Naila Scargill; Martin Unsworth; Barbie Wilde; and James Zborowski. Thanks also to David J. Skal and Donald F. Glut for answering my queries regarding Tod Browning's *Freaks* and *Shock Theater*, respectively. Special thanks to Dawn and Craig Clark at Roundabout Entertainment, Burbank, California, for their generosity and hospitality, without which this book could not have been written; to James Gracey, for his careful proof-reading and analysis; and, to my wife, Joanne Rudling, for her invaluable help during the research and in the preparation of the final manuscript.

This book is an expansion of an article I wrote for the magazine *Paracinema* ("Endemic Madness: Subversive 1930s Horror Cinema," issue 17, September 2012); I am grateful to Dylan Santurri for granting permission to reprint material from that article in this book's introduction.

Introduction
"Misery likes reality for company"

Horror's First Golden Age

Why did the 1930s become horror's first golden age? There had, of course, been "horror" films in the silent era, but not as concentrated, popular and controversial a cycle as emerged in the thirties. As Tom Johnson remarks in *Censored Screams*, "despite well over 50 silents that could reasonably be classed as horrific in intention (if not in fact), few even today choose to see them as a unified group." Johnson goes on to observe: "These pictures contained most of the elements that would resurface in the 1931–1936 cycle of horror films, yet they apparently offended very few. The silent cycle lasted a quarter of a century, seemingly without serious controversy or censorship, yet the sound wave started by *Dracula* lasted a mere five years. But what a five years!"[1] Indeed, during those five years following *Dracula* upwards of 50 horror films were produced in America, of which over 30 were released in Britain (and other overseas territories) before the so-called "ban" of horrific films in that country led to the discontinuation of the cycle by Universal and the other major Hollywood studios in 1936.[2] While the thirties cycle did not give birth to the horror film, it represented a level of popularity and controversy for horror pictures that was unprecedented.

Critics and historians have posited a number of cultural and socio-economic reasons for horror's popularity in the thirties, factors that led to the cycle's rapid growth during that decade. First is the effect of the Modernist movements in art, literature, theater and film that took place in the early 20th century following World War I, in particular the influence of German Expressionism on silent horror films, which continued into the sound cycle, often via the émigrés working in Hollywood in the thirties. Thomas Schatz points out in *The Genius of the System* that Universal had been cultivating the genre for years, as Carl Laemmle, Sr., signed "scores of European film-makers during his annual trips abroad." Many of these were German, such as cinematographer and later director Karl Freund, and schooled "not only in the European tradition of gothic horror, but also in the German Expressionist cinema of the late teens and early 1920s." Schatz describes these émigrés as bringing with them a "fascination for the cinema's distinctly unrealistic qualities, its capacity to depict a surreal landscape of darkness, nightmare logic and death."[3]

The tradition of Gothic horror that Schatz mentions is, of course, another factor, providing a continuum to literary precursors, although it is perhaps less tangible an influence on the thirties horror film than is often thought. Joseph Maddrey, in *Nightmares in Red,*

White and Blue, discusses American Gothic as a relatively recent cultural development dating back to Edgar Allan Poe: "The Gothic has been ... re-defined in 20th century literature and film. Visual motifs and other elements have been subsumed into the horror genre, making the classic Gothic an elusive undercurrent in the narrative." A number of thirties horror films, such as *Dracula, Frankenstein* and *Murders in the Rue Morgue*, were based on literary adaptations and plays, but given a distinctly modern spin: some of the recurring plot devices and themes which, according to Maddrey, define the Gothic—the haunted settings and the supernatural forces—are downplayed in favor of others—sadomasochism and "the brutality, cruelty and superstition of the Middle Ages"—although the thirties films retain what Maddrey describes as the most common thread of Gothic, the "pessimistic tone of the works, a sense that human nature is innately corrupt and transcendence inherently dangerous."[4]

Equally crucial to our understanding of the thirties cycle is the advent of sound cinema. As Rhona Berenstein notes in *Attack of the Leading Ladies*, "it was in the 1930s that horror became a significant American sound film phenomenon." Sound gave film directors a new medium of expression, bringing a greater sense of realism that they were quick to exploit, especially in terms of horror's representation of sadism and pain: many horror films of the thirties feature "bloodcurdling renditions of the female scream."[5] Moreover, sound gave filmmakers the opportunity, in the words of Stephen Prince, to "aesthetically stylize acts of cruelty and violence and to make these vivid and disturbing at a new and evocative sensory level." Directors such as Browning, Whale and Mamoulian were open to the expressive possibilities of this new medium early on. However, the potency of sound in horror cinema only became apparent to the studios and the censors when, as Prince points out, "the escalation of violence in horror films, which sound was helping to make possible, exposed the industry to serious risk."[6]

This brings us to another important factor in horror's growing popularity in the thirties—perhaps the most significant. On April 3, 1932, the trade journal *The Film Daily* printed this editorial:

> Early last season exhibitors were unanimous in crying out for more comedy and more cheerfulness in feature pictures. They argued that, in times of general gloom, the public wants the kind of entertainment that will bring out smiles.
> It sounded very plausible.
> So the producers immediately responded that they would make this a "laugh" year.
> And what has been the result?
> Feature comedies, including some very good ones, have had an uphill fight all season, whereas the horror, shock and thrills dramas have done the big business.
> Proving, it would seem, that misery likes reality for company.[7]

Without question, the Great Depression, as Berenstein writes, "fostered a climate in which the destruction of the social fabric by monsters was greeted by spectators with a sense of familiarity if not relief."[8] Moreover, the early thirties horror film arguably gave vent, as *The Film Daily* editorial implies, to widespread discontent in the midst of economic collapse. As Thomas Doherty puts it in *Pre-Code Hollywood*, "the economic catastrophe of the 1930s ... was the central American trauma of the twentieth century, the last time that the foundational beliefs of the nation were seriously up for grabs—not only its political system and economic structure but (more to the Hollywood point) its animating myths and cultural values." Identifying the horror film of the early thirties as part of pre–Code Hollywood discourse in terms of its cultural significance, Doherty goes on to argue that pre–Code Hollywood "negotiated cultural dislocations by venting insurrectionist impulses and reformulating American myths during a time uncongenial to their straight-faced assertion. Newly audible and becoming articulate, relatively free and open to risk, it uttered challenges to traditional verities and flirted with political controversy, anything to lure back a lapsed audience with depleting reserves of discretionary income."[9] Doherty posits that the pre–Code horror film of the thirties, in particular, gave free rein to "psychic turmoil and social disorientation" because it possessed a unique freedom from censorship: *Frankenstein* brought to light "a censorial oversight regarding the quality of gruesomeness"—there was no provision in any censor law or in the Production Code that ruled on the quality or extent of "gruesomeness." And it was this loophole, according to Doherty, that gave the horror genre its "singular thrill."[10]

It is not surprising, then, that *Frankenstein* became such a trailblazer at the box office at the height of the Depression, generating a cycle of "horror, shock and thrills dramas." Universal and the other studios, hard hit by falling audiences, recognized the profitability of the cycle—its scope for shocking, thrilling and gruesome content—and 1932 alone saw the release of *Freaks* (MGM), *Dr. Jekyll and Mr. Hyde* (Paramount), and *Dr. X* (Warner Bros./First National) as well as others made by poverty row outfits such as Republic and Monogram Pictures—thereby ushering in horror's first golden age.

Defining 1930s Horror Cinema: Classic vs. War Years Horror

This first cycle of horror films produced between 1931 and 1936 is often characterized as the classic period, although many film scholars also include the films produced during the war years within this period. There are, however, several reasons why a distinction should be made between films produced in the classic period and those produced in the war period.

Firstly, the majority of films of the classic period were made before the stricter enforcement of the Production Code from July 1934, which subjected filmmakers to more rigid restrictions on the content and treatment of subject matter in their films. Although prior to 1934, the studios had exercised an element of self-regulation under the Studio Relations Committee, the tightening of the Production Code under Joseph Breen's administration reflected a renewed moral conservatism that gradually changed Hollywood filmmaking in the lead up to the Second World War. Producers were actively discouraged from making horror pictures and scripts were more closely vetted by the Production Code Administration than they had been previously. An amendment eventually made to the Production Code itself stipulated that scenes of "excessive brutality and gruesomeness" must be cut to "an absolute minimum."[11] There were, in other words, fewer opportunities to slip offensive content into films after 1934, although directors such as James Whale (to name but one example) were renowned for using their powers of diplomacy, as David J. Skal says, "to get the Production Code seal while keeping subversive material intact."[12]

Secondly, the pre–Code period of the horror film coincided with a time of greater autonomy for Heads of Production in the major studios. Carl Laemmle, Jr., at Universal had almost complete authority over what projects would be produced partly because his father owned the studio. Irving Thalberg at MGM was known to be a gifted supervisor of production. To an extent these studios heads were sympathetic to the horror genre and respected their writers, producers and directors. It was Junior Laemmle, for example, who turned the horror film into Universal's signature genre after the success of *Dracula*. Thalberg produced *Freaks* in 1932, having previously worked with Tod Browning at MGM. However, when the Laemmles lost Universal to a corporate investor, J. Cheever Cowdin in 1936, Junior Laemmle was replaced by Charles Rogers as production chief. According to film historian Douglas Gomery, "Cowdin approved budgets and scripts and, once these were prepared, directors and production supervisors had no power; they had to shoot as written. After *Dracula's Daughter* (1936) Rogers ended the production of horror pictures entirely."[13] The autonomy that many heads of production enjoyed ended as corporations took over the studios in later years.

A third distinction to make between the horror films of the classic period and those of the war period is arguably the talent of the filmmakers involved. James Whale, Tod Browning, Edgar G. Ulmer and Michael Curtiz are recognized as major directors, whereas the Universal horror films of the war period in particular produced almost no filmmakers of comparable note. Directors such as Albert S. Rogell (*The Black Cat* [1941]), Erle C. Kenton (despite making the classic *Island of Lost Souls* [1932]) and Charles T. Barton (*Abbott and Costello Meet Frankenstein* [1948]) were efficient but undistinguished technicians hired to shoot the script as written quickly and cost effectively. Moreover, Ulmer and Curtiz, as well as many other directors and technicians, had escaped Europe before the rise of Nazism and brought with them a deeply pessimistic view of human nature that translated into the doom and sadism of the horror film (and later the film noir). The mainstream Universal horror film of the forties is arguably lacking such auteur directors.

This is not to say that war years horror should be "written off" as inferior to the classic period, as is so often the case; indeed, much of the recent work undertaken by scholars such as Mark Jancovich and Tim Snelson to re-evaluate forties horror cinema—particularly in terms of the emergence of psychological horror in the forties—has, in fact, served not only to recover forties horror but also to highlight key differences between the 1930s and 1940s horror cycles. Jancovich, for example, suggests that one of the reasons for the development of psychological horror in the 1940s was to circumvent the Production Code Administration's objection to "gruesome and brutal" content. Psychological horror of the 1940s, as Jancovich points out, eschewed the visual explicitness of the 1930s cycle "in favor of suggestion and suspense,"[14] and this is perhaps the most important distinction to be made between the two cycles.

1930s Europe as Torture Chamber: Allegorical Gruesomeness

Ulmer's *The Black Cat* (1934) illustrates very clearly the allegorical concerns of the horror film in the mid–1930s, which manifested in scenes of gruesomeness. *Frankenstein* and *Freaks* had reflected the raised class consciousness brought about by the Depression which had led to Roosevelt's New Deal. However, with the clouds of war gathering in Europe following Hitler's rise to power, filmmakers, by 1934, had become increasingly concerned with the specter of catastrophe arising, once again, from Germany.

Essentially an allegory of the dark forces at play in Germany and the Austro-Hungarian empire following World War I, *The Black Cat* concerns the unfinished business between Austrian psychiatrist Dr. Werdergast (Bela Lugosi) and his architect friend Poelzig (Boris Karloff), whose Bauhaus house (an ex-fortress) is built on the corpses of a battleground and undermined by dynamite. During the war Poelzig commanded the fortress which he is accused by Werdegast of having betrayed to the Russians, causing the death of thousands of Hungarians. A naïve American couple is drawn into this vendetta scenario with the two adversaries competing for their souls. Ulmer alludes to the occultism underlying the Third Reich in the character of Poelzig, a Satanist. The film culminates in the sadistic (off-screen) flaying of Karloff by Lugosi in the former's underground torture chamber and the subsequent detonation of the dynamite that brings about a new conflagration.

Ulmer's film clearly conveyed the message that World War I had not been resolved: the forces of chaos which had started that war could easily spark another. "The slightest mistake by one of us could cause the destruction of all," Werdegast warns at one point, voicing popular opinion at the time that World War I had been started by mistake.

It is easy to see why overseas censors baulked at the film in 1934, what with Hitler

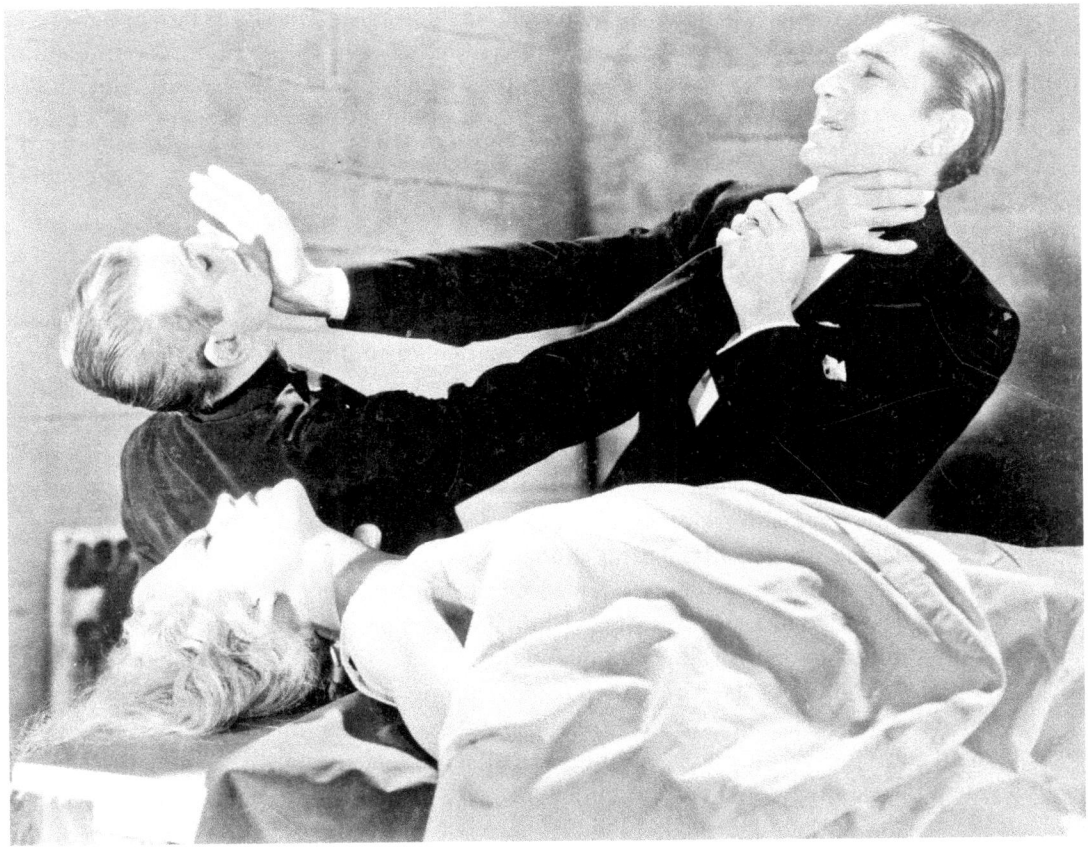

Werdegast (Bela Lugosi, right) and Poelzig (Boris Karloff) fight over the lifeless body of Karen (Lucille Lund) in this rather staged production still from *The Black Cat* (1934, Universal).

drawing on the Eugenics doctrines to preach Aryan superiority and international tensions rising following Germany's massive rearmament program. America had invested heavily in European war debts to keep the European economy afloat as a large consumer market for American goods. In effect, American commercial interests had financed Germany's rebuilding and close relationships between American and German businesses now became an embarrassment following the Nazi rise to power.

In Hollywood many were alarmed by Hitler's anti–Semitism (including Curtiz, whose extended family was to perish in Auschwitz). Even conservative studio heads such as Louis B. Mayer joined the Anti-Nazi League. However, Joseph Breen was sensitive to the industry's commercial interests in Germany and anti-Nazi films were almost impossible to make under the Production Code.

But, as Richard Maltby has remarked of the Production Code, it "forced Hollywood to become ambiguous."[15] It can be seen that the horror films of the time addressed the issue of the increasing Nazi threat *allegorically*. Gruesome images of sadism and the torture chamber as featured in *The Black Cat* became increasingly prevalent in films of the era, featuring strongly in *Mad Love* (1935) and *The Raven* (1935), to name just two examples. The latter caused international protest at the potent image of its swinging pendulum: a literal sword of Damocles hanging over Europe. (In addition, as Donato Totaro points out, one could add the risqué thematic treatments of the libido in *Dr. Jekyll & Mr. Hyde* and lesbianism [e.g., *Dracula's Daughter*] as "elements that unsettled studio heads, to the point where censorship eventually emasculated the more adult and subversive elements" of the 1930s horror films.[16])

"Endemic madness"

Europe as torture chamber, presided over by monsters and madmen: these films are remarkable in their portent of things to come, particularly of the Holocaust. That many of the filmmakers who made these cautionary tales were Jewish should come as no surprise.

No surprise either that these films were followed by a moral backlash against the horror genre, particularly in Britain, where prime minister Chamberlain was taking an appeasement stance following the horrors of World War I. Britain, nervous that Hitler might bomb the population with bio-chemical weapons, did not want the public subjected to these shocking images. Many local councils banned horror films in their areas. The British censor eventually introduced a new certificate, the "H," ostensibly to prevent children from being admitted to see horror films. Church groups pressured for greater censorship generally—not just of horror films but of all films.

Britain had also seen its share of class conflict during the Depression. The conservative-dominated government, in direct contrast to the Roosevelt administration, had concentrated on cutting government expenditure and raising protective tariffs, leading to unemployment rates as high as 70 percent in the northeast of England, prompting a number of hunger marches on London such as the 1936 Jarrow Crusade.[17]

In America, faced with similar pressures to increase censorship, the Production Code Administration, through active campaigning and dissuasion (using the prospect of a British "ban" as leverage), had succeeded in deterring studios from horror production by the end of 1936.[18] After Universal took horror productions off its schedule, other studios followed. By the time production resumed in 1939 with *Son of Frankenstein*, the classic period was in effect over. Hollywood had changed, the production teams were different, Breen's Production Code Administration had tightened practice: the films being produced were "safe."

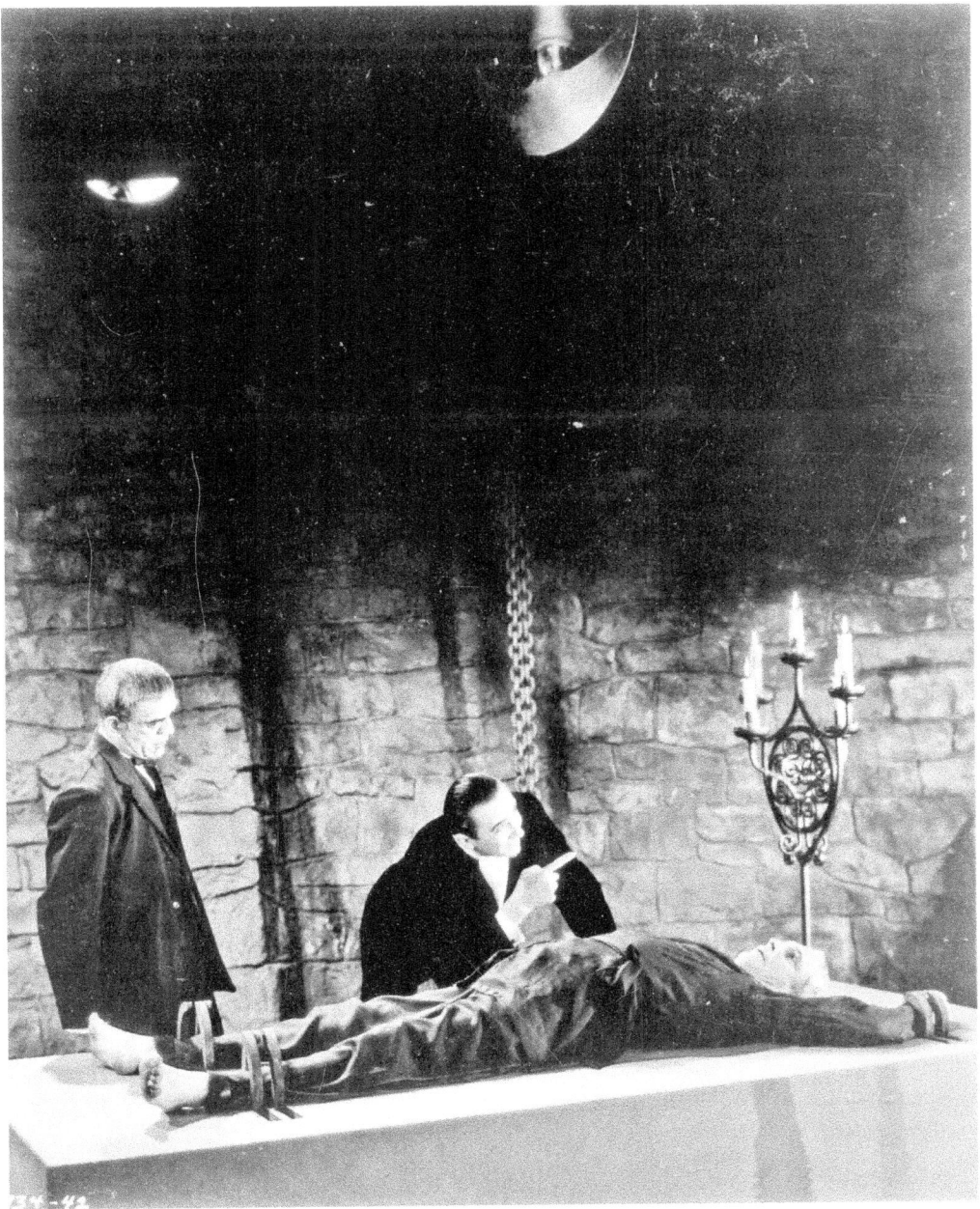

"Torture waiting, waiting!" The sadistic Dr. Vollin (Bela Lugosi) subjects Judge Thatcher (Samuel S. Hinds) to the pendulum in *The Raven* (1935, Universal). A disfigured Bateman (Boris Karloff) looks on.

Ideologically, the Universal horror films of the war period reflect the moral conservatism of the war years. They generally lack the genre innovation and radical commentary of the 1930s horror film, and they particularly lack its gruesomeness and brutality.

Reviewers, by the time of *The Raven*, had begun to object strongly to the "lurid" treatment of subject matter, the prominent "torture aspects" of the narrative and the emphasis on "horror for horror's sake."[19] Elements, in other words, that made the burgeoning genre popular with, and relevant to, Depression-era audiences. Clearly, for audiences and reviewers, normative order was not being restored in these films and that was precisely what the audience was responding to. As the decade rolled on, it was becoming increasingly apparent to the British and American public that the only way out of the Depression, it seemed, was to prepare for another war. As Britain and America embarked on programs of rearmament, the injections of government money served to stimulate the economy and reduce unemployment, making war seem not only inevitable, but economically desirable. Little wonder, then, that the 1930s horror film, as theorist Andrew Tudor has noted of *The Black Cat*, leaves the overall and lasting impression of "endemic madness, a world at odds with itself."[20]

And yet, many film theorists and academics, when discussing thirties horror cinema, speak of it as constructing a "secure" universe. In her book *Recreational Terror*, Isabel Pinedo, for example, writes: "The classical horror film constructs a secure universe characterized by narrative closure, one in which the (hu)man agency (human agency understood as male agency) prevails and the normative order is restored by the film's end."[21] This is an overly-simplified evaluation when it comes to the 1930s horror film (based as it is on the lumping together of classic period and war period horror films), and one that needs further discussion. As the "secure universe" that Pinedo proposes is "characterized by narrative closure," it is necessary to examine the nature of the 1930s horror film restorative ending.

"Happy endings"

It is, of course, common practice in Hollywood to revise a film's ending if the film has tested poorly with audiences during preview screenings. This was the case in the thirties as it is today. *Frankenstein*, *Freaks* and *Bride of Frankenstein* (1935) are but three examples of films in which the endings were changed by the studio at a late stage in production in an attempt to give the audience a "happy ending." In the case of *Frankenstein*, according to historian Thomas Schatz, the original ending saw the destruction of both Frankenstein and his creation, but after previews, Laemmle ordered this "vaguely dissatisfying" ending revised so that Henry Frankenstein (Colin Clive) would be allowed to live.[22] In fact there had been a certain ambiguity to the original ending in the way that Whale shot it that left the audience uncertain as to whether Frankenstein had actually perished. It can therefore be seen that the added tag ending was, in part, an attempt to provide the audience with a greater sense of narrative closure than Whale had originally intended. In the case of *Bride*, the ending was again changed late in production to allow Frankenstein to live, while *Freaks* had an epilogue added after preview in a bid to soften the impact of the climactic uprising of the circus freaks. In both *Bride* and *Freaks*, these changed endings can be seen as an attempt to restore normative order, a feature noticeably absent in the early scripted versions of these films.

The changed ending of *Bride* ran counter to Whale's original intention that "nothing will be resolved."[23] Likewise the tag ending of *Freaks* went against Browning's original intention, as is clear in the final screenplay, to leave the audience with a subversion of normality. In *The Classical Hollywood Cinema*, David Bordwell discusses the classical ending of resolution and epilogue in terms of its tendency to "usher in the narration as self-conscious and omniscient presence," and goes on to say "this overt narration should harmonize with the story action and generic demands."[24] However, the changed endings of *Frankenstein*, *Freaks* and *Bride* fail to harmonize with the preceding story action precisely because neither Whale nor Browning originally intended to restore normative order at the end of their films: these tag endings are clearly tacked on to the main body of each film, running counter to that film's thrust. It is possible that Browning and Whale agreed to these endings knowing that they would appear so obviously tacked-on. Indeed it may be possible that Browning and Whale actually *designed* these epilogues this way, to foreground the arbitrary conventionality of these imposed endings—the very fact that they do not "fit."

Other endings—even those not subject to revision after preview screenings (such as that of *The Raven*, for example) —can be seen as arbitrary and ill-fitting in the same way.

Formula Endings

As film theorist Rick Worland notes: "Classic horror films end in a certain way: the monster is definitely destroyed in a manner that permits a sense of catharsis; and the restoration of 'normality' is usually signaled through the formation (or preservation) of a heterosexual couple or family group."[25] This formula ending, added arbitrarily, is emblematic of the 1930s horror film. By arbitrarily I mean it is applied by the filmmaker in a cursory manner, with a lack of conviction, primarily as a sop to the Production Code and state censors. By applying this formula ending, no matter how perfunctorily, studios were able, at least before July 1934, to satisfy the Production Code's demand for "compensating moral values," while still including elements of sadism in the main body of the film. Naturally, filmmakers like Ulmer would have been aware of this: by adhering to the Code in terms of an obligatory happy ending, they were able to add risqué elements elsewhere. To illustrate how cursory these endings actually are it is necessary to provide some examples. Let us look first at the epilogue of *The Black Cat*:

> Werdegast flays Poelzig. Peter Allison (David Manners) shoots Werdegast who nevertheless allows him to escape with his wife, Joan (Jacqueline Wells). As Werdegast detonates the dynamite undermining the house, Allison and Joan flag down a passing car (!) and from there take a train to Budapest. In the epilogue, Allison happens upon a newspaper containing of his latest play: "we feel that Mr. Allison has, in a sense, overstepped the bounds of the matter of credibility. These things would never, but with a further stretch of the imagination, actually happen."

The epilogue mirrors the opening scene introducing the newlyweds (also set on a train), thus substituting symmetry and "book-ending" in place of any genuine restoration of narrative equilibrium. Ulmer was a designer who understood the concepts of architectural balance and this epilogue uses formal means to restore balance, but only on a surface level. The ironic tone of the scene—the newspaper review's reference to incredible events— further masks its irrelevance. The final couple is ostensibly preserved but Ulmer slyly undermines them by emphasizing their triviality. It could be argued that Ulmer's intention was to show that the Americans are as uncomprehending at the end of the film as they were at the beginning; however, this is countered by the fact that, despite learning something of the vendetta between Werdegast and Poelzig during the course of the film, Joan appears to be unaffected and unchanged in the epilogue. Again this shows that the epilogue is not in harmony with the preceding story action, and displays elements of self-reflexivity.

The Raven features a similar epilogue where the heterosexual couple is ostensibly preserved—but again their irrelevance is emphasized by the inanity of their dialogue:

> Jean (Irene Ware): Poor Bateman—he gave up his life.
> Jerry (Lester Matthews): Yes, darling. He saved us from being crushed alright (embracing her). I think I'd better finish the job, don't you? Only a little more gently.

The resolution of *The Raven* is also perfunctory by way of its brevity, so that the audience scarcely has time to feel any sense of catharsis: "Bateman (Karloff) turns against Vollin (Lugosi), causing both their deaths, the victim is saved from the pendulum and heteronormative values are reaffirmed, all in less than 3 minutes of screen time."

The ending of *Mad Love* is even terser, taking place in one minute of screen time: "Gogol (Peter Lorre) attempts to strangle Yvonne (Frances Drake), whom he loves obsessively. Her husband, Orlac (Colin Clive) arrives with the police. He manages to throw a knife through the open door and kill Gogol in time. Husband and wife are reunited."

The arbitrary conventionality of these endings, their under-motivation and extreme brevity belie Worland's claim that the monster is definitely destroyed in the mind of the audience. They work against any genuine sense of catharsis following the monster's on-screen death. Any return to normality promised by the ending is at best fleeting and the monster remains protean in the mind of the audience after the film has ended.

Following David Bordwell's argument, foregrounding the arbitrary conventionality of the ending can, in itself, be seen as subversive. Bordwell quotes German director Rainer Werner Fassbinder: "A good director can contrive a happy ending that leaves you dissatisfied. You know that something is wrong—it just can't end this way."[26]

It is possible, therefore, that some horror filmmakers deliberately contrived these happy endings to raise questions of ideology. Furthermore, by contriving a cursory resolution or epilogue, the filmmaker can, according to Bordwell, "put on display the requirements of social institutions (censorship agencies, studios) which claim to act as delegates of audience desires. The happy ending may be there, but to some extent the need for it is criticized."[27] These endings can also be seen, then, as a form of protest against the demands of censorship (the Production Code was despised by many Hollywood filmmakers, especially after 1934).

In any case, the effect of these endings is to present a lack of true resolution—the monster may appear to die on screen but the threat to normality that the monster represents is barely vanquished and *the wider crisis remains*.

Foundational Works for a Re-Evaluation of 1930s Horror Based on Its "Gruesomeness"

"In a sense critics are parasites," Robin Wood has written, "very much dependent upon the work of theorists and scholars, which they ignore at their peril. Theory and scholarship supply materials upon which critics can build, applying the theories relevant to their work, using the data for accuracy and factual support."[28] When, in 1979, Wood authored his seminal essay on the modern horror film, "The American Nightmare," there was little in the way of foundational scholarship on classical horror cinema. There were, of course, two highly regarded works, Carlos Clarens' *Horror Movies: An Illustrated Survey* (1971) and William K. Everson's *Classics of the Horror Film* (1974), but neither positioned gruesomeness as central to the thirties horror film. In his chapter on classical horror cinema ("Children of the Night: Hollywood, 1928–1947"), in which he presents the late silent, thirties and forties periods as a single largely unified era, Clarens refers to gruesomeness in his discussion of those films made in the 1930s, but only in passing, and falls short of identifying gruesomeness as a defining characteristic of thirties horror generally, and one which distinguishes it from the forties cycle[29]; Everson, in his overarching argument that "the best horror films have always been those that relied more on suggestion than on outright statement,"[30] tends to gloss over the visual explicitness of pre–Code horror. In his praise of *Murders in the Zoo*, for example, Everson writes: "Tastelessness is a matter of relativity ... in comparison with the physically repellent obsession with gore and clinical detail that has marked recent horror films, and especially those of Hammer, *Murders in the Zoo* seems a model of restrained decorum, and if there is any tastelessness at all, it is primarily in the healthy vulgarity of some of Charlie Ruggles' comedy."[31] Although he admits that *Murders* is "sometimes quite grim stuff," and mentions that the film suffered heavy censorship, he fails to detail the censorable material in question, referring to the infamous opening in which a man's lips are sewn together (described by *Turner Classic Movies* as "one of the most shocking scenes in 1930s horror cinema"[32]) as merely "colorful." Is it any wonder, then, that in his comparison with 1970s horror ("the period in which the evolution of the genre produced films more gruesome, more violent, more disgusting, and perhaps more confused, than ever before in its history"[33]), Wood, dependent as he was on these types of historical accounts for "materials" on which to build his critical ideas, seems content to characterize classical horror primarily by restorative endings that see "the monster destroyed [and] the young lovers (sometimes the established family) united and safe," with no reference to the gruesomeness and brutality of the 1930s cycle, or discussion of its significance? (Even Wood's detailed analysis of *Murders in the Rue Morgue* makes no mention whatsoever of the controversial "rotten blood" scene.) In following this example, subsequent critics have sought to emphasize *differences* between the modern and the classical period of horror cinema, rather than examine *similarities* and what these similarities might represent in terms of the genre's inherent values and essential continuities.

In many ways, however, the foundational works for a re-evaluation of 1930s horror based on its gruesomeness are still those written by historians and scholars rather than by theorists. Since the late eighties and early nineties and the age of home video and DVD a new generation of horror movie scholars have (with the help of archivists, film restorers, and, to an extent, the studios themselves who have, in recent years, reissued restored uncensored versions of their classic horror movies on home video) further examined the 1930s horror film, uncovering its production history and its censorship, helping to bring more fully to light the gruesomeness of the thirties cycle, in the process coming to acknowledge gruesomeness (whether they approve of it or not) as a key characteristic of classic thirties horror. Historian Tom Weaver, for example, in his foreword to Tom Johnson's *Censored*

Screams, starts out the way of Everson, stating: "part of the appeal [of 1930s horror films] is that they leave a lot to the imagination," before correcting himself with the evidence at hand:

> Remember that in the pre–Code *Murders in the Rue Morgue* Bela Lugosi wanted to find the Right Girl for his pet gorilla to have sex with. A man with sewn-up lips gets a big screen-filling closeup in *Murders in the Zoo*. There's more proposed inter-species sex (and Charles Laughton being hacked to pieces by animal-men with surgical knives) in *Island of the Lost Souls*. Those are just a few examples.
>
> There was every indication that Hollywood intended to continue to "push the envelope": Before the Hays Office started flexing its muscles, the script of *The Black Cat* called for Bela Lugosi to put Boris Karloff on a rack, a prelude to the audience seeing in shadow "[Lugosi] splitting the scalp slowly, pulling the sheath of skin over [Karloff's] head and shoulders." We were then to see Karloff (sans skin) free himself, fall to the floor and, "still living as a hideous pulp of blood," drag his putrid body across the room toward the heroine. John L. Balderston sounded envious when he wrote in a memo to Universal that Cecil B. DeMille had a monopoly on the "great box office values of torture and cruelty"; he wanted to include in his script of *Dracula's Daughter* such scenes as a baby in a sack being presented to one of Dracula's ravenous vampire brides. If there were no censor's office to nix scenes like this, what would horror films have been like by the forties and fifties?[34]

Like Everson before him, Weaver dislikes the "new era" of horror that requires the viewer to "have a cast iron stomach." Crucially, though, unlike Everson, Weaver—in advocating the Hays Code for preventing "what's happened to horror movies in the last 30 or 40 years" from "getting a good running headstart back in the mid-thirties"[35]—makes the tacit connection between classic and modern horror in terms of its visual explicitness. Horror started out as already gruesome—and it continued to get more so as time went on.

The evidence, then, speaks for itself when allowed to do so. My approach during the writing of this book has been to try to let it. In this, I am very much indebted to those historians and scholars as listed in my bibliography who have provided the factual support, and to the archivists noted in my preface who supplied the raw data.

1

"Nightmare pictures"
Thirties Horror and the Hollywood Film Industry

> With *Dracula* making money at the box office for Universal, other studios are looking for horror tales—but very squeamishly. Producers are not certain whether nightmare pictures have a box office pull, or whether *Dracula* is just a freak.
> —*Variety*, April 8, 1931[1]

The crisis that Hollywood faced in the Great Depression was manifold. The 1920s had seen the Hollywood studios grow into big businesses: through a series of mergers, Fox, Warner, MGM/Loews, Paramount and RKO had become, by 1930, a mature oligopoly, dominating the industry. They owned the best first-run theaters in metropolitan areas, accounting for 70 percent of the box office, and operated a "community of interest" whereby preferential treatment was given to one another's pictures in towns and rural areas; this was to the detriment of independent exhibitors and small theater chains, and to some extent, the minor studios, such as Universal, who supplied low cost pictures to the majors but lacked theaters of their own to fully profit from first-run prestige productions.[2]

Steffen Hantke has stated that capitalism "contains within itself contradictions, schisms, ruptures."[3] Of course, horror cinema in the thirties (along with the sex picture and underworld crime film) itself represents such a contradiction, schism, rupture. Sensational screen content in the pre–Code era arose from an economic imperative: to draw audiences back into theaters by ramping up the sex and violence. But such content also posed moral and ideological threat, a schism between economic base and ideological superstructure, which ultimately necessitated the introduction of tighter industry regulation and censorship in order to bring base and superstructure back into alignment. Moreover, the schisms of capitalism also manifested in other ways beside censorship troubles in the American film industry of the early 1930s: in the cultural conflict between provincial and urban, Catholicism and Protestantism, and federal and state. Except for a brief period between 1933 and 1935 when Roosevelt's National Recovery Act encouraged monopoly in business,[4] the major Hollywood studios were constantly under the threat of prosecution under longstanding monopoly legislation; they were under attack by consumer groups, Congress and the Federal Trade Commission alike for block-booking films in theaters[5] (the practice by which the studios imposed their product—regardless of quality or subject matter—on independent theater owners, thereby stifling competition); they were under attack by the

Catholic Church and other pressure groups who objected to "indecent and immoral pictures, and those which glorify crime and criminals" and whose Legion Of Decency threatened to order a boycott of films and movie theaters unless the industry cleaned up its act.[6] The emergence of the horror film in the thirties must therefore be understood within the context of industry politics and cultural struggle.

Perhaps unsurprisingly, given these stresses, the horror film's growth into an established niche market by the mid-thirties was not altogether a steady one. Indeed, there was doubt that the first horror films of the thirties would flower into a successful film cycle. As early as February 1932, industry commentators were asking, "Is the cycle on the wane?"[7] However, as we shall see, the horror film, from the very beginning, exhibited a morphing quality, an ability to mutate itself to meet public demand by incorporating elements of other popular cycles of the time (such as the jungle movie, for example). Supernatural monsters gave way to mad scientists, animal-hybrids and maniacs. Intriguingly, by the time of *The Raven* and *Mad Love*, an element of self-parody already began to set in, something that would become a genre trait in later decades. Constant throughout the thirties, however (at least until Breen's strict enforcement of the Production Code after July 1934), is the gruesomeness and brutality depicted in the horror film, which, if anything, intensified as the cycle developed, and which remained problematic for censors.

The Emergence of Horror Pictures in the 1930s

In 1931, the American film industry was ailing: the Great Depression meant declining audiences and the industry sought ways to boost cinema attendance. Although sound had staved off the Depression for over a year, by 1931 the novelty of talkies was beginning to wear off.[8] Producers desperately cut costs and exhibitors tried double-features and giveaways to bring audiences back into theaters.[9] Because the major studios had over-extended themselves in the twenties, buying up theaters in a bid to control exhibition, they were now struggling to pay their mortgages. In 1931, Warner Bros. had lost $8 million over the previous year; Fox $3 million; and RKO $5.6 million. Only Paramount and MGM/Loews remained in the black.[10] Of the minor studios, United Artists and Columbia were fighting to survive, and Universal had suffered losses of over $2 million.[11]

Studios needed a general audience in order to try to fill theaters, but at the same time realized that promoting films for "adults only" (a practice known as "pinking") attracted audiences of all ages in great numbers. After the success of *Little Caesar* (1931), producers rushed out a series of crime pictures that capitalized on the public's obsession with true-life gangsters like Al Capone. However, there was a growing backlash against these films by civic groups, exhibitors and state censors. Likewise, the sex picture, which had already made an appearance in the late 1920s (as had the gangster film), met the disapproval of government state censors and the Hays Office. Not that this particularly bothered the studios—as long as audiences continued to turn out for these types of films, and state censors still passed them, studios would continue to make them. Except that the moral objections made by women's groups and parent-teacher associations concerned about their children's well-being often went hand in hand with their criticism of the industry's business practices: the violence and smut that studios were peddling to the children was seen to be forced upon exhibitors in unfair contracts that obliged neighborhood theaters to show whatever the studios wanted, irrespective of the wishes of the theater manager or the local community. These moral reformers, and many independent exhibitors, wanted to extend federal regulation, and that would threaten the monopolistic business practices of the studios.[12] With the gangster pictures and sex films, studios were walking a political tightrope, and they knew it.

At Universal, Junior Laemmle had been looking around for an alternative to "fallen woman" pictures and gangster films (which Universal, however, still continued to make). In spite of his recent success with big-budgeters like *All Quiet on the Western Front* (1930) and *Showboat* (1929), Universal did not own the first-run theaters necessary to exploit such high-budget product, so when the Depression hit, Junior Laemmle had been forced to revise studio strategy. He capped budgets at $1 million per picture for the "super-productions," and concentrated on producing modestly-budgeted, sensational features suited to double bills outside the first-run market in outlying urban, small town and rural theaters.[13] A revival of the "mystery thriller" which had become a Universal specialty in the 1920s— with films like *The Hunchback of Notre Dame* (1923), *The Phantom of the Opera* (1925), *The Cat and The Canary* (1927) and *The Man Who Laughs* (1927)—seemed like the ideal solution to both problems. Relatively inexpensive to produce, this type of picture did not require star names or romantic leads, and as Universal was still in the process of fully equipping its studio facilities for sound (according to Junior Laemmle, Universal would continue to rely upon the RCA discs system "where the sound was on records made back in New Jersey" until as late as 1932),[14] Junior Laemmle saw the horror film as a means of making the transition from silent to sound cinema as economical as possible—reliance could be placed on the visual qualities of horror pictures, and sound kept to a minimum.[15] (In 1930 Universal had already reissued the silent *The Phantom of the Opera* [1925] with new dialogue sequences.) Moreover, unlike sex films and gangster pictures made in the silent era, mystery pictures made in the twenties had never caused a major problem with state censors or pressure groups.

Still, Junior Laemmle proceeded cautiously in terms of any plans for a cycle even after the success of *Dracula* (1931). The controversy of gang and sex pictures had made the state censors—and some exhibitors—anxious about what new type of lurid picture cycle might come next in the studios' bid for box office returns. (At the height of the furor over *Scarface* [1932], Will Hays would send Jason Joy to assure state censors that *Scarface* was the end, not the beginning, of the gangster cycle.[16]) There was also growing controversy over the routine violation by the studios of the Advertising Code: Universal had, itself, toned down its "sexy" advertising campaign of *Dracula* (early artwork depicted the vampire descending on a sleeping female victim with prominent nipples) prior to the film's release.[17] Besides, the longevity of such a cycle of horror pictures was hard to predict, and depended, of course, on its continued popularity with audiences.

Universal had first considered an adaptation of *Dracula* as early as 1915, and then again in 1920 and 1925[18] (according to some sources, also in 1927, after the play's successful run in London and on Broadway). Carl Laemmle, Sr., himself had vetoed the adaptation, afraid that it would be too gruesome for the rural market.[19] The assessments of Universal's in-house story department had been mixed. Some readers had been enthusiastic about adapting the property, based on its sensationalism and gruesomeness, others had been revolted by it for those same reasons.[20] Universal had decided not to take the chance so as not to alienate the market with horrific product. Paramount subsequently toyed with the idea of an adaptation in 1930 but they too had concerns about the morbid subject matter, and about the new Production Code which could "prohibit the very things that made people talk and gasp about [*Dracula*]." They also worried that state censors would cut the film because of its potential effect on children.[21] Indeed, when Junior Laemmle was again considering *Dracula* in 1930 after Paramount passed on it, he sent a letter to Jason Joy, an executive at the Studio Relations Committee, hoping to elicit "censorship angles" on both the play and novel. Ever circumspect, Junior Laemmle had also submitted the developing script to the SRC over a three-month period, and the script, sent in sections, had raised no objections.[22] If Laemmle had waited another year to make *Dracula*, Joy may have taken a different view, given the *Scarface* controversy and the growing concern over film cycles generally. As it was, staff and executives at the SRC felt that the gruesome elements of the film did not fall under the Production Code guidelines, and did not seem particularly offensive anyway. Universal had also exercised caution in terms of not publicizing *Dracula* as a gruesome picture—at least initially. As the *Exhibitor's Herald-World* reported on October 4, 1930: "After puzzling for a week as to whether "Dracula," soon to be produced by Universal, should be a thriller or a romance, Carl Laemmle Jr. and Tod Browning decided to make it both."[23]

Thus, when *Dracula* previewed in December 1930, in a bid to appeal to a general audience it was billed in pre-release publicity as both thriller and "sexy" romance ("The story

Dracula (1931, Universal). The studio revised its marketing strategy for the film after reviews praised it as a "chiller." Universal had originally billed it as a thriller and a sexy romance.

of the strangest passion the world has ever known"). However, following the film's release on February 12, 1931, reviews began to emphasize the audience's enjoyment of the film as a "chiller." In an advert placed in the trades on February 16, to promote the film's New York premiere at the Roxy, Universal highlighted this in its use of critic quotes: "A THREE STAR SPINE CHILLER," "A CREEPY, BLOOD CURDLING THRILLER," "HAIR-RAISER," "EXCITING and THRILLING," "EERIE," "SHIVERS and THRILLS."[24] Pretty quickly, Universal began to rethink its publicity strategy again. By February 18, 1931, Carl Laemmle, Sr., had forgotten any concerns he'd had about the gruesome nature of *Dracula*. In a "Straight from the Shoulder Talk" advertisement placed in *The Film Daily* he enthused to theater managers that *Dracula* was "so realistic, so daring, so blunt and uncompromising" that it was going to "knock the spots off the tremendous business" done by Universal's previous hit, *All Quiet on the Western Front*. *Dracula*, according to Laemmle, was "proving to be exactly the change of movie diet that the fans have been waiting for."[25]

The success of *Dracula*, then, and the relative ease with which it had received Production Code and state censor approval, had convinced Universal that there was an opening for more horror pictures—at least enough for Junior Laemmle to have, by early April 1931, tentatively scheduled two more such productions for the coming season. On April 8, *Variety* reported that Universal was to make *Murders in the Rue Morgue* as the follow up to *Dracula*; then *Frankenstein*, described as a "mid–Victorian melo of a medical student who finds the secret of life and chemically creates a man." "Bela Lugosi," *Variety* reported, "goes in the latter." The article noted that Universal had made horror films in the past, "Carl Laemmle being one of the few to spend money on such stories." The other studios were looking for horror properties, *Variety* reported, but very cautiously: "To date no other studio has tried to follow in U's steps, one of the few occasions when a hit wasn't followed by a cycle of similar pictures."[26]

It wasn't just uncertainty about the box office pull of nightmare pictures that was making the other studios squeamish about joining another sensationalistic cycle: during the spring of 1931 the controversy over gang pictures had continued to build up steam. In March, M.A. Lightman, President of the Motion Picture Theater Owners of America, had warned the studios against over-saturating the market with underworld and gangland pictures as "they exercise a bad psychological influence over children" and—perhaps more to the point—made "excellent ammunition for reformers." Instead, Lightman urged producers to hang fire on cycles—including musicals—assuring them that business conditions throughout the country were showing improvement compared to three months before, without the need for cycles.[27] In conflating his comments about the psychological effects of crime movies on children providing ammunition for reformers, Lightman was making reference to a newly commissioned series of reports that sought to "evidence" the influence of films on the children of America. The Payne Fund Studies conducted by the Motion Picture Research Council, a collective of socially-minded citizens (i.e., federal censorship advocates), had been set up to examine the effects of movies on children's attitudes, emotions and behavior. Naturally, the way that movies colored sexual and criminal behavior in the nation's youth was of particular interest to investigators.

Lightman's warning had not been lost on the Hays Office. On March 9, *The Film Daily* had reported that the Hays Office was conducting a jail investigation to determine whether motion pictures had any influence in prompting crime. Among the cases being checked was that of three youths who had received long sentences after holding up a bank; the boys had said they got the idea from the movies. The Hays Office clearly had to be seen to be doing something. "Various surveys along this line in the past," *The Film Daily* reminded readers, "made by different welfare bodies, have shown that pictures played little or no part in influencing lawbreaking."[28] Hays had also hired respected former Police Chief August Vollmer to analyze crime films for their impact on children. Vollmer had concluded that gangster movies, although trashy and vulgar, were not harmful in any way.[29]

Nevertheless, the state censors had stepped up their own activities. In the same month that the Hays Office mounted their PR-driven investigations, the Virginia censor made deletions in 14 out of 77 pictures in the space of less than a month. "The number of cuts," reported the trades, "is unusually high."[30] Sure enough, trouble was brewing. In April 1931, just as Junior Laemmle was announcing the production of *Frankenstein* and *Rue Morgue*, the first legislative move to ban underworld and gangster pictures was raised in California. The Assembly bill, prohibiting pictures with scenes depicting crime and imposing a serious penalty, was killed in the judicial committee.[31] However, this was to be the start of a public outcry against crime pictures: by July, cities like Syracuse were banning gangster films from their screens.[32] On April 12, two days after defeat of the Assembly bill in California, Dr. Clinton Wunder, Executive Manager of the Academy of Motion Pictures Arts and Sciences, sought to quell the growing hysteria over gangster pictures in an address to the trade papers, citing figures that showed the output of sex and crime films was in fact dropping:

> In January and February this year, out of 48 features released by studio members of the Hays group, only nine contained crime or sex in any degree of prominence ... and of these nine, eight received endorsement by one or more of the official reviewing groups representing great national organizations, including the D.A.R., University Women's Ass'n, Y.M.C.A., Federated Women's Clubs, International Federation of Catholic Alumnae, and others.
> From January to June, 1930, the representatives of public groups who examine pictures here reviewed 607 new productions and nine out of every ten pictures won the endorsement of at least one group.[33]

If Wunder's comments seem disingenuous, it is well to remember that only a small output of Hollywood product was intended to be "adults only"; indeed, the vast majority of movies made by the studios were family-centered and made with juvenile patronage in mind. In fact, at the time of the controversy over sex and crime films, the studios and distributors mounted a campaign to "bring back the kiddies into the movie theater." The child audience was potentially huge, but with the advent of sound fewer children were attracted to the movies. Now, clean juvenile films were seen as a timely tonic, and studio heads, for a brief period in April 1931, fell over themselves to be seen rushing out child-friendly comedies that would also appeal to adults (like the 1931 re-boot of *Our Gang* with Jackie Cooper). But like other desperate attempts to increase audiences in the 1930s (such as "revival" pictures, for example) the move to restore juvenile attendance was short-lived and yielded disappointing box office results—perhaps it was never really meant to be anything more than a PR exercise by an industry worried about negative publicity. *Dracula*, on the other hand, in the same month, was going through the roof.

Dracula *Raises the Stakes*

Gary D. Rhodes has noted how journalists and exhibitors increasingly used the term "horror" to describe *Dracula* during the film's general release in 1931; that the gradual rise of the term, "horror," as "the nascent genre's name during the period from February to April 1931 [and thereafter] represents one of the key legacies of *Dracula*'s original release."[34] Also important to note is that reviewers of the film increasingly used the word "gruesome" in tandem. By early 1932, and the release of *Murders in the Rue Morgue*, not only was the term "horror film" in general use, but Universal was routinely using the word "gruesome" in their publicity—much to the chagrin, no doubt, of the Hays Office. The industry, in other words, quickly came to see gruesomeness as a defining characteristic—and key attraction—of the horror cycle.

Buoyed, then, by *Dracula*'s box office success, in May 1931, Universal released plans for its 1931–1932 season. *Dracula* had increased Universal's visibility in the first-run market[35]; also, expediently, Universal had adopted the policy of renting its films in groups of five or as singles, with no requirement for exhibitors to block-book films they did not want.[36] The 1931–1932 season therefore combined Junior Laemmle's ambitious strategy of targeting first-run houses with prestige productions, and the pragmatic production of "programmers," including 52 two-reel comedies; 26 sports one-reelers; 13 two-reel shorts based on the popular Detective Story Hour radio show, *The Shadow*; and four "all-talking serials," *Danger Island, Battling with Buffalo Bill, Heroes of the Law*, and *The Airmail Mystery*; plus newsreels and 13 John Hix *Strange as It Seems* shorts to be produced in color. The 26 proposed full-length features ran a mix of genres including a few low profile gangster pictures, such as *The Homicide Squad* (1931), and the rather more provocative *Baby Faced Gangster* written by Donald Henderson Clarke (who had scripted *Born Reckless* which John Ford directed at Fox in 1930). The latter was never made, possibly because it was deemed too near the knuckle after the real-life Baby-Face Nelson graduated from bank robbery to murder that same year. ("Gangsters are an important part of contemporary affairs," Carl Laemmle, Sr., had justified in response to newspaper columnists who criticized the studios for glorifying gangsters). Women's pictures were also included in the program, with titles like *Marriage Interlude, Nice Women* (1931) and *Impatient Maiden*, all to star Sidney Fox.[37] That petite brunette ingénue would also, of course, appear in *Murders in the Rue Morgue*, which, along with *Frankenstein* (still "starring Bela Lugosi") represented the extent of Universal's plans for a horror cycle at that point.

"The industry should be made to feel a demand for more socially useful pictures." On June 29 a report prepared by the Department of Research of the Association of Protestant Denominations, the Federal Council of Churches of Christ in America, lambasted the Hays Office, claiming that no amount of "cuts and eliminations" could improve the moral content of motion pictures, and urging community agencies to demand the help of the industry in promoting responsible citizenship and "all-round betterment." The report voiced the Council's lack of confidence in Hays himself "traced to the fact that the public has been encouraged to expect more from Mr. Hays than he has had the power to accomplish." This fresh attack on industry self-censorship and immoral industry practices—including block-booking—sent the Hays Office into a frenzy of retorts: Carl Milliken, the MPPDA's executive secretary and chief spokesman, immediately resigned as attaché to the Council. In response to the report, Will Hays accused the Council of "pamphleteering," and cited the case of the Rev. George Reid Andrews, the former chairman of the Council who had demanded 10 percent of the box office gross of *The King of Kings* (1927) in return for acting as technical advisor on the film, and who had subsequently launched an attack on the film industry when his demands were not met. "The task of self-regulation in the film industry is nowhere near accomplished," Hays stated, and in a remark that can be seen as a harbinger of things to come, he went on to comment, "only by sincere constructive cooperation from church and other bodies can the task be made lighter."[38] That cooperation was eventually to be obtained from the Catholics who endorsed the industry's tightened-up program of self-regulation when the Production Code Administration was set up in July 1934 to rigidly enforce the codes of censorship, thereby staving off any further calls for federal censorship. But the feud between the Hays Office and the Protestant Federal Church Council raged on into July 1931 as newspapers latched on to it, with many taking the Church's side.

So it was in a climate of ongoing controversies and general trepidation that Universal released *Frankenstein* in late November 1931. *The Film Daily* (November 12, 1931) reports that RKO had already determined pre-release to ban children from seeing the film in its 175 theaters: "Children under 12 years old will be barred from all RKO theaters during the showing of Universal's *Frankenstein*, according to orders sent to all RKO managers yesterday. Because of the nature of the story and the leading character monstrosity, the ban includes the kids even though they are accompanied by parents and guardians. All newspaper cuts and mats will carry the 'No children' line."[39]

Universal's nervousness and desire not to cause unnecessary controversy within the industry can also be seen in several announcements it made through the trades that month. Firstly, *Variety* reported on November 17, that Universal had made the decision to separate the releases of *Frankenstein* by three months to avoid having similar pictures hitting theaters at the same time[40]; however, Paramount's *Dr. Jekyll and Mr. Hyde* (1931) had finished shooting earlier that month and Zukor had already released *Murder by the Clock* (1931) (touted as the "female Dracula") in July. Universal may well have wanted to avoid accusations of deliberately trying to create a cycle. Two days later on November 19 Universal announced that it had made arrangements to buy the world rights to Robert Louis Stevenson's *The Suicide Club*, but was at pains to point out that this would be the last of its horror films that had started with *Dracula*.[41] The following week (November 25) Universal told *The Film Daily* that it had decided to discard two gangster films, *A Lady of Resource* and *Bullet Proof* (scripted by W.R. Burnett, who had written the original novel of *Little Caesar*), from its schedules.[42] But if Universal had been nervous prior to *Frankenstein*'s November 20 out-of-town tryout in such cities as Detroit, Washington and Milwaukee, it would throw caution to the wind afterward. "*Frankenstein* unreeled at RKO Downtown theater yesterday before audience that jammed place to doors and kept long line of standees waiting to get in for the second showing. It chilled them. It thrilled them. Everybody shivered and all had a great time,"[43] reported the *Detroit Mirror* on November 21. The film was an instant smash. Universal received a flock of telegrams from ecstatic theater owners reporting on *Frankenstein*'s blockbuster premiere screenings:

> Fred S. Meyer of Milwaukee wired that the first week broke every box office record at the Alhambra and the second week was starting even bigger. Ned Gerber of Cleveland said it opened to the best business in the history of the Hippodrome. Manny Gottlieb of Detroit reported that a riot squad had to be called after the house had filled in 45 minutes and an even bigger crowd was still waiting outside. Duke Hickey of the Boston Keith said it beat all opening day and daily records there. J. Matt Skorey of Omaha wired that the Orpheum had its longest lines in more than a year.[44]

"*Frankenstein* clicks," *The Film Daily* enthused on November 27: "Results of premiere showings of Frankenstein in Detroit, Washington, Milwaukee, Lawrence Mass., and Providence have convinced Universal that the public is still going for 'shockers.' In all these

Murders in the Rue Morgue (1932, Universal). By 1932 Universal was using the term "gruesome" in its advertising of horror films, indicating that this aspect was seen as a key selling point.

cities where the grotesque drama has been given a pre-release showing the critics' comments and the b.o. reactions have been highly favorable."[45]

But what exactly was it about *Frankenstein* that made it "click" with audiences and critics of the time? In his review of the film for the *New York Times* (December 5, 1931), Mordaunt Hall described it as "a stirring grand-guignol type of picture.... It is naturally a morbid, gruesome affair, but it is something to keep the spectator awake, for during its most spine-chilling periods it exacts attention."[46] Leo Meehan (*Motion Picture Herald*, November 14, 1931) objected to the film's "dreadfully brutal" scenes which carry "gruesomeness and cruelty just a little beyond reason or necessity," but added, "I have a hunch that ... people may rush to see *Frankenstein*."[47] *Variety* (December 8, 1931) commented that "appeal is candidly to the morbid side.... [The] maximum of shock is there"; the terms "gruesome" and "gruesomeness" are used three times during the course of the review.[48]

Scholar Kyle Edwards has noted the emphasis on "the ambivalent allure of *Frankenstein*" used in advertisements for the film. Indeed, an advertisement placed by Universal in the *Atlanta Constitution* (November 29, 1931), that Edwards cites as an example, carried a "friendly warning" that Frankenstein would agitate those with "a weak heart [who] cannot stand excitement or gruesomeness."[49] The term "gruesome" would be used again by Universal in its promotion of *Rue Morgue*, and marks a significant development in the evolving horror cycle: the very characteristic that had led Carl Laemmle, Sr., to reject *Dracula* as a property in the 1920s, had, by late 1931, become the cycle's key selling point—and would soon become the source of a new censorship controversy.

Universal prepared two special trailers for *Frankenstein*: a 100-foot teaser to run two weeks in advance of the opening, and a "remarkable de luxe" trailer to show one week before screenings.[50] Although neither of these 1931 trailers appear to have survived, *The Film Daily* (December 2, 1931) tells us that "the trailer everywhere is plugging the negative quality of the film ... and selling the nation."[51] A re-issue trailer circa 1933–1934 (featuring "The Uncanny Karloff") highlights the Monster's creation, its stalking Elizabeth (Mae Clarke) in her bedroom and its attempt to strangle its creator, Henry (Colin Clive), evoking that very same negative quality.

"Is this the beginnings of a cycle that ought to be retarded or killed?"

With *Frankenstein*, according to trade ads, "smashing all records wherever it plays"[52] and on its way to becoming the biggest money-maker of the season, by December 1931, Junior Laemmle was now looking to extend the horror cycle beyond *The Suicide Club*. Other studios, cottoning on to *Frankenstein*'s success, also began to cast around for "novelty material off the beaten path," as *The Film Daily* reported on December 7. However, "the likelihood of another 'cycle' is not very probable," the trade paper announced, "as the novelty angle is expected to make each production more or less an oddity of its own."[53] Considering the "favorable rumblings emanating from MGM over *Tarzan, the Ape Man* and *Freaks*,"[54] the case for "novelty" makes sense. Certainly some of the ballyhoo accompanying *Frankenstein* had played up the weird thrills of the picture, with novel stunts including exhibitors planting "hysterical" young girls in the audience and firing off gunshots behind the cinema

Fritz's torture of the Monster features prominently in this lobby card for the 1951 Realart re-release of *Frankenstein* (1931, Universal).

screen during the *Frankenstein* trailer.[55] However, the downplaying of the likelihood of another cycle, especially a horror one, can also be seen as the studios still trying to avoid unnecessary controversy and bad publicity. Indeed, on December 1, the trade papers reported that producers were—somewhat implausibly—claiming to be considering abolishing film cycles altogether: "past experience shows that the run to imitate successful pictures has been costly all around in the long run," *The Film Daily* reported. "Box Office results indicate that the cycle system is destructive from a patronage viewpoint."[56]

The Hays Office knew better than to believe this. Moreover, by December, *Frankenstein* had gotten the Hays Office alarmed, and for several good reasons. On November 2, the Hays Office had declared *Frankenstein* satisfactory under the Code, and "unless some of the official censor boards consider it gruesome, reasonably free from censorship action."[57] However, an editorial that appeared in *Variety* two weeks later on November 17 is almost certain to have made the Hays Office regret taking the same laissez-faire approach to *Frankenstein*, despite the concerns about gruesomeness, as they had to *Dracula*:

> Picture producers have discovered what is the first loophole in all forms of censorship as well as their own Hays Production Code. There is no provision, it is officially conceded, in any censor law which rules on the quality and extent of gruesomeness.

> Sex, crime, ridicule, politics, church and school—all are taken care of in the censor book.
> Universal's "Frankenstein" is bringing the censorial oversight of gruesomeness into the light. The Hays office admits that under the code it is powerless to take a stand on the subject. The same goes for the censors, it is also added. Only way in which the gruesome picture can suffer, it is pointed out, is by the fans themselves, staying away.[58]

Clearly such industry word-of-mouth threatened the public perception of the Hays Office as an effective censor, and also sent a signal to the studios that they had carte blanche when it came to horror films—irrespective of what studio heads might say publicly about "abolishing film cycles."

> We saw a preview of the Fox picture, ALMOST MARRIED. While it contains nothing contrary to the Code, it is another "gruesome" picture which falls in the same class with DRACULA, FRANKENSTEIN, DR. JEKYLL AND MR HYDE and FREAKS. Maybe we are starting a cycle. We would be pleased to have from New York any advice that can be given to help us to come to conclusions about it.[59]

Such was a RESUME placed in the Hays Office files on December 4, 1931. The possibility of another potentially controversial cycle particularly worried Jason Joy who wrote Will Hays the following day for advice. "Perhaps it would be wise to obtain an early estimate of the audience reaction and critical opinion concerning *Dracula* and *Frankenstein* by Universal; *Dr. Jekyll and Mr. Hyde* by Paramount; and *Almost Married* by Fox, all of which are in distribution or about to be distributed," Joy fretted, adding that MGM had "one-half shot" *Freaks* and that "Paramount has another 'gruesome' picture about to be put into production." He then asked Hays outright: "Is this the beginning of a cycle which ought to be retarded or killed? I am anxious to receive your advice."[60]

Certainly the phenomenal box office success of *Frankenstein* was something that contributed to Joy's unease about the growing cycle. In a later letter to Hays (January 11, 1932) he would talk about the studios being "much intrigued" by the fact that *Frankenstein* was taking in big money at theaters that "were about on the rocks."[61] Indeed *Frankenstein*'s success was front page news in the trades. On December 9, 1931, *The Film Daily* ran a front page editorial, "Frankenstein—A Story and a Moral": "When we saw 'Frankenstein' on the Universal lot during our recent trip to Hollywood," gushed Jack Alicoate, Editor-in Chief, "we predicted in this column that it would be the outstanding thriller of the year. It has proven itself to be a smash. Everywhere it plays, receipts go skyrocketing. Funny that it should conjure up hazy thoughts of this very business ... 'Frankenstein,' the picture, will no doubt do its share toward slaying the frankenstein picture bugaboo."[62]

"I thank the publicity and marketing men," Carl Laemmle, Sr., announced in another "Straight from the Shoulder Talk" advertisement (*The Film Daily*, December 14, 1931). In an extraordinarily brash—and some would say ill-advised—address to the industry he boasted of the advertising campaign for *Frankenstein*, "instead of soft-peddling on the fact that the picture is gruesome, grisly and shocking [the advertising men] made capital out of the fact. They dared people to see it. They warned them not to see it unless they had good nerves. They taunted the faint-hearted." Then Laemmle dared the marketing men to do the same with *Rue Morgue*, which he was now billing as a "super-shocker": "Take it from me it's no Pollyanna," Laemmle wrote. "It's red hot and grisly, and packed with the kind of dynamite that can be detonated by smart brains."[63]

Laemmle Sr. was, of course, simply exercising his showmanship during hard times. However, those in the Hays Office must have been wondering if Universal hadn't inadvertently created a "Frankenstein's monster" in other ways too. Several days before Laemmle's big exploitation speech was printed, Universal had received a "super-shock" of its own, one which would see the studio running to the Hays Office for protection. On December 15, *Variety* reported the drastic cuts that Kansas censors had demanded made to *Frankenstein*:

> *Frankenstein*, Universal's thriller may be kept out of Kansas by the state's board of picture censors through 34 cuts made in the talker, which practically destroys it as a picture.
>
> The entire eighth reel with the exception of a short interior in the home of Baron Frankenstein, is ruined. This reel shows the destruction of the man-made creature on the roof of the mill, by fire, set by an angry mob. The boards report says the film shows cruelty and tends to debase morals.
>
> Action of the censors will hold out the film from some 400 picture theatres in Kansas.... The picture was shown at the Mainstreet here last week to capacity business.[64]

Universal was understandably dismayed by this list of cuts which, to all intents and purposes, amounted to a barring of the film from the state of Kansas. Universal's Ted Fithian hastily sent a letter to Joy at the SRC accompanied by the list of cuts: "As you will readily see, these deletions destroy all the dramatic power of the picture and Junior urgently requests that you do anything you can to have these cuts re-considered."[65] Joy and Joseph Breen intervened, and the Kansas censors reduced the number of cuts, ultimately shortening the running time, according to a report in *Motion Picture Herald* (December 26, 1931), by "only" four minutes.[66] A resume in the Hays Office files dated December 17 states: "Word has been received from Mr. Breen that Universal's production, *Frankenstein*, has been passed by the Kansas State Board of Censors, This, of course, pleases us very much, as it does Universal. This news will be happily received by the other companies too, because the trade papers carried the word of the original rejection which created a wave of acrimonious anti-censor feeling among the folks of the industry."[67] Indeed, as those trade papers made clear to readers, it may well have been the "deluge of protest which had poured in from exhibitors and the public," as much as Joy and Breen's intercession, that had persuaded the Kansas censors to reconsider, especially as it had been thought that Harry H. Woodring, the governor of Kansas, would be asked to intervene otherwise, "since the censor board was appointed by him."[68] *Motion Picture Herald*, on December 19, reported that Kansas had been "up in arms over the action of the Kansas state censor board in barring *Frankenstein* from the entire state," with letters of protest "pouring in from all sides and newspapers ... adding their voice to the general resentment." The article relates how John C. Moffitt, film critic of the *Kansas Star*, had delivered a "scathing denunciation of the censors," likening the board to the Frankenstein monster, "that has been blindly butting and stumbling about the state for eighteen years, making it look ridiculous and interfering with the taxpayers' simple and inexpensive amusement." Moffitt had concluded in reference to the all-female Kansas state censor board: "When it comes right down to cases, 'Frankenstein,' the most popular picture of the year, is being kept from Kansans because it is not suitable for children and because three women do not like it."[69] Moffitt had, in fact, just returned from a year's stay in California as a film editor for Universal; at Laemmle Sr.'s request he oversaw the final re-cutting of *Frankenstein* for the Kansas censors who gave it the okay.[70]

Although Universal would encounter similar censorship difficulties with *Frankenstein* in Quebec, and the film would receive significant cuts in a number of other towns and cities (including outright bans in Arlington and Cohasset in Massachusetts, which Universal again called on the SRC to help overturn), the "victory" in Kansas was seen by Hollywood as somewhat of a vindication. In response to the considerable animosity that the episode had aroused in the studios towards the regional censors, James Wingate, then head of the New York Board of Censors (at that time one of the strictest and most influential of the state censorship boards), advised rebellious producers that adherence to the Production Code and its provisions would save them time and money and avert further threat of disciplinary action.[71] But the studios, buoyed by the extraordinary financial success of *Frankenstein* and the victory in Kansas, now saw opportunity to cash in on the potentially lucrative new "horror" cycle by exploiting the "gruesomeness" loophole in the Code.

A Flood of "Horror"

At the end of December 1931, the major studios started to dust off their gruesome thriller scripts, "buys of the past," as *Variety* put it, "that went into oblivion when studios laughed at what looked like the impossible." *Variety* reported that "Metro's *Freaks* was getting a horror slant," and that Paramount was dusting off an adaptation of Karel Čapek's futuristic robot rebellion play, *R.U.R.*, for Rouben Mamoulian (who was just coming off

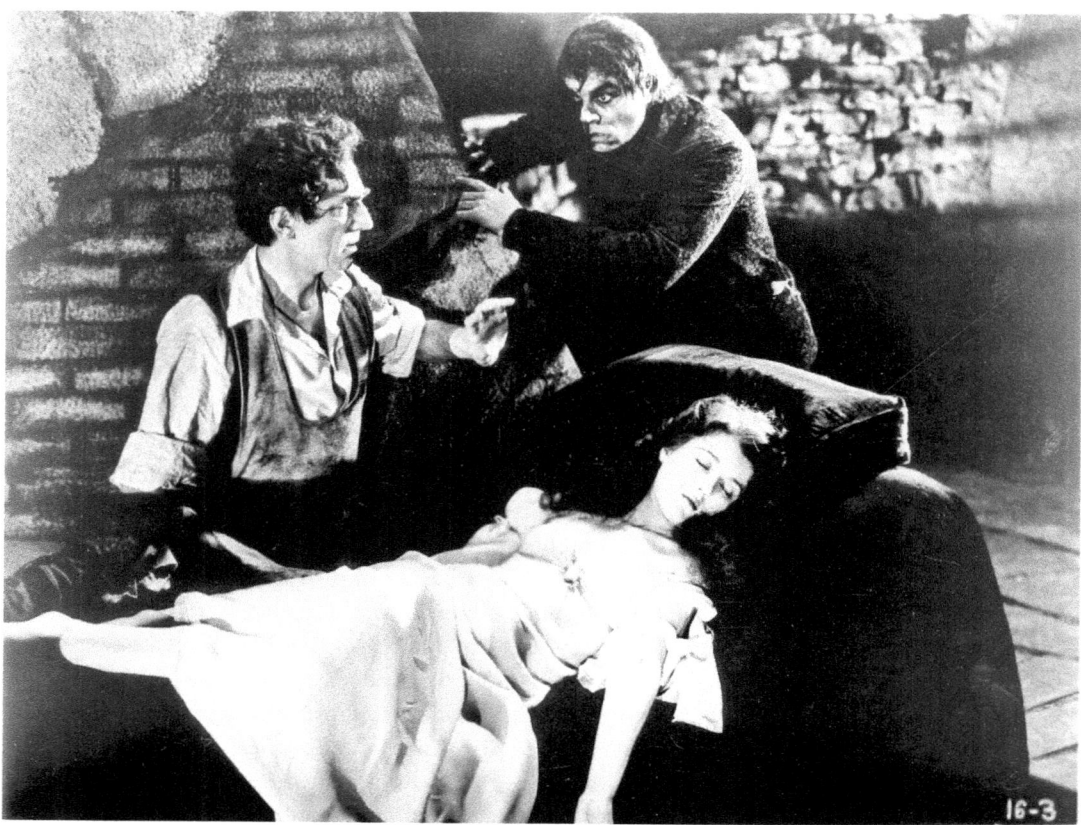

In *Murders in the Rue Morgue* (1932, Universal) Dr. Mirakle (Bela Lugosi) orders his manservant Janos (Noble Johnson) to hold off the police, while he prepares to mate Camille (Sidney Fox) with Erik the gorilla.

Dr. Jekyll and Mr. Hyde) to direct. *Variety* also reports on an intriguing anthology horror planned by one studio, concerning three men sentenced to hang, of whom the one who can tell the most horrible story will be permitted to live: "Studio will weld the three grewsome [sic] tales into one." Also reported were "stories involving apes, a' la *Murders in the Rue Morgue*, hypnotism, and highly imaginative themes are now getting serious attention from editors and readers."[72] With the Poverty Row studios and other small independent outfits all wanting to make a quick buck as well, the market looked set to be flooded with horror pictures, much as it had been with gangster movies earlier that year.

And, as he had done back in March, M.A. Lightman, President of the Motion Picture Theater Owners of America, issued another warning to the industry—this time not against gangster pictures but against too many horror films. "Declaring that drastic consequences will result to juvenile and family attendance if a flood of 'horror' films is put out as a result of the success of two or three such films already released," *The Film Daily* reported on December 28, "[Lightman] issued an earnest warning to producers to take immediate steps to prevent calamity":

> If Hollywood runs true to form the market will be flooded with horror films during the next four to five months. The success of *Dracula*, *Frankenstein* and the probable success of *Dr. Jekyll and Mr. Hyde* will, no doubt, lead a number of producers to believe that they can get away with similar productions ... if 15 or 20 of them are released during the next few months it is going to be very unfortunate. All that is necessary now, on top of all our other trials and tribulations, is to start frightening our child patrons to a point of hysteria and have them jumping about in their beds at night. Parents will certainly rise up in arms if this condition is permitted to develop. The far-sighted exhibitor will register protest to the producers in an effort to curtail the number of pictures of this type to be released. It is earnestly hoped that the large circuits will foresee the danger and stop it before it is too late.[73]

But at that point the large circuits—including the studios—had no intention of stopping the go-ahead for the production and exhibition of more horror films, and, by mid–January, any plans of "bringing-the-kids-back-to-the-theater" had been abandoned—at least for the time being. While horror movies were hot, the studios decided to hold off production of juvenile interest stories until the spring—it was felt that the public would probably have tired of the morbid by then, and that the demand may be for an entirely different kind of movie; a play for the kids might then also hit the fancy of the adults. During the run of *Frankenstein*, theaters such as the Orpheum in Los Angeles, had discouraged juvenile patronage of the film by raising children's admission to regular adult prices. Now more theaters planned to do the same during the playing of future horror films.[74]

Nevertheless, horror films, like gangster movies, were increasingly seen as posing a social and psychological threat to children and adolescents. Joy, in particular, expressed concern that the cycle would lead eventually to a straining for more and more horror "until the wave topples over and breaks." In a letter to Hays (January 11, 1932), he urged that they had a moral responsibility to define what was acceptable as screen content and what was not, as they had recently done with *Scarface* (1932), which through their censorial powers they had effectively turned into anti-gunmen propaganda. "If something as effective could be done about the so-called horror pictures we'd be very much happier than we are," Joy wrote.[75]

However, by February 1932, there were already doubts in some quarters that many more horror films would be made. "Producers are taking second thought on the advisibility of going into a tail-spin of horrors," the *New York Times* (February 14, 1932) reported. "By the time a new crop could be made ready for the harvest the balmy days of Spring will be abroad in the land, and the public mind conceivably in lighter mood."[76] By February 16 disappointing box office returns in Cincinnati for both *Rue Morgue* and Warner/First National's *The Hatchet Man* (1932) led the trades to speculate that the "horror cycle seems on the wane."[77] Ten days later, *The Film Daily* (February 26, 1932), reporting on the failure of MGM's *Freaks* to "draw any substantial business" in Baltimore as a possible indication that the public had already had enough of the shock and horror cycle, again posed the question "Is the cycle on the wane?"[78] *Freaks* went on to divide audiences at the box office but met with almost blanket condemnation by the critics. As Elias Savada has pointed out, the reviews of *Freaks* all had one thing in common: "an attempt to keep the younger patrons' morals from being corrupted by the 'shock' nature of the picture."[79] A letter from Idaho theater owner Herman J. Brown, printed in *Motion Picture Herald* on March 5, 1932, airs an opinion shared by many in the industry who were against horror pictures in general:

> I would like to add my voice in protest to that of other distributors, who foresee a prolonged cycle of "horror" pictures. One company has already announced a forthcoming "horror" picture. The only hope for this industry lies in getting away from the rubber stamp "cycle" film executive. I say film executive advisedly, as they are in no sense producers.
>
> Universal is to be congratulated; it has originality, it brought out "horror" pictures when the other rubber stamps were still making crook and third-rate sex pictures by the hundreds. It will know when to quit "horror" pictures, too.[80]

Thus, by early 1932 it was already clear that a moral backlash against the horror cycle was beginning to build.

The Horror Cycle Falters

Freaks, Dr. X, The Most Dangerous Game, The Mask of Fu Manchu, The Mummy, Island of Lost Souls, The Old Dark House, White Zombie, et al.—although 1932 looks to us now like a vanguard year for horror, it was in fact a crisis year, not only for the burgeoning genre but for American movies in general. It was at the height of the Depression and one of the worst years ever for cinema attendance. Admissions fell from 80 million per week in 1930 to 50 million by the start of 1933.[81] Worse yet, it seemed that nobody could agree upon the best strategy to combat declining theater revenues. This general lack of confidence translated into wild betting on pictures that emulated current box office successes, which led to yearly cycles, but cycles were rarely seen as anything other than short lived by the industry as trends were constantly changing (the term "genre," which suggests an evolution of filmic tropes over time, is never used by the industry commentators of the thirties). Instead, the studios responded to changing trends by rushing out films as quickly as possible, and by rewriting scripts to include topical content. The success of *Frankenstein* thus led to a sudden wave of gruesome mystery thrillers, but nobody was convinced that "horror" pictures had staying power, and it seemed unlikely that their production would continue past this first wave. An April 12, 1932, review of Lugosi's ill-fated horror play *Murdered Alive* described it as coming "at the tail end of the horror cycle with public presumably having its stomach full."[82] Undeniable, however, was the opportunity for sensational content that the horror picture afforded. "Stories classed as sensations are the only kinds being sought by studios," *Variety* opined (April 19, 1932). "Anything that doesn't bring a gasp isn't wanted and will only be sought out of necessity." The article goes on to speculate that this has been brought about by "Hollywood's realization of the wide difference in grosses between average pictures and those hitting public fancy," such as *Frankenstein*, whose success the studios attribute not to its horror angle "but because it was different to the ordinary run of stories." *Variety* concludes: "Hollywood is in for an era of what is good tabloid, outré, startling and black magic."[83]

Some studio executives certainly shared this opinion. Darryl F. Zanuck at Warner Bros. decided to adapt mystery play *Dr. X* (1932) as a newspaper-thriller-comedy rather than as a straight horror, and the studio continued to avoid the horror label with *Mystery of the Wax Museum* (1933), which Zanuck billed as a newspaper picture despite its including some of the most gruesome scenes of the whole of the thirties cycle. One reason for this disavowal of the horror tag was to mollify the Hays Office and the state censors, and the ploy worked, as both films were passed with their gruesome scenes intact as it was thought that the comedy element lightened the gruesomeness. This hybridization of the horror film and other popular cycles also seemed to appeal to audiences because of its inherent novelty value.

It was also becoming apparent by mid–1932 that straight "horror" pictures—like gangster movies—were increasingly frowned upon by ordinary parents as well as educationalists with a sense of moral responsibility. As early as February 20, 1932, B.O. Skinner, Director of Education at the Ohio State censor board, had written to Jason Joy at the Hays Office concerned by the "increasing tendency in the past few weeks to include in pictures scenes of horror and realism which we have found to be offensive to many people," citing *Rue Morgue* as an example: "scenes where 'Doctor Merkel' [sic] has woman tied with her hands above her head and is threatening and torturing her."[84] Herbert Blumer, a sociologist commissioned by the Payne Fund Studies to investigate the effects of movies on the nation's youth, was to include in his subsequent report—the influential *Movies and Conduct*—a chapter on horror pictures, showing in particular how they might arouse terror and fright in children. A letter which appeared in the movie magazine *Screenland* (June 1932) voices the opinion of a typical American father worried about the effects of horror pictures on his children:

> Now with the demise of gangster pictures, producers are turning again to the mystery and horror kind to give Mr. and Mrs. Public their full quota of thrills. During the past year or so we've had *Dracula, Dr. Jekyll and Mr. Hyde, Frankenstein*, and now, *Murders in the Rue Morgue*.
> I've seen them all once, some twice. They produce a kick as no other type of movie can. Fine stuff, say I, for the adult mind. But what about children?
> My neighbor's little boy, aged eight, had a wild nightmare after seeing one of the morbid movies. His mother confided he was scared nearly to death when his bedroom light was out. A child's mind is easily upset, (I recall my own nightmares after Dad told me a spooky story), and such shivery horror is, in my opinion, unfit fodder for childhood. Wonder what your other readers think?[85]

The editor saw fit to print this under the heading "Mothers Should Be Their Own Censors"—perhaps to argue that such films were not intended for children. However, the letter, and its inclusion in a popular movie magazine, illustrates how the notion of horror pictures as a source of moral concern was filtering down from regulators like Joy and Skinner to moviegoers, via newspapers and magazines.

In actual fact, underworld crime pictures would continue to concern the Hays Office for some time to come but, as the author of the above letter rightly claims, the gangster film in its pure form á la *The Public Enemy* and *Scarface* met its demise in the summer of 1932. In his book *Pre-Code Hollywood*, Thomas Doherty describes how protests from the general public as well as from moral guardians and state censors compelled Will Hays to publicly denounce the genre and to privately secure from the studios a tacit agreement that there would be no more "sawed off shotgun stuff." This, combined with, as Doherty puts it, a "sharp downturn in the box office mandate," made the gangster film more trouble than it was worth in the eyes of the studios.[86] All signs pointed to this happening with the horror cycle as well—there was "a growing public revulsion at too much horror"[87]—such that by June 1932 the trade papers were predicting that "pictures of gangdom, horror, courtroom and newspaper yarns are out for the coming season." "Horror," *Motion Picture Herald* announced with certainty on June 11, 1932, "has run its course."[88]

* * *

Come August 1932, the trades were surprised, then, that some studios still had horror pictures on their rosters. "Schedules show cycle of 'horror' pictures continuing," gasped the front page of *The Film Daily* (August 1, 1932). "At least four pictures of this type set for 1932–1933." The pictures in question were "Isle of Lost Souls" for Paramount and "Kong" for RKO, with United Artists' "Zombie," Fox's *Almost Married* and RKO's *The Most Dangerous*

Ivan Igor (Lionel Atwill) works on his sculpture in *Mystery of the Wax Museum* (1933, First National/Warner Bros.). The film was intended by the studio as "a thriller, away from the horror angle."

Game in current release. However, other studios were playing it safe: Warner Bros., First National, MGM, Fox, United Artists, Columbia and Worldwide had "no plans for productions with 'horror' themes during the next season."[89] Of those pictures in current release, box office was generally disappointing, indicating that the public was indeed tiring of horror pictures—at least those of the supernatural, mystery and mad scientist kind. In September 1932, in Chicago, *White Zombie* (1932) stayed for one week only at the United Artists Theater. Its advertising campaign failed to bring in the estimated $16,000, taking only $10,000: "Feeling here," *Variety* (September 6, 1932) reported, "is that the horror cycle is over and that more bookings of that kind only invites deficits."[90] In the same week Warner Bros. announced that in doing *Wax Museum*, it was in hopes of developing a new type of cycle, "intended as a thriller, but away from the horror angle."[91] Likewise, Paramount was rethinking how it would sell *Island of Lost Souls* in light of the public's turn against horror pictures. It was "admittedly a horror picture," *Variety* wrote, "but Paramount is trying to find a selling angle ... that will eliminate reference to it as such." The "cycle of blood and thunder," it seemed, was now officially deemed passed, and studios were afraid that their pictures would, in *Variety*'s words, "do a dive unless the creepy angle is eliminated."[92]

A general feeling that the horror cycle was over increasingly colored the trade reviews. In July, *Hollywood Filmograph* wrote of *The Old Dark House* that "we don't predict box office returns for this one, as the subject is passé and is not 'entertainment,' at the present day."[93] *Variety* (November 22, 1932) adjudged *The Most Dangerous Game* a "fantastic would-be thriller whose effects at horrifying are not very effective. It's not so much that the cycle is passed, but that 'Most Dangerous Game' is lacking in that which superior pictures of this type possessed."[94]

Finally, in December 1932, even Universal seemed to admit that the horror cycle was passed. Having originally announced an adaptation of Robert Louis Stevenson's "The Suicide Club" as early as November 1931, Universal had shelved the project six months later when the horror cycle began to show signs of flagging at the box office. Junior Laemmle now decided to revive the project for his cousin Edward Laemmle to direct, but had the story rewritten to remove the "horror." "Much of the early horror in the first treatment is being taken out," *Variety* noted, "with the feeling now at U that the creepy cycle has about exhausted its box office appeal."[95] Indeed, "The Suicide Club" was never made. As 1932 ended, so, it seemed, had the horror picture.

However, its controversy had not.

In January 1933, the Virginia censor banned *The Island of Lost Souls* on the grounds of it being "too extreme."[96] Although this was the only banning of the film in the United States, overseas *Lost Souls* was refused in several countries including Singapore, New Zealand, Holland, Tasmania, Germany, India, Hungary, Italy, South Africa, The Netherlands, Latvia and—most famously—the United Kingdom. In June 1932, Jason Joy had read the H.G. Wells novel *The Island of Dr. Moreau*, on which the film was to be based, which Paramount had sent to him, and warned production head B.P. Schulberg that any suggestion of "crossing animals with humans" should be abandoned in the screen treatment of the story as "you would never be permitted to suggest that sort of thing on the screen."[97] Paramount had subsequently made a film that had retained that very suggestion; however, not everyone seemed to spot it, not even Joy himself nor James Wingate, his successor at the Studio Relations Committee, who even praised Paramount on doing a "splendid job" in "handling a difficult subject."⁹⁸ Moreover, Joy and Wingate may well have been influenced by their faith in Paramount's ability to create a prestigious picture from an H.G. Wells novel. A review by critic Maude Latham expresses what Joy may have secretly felt in terms of the film's likely public reception: "[*The Island of Lost Souls*] would be expected only to attract the morbid-minded, but when your neighbors hear about it, they will all be there, and we predict the picture will make money..."⁹⁹

But, as did *Freaks*, *The Island of Lost Souls* seemed to polarize reviewers and audiences alike, and in some ways, illustrates the abiding attraction of "horror" as a niche product. Whereas *The Film Daily* denounced *Island of Lost Souls* as a "horror picture with a rather unpleasant theme about a mad scientist creating human-animal-monstrosities,"¹⁰⁰ other reviewers, such as Arthur Forde, writing in *Hollywood Filmograph* (December 10, 1932), seemed to appreciate its ability to challenge an audience:

> What the general reaction to this picture will be, one cannot with certainty say. Personally, I am for it one hundred percent. In other words, I ate it up and yelled for more. It is an example of the free use of imagination on the screen. I think the screen needs imagination—lots of it—even if it is morbid. I should say approximately half of the Pasadena audience agreed with me in this stand. The other half divided into two sections. One section left the theater during the preview, grunting and denouncing. The other remained, hair standing on end, also grunting and denouncing, but fascinated by the eerie tale being unfolded before them.¹⁰¹

Moreover, further reviews identified the "mutant" quality of the film, itself a suggestion of the future direction that thirties horror would take. "Literally the proper title is 'Island of the Lost Freaks,'" pronounced *Variety* (January 17, 1933). "It is decidedly a freak picture." The reviewer then goes on to describe the film as an "adventure story" of the type which rates high in the "cheaper magazines with the greater circulations."¹⁰² Intriguingly, the term "horror" appears nowhere in the review; instead, like Moreau's mutations themselves, *Island of Lost Souls* is seen as a hybrid, and a harbinger of things to come. "Kathleen Burke, Paramount's new 'Panther Woman' looks as though she is going to cause quite a stir," *The New Movie Magazine* announced that same month in its forecast of "What will happen to movies in 1933?" "There will be unusual cycles [in 1933]," the article predicts. "Last year we had a Gangster cycle, a Doctor cycle and a Grand Hotel cycle, which is carrying over into the New Year. This year expect a Fashion cycle, a Rural cycle and a Novelty production cycle with modified horror pictures."¹⁰³ Indeed horror pictures in a modified form would find new life after the extraordinary success of *King Kong*, and then in the self-parody of *Mad Love*, *Bride of Frankenstein* and *The Black Cat*—films which, if anything, exceeded the gruesomeness and brutality of what had gone before. "Graveyard-at-midnight cycle has passed like any number of given cycles," *Variety* (January 24, 1933) concluded in its review of Majestic Pictures' box office flop *The Vampire Bat* (1933), a "shiver picture, well enough done but coming along too late in the cycle to figure in the money ... there is the horror side of the 'Dracula' idea and also the pseudo-scientist angle of 'Frankenstein' ... now the fans know all those tricks and at this late date they're shock-proof from those devices."¹⁰⁴

The Cycle Revives Itself—"confidence restored!"

Just as the election of Roosevelt in March 1933 restored confidence in America's recovery from economic depression, the flood of animal and expedition films that came after

King Kong revitalized thirties horror by moving it towards novelty. That is not to say that films in the horror cycle lost their gruesomeness and brutality; on the contrary, the exotic savagery of the jungle movie seemed to lend itself to scenes of graphic horror: witness the opening of *Murders in the Zoo* (1933), for example, in which a man has his lips sewn together with catgut. Likewise, many 1933 reviews of *King Kong* recognized the film's "shocker stuff" and terror heightened by Fay Wray's continuous screaming in the film (*The Film Daily* warned that "some women and children may find it strong").[105] Sadism, captivity and torture—already present in the horror picture since *Frankenstein* and *Rue Morgue*, but heightened in *Murders in The Zoo* and *King Kong*—would be taken to new levels in *The Black Cat, Mad Love,* and *The Raven*.

Before then, though, in 1933 the MPPDA's board of directors, at the request of Will Hays would sign a Reaffirmation of Objectives of the Production Code, the first step towards widespread industry self-censorship via the Production Code Administration under Joseph Breen. An addendum would eventually be made to the Production Code itself removing the "gruesomeness" loophole, requiring producers to reduce scenes of excessive brutality, horror and gruesomeness to an absolute minimum, whilst also empowering the PCA to refuse the Production Code seal of approval on this basis.

As Thomas Schatz points out in *Genius of the System*, this signing of the Reaffirmation took place—significantly—on March 5, 1933: the same date that Roosevelt closed the banks for four days, thereby ending the bank runs that had plagued the Depression. The bank holiday, according to Schatz, heralded heavy federal subsidy via the National Industrial Recovery Act, a financial godsend to the Hollywood Studios which was, nevertheless, closely tied in with the industry's decision to reaffirm the Production Code.[106]

On March 4, 1933, *The Film Daily* celebrated Roosevelt's election into office with the headline "Industry Set for 'New Deal' Under Roosevelt." Industry chiefs, including Will Hays and Carl Laemmle, Sr., lined up to welcome the incumbent president and his New Deal which promised relief, recovery and reform. "Leaders in the film industry see renewed hope for the speedy enactment of measures that will restore the country, and motion picture business with it, to normal prosperity," announced the editorial.[107] These measures would come to include direct subsidy of the major chains and permission, for the time being, to exercise monopolies, thus enabling the chains later to establish a run zone clearance system of exhibition that would ensure the Hollywood majors maximum profits. The New Deal promised the film industry reconstructed prosperity, at least for the Hollywood majors. Meanwhile, *King Kong* itself seemed to represent a New Deal for the industry too. "*King Kong* Inaugurates a New Deal for the Forgotten Showman," ran an advertisement for the film, promising "Greatest Attendance in Show History."[108] Indeed, *King Kong*, which had opened on March 4, had already become a box office phenomenon. The banks may have been closed but people were flocking to theaters to see it. "No Money Yet New York dug up $89,931 in 4 days to see *King Kong*," RKO crowed in another advertisement on March 10.[109] Tying in their campaign to Roosevelt's extraordinary first weeks of presidency even more closely, on March 20 the studio announced: "Banks open! Confidence is Restored! America is 'around that corner' and America is going to spend! *King Kong* heads the parade of hit pictures that start a new deal in show business."[110]

Kong also led a parade of what *Variety* had called "freak pictures," modified horror pictures that played up the novelty angle. "RKO flashed something ingenious and brand-new in *King Kong*," *Movie Classic* announced in January 1934, "Universal toppled even its own previous horror tales with *The Invisible Man*—giving terror talkies a new boom."[111] "It has novelty and mystery and gets away from the *Frankenstein* type," added *Motion Picture Herald* (January 6, 1934).[112] The enthusiasm with which the reviewers received *The Invisible Man* (1933) speaks to the rebirth of the horror film in its new form as Novelty picture in 1934; by May, and the release of *The Black Cat*, the novelty angle was still modestly paying off: "Horror pix has two great exponents of the school, Karloff and Lugosi. Doing Grand Thrill Job" (*The Film Daily*, May 19, 1934).[113] Universal had, by this time, separated its horror output into prestige and programmer units, reflecting Junior's desire to build a first run presence with "A" pictures like *The Bride of Frankenstein* while also supplying low-budget pictures like *The Black Cat* to exhibitors for dual-features.[114] However, both films breached the boundaries of acceptability under the Production Code, due largely to their gruesomeness and brutality, and the former was heavily censored.

By 1936, along with the gangster picture, horror films would be largely outlawed by the Production Code Administration. The economic stability that Roosevelt's New Deal had brought to the Hollywood film industry meant that studios no longer had to gamble on the box office attraction of sensational screen content to keep going. Adopting greater self-censorship would enable the industry to head off pressure groups and avoid further calls for federal censorship. As Thomas Schatz observes, "If the PCA could forestall external threats and maintain public relations, the studios would learn to live with it."[115]

By then, however, the horror film was well and truly established, and rooted from the very start in gruesomeness.

2

"Five reels of transgression followed by one reel of retribution"

Thirties Horror and the Studios

"Some years ago the industry discovered that suggestiveness and sensation were necessary to its profits but that truth and consistency were not. Accordingly, it invented the perfect formula—five reels of transgression followed by one reel of retribution."
—*The Nation*, April 16, 1930[1]

Industry politics during the Great Depression allows us to understand the context of the thirties horror cycle in terms of its emergence and growth into an established genre—in other words *how* the cycle developed. However, a number of factors influenced the actual content of the thirties horror films, including: the work of producers, screenwriters and directors; the input from the Hays Office and later the Production Code Administration; and, as explored in this chapter, the Hollywood studio system itself, and its mode of production from the thirties onwards, which shaped not only the content of the classic horror film, but also its form.

As Thomas Doherty notes, "gruesomeness was to the horror film what sex was to the vice film."[2] Hollywood studio production chiefs trod a line between encouraging brutal and gruesome screen content in a bid to attract audiences to horror pictures, while also pacifying the Hays Office and state censors with happy endings which provided mitigation and moral recompense. In several instances this required endings to be reshot, or tag endings added after preview screenings (*Frankenstein, Freaks*); endings were often changed during the late stages of the scripting process in order to provide the necessary "compensating moral values" (*The Bride of Frankenstein*), or added to the narrative in a formulaic, somewhat obligatory manner during production (*Mystery of the Wax Museum*). In this way, it can be seen that producers were playing the same game with horror pictures as they were with gangster and vice films. "Producers have learned to get away with almost anything suggestive and immoral, if it only has the proper moral ending," wrote the National Council on Freedom from Censorship in 1933.[3] Certainly, the "proper moral ending" enabled producers of early thirties horror to get away with some strikingly gruesome and brutal scenes in the main body of the film.

As well, other industry factors, beyond the need for a happy ending, shaped the thirties horror film: movies were routinely cut to almost minimum feature length to satisfy the demands of exhibitors; retakes and additional scenes were often made after preview screenings to maximize audience approval (a system that became policy at most studios by 1930); and often numerous writers contributed to the development of a script under the control of a producer looking to capitalize on the success of a cycle. These were standard practices operated by the Hollywood studios and, as such, account for much of what made the thirties horror films what they are. In addition, studios withdrew a number of films from distribution for many years: *Dr. Jekyll and Mr. Hyde, Freaks, Mad Love, The Old Dark House, Mystery of the Wax Museum, Dr. X* and others languished in studio vaults for decades; their relatively recent rediscovery helps to give us a more complete understanding of the thirties cycle and the role played by the studios in formulating the genre.

Hollywood's Mode of Production in the Thirties

By *Dracula* in late 1930, the mode of production that is now commonly referred to as the "producer-unit system" was in operation throughout Hollywood. Developed by Irving Thalberg during his time as vice president in charge of production at Universal at the start of the twenties, and later perfected after he moved to Louis B. Mayer Productions (later merged to become Metro-Goldwyn-Mayer) in 1923, this new mode of production marked a shift in power away from the director to the producer. Under Thalberg's system, as Thomas Schatz observes, "It was no longer the director's responsibility to orchestrate the entire filmmaking process from conception and story development through editing to release [as it had been in the early silent era]. That responsibility steadily shifted to the producer."[4]

It was the vertical integration of the studios during the twenties that spurred Thalberg to find a mode of production that would enable him to control the flow and quality of product, so as to fulfill the quota of pictures ordered by the front office in New York, based in turn on the needs of its own theaters. Like any other mass production industry, the cinema developed its own version of the assembly line, as Schatz notes, "with an appropriate division and subdivision of labor."[5] The necessary use of sound stages for principle photography during the early sound period facilitated this shift of control to the producer, as filming was confined to the lot and therefore close to studio supervision in Hollywood, rather than on some distant location away from studio interference.

Thalberg himself took editorial control of the script development and planning of his films during preproduction and in the cutting of them after shooting. A strict regime of continuity shooting script, production schedule and detailed budget was seen as essential to ensure quality and efficiency. Associate producers oversaw the progress of individual productions; directors were brought in just before shooting—with the screenplay often already well developed by the time the director arrived—and stayed on for the first cut of the film, after which the film was previewed to an audience, and any necessary changes made. Thalberg, as Tino Balio writes, thought of the first cut of any film as basic raw material: "After sneak previews, he ordered entire scenes reshot and altered endings for greater audience appeal."[6] The director, by this stage, had often been moved on to his next production, and these reshoots taken by a different director. Thalberg's preview-retake system—a lengthy process of rewrites, reshoots and fine tuning—was costly but enabled him to tailor the film to audiences, which ultimately proved a profitable strategy for the studio.

Screenwriters were hired for their specialisms—whether it be dialogue, story construction, or rewriting. Scripts underwent various stages of development through basic scenario, longer visual treatment, and detailed shooting continuity which broke the film down into numbered sequences, scenes and shots. It was rare for one writer alone to see a screenplay through from concept to finished shooting continuity; more often different writers—or even writing teams—were assigned to each stage in the script development process, with Thalberg exerting editorial control overall, holding regular script conferences with the writers, associate producer and—during the later stages of the scripting process—the director.

Schatz makes the comment that even with the increased specialization and division of labor that came with Thalberg's system, "there was a good deal of interaction and collaboration among the principal creative personnel, all of which was orchestrated by Thalberg and one or more of his associates."[7] Although the director's authority and sense of ownership was necessarily minimized under Thalberg, it is also important to note that some directors had more say than others during the scripting stage and in the fine tuning of the finished picture. Under Thalberg's system, directors were generally left alone during the shooting—provided they stuck to the budget and didn't go over schedule. Likewise some writers, cinematographers and editors had more influence on the style and content of the movies they worked on than others. However, it was altogether a highly regimented system, and one quickly adopted by the other studios—Zanuck at Warner Bros.-First National, Selznick at RKO, Junior Laemmle at Universal. Its influence can be seen on almost all studio-produced horrors of the thirties, starting with *Dracula*.

"Bearing gruesome cargo": Dracula *(Universal, 1931)*

As Gary D. Rhodes has speculated, Universal may never have finally committed to a screen adaptation of the Bram Stoker story had it not been for Junior Laemmle.[8] Famously, Carl Laemmle, Sr.'s aversion to the horror film led him later to confess to journalists that he'd had reservations about his son creating such a cycle with *Dracula* and its follow-up, *Frankenstein*: "I said to Junior, 'I don't believe in horror pictures. It's morbid. None of our officers are for it. People don't want that sort of thing.' Only Junior wanted it. Only Junior stood out for it and he said to me, 'Yes, they do, Pop. They do want that sort of thing. Just give me a chance and I'll show you.' Well, he showed me. He showed us all."[9]

Junior Laemmle's more daring business approach at Universal and his claiming to understand the youth market may well have led him to give the go-ahead to *Dracula* precisely because of those same factors that had caused Universal and other studios to reject the project previously: things "that made people gasp and talk about it [on stage], such as the blood-sucking scenes."[10] Indeed, Junior Laemmle and Browning actually front-loaded the gruesome in *Dracula*—in the early scenes depicting the Count and his brides emerging from their coffins. This macabre reveal near the beginning of the film undercuts normal mystery-thriller conventions by presenting Dracula as a supernatural being upfront, rather than waiting to uncover the fact later in the story (as the novel had done). The strategy of

Universal front-loaded the morbid and grotesque into *Dracula* (1931, Universal) in this scene which shows the vampire brides (Geraldine Dvorak, Dorothy Tree and Cornelia Thaw) emerging from their coffins.

this approach is precisely to foreground the gruesome appeal of the subject matter, its sensationalism, which is what Junior Laemmle seems to have intended from the start; although he was equally careful to ensure that *Dracula* did not exceed the boundaries of acceptability in the eyes of the Hays Office or, indeed, the audience.

As Rhodes notes, at least five different writers attempted to adapt *Dracula* in 1930, producing numerous drafts, treatments and scripts, overseen by Junior Laemmle, associate producer E.M. Asher and Tod Browning.[11] Browning himself contributed to the final screenplay written with Garrett Fort (based on earlier drafts by Louis Bromfield and Dudley Murphy), on which Junior Laemmle gave notes. These notes clearly indicate awareness on Junior Laemmle's part of the line it was necessary for them to tread to bring *Dracula* to the screen. On the one hand, Junior Laemmle was keen to take a realistic approach to the picture (which later translated into the promotion of the film as being of "such convincing sincerity that it conveys the impression of actual reality [so that] the audience sit enthralled by its gruesome horrors"[12]), a desire on Junior Laemmle's part to proffer, in Rhodes' words, "horror for horror's sake."[13] On the other hand, other notes given by Laemmle suggest the removal of several gruesome scenes, such as one in which the three vampire women were to bite Renfield after opening his shirt,[14] and others (including a scene in which Renfield

2. "Five reels of transgression followed by one reel of retribution"   43

eats a fly from a lump of sugar) which he worried might be "awful strong."[15] In general, Junior Laemmle was careful to ensure that the final script complied with dictates of good taste in the treatment of "low, disgusting, unpleasant, though not necessarily evil subjects" required by the Production Code as adopted by the industry in 1930.[16]

Tod Browning followed Junior Laemmle's wishes in the shooting of the film, except, notably, in the scene in which Dracula bites Renfield. Perhaps again bearing in mind the Production Code, Junior Laemmle had advised that Dracula should "go only for women and not men."[17] However, in following Junior Laemmle's note to remove the gruesome scene in which the three vampire women bite Renfield, Browning substituted the perhaps even more transgressive action of Dracula's biting another male (the discrete fade to black as Dracula advances on the prone Renfield heightens the homoeroticism). Arthur Lennig suggests in his book, *The Immortal Count*, that Junior Laemmle viewed Dracula not only as a vampire but as a sexual being.[18] Critic Elliot Stein, writing in 1980, pinpoints what Junior Laemmle may have seen as being the sensational sexual appeal of *Dracula*: "the vampire is a coherent variation of one of the great figures of Western literature—Don Juan, the insatiable libertine."[19] In the same way that *Dracula* front-loads the morbid and grotesque in the scene showing Dracula emerging from his coffin near the start of the film, it is also remarkably frank and upfront in its portrayal of Dracula as a sexual predator. In the scene where Dracula first enters Lucy's bedroom to drink her blood, Browning and Junior

Dracula (1931, Universal). The studio emphasized the erotic undercurrent of the story in bedroom scenes such as this one, where the Count (Bela Lugosi) stalks Lucy (Frances Dade) while she apparently sleeps.

Laemmle make the choice first to show Lugosi standing outside Lucy's bedroom window staring up at her from the street below. We see from his point of view as Lucy opens the window, possibly to allow him entry. The film then switches to Lucy's point of view as she lies in bed reading a book, and Dracula as a bat appears in the open window. Lucy closes her eyes, and Dracula materializes in human form, advancing on her as she—seemingly—sleeps. The sequence is thus presented in a very matter of fact way which only serves to emphasize its erotic undercurrent. It is a classic seduction scene, with perverse intent. At this point *Dracula* becomes a "sex picture" pure and simple, and Browning's presentation of it is as such—something which Junior Laemmle would have been entirely aware of and no doubt encouraged.

There are indications that Browning and Junior Laemmle may have originally planned to emphasize more strongly the carnal aspects of the vampire's actual bite itself. Rhodes suggests that having Dracula bite his victims off screen may have been a concession to the Production Code edict that "brutal killings are not to be presented in detail."[20] (This particular aspect of the Code may also have influenced the staking of Lucy and the Count later in the film taking place off-screen.) However, there is evidence in the final shooting script that during the blood-sucking sequences Dracula was to display "fang-like teeth," and that bite marks on Lucy's neck (now mentioned only in the dialogue) were to have been shown in close-up in other scenes. Again, the reason for these deletions seems to have been to avoid censorship problems.[21] It is also possible, however, that the censorship trade-off for losing these gruesome details was a greater emphasis on the sexual angle in the film, as the decision seems to have been taken at some point during production to increase the number of Dracula's visits to Mina's bedroom from one to two, in effect adding a further scene of seduction in the film.[22] In this way, Junior Laemmle carefully weighed up the appeal of the gruesome and the morbid with that of sex in order to find a balance between the two that would gain censor approval and titillate rather than turn off audiences (of course, in *Dracula*—and horror films generally—these two factors of appeal are closely interconnected).

DRACULA AND THE PREVIEW-RETAKE SYSTEM

Although *Dracula* was not to suffer the same level of editorial revision during post production as Universal's subsequent pictures in the thirties cycle, such as *Frankenstein* and *Murders in the Rue Morgue*, it is noteworthy as one of the first sound productions for which Universal had adopted Thalberg's preview-retake system in late 1930. A report in *Motion Picture News* (September 20, 1930) described how Universal's new system would operate:

> The plan is this: Talkers are previewed in a very rough form with a lengthy footage. Scenes which are not even planned to be used are judged and scenes that are expected to go over well and fail are to be remade. The policy is retaking scenes that are weak and in some cases adding sequences in places that will bolster up the film. Three pictures have recently been "overhauled" at Universal, "The Cat Creeps," "East is West" and "Command to Love." When finished it is expected the talkers will show about fifty percent improvement.[23]

It seems unlikely that studios would want to include scenes that are "not even planned to be used" (to what purpose?), however, the overall aim of the policy seems clear: films would be recut based on audience's reactions in the preview screening, and if necessary new scenes added to "bolster up" interest within the narrative.

How did this affect Universal's handling of *Dracula*? Certainly, the shooting schedule indicates that retakes and additional scenes were made, with some of these shot following a preview screening of the film.[24] What exact footage was reshot and/or added to *Dracula*—and why—is still open to conjecture. Some writers have claimed that Laemmle Sr. had the "violent heebie-jeebies" over *Dracula* when it was screened for him and ordered retakes.[25] Mark Vieira claims that "Browning had made too many master shots and too few cutaways. It was too slow and there were not enough close ups of Lugosi."[26] Given that Browning had been under pressure to complete the film having gone over schedule, there may be an element of truth to this: "pick-ups" were shot at the end of production in November 1930, and retakes were made, including scenes with Lugosi, on January 2, 1931, following an audience preview.[27] It may be possible, however, that the retakes of Lugosi in Dracula's chambers were due to technical problems which left the dialogue inaudible to the audience (the original *Dracula* pressbook mentions how the sound recordist had to wait until the crackling flames in the fireplace had died down before the shooting of that scene could commence).[28] It is also possible that the preview audience found Lugosi's performance too mannered or his intonation difficult to understand in his early scene with Renfield (Lugosi's performance, in the retaken section of this scene, is noticeably toned down in comparison to the rest of the sequence.) Likewise, the "added scenes" to *Dracula* are difficult to determine as the film contains only a minor amount of material that was not indicated in the script, and, as Rhodes points out, the extra footage was filmed in only one day, likely suggesting it was limited (perhaps most significantly, new footage may have been needed when Dracula's visit to Mina's bedroom was split into two scenes).[29]

In any event, neither the main body of *Dracula*'s narrative nor its ending was drastically changed after preview, although—importantly—Junior Laemmle would take what he had learned through trialling the preview-retake system on *Dracula* to give the audience greater gruesome thrills (while simultaneously providing the necessary "compensating moral values") in subsequent horror pictures. In the case of Universal's next horror picture, the considerably more brutal *Frankenstein*, this would involve shooting a completely new compensatory epilogue to the film.

But what about *Dracula*'s ending as it stands? Truncation of the final scene depicting Dracula's demise in the abbey, his off-screen staking, and the removal of a scene in which Van Helsing saves the dead Renfield's soul by driving a stake through his body[30]—probable results of the film being tightened up for pace in the final stages of editing, and of the need to meet the Production Code—leaves the film feeling curiously unresolved, robbing the audience of catharsis, as several critics have noted.[31] What we are left with instead, as Kendall Phillips observes, are "Mina's almost erotic reaction to the vampire's death moans rather than the act itself," and "this sense that the threatening chaos of the vampire [is] not ended but only held off for the moment."[32] This may or may not have been Junior Laemmle or Tod Browning's intention; however, in *Dracula*, sex and death, the Freudian driving forces of horror films, come to the fore in the narrative, bolstered by the studio's handling of the film throughout its various production stages. Thus the basic formula is set for subsequent pictures in the cycle, which would continue with *Frankenstein*.

"Gruesomeness and cruelty beyond reason or necessity"
—Frankenstein *(Universal, 1931)*

Although *Dracula* was generating large profits by March 1931, Universal's annual fiscal report released that month showed a loss of over $2 million for the previous year.[33] This was due, in part, to falling theater attendance as a result of mass unemployment, but also because of the costs of Universal's super-productions like *All Quiet on the Western Front*. Subsequently, Laemmle Sr. had to reduce overheads by firing 350 people and shutting down production at the studio for six weeks until the end of April.[34] Despite these measures Universal continued to lose money; by May, it had begun to cut the salaries of its remaining employees and quietly reduce production budgets. As Schatz reports in *The Genius of the System*, Junior Laemmle's strategy of high-budget prestige production for first-run houses had required Universal to take out loans, but the studio's inability to keep borrowing, due to its lack of real-estate holdings with which to leverage further loans, meant that Universal had to revert to the kind of "closely regulated, high-efficiency system that Carl Sr. had relied on for decades."[35]

Although Junior Laemmle had to withdraw from high-budget super-productions, he did not want to relinquish the first-run market, and formula pictures seemed to be the only way forward. *Dracula*'s unexpected success amid this financial crisis no doubt prompted Junior Laemmle's decision to seek out more "gruesome" pictures, despite the objection of many at Universal who felt that the success of the first film had been a fluke, a one-off, and that Junior's proposed follow up, *Frankenstein*, was "a repeat, but more horrible as a shocker."[36] This may well, of course, have been what attracted Junior Laemmle to *Frankenstein* in the first place.

Historian Rudy Behlmer asserts that even before *Dracula* was in theaters, there had been discussions of a follow-up, and that "*Frankenstein* was a logical choice."[37] This may well be the case: the Peggy Webling play would have been known to Universal through Junior Laemmle's association with the *Dracula* playwright John L. Balderston, who was adapting it for the American stage and ramping up its sensational aspects in the process. Later, as a screenwriter, Balderston would go on to make significant contributions to a number of films in the 1930s horror cycle, and actively push the sex and cruelty angle in his scripts, as explored later in this book.

GRUESOMENESS AND BRUTALITY IN THE SCRIPT OF *FRANKENSTEIN*

As Schatz points out, for 18 months between August 1930 and February 1932, Junior Laemmle stopped supervising individual films altogether, concentrating instead on overseeing the entire feature schedule: part of his drive for high-efficiency at Universal.[38] The supervision of *Frankenstein*'s script development thus fell to scenario editor Richard Schayer, a former theatrical press agent and war correspondent who started in the film business as a publicity manager for Lewis J. Selznick before working as a scenarist at Vitagraph, Goldwyn, and, later, MGM. Like E.M. Asher (who had been an independent producer before joining Universal as an associate producer in 1930), Schayer was a creative executive employed to interface with Junior Laemmle and the various writers, directors and other key personnel involved in the making of the pictures. During his time at Universal, Schayer worked on a number of horror films—as did Asher—including *Rue Morgue*, *The Mummy*, *The Invisible Man* and *The Devil Doll*, for which he actively contributed story and/or dialogue[39]; it also seems that, as well as supervising the scenario of *Frankenstein*, he wrote without screen credit additional scenes, or at least versions of them, after the completion of principal photography.[40] As with Asher, it is difficult to be certain of the exact contribution that Schayer made to *Frankenstein*—and indeed the horror pictures that followed—and given the complexities of studio production we are unlikely ever to know for sure. What we do know is that Schayer was unable to write the script of *Frankenstein* himself, due to his administrative duties at Universal, and so he suggested to Junior Laemmle that they contract Robert Florey to co-write the script with Garrett Fort.[41]

Florey and Fort's resulting screenplay, based on a five page outline written by Florey, took the same approach to Mary Shelley's story that Balderston had adopted in his American adaptation of the stage play. Balderston had added a strong element of cruelty to the Webling version: Frankenstein seeks dominance over his creation with a whip and hot irons, and subjugates it into performing tricks like a dog. The relationship between Frankenstein and his creature is therefore that of master and slave.[42] The Florey and Fort script retained this

Fritz (Dwight Frye) terrorizes the Monster (Boris Karloff) in a brutal scene from *Frankenstein* (1931, Universal) (courtesy Ronald V. Borst/Hollywood Movie Posters).

dark, brutal tone, and included similar scenes of Frankenstein savagely whipping the Monster into submission.[43] Indeed, the relentlessly grim tone of the Florey-Fort script was of some concern to Universal executives, such as Henry Henigson, Universal's studio manager, who complained about the lack of comedy relief in the script. Fort sent a memo to Schayer admitting, "There is undoubtedly some need for comedy relief, but owing to the character of the story and the length of the script in its present form, I see no way to interject this beyond utilizing minor characters in whatever sequences such comedy can be used without appearing dragged in."[44] This suggests that a tone of gruesomeness and brutality had been the intention from the start, no doubt advocated by Junior Laemmle, and communicated by Schayer to his writers.

When James Whale took over from Florey as the film's director, he oversaw rewrites of the Florey-Fort script (by Fort and later Francis Edward Faragoh) which sought to make both Frankenstein and the Monster more sympathetic as screen characters, but the grim tone, for the most part, remained despite these changes (and some added "mild" scenes—such as the romantic interludes between Henry and his fiancée, Elizabeth—intended, no doubt, to help palliate the gruesomeness and brutality of the main plot). This perhaps prompted Jason Joy of the Studio Relations Committee to caution Universal on the final shooting script which Universal sent voluntarily to the Hays Office in August 1931: "We think that you ought to keep thoroughly in mind during the production of this picture that the telling of a story with a theme as gruesome as this will not permit the use of superlative incidents of the same character. Therefore, consideration should be given to scene A-12 showing the body of the hanged man, and scene H-4 showing the dwarf hanging by a chain; and several other gruesome incidents which make up a part of the script."[45] Whale and Universal ultimately decided not to take Joy's advice; these gruesome scenes would stay in.

"WE THOUGHT THAT MR. HENRY COULD DO WITH A GLASS OF HIS GREAT-GRANDMOTHER'S WINE": A COMPENSATORY HAPPY ENDING FOR *FRANKENSTEIN*

Junior Laemmle was shown a rough cut of *Frankenstein* in October 1931 and found the ending, in Schatz's words, "vaguely dissatisfying."[46] Whale had essentially shot the ending that Florey-Fort had devised in their draft of the script. Florey and Fort had, in fact, disagreed over Fort's idea to have the Monster hurl Frankenstein to his death from the burning windmill before itself perishing in the flames. Schayer, as scenario editor, had taken the final say on the matter, instructing the writers to proceed with killing off both Frankenstein and the Monster.[47] However, Junior Laemmle was now concerned that the final screen version, which ended thus, would leave the audience without any sense of hope or redemption for Henry Frankenstein—and that it also precluded the possibility of a sequel if the film proved successful at the box office. Whale resisted pressure to change the ending, at least until after the preview.[48] In fact the ending, as Whale shot it, includes an element of ambiguity: Frankenstein's seemingly lifeless body is retrieved by the mob and the Burgomaster orders it to be taken home, but the film leaves it unclear as to whether Frankenstein is actually dead or just unconscious, his fall having been broken by the sails of the windmill. Whether this was the intention, we do not know. Subsequent comments made to the press by Colin Clive suggest that he, at least, was under the impression that his screen character had perished.[49]

Whatever the case, the preview of *Frankenstein,* which took place on October 29 1931, seemed to confirm Junior Laemmle's suspicions about the ending. Moreover, although he had actively encouraged the film's gruesomeness from the start, having rejected the science fiction approach of Balderston's adaptation in favor of the horror angle, Junior Laemmle had not anticipated the audience's strong reaction to the film, which arose partly from the shock effects of the film's sound. From the opening scenes of grave robbing, to the shots of the body hanging from a gibbet that Jason Joy had cautioned Universal against, to shots of medical cadavers and human brains, to the reanimated corpse of the Monster itself, the preview audience, in 1931, had no cinematic frame of reference for the gruesome imagery of *Frankenstein.* And while audiences may have been used to horror pictures of the silent variety, they were caught off-guard by the heightened realism that sound brought to screen horror, the impact of which, in the hands of a knowing director like Whale, could be positively brutal on the unsuspecting viewer.

Indeed, the preview audience's startled response was such ("As it progressed, people got up, walked out, came back in, walked out again. It was an alarming thing")[50] that Universal executives, including Junior Laemmle himself, went into panic and immediately started to order changes to the film, involving the elimination of gruesome scenes such as the drowning of the child by the monster ("No little girl is going to drown in one of my pictures!" Carl Laemmle, Sr., apparently exclaimed).[51] Whale successfully argued for the scene to stay in, having already abbreviated it himself prior to the preview (although several state censor boards would later cut it out of the picture anyway). Still, Junior Laemmle needed to be sure that the film had not over stepped the mark of public acceptability before he relented from making extensive cuts to *Frankenstein.* Schayer and Whale, knowing how much was riding on the success of *Frankenstein* for Universal, agreed to write a new epilogue that would soften the overall impact of the film and provide the audience with the required closure and happy conclusion to the story.[52] Frankenstein would be allowed to live and in returning him to the bosom of his family and fiancée, normality would be restored, thus providing the traumatized audience with much-needed reassurance.

That was the plan, at least. The addition to the end of a horror film of a short tag scene delivering a happy conclusion would become as much a part of the horror formula as gruesomeness; only gruesomeness and brutality would become more extreme as the cycle progressed while the happy endings remained anything but convincing. Rick Worland has noted of *Frankenstein*'s epilogue: "to regard the ending as a categorical endorsement of the status quo we must forgive and forget a lot about Henry Frankenstein."[53] Perhaps, as the cycle progressed, audiences came to need the reassurance of the "happy ending" less, enjoying the thrills and the horror more.

Despite being awarded MPPDA approval, Junior Laemmle took the extra precaution of asking Will Hays to view *Frankenstein* personally, perhaps to get his opinion on the likelihood of state censors taking action against the film. Fred Beetson of the MPPDA had written to Junior Laemmle on November 2, 1931: "Some censors probably will object to Frankenstein's cry, when he creates the man: "In the name of God" and his line: "God—now I know how it feels to be a God." We still are of the opinion that these lines are usable because they are not spoken profanely, but it is very likely that they will not be accepted as such by some censors."[54]

Junior Laemmle was in the business of taking risks but Universal could ill afford to have audiences boycott the film on religious grounds (especially as Paramount were already mounting their production of *Dr. Jekyll and Mr. Hyde*, which threatened to rival *Frankenstein* in terms of its sensationalism) so before prints were struck, the now famous "warning" prologue delivered by Edward Van Sloan was added to assuage parents, religious groups, censors and any others who might take exception to the film's theme of divine presumption. The wording of the prologue ("I think it will thrill you. It may shock you. It may even horrify you"), of course, served to titillate audiences into the bargain, an irony that did not go unappreciated by industry wags, one of whom dubbed it "a brand new idea in film advertising ... warning the public against Unfavorable Reactions of a picture."[55]

Other trade journalists were less welcoming of the film's unprecedented scenes of horror. Leo Meehan, reviewing the film in *Motion Picture Herald* (November 14, 1931), particularly deplored the drowning of the girl, calling the scene "too dreadfully brutal, no matter what the story calls for.... It carries gruesomeness and cruelty just a little beyond reason or necessity." Meehan was right, however, when he went on to predict that these very aspects would draw sensation-seeking audiences to the film and ensure its word of mouth, "I have a hunch [audiences] may go 'just to see if it is as bad as Mrs. Jones said it was.'"[56]

Universal desperately needed a hit to stay afloat, and *Frankenstein* provided them with one, and for this very reason, the gruesomeness and cruelty of *Frankenstein*—for Junior Laemmle and Universal—*was* a necessity. Moreover, by tempering that gruesomeness with an upbeat narrative conclusion, so that audiences could go home feeling good about feeling bad, Junior Laemmle had found in *Frankenstein* the perfect box office formula, one which other studios would soon be trying to repeat.

"I'll show you what horror means!" Brutality and Sexual Sadism in Dr. Jekyll and Mr. Hyde *(Paramount, 1931)*

With Universal's *Dracula* all set to hit big at the box office, Paramount's Head of Production B.P. "Ben" Schulberg no doubt regretted turning down the property the previous year after colleagues called it too "morbid" to get past the censors. Paramount had started 1931 in the black, but thanks to the Depression had seen its profits fall from $18 million to $6 million in the space of 12 months.[57] Following a decade of aggressive expansion, Paramount had become the biggest studio in Hollywood but had gone into massive debt in the process. Now, like Universal, the studio was forced to make cuts to salaries and to reduce production budgets in order just to stay in business. Paramount desperately needed a box office hit, and *Dracula* showed signs of becoming one for Universal. As the cameras were starting to roll on Browning's picture, Schulberg was already planning a remake of *Dr. Jekyll and Mr. Hyde*. Paramount had last made a version of Stevenson's classic novella in 1920, starring John Barrymore as both the titular scientist and his evil alter-ego. Indeed, story synopses for a new adaptation of *Dr. Jekyll and Mr. Hyde* had been written as early as September 1930, by Enid Hibbard and Karl Owen Tunberg, among others.[58]

To direct the new version, Schulberg chose the artistically daring, formally innovative Rouben Mamoulian. The Russian émigré had been recruited from the Broadway stage in 1929 to direct talkies for Paramount, and had quickly established himself as one of the studio's top directors. *Dr. Jekyll and Mr. Hyde* would be a prestige production at Paramount. As was Schulberg's way, prestige pictures were left relatively free of executive control or front-office interference, as Schulberg and his associate producers preferred instead to concentrate their supervisory powers on standard features. Prestige productions were entrusted to star directors, like Ernst Lubitsch, Josef von Sternberg and Mamoulian himself, who generally acted as their own producers. Thus, Mamoulian, while at Paramount, enjoyed a degree of freedom rare within the Hollywood studio system of the 1930s.[59] Under his direction and Schulberg's nominal supervision, *Dr. Jekyll and Mr. Hyde* would push the Production Code to its absolute limits in terms of brutality and sheer sexual sadism. However, Mamoulian would also see his film shorn of almost nine minutes by Paramount for its general release, and the film would be withdrawn from distribution in 1941, remaining unseen for almost 25 years.

"Isn't Hyde a Lover after your own Heart?" Jekyll's Sexual Repression/Hyde's Sexual Sadism

In his 1969 monograph on Mamoulian, critic Tom Milne writes, "[T]he first thing that strikes one about Mamoulian's *Jekyll and Hyde* is its unequivocal sexual basis."[60] Indeed, Mamoulian turned Stevenson's classic into a story of the "struggle between Victorian sexual repression and sexual expression."[61] Where *Dracula* and *Frankenstein* had only hinted at sexual sadism, *Dr. Jekyll and Mr. Hyde* would become horror cinema's first full blown depiction of it. As Tom Johnson notes, "The monster's sadistic baiting and beating of the unfortunate Ivy must have been quite an ordeal for 1931 audiences; it's shocking enough today, and presents a dictionary definition of sexual harassment."[62] The character of Ivy (played in the 1931 film by Miriam Hopkins), a dancehall prostitute who becomes the focus of Hyde's sadistic attentions, did not, in fact, feature in Stevenson's story, but originated in Paramount's 1920 version, appropriated from Oscar Wilde's *The Picture of Dorian Gray*, and remained a staple of *Jekyll and Hyde* adaptations ever since.[63] The Ivy character brings a certain thematic symmetry to the story in terms of Victorian morality: Jekyll is engaged to the virtuous Muriel, but harbors desire for Ivy, a woman of ill-repute; Hyde embodies the eruption of this repressed sexual desire in degenerate, sadistic form.

As film critic Russ Hunter observes of the 1930s horror film, "Among the more significant innovations was the deepening of female roles. Productions became ever more creative in establishing soiled objects of desire around whom the story would unfold, and this had the effect—at least for many viewers—that the films exude a sense of sexual repression, impurity, anxiety and hysteria from both men and women."[64] If we take Ivy's story—dancehall girl caught between the advances of a kind, wealthy doctor and a sadistic underworld killer—we have a premise very much akin to that of an early 1930s "sex picture." Indeed, Jekyll and Hyde's principal screenwriter, Percy Heath, had made his name authoring the scripts of many risqué comedies of the late 1920s, several of which starred Clara Bow and Louise Brooks as similar fallen women.

The sexual repression, impurity, anxiety and hysteria of which Hunter speaks are already present in the early drafts of the *Jekyll and Hyde* script. In a 16-page treatment written by Heath, dated June 11, 1931, Jekyll and Lanyan, early in the story, help a "pretty but overdressed" young woman who trips on a curb after hastening to avoid being run down by a cab. She lifts her skirt to examine her knee. "Jekyll looks after her with a frank expression of desire," writes Heath. Lanyan chaffs Jekyll about this, and Jekyll "points out that both of them at times would like to give play to the purely animal instincts within them, times when they would like to defy the conventions and restrictions that hedge about men of their calling and position and to turn loose the baser half of each dual personality. He admits that it is, principally, the fear of sacrificing these benefits which accrue to a life of rigid respectability which keeps him (and other men) in the straight and narrow path."[65]

Hyde's sexual sadism, too, is already present in the first draft, written by Heath and Samuel Hoffenstein and dated June 23, 1931. The scene in which Hyde torments Ivy in her boarding house chambers is already fully written with much of the dialogue remaining unchanged in the final film. However, whereas in the film the scene is extended to highlight Hyde's sadism, in the first draft script the scene ends with Hyde's pronouncement that he is going to spend the night with Ivy before going away the next day. Also missing in the first draft is Ivy's famous striptease. Instead, the script cuts away from the scene as Ivy begins to undress, the script cuts away from the to scene as Ivy begins to undress, to Lanyan reporting the assault to a policeman—then returns to the scene to find "Ivy, in bed, is drawing the covers up over her."[66]

Thus, we can see that as they took the screenplay through the process of redrafting and revising, through to shooting, Mamoulian and his writers actually *increased* the level of sexual sadism in the story. Consequently, the complexities of the scripting process of *Jekyll and Hyde* (at least six drafts in all written by Heath and Hoffenstein between June and August 1931, plus numerous rewrites of certain scenes) arose partly from the challenges that the script posed to the Production Code, which, even in the pre–Code era, were considerable.

"Over the line": Hyde and the Hays Code

From the start, the sexual angle of *Dr. Jekyll and Mr. Hyde* made the project quite risky from the point of view of the censors. Paramount sent the *Jekyll and Hyde* script to the SRC in July 1931. James B. Fisher read it, and discussed the censorship aspects in detail with the associate producer, Richard Diggs. "Our suggestions were in regard to brutality contained in many situations in the script," Fisher wrote in a memo for the files, "and also to the lines in that portion of the script which deals with the relationship between Ivy and Hyde." Fisher pointed out that many lines of dialogue were dangerous from the standpoint of the Code and censorship and suggested that Diggs work with the writer in revising them.[67]

However, the next draft of the script, dated August 7, 1931, included essentially the same potentially objectionable material to the censors as the July draft. This time John V. Wilson wrote Ben Schulberg:

> Our chief concern is with regard to some of the dialogue and action incidental to Hyde's characterization which may appear to a portion of the public, as well as to the censors, as being overly brutal and at times somewhat too suggestive. We realize that the nature of the story necessitates the portrayal of evil and it is possible that for this reason you may find it possible to go a step further in both dialogue and action than would ordinarily be the case. However, we are of the opinion that the following material may be looked upon as being "over the line"[68]:

Wilson itemized material that was "over the line." This included the early scene where Ivy is beaten by one of her customers, which Wilson adjudged overly brutal. The August 7 script also had Hyde rescue a kitten from a tree only to drown it in the river; then (in a blackly comic scene reminiscent of Buñuel's surrealist classic *L'Age d'Or* [1930]) Hyde was to help a blind man cross the street only to leave him in the middle of a busy road.

Not surprisingly, the scene in which Hyde torments Ivy in her room caused the most concern in terms of its sadism and suggestiveness. Among the lines of dialogue that Wilson urged the studio to "tone down" were Hyde's taunting: "You wouldn't let me go tonight would you?... Now would you let me go tonight?... I am going to spend the night here with you ... the last night is always the sweetest

The brutality of *Dr. Jekyll and Mr Hyde* (1931, Paramount) caused much concern to the Studio Relations Committee. Here Frederic March as Hyde terrorizes Ivy Pearson (Miriam Hopkins).

you know ... and what a farewell this one will be! I don't know whether even when the dawn breaks I shall be able to tear myself from your living arms and your kisses."[69] In the same scene, the action in which Hyde is shown snapping Ivy's garter was also considered "over the line," as was Hyde's dialogue, "Look, my darling, how tight your garter is. You mustn't wear it so tight. It will bruise your pretty tender flesh." All of this dialogue and the action with the garter were to remain largely unchanged, with the exception of "tonight" and "night" being replaced by the less suggestive "evening," but this, the film's most disturbing scene of sexual sadism remained intact, with Paramount going all out for sensationalism.

In his book *Classical Film Violence*, Stephen Prince observes "filmmakers would never wholly subscribe to such a restrictive philosophy [as the Production Code], and the Studio Relations Committee found great difficulty in getting filmmakers to work within the Code."[70] Such is the case here. Although Paramount and Mamoulian made minor changes to the script of *Jekyll and Hyde*, they very likely failed to tone it down to a level that would completely satisfy the Hays Office. Nevertheless, on December 1, 1931, after seeing the finished film, Joy wrote to Schulberg to inform him that only one scene needed to be changed for Code reasons. Tellingly, the scene was not one that the SRC had previously voiced concerns about (Joy expresses the hope that "the excellence of the production will offset any apprehension that the theme is too harrowing"). Instead, the scene in question was Ivy's strip. Mamoulian had cut away from it in the script, but in the finished film, he had let the scene run on, showing Jekyll watch in anticipation as Ivy takes off her clothes before she gets into bed. Paramount and Mamoulian were clearly hedging their bets, whether the scene was justified by the needs of the story or not. Joy wrote that the scene should be considerably shortened, that the undressing should not be watched by Jekyll and that, "under no circumstances, should the audience know that Ivy has taken off all her clothes" in front of Dr. Jekyll.[71]

Paramount and Mamoulian then did an extraordinary thing: they ignored Joy's dictates.

According to Greg Mank, Paramount previewed *Jekyll and Hyde* on December 13, 1931, at Westwick Village Theater in Los Angeles. Jason Joy was there and after the screening demanded some eliminations in the second reel which most likely related to Ivy's strip scene.[72] A rather terse note in the PCA file, dated December 11, reads, "We again saw one reel of Paramount picture, *Dr. Jekyll and Mr. Hyde*. In our judgment it still contains matters inimical to the Code (Joy and Fisher)."[73] Today, only a cut down version of the striptease scene exists. In his DVD commentary to the film, Greg Mank claims that "the entire strip apparently does not exist anymore due to various cuts over the years."[74] Arguably, however, the most damaging cuts to *Dr. Jekyll and Mr. Hyde* were not made by the state censors or at the behest of the Hays Code or the Production Code Administration (when the film was reissued in 1935 the PCA requested the entire deletion of the undressing scene), but by Paramount after the film's Broadway premiere on New Year's Eve 1931.

HYDE GETS CUT BY THE STUDIO

Paramount made extensive cuts to *Jekyll and Hyde*, most likely in the intervals between the film's New York opening, its "deluxe run" and its subsequent general release. However, these cuts were not made to lessen the film's brutality and suggestiveness, as one might expect; if anything, the studio wanted to boost *Jekyll and Hyde*'s popular appeal by removing other scenes which might reduce the film's overall sensational impact on a mass audience.

Schulberg must have studied reviews of the film closely, especially *Variety*'s write up (January 6, 1932) which assessed *Jekyll and Hyde*'s box-office potential thus: "Elaborated, artistic version of the old standby. Promises abundant shocks and returns now that the fan public is horror conscious. Probably loses something in popular appeal by highbrow treatment, but will create talk. Runs 98 minutes in Broadway form, but easily adaptable to cutting."[75] The studio, more desperate for box office returns than artistic kudos, took its scissors to the film in the prescribed manner, and judging from the cuts that were made, quite possibly used the review in *Variety* as a guide.

Among the scenes to go was the now-celebrated opening sequence which adopts the use of subjective camerawork to show the world through Jekyll's eyes. The studio probably looked upon this sequence as the kind of "labored adornment" that *Variety* thought would weaken the production "for mob appeal." Also to be cut, possibly for the same reasons, was Jekyll's recitation of Keats' *Ode to a Nightingale*, prior to his first involuntary transformation into Hyde. The studio no doubt felt that the literary reference, despite its thematic relevance, would be lost on a mass audience, and also feared that the picture might get some bad laughs. Hence, other cuts included approximately 25 seconds from Jekyll's first transformation into a joyful, puppy-like Hyde, and two minutes from the final scene between a fraught Jekyll and Muriel, which the studio may have considered too theatrical. The studio may also have cut this scene down because it delayed the film's climax; the *Variety* reviewer had thought the film generally too long and that it dragged in places, which detracted from its highest box office possibilities. "The picture doesn't build to an effective climax, and it seems that the reason is the too slow and especially too labored approach to the climaxes."[76] Elsewhere in the review, the first transformation from Jekyll into Hyde is praised for carrying a "terrific punch," but the point is made that in each successive use of the device "it weakens for hair-raising effect." The reviewer also complained that this new version of the story had "brought up too many complications."

Paramount's solution was to make drastic cuts in an early part of the film, removing six minutes of footage from the third reel, and with it a whole section of the story, including one of the Jekyll/Hyde transformations. The cuts helped the pacing of the film but weakened Jekyll's motivation for wanting to take the potion that turns him into Hyde. Indeed, by seeking to play up the "vital reaction" of horror in the audience, Paramount chose to disregard what *Variety* (in its sidebar review, "The Woman's Angle") described as the film's appeal to female spectators: "Classic shocker loses much of its stark horror and consequent unpleasantness for women, by growing logical with psychoanalytical [sic] motivation and daringly presented sex appeal. Latest version made enticing instead of repellant to the girls."[77]

The cuts to *Dr. Jekyll and Mr. Hyde* raise some interesting cultural assumptions made by studios (and reviewers) in the 1930s about the horror conscious fan public; perceived as predominantly male, under-educated and provincial. Psychological depth was fine for the urbane "deluxe run" film-goer, but general release audiences wanted sensationalism—pure and simple.

HYDE IS HIDDEN FROM THE PUBLIC

While cuts to *Jekyll and Hyde* did not reduce the film's sexual sadism, the film was destined to become withdrawn from circulation for many years following the release of MGM's 1941 version, to resurface only in 1967. For that reason, *Dr. Jekyll and Mr. Hyde* was not included in the classic horror retrospectives that took place on television in the late 1950s and early 1960s; likewise, detailed writing about the film in magazines like *Famous Monsters of Filmland* (which included an article on *Jekyll and Hyde* as early as April 1961) was inevitably based on the cut version, and, due to the film's unavailability, more often than not drawn from the memory of the few who had seen it many years before. Consequently, Mamoulian's *Jekyll and Hyde* remained unseen and little known during the *Famous Monsters* era, and the subject of much speculation. In short, not many horror fans and critics of the *Famous Monsters* era would have been fully aware of the film's sexual suggestiveness and brutality (and this would have been the case for the majority of the early 1930s horror films which would have only been seen in versions censored by the PCA), or at least have witnessed it first-hand.

Why had *Jekyll and Hyde* been hidden away? When MGM embarked on the 1941 remake, the studio bought up all the prints of Mamoulian's film from Paramount and buried them in the vaults, so as to avoid comparisons between the two films[78] (the 1941 film was closely based on the 1931 Heath and Hoffenstein screenplay). The film collector and distributor, Raymond Rohauer, discovered the film in the MGM vaults in 1967. There is some disagreement as to whether the version he discovered was the one cut by Paramount or the original longer version prepared by Mamoulian (Tom Milne's detailed analysis of the film in his book *Mamoulian*, written in 1969, appears to be based on the longer cut); however, the full version was eventually restored for home video release in 1989.

"One of the most shocking instances of violence in early sound cinema": Murders in the Rue Morgue *(Universal, 1932)*

Much has been made of the politicking behind Junior Laemmle's decision to replace Robert Florey with James Whale as the director of *Frankenstein*, and Florey's subsequent "demotion" to the lower budgeted *Murders in the Rue Morgue*. Whatever Junior Laemmle's reasons for making these changes, it is likely that pragmatism played a large part in that decision. Indeed *Frankenstein* and *Rue Morgue* were but two of the "horror" properties that Junior Laemmle was considering after *Dracula* in 1931: other potential projects included a proposed remake of *The Hunchback of Notre Dame*, an adaptation of HG Wells' *The Invisible Man* and a version of the legend of *Cagliostro*.[79]

Hollywood studios, then as now, rarely commit to a feature project fully until the project reaches an advanced stage of development. Instead, a film property goes through various phases of scripting and pre-planning, and can be dropped from the slate at any point before the "greenlight" is given for actual production. Junior Laemmle likely did not fully commit to *Frankenstein* (or *Rue Morgue* for that matter) until after he had secured Whale, Universal's rising star, as its director. Even then, it is probable that the go ahead for *Frankenstein* was only given late in its development in June 1931 after Junior Laemmle had returned from meetings with the front office in New York having secured the finances for his planned 1931–1932 season.[80] Such was the antagonism within Universal towards the production of more horror pictures, even after *Dracula*'s success, that Junior Laemmle would have needed to shore up a very strong argument during those meetings to secure the finances for *Frankenstein* and *Rue Morgue* from the executives and shareholders. Selling Whale as the director of *Frankenstein* (and *Rue Morgue* as a low budget horror vehicle for Lugosi) may have been a tactic Junior Laemmle used to help win over the New York front office, by using his "stars" as leverage to obtain funds for the two films.

As it was, script difficulties held up *Rue Morgue* anyway, and so Junior Laemmle shifted the slate so that *Frankenstein* would go before the cameras first, the original plan having been for *Rue Morgue* to be produced before *Frankenstein*. But even by standards of the studio system, *Rue Morgue*'s script development was a protracted one. According to Arthur Lennig, an original treatment was submitted by Leo Birinski in April 1931; Tom Reed revised the treatment in May; screenplays were then submitted by various writers between June and October 1931, including drafts by Birinski, Reed, Francis Edwards Faragoh, Dale Van Every and John Huston[81] (other sources attribute the original treatment and final shooting continuity to Florey). Part of the difficulty early on seems to have been in determining the direction and approach of the story, especially as Poe's original had little in the way of plot. The adaptation might have emphasized the mystery-thriller angle that had been a staple for Universal in the 1920s. However, as the script developed, the studio ultimately opted for "horror"—with its attendant gruesomeness and brutality— which *Frankenstein* had concurrently adopted, and sexual sadism à la *Jekyll and Hyde* (then in development at Paramount, and a project known to Junior Laemmle via his friend E. J. "Eddie" Montagne, a story editor at Paramount). Thus *Rue Morgue*, as Kyle Edwards notes, "gradually morphed from a pensive, nonlinear detective story that kept physical contact with its grisly subject matter at arm's length into a grisly tale of bizarre characters and gruesome events."[82]

The most gruesome event in the picture was front-loaded to the first scene of the script, much as Junior Laemmle front-loaded the morbid and grotesque in *Dracula* and *Frankenstein*, and for similar reasons: to attract an audience through sheer sensationalism. It was another pragmatic move on Junior Laemmle's part, and one found to be highly questionable by the SRC, who, after *Frankenstein* and *Jekyll and Hyde*, were becoming alarmed not only by the gruesomeness in horror pictures but also by the strong undercurrents of sadism and sexual violence.

"We have read with interest your script of 'Murders' and believe it satisfactory under the Code and reasonably safe from censorship difficulties, provided the picture is not regarded as too gruesome and full of horrors," wrote SRC executive Fred Beetson to Junior Laemmle in October 1931. "It seems to us the two major situations which offer concern are: first, the scenes in which the unknown woman is murdered in the opening episode, especially shadows of her apparently strapped to a cross and second, the scene when the body of Camille's mother is discovered in the chimney."[83]

Despite the SRC's concerns, both scenes would stay in the script, the opening episode going on to become, according to Stephen Prince, "one of the most shocking instances of violence in early sound cinema."[84] However, Universal would be obliged to rethink the gruesomeness and brutality of the opening sequence of *Rue Morgue* and subsequently restructure the film so as to give the sequence less dominance; an unusual step to take and one that has led to much speculation by scholars in the intervening years.

"Our Feeling is that the screaming of the woman of the street … is over-stressed"

By *Rue Morgue*, Junior Laemmle was taking full advantage of the preview-retake system devised by Thalberg and adopted as studio policy by Universal in 1930. *Variety* reported on December 8th, 1931 that following the big reception of *Frankenstein*, Universal was adding $10,000 more worth of "sensational stuff" for *Murders in the Rue Morgue*.[85] On December 22, *Variety* revealed: "'Murders' is deemed to lack action and new sequences are being inserted."[86] A second Universal film, *Law and Order* (1931) was also having retakes for the same reason, indicating that Junior Laemmle was routinely adding sensational scenes to films that he felt needed to be bolstered up. The schedule for *Rue Morgue* indicates: "Dec 10, 7–10 days of retakes and added scenes, inc. INT. Mirakle's lab & Duel sequence (on Dec 10 for 1 day); 4 nights of filming on roof tops; process shots of roof tops; 3 days filming close ups of monkey in Selig Zoo & Dupin's room. $22k of retakes taking total budget to $186,090. The main action augmented being the climactic rooftop chase."[87]

Junior Laemmle, at some point, also made the decision to reorder the early sequences of the film, in effect foregoing a sensational opening by moving the "rotten blood" scene to later in the story. Exactly why this decision was taken is not clear. It may have been on the advice of the SRC: However, the change appears to have been made *before Rue Morgue* was screened for Jason Joy of the SRC in early January 1932, as a synopsis, written by the SRC shortly after the screening, begins the story as it is now.[88] It might have been because the preview audience had reacted badly to the scene, but this doesn't seem to have been the case either: *Rue Morgue* was previewed in January 1932 and the test screening was apparently a success; the *Hollywood Reporter* (January 6, 1932) described the film as a "perfectly delightful scare."[89] Junior Laemmle, as we know, was concerned that *Rue Morgue* lacked action: moving "rotten blood" further into the film may have been an attempt to inject more thrills and excitement into an otherwise draggy mid-section. Bryan Senn claims that the scene had been "deemed too downbeat an opening": this might also have been a reason for moving it.[90]

Whatever the reason for the change, the SRC objected to the scene anyway. Joy wrote to Junior Laemmle on January 8, 1932:

> Our feeling is that the screaming of the woman of the street in the scene ... is over-stressed, not only from the standpoint of possible audience reaction but also censorship objection. Because the victim is a woman

"Rotten Blood": A gruesome and much censored scene from *Murders in The Rue Morgue* (1932, Universal). Dr. Mirakle (Bela Lugosi) laments the death of the streetwalker (Arlene Francis) (courtesy of Ronald V. Borst/Hollywood Movie Posters).

2. "Five reels of transgression followed by one reel of retribution" 59

in this instance, which has not heretofore been the case in other so-called "horror" pictures recently been produced, censor boards are very likely to think that this scene is overdone in gruesomeness. We therefore suggest that you ought to consider making a new soundtrack for this scene, reducing the constant loud shrieking to lower moans and an occasional modified shriek.[91]

Although *Dr. Jekyll and Mr. Hyde* had presented sexual sadism to a 1931 audience, Hyde's onscreen brutality towards his female victims had largely taken the form of psychological cruelty; the torture in *Rue Morgue* by contrast, was physical, graphic and unprecedented. Inherent in the scene, in which the woman of the streets (Arlene Francis) is bound and bloodied, wearing only her underslip, was a sense of, in the words of Stephen Prince, "sexual bondage and fetishism"[92]; moreover, the soundtrack made the scene completely unremitting in terms of its focus on the victim's pain. *Dracula*, *Frankenstein* and *Jekyll and Hyde* had included female screams, but not the *sustained* screaming of *Rue Morgue*: this was something new and disturbing to the censors, and would, of course, be used to similar effect in *King Kong* in an attempt to titillate the audience.

According to Kyle Edwards, Junior Laemmle did address many of the concerns raised by the SRC including toning down the soundtrack of the woman screaming.[93] However, this was not enough to stop *Rue Morgue*, along with *Frankenstein*, from facing objections from a number of state censors, including bans in several towns in Massachusetts. This was in addition to *Frankenstein*'s problems with the censors in Kansas and Quebec. In these instances, Universal was not averse to making deep cuts to their films in order to secure their release in these states. In a letter to Joy, regarding the Massachusetts bans, screenwriter and executive Ted Fithian assured the SRC that loss of potential revenue as a result of these bans was sufficient for Universal to do "whatever we can to have these pictures released in those markets."[94] In the case of *Frankenstein*, Fithian was even prepared to cut the added happy ending, so that the film would fade out on the windmill burning, leaving the impression that Frankenstein was dead, "for this would help the moral support of the story."[95] An interesting reversal, given that Whale's original intention had been to end *Frankenstein* this way. More predictably, Fithian offered to cut out shots that "would apt to be construed as too gruesome," such as, in *Frankenstein*, "the dwarf bedeviling the monster with the whip and fire." In the case of *Rue Morgue*, Universal ended up cutting three minutes from the film in order to get it passed by a number of state censorship boards; inevitably, perhaps, the "rotten blood" scene was cut almost in its entirety in some states, including in New York State whose Censor Board specified:

Reel 2—Eliminate all distinct views (5) of girl bound and tied to cross beams in Dr. Mirakle's laboratory—all views of her writhing in agony—all views of Doctor standing over her, holding her arm while he tortures her.
Eliminate all sounds of girl and loud cries and moans of agony and fear, and accompanying dialogue: "Be patient. Are you in pain, Mademoiselle? It will only last a little longer."
"Ah! "You are so stubborn! Hush! It will only last one more minute and we shall see. We shall know if you are to be the bride of science."
"Oh! Hush! Hush! Now, Madamoiselle, now."
"The clots—the black spots! Your blood is rotten—black as your sins. You cheated me. Your beauty was a lie."
"Janos! Janos!"
"Get rid of it—get it away."[96]

On February 26, 1932, MPPDA general counsel CC. Pettijohn sent a memo to Jason Joy informing him that "for the first time in 27 years we have had action by the Seattle Censorship Board—they have ordered 247 feet removed from Universal's 'Murders.'"[97] A week earlier, B.O. Skinner had also written to Joy complaining about "scenes of horror and realism" in a number of recent pictures, specifically citing the "rotten blood" scene in *Rue Morgue* as a prime example.[98]

Despite the growing objections to horror pictures and the costs incurred in making the cuts demanded by state censors, Junior Laemmle, still buoyed by *Frankenstein*'s success despite relatively poor reviews and box office for *Rue Morgue*, announced to the *New York Times* in April 1932 that Universal had started a cycle of horror pictures and was "going to continue along that line."[99] Other Hollywood studios, suffering badly in the Depression, were already looking to the examples set by Universal and Paramount, and dusting off their novelty thriller scripts: Warner had *Dr. X*, based on a 1931 mystery play by Harry Warren Comstock and Allen C. Miller; RKO, an adaptation of Richard Connell's short story "The Most Dangerous Game"; and Paramount was following up *Jekyll and Hyde* with a script they called *Isle of Lost Souls,* taken from the H.G. Wells novel, *The Island of Doctor Moreau*. Even Irving Thalberg at MGM had been tailoring a short story property called "Spurs" into a screenplay with a horror slant. The resulting film, *Freaks*, would become one of the most mutilated in horror movie history; however, no amount of tinkering even by "The Boy Wonder" himself—including drastic re-cutting, retakes and a new tag ending—would save it at the box office. Indeed, MGM would eventually disown *Freaks*.

"Shudders of genuine distaste and horror": Freaks *(MGM, 1932)*

Of the Hollywood majors MGM/Loews was the least hard hit by the Depression. Nick Schenck, President of Loews Theaters (which owned MGM), had located most of its theaters in New York City which suffered less from the economic downturn than smaller cities and towns. In 1931, while other studios were facing bankruptcy and receivership, Loews was able to operate its theaters debt-free, having used its profits to pay off bank loans.[100] As the Depression worsened, however, by the end of that year, and into 1932, Schenck was forced to take steps as profits began to plunge (from $10 million in 1930 to $1.3 million in 1933[101]). He slashed salaries at the studio and began to restrict the number of films being produced. The pressure was on Irving Thalberg therefore to make each of those pictures a hit.

Thalberg's intention with *Freaks* was to cash in on the box office success of *Dracula* at Universal. The MGM archives show that Thalberg had been in possession of the Tod Robbins short story "Spurs" since 1928.[102] Some accounts cite director Tod Browning as first bringing the story to Thalberg's attention,[103] possibly as a vehicle for Harry Earles, the diminutive actor whom Browning had directed in *The Unholy Three* (1925, also based on a novel by Robbins, and produced by Thalberg). As *Variety* reported in its December 22, 1931, survey of horror productions being currently undertaken by the studios, *Freaks* was deliberately "getting a horror slant."[104] Thalberg, according to Elias Savada, sensing an upcoming horror cycle, was keen to outdo rival studios with a "shocker" that would be "more horrible than all the rest"[105] and commissioned screenwriter Willis Goldbeck to work up a suitable script, with instructions to that effect. As was his way, it is likely that Thalberg exerted overall editorial control over the script for *Freaks*, and developed the

2. "Five reels of transgression followed by one reel of retribution" 61

story in conference with Goldbeck and Browning before sending off Goldbeck to write the screenplay.

In their biography of Tod Browning, *Dark Carnival*, Savada and David J. Skal suggest that Browning had not liked that Thalberg and Goldbeck had taken the melancholic short story and turned it into a wild tale of revenge. They quote an interview with Browning's friend, William S. Hart, Jr., who claimed that Browning had originally envisaged a narrative fade out to *Freaks* that would underscore "the sadness of the poor people that couldn't ever be part of the other people." But that the studio had subsequently "forced on him ... this wild revenge to make a macabre ending."[106] Thalberg's box office imperative to emphasize the gruesome apparently won out over Browning's artistic aspirations for the picture. Any sour feelings on Browning's part are likely to have been exacerbated by his having that year signed a long-term contract with MGM at the expense of losing a more lucrative one at Paramount, a studio which may also have granted him more autonomy as a producer-director.[107] Browning would not flourish at MGM, and after *Miracles for Sale* (1939), would sink into obscurity.

Despite this initial disagreement between parties, Goldbeck's script came together quickly. Goldbeck submitted a temporary incomplete screenplay of 55 pages (with addi-

The cast of *Freaks* (1932, MGM) stare accusingly into the camera in this stark publicity still from the film.

tional dialogue written by Leon Gordon) to Thalberg on October 26, 1931, which Thalberg okayed (famously remarking, "I asked for something horrifying, and I got it"[108]). Goldbeck and Gordon then turned in a complete 107 page draft three days later, and it was with this script that Browning went into production. Scholars have reported that the project met considerable resistance from executives at MGM, including Thalberg's mentor, Louis B. Mayer.[109] However, Thalberg would not have been able to approve the production without receiving the "greenlight" from Schenck himself.[110] Significantly, Goldbeck and Gordon's script (dated October 29, 1931) was okayed by Eddie Mannix, Schenck's right-hand man at the studio, indicating support for the project by the New York front-office if not on the West Coast.[111]

THE MUTILATION OF *FREAKS*

Over the course of nine weeks at the end of 1932, Browning shot *Freaks* as per the Goldbeck/Gordon screenplay, including the gruesome revenge climax. However, it was to be the casting of real-life disabled performers in leading roles—which Thalberg no doubt saw at the time as a great publicity stunt and novelty attraction—that proved to be the undoing of *Freaks*. Preview screenings were met, according to Senn, by an "almost violent reaction."[112] A letter sent to the editor of *Photoplay* (May 1932) by a reader from San Diego professing to having seen "that picture *Freaks*" expresses how preview audiences likely received the film: "I certainly think that whoever directed it should be ashamed to have put his name to it. I didn't mind its gruesomeness so much, but its cheap vulgarity is something that left a bad taste in my mouth."[113]

Shortly following preview, in early January 1932, Thalberg ordered Browning to cut the film's most offensive scenes, including the opening which introduced the freaks playing "like children" in a country estate, and the gruesome ending involving castration of the strong man, Hercules, and the mutilation of his lover, Cleopatra, by the vengeful freaks. According to Senn, Browning himself hastily wrote the framing device of a carnival barker introducing the freaks, which served to bridge the missing sequences.[114] Browning shot four days of retakes, including an epilogue designed to soften the film's shock impact and give audiences a happy ending. A dialogue cutting continuity prepared by the film's editor, Basil Wrangell, dated January 29, 1932, confirms that the storm sequence climax was to segue into the Spieler revealing Cleopatra as the "Duck-Woman," followed by the Hans and Frieda tag ending.[115] Wrangell confirms the final footage count as 8200 feet, or approximately 90 minutes. It seems likely, at this point, that Thalberg and MGM were hoping that these changes would be sufficient to make *Freaks* viable at the box office (after all, *Frankenstein* had also suffered a disastrous preview, and had, after retakes and fine-tuning, gone on to become a great success)—such was Thalberg's belief in his own preview/retake system. However, a damning review by Leo Meehan (*Motion Picture Herald*, January 23, 1932) questioning the film's moral effect on the industry is likely to have further dampened enthusiasm for *Freaks* at MGM in the lead up to the film's release:

> Private lives of side show freaks are exposed and rather gruesomely dramatized for the edification (or education) of those morbid persons who enjoy gazing upon unfortunate, misshapen, cruelly deformed humanity.... [T]he playgoer who sees Boris Karloff in the role of the monster, or Frederic March as the hideous Mr. Hyde, know [sic] full well they are seeing only imaginary figures, created by the actor and the make-up man. Not so with these "freaks".... [T]his may, or may not, make the psychological reaction of the public entirely

different.... [T]hat the production is bold and novel in conception and execution is unquestioned.... [T]he question of the taste that prompted it, and the still more important question of the moral effect it will have on the industry with the large portion of the public—these are quite other matters.... [I]f a feeling of revulsion greets it, the picture may serve [a] good purpose: a warning to producers against offending the finer sensibilities of a vast number of people, and consequently acting as a dam to stem this rising tide of goose-flesh drama.[116]

MGM postponed the film's planned January 30 release date, while Thalberg set about drastically truncating the film, reducing its running time by 26 minutes, to the length of a double feature presentation. Like Universal, MGM would eventually move into double-features and develop its B picture unit; in MGM's case, Schenck would, after 1936, convert all subsequent-run Loews theaters to double features in response to the changing realities of the movie business.[117] However, MGM's motives for producing a 64-minute "revised version" of *Freaks* seem less to do with any plans they might have to bury the film in a double bill, than an attempt by the studio to cut aspects of the film that might cause further offence and bring the industry into disrepute. Although it is frequently claimed that what was cut from *Freaks* was merely "background," closer inspection of the script (the actual excised footage remains lost) reveals that much of what MGM cut is likely to have been considered risqué by the Hays Office. For example, the original script presents Venus as a "fallen woman" (it is suggested she may be a former prostitute) who is trying to reform; however, scenes which establish this were excised from the film during the preparation of the revised version. As David Gasten observes, "the cut footage reveals that the original plan was for Venus to be a bad girl who is trying to reform and to portray the difficulty she has in adjusting to the straight life. But in the final cut, Venus appears to be a good girl who was briefly and naïvely led astray by a bad man."[118] Preparation of the revised version, then, seems to have been a damage limitation exercise on the behalf of Thalberg and MGM.

There is apparently no surviving PCA case file of *Freaks*. Therefore it is impossible to ascertain what influence the Hays Office actually had in terms of the revisions made by MGM to *Freaks* before its release in February 1932. The studio would certainly try to downplay the "horror slant" in its advertising of the film, promoting it instead as a "thrilling and astounding love drama."[119] However, its box office was generally poor, affected by almost universally negative reviews. After its brief New York engagement, MGM withdrew *Freaks* from distribution in August 1932.

The disappearance of the *Freaks* PCA file (alongside that of *Kong Kong*) is itself a mystery: was *Freaks* an embarrassment to the Production Code Administration in later years? *Freaks* was one of the few 1930s horror films to be officially denied certification in Great Britain, banned on the grounds that it "exploited for commercial reasons the deformed people that it claimed to dignify."[120] Given this state of affairs, it seems highly unlikely that the PCA, after 1934, would have granted the seal for a re-issue, even with further cuts. Exploitation producer Dwain Esper may have attempted to circumvent the Production Code when he obtained the distribution rights in 1947, passing off the film as educational (hence the written prologue—or to use Doherty's term, exculpatory preface: "an inscription or precredit epigraph affirming the social import and theological worth of the forthcoming motion picture photoplay"[121]—tacked onto the beginning of *Freaks* by Esper for the re-release). Certainly Esper was known to play "cat-and-mouse" with the Breen Office, according to Eric Schaefer: "getting approval for ... motion pictures but never actually making the cuts dictated by Code officials."[122] Esper may have chosen to ignore the Breen Office altogether in the case of *Freaks*, releasing it without a seal in unaffiliated theatres or as an "adult-only" road show attraction under a variety of alternate titles: *Nature's Mistakes, The Monster Show* and *Forbidden Love*. In 1938 F.S. Harmon had written to Breen regarding another Esper picture, *Angkor* (1937) that had been awarded the seal after agreed cuts for female nudity, but which Esper exhibited under the title *Forbidden Adventure* with the nudity reinstated. "I am reasonably sure," wrote Harmon, "that in states without censor boards these people are showing this picture in a form different than they agreed to."[123] Breen considered Esper "a gentleman who is not responsible."[124] Furthermore, as Schaefer observes, the "states' rights" distribution system under which Esper and other exploitation exhibitors operated worked against the MPPDA in their efforts to enforce the Production Code: "Because regional distributors could insert scenes—or take them out—with a large degree of impunity, the MPPDA was always at risk when it passed a states' rights film."[125]

All in all, the film intended as "more horrible than all the rest" had turned into an embarrassment for Thalberg, MGM, the Hays Office and the industry in general. *Freaks* itself, by the time it resurfaced at the Cannes Film Festival in 1962, had been mutilated almost beyond recognition. However, the studios did seem to learn something from the fiasco, as Meehan suggested. The failure of *Freaks* did *not* deter studios from gruesomeness: if anything, producers were even more determined to smuggle gruesomeness into their stories than before—only, they became more adept at doing so.

"PRODUCERS HAVE LEARNED TO GET AWAY WITH
ALMOST ANYTHING SUGGESTIVE AND IMMORAL,
IF IT ONLY HAS THE PROPER MORAL ENDING"

If, as *The Nation* opined, "five reels of transgression followed by one reel of retribution" had proved the perfect formula for Hollywood on the introduction of the Production Code in 1930, the period following *Freaks* saw studios consolidate the horror film formula by pushing gruesome content while avoiding the problematic "horror" label in their marketing, and by conventionalizing the restorative happy ending in the form of the (re)union of the heterosexual couple. As *Frankenstein* and *Freaks* required upbeat epilogues to be added after preview, scriptwriters from thereon in were careful to write such happy endings into their initial screenplays—regardless of how (il)logically they fitted the storyline. Similarly, gruesome scenes were devised early on for sensational effect, and fed into the script development process from outline to treatment to screenplay.

In *Happy Endings and Hollywood Cinema*, James MacDowell comments on the flexibility of the "final couple" ending: quite apart from any ideological premises that it may convey as a "moral conclusion," the convention offers, according to MacDowell, "greatly varying kinds of ... happiness, closure and unrealism."[126] It is therefore not surprising that studios should opt, in the horror cycle as well as in other thirties cycles, to deploy such a "fit all" convention primarily to meet the requirements of the Production Code. Moreover, the final couple was, as MacDowell points out, a movie cliché back in the 1930s just as it is now: therefore, it is not so much that the horror films of the thirties have final couple endings as the fact that such endings were *added* to them to satisfy the Code that is significant. So, in *Mystery of the Wax Museum*, for example, we are presented in the last scene with a marriage proposal so out of the blue as to invoke unrealism; the viewer can make sense of it only by recognizing it as a convention. Hence the criticism leveled at the Production Code by censorship campaigners claiming that "producers have learned to get away with almost anything suggestive and immoral, if it only has the proper moral ending." Likewise, screenwriters were careful to ensure that gruesome set-pieces were not central to the plot, that they could be eliminated in part or whole by state censors without affecting the coherence of the story. Gruesomeness, therefore, became a part of the marketing mix for horror pictures.

"Synthetic flesh": Doctor X *(Warner Bros./First National, 1932)*

Warner/First National had, in fact, bought the rights to the play *Doctor X* with Bela Lugosi in mind.[127] However, Production Head Darryl F. Zanuck ended up steering *Doctor X* in a rather different direction to what was originally intended. Instead of making it a "gothic shocker," historian Scott MacQueen suggests that Zanuck and his writers, Robert Tasker and Earl Baldwin, sought to "flip" Universal's formula of "eighty percent horror, twenty percent comedy" on its head, turning *Doctor X* into a "newspaper thrill comedy" instead "but ensuring that the limited horror scenes would be the grisliest yet."[128] There are several possible reasons for this change. It has been suggested that Jack Warner's personal dislike of horror films may have influenced Zanuck to downplay this aspect of the play, reframing the story instead as a *The Front Page* (1931)–style newspaper film complete with a wisecracking reporter (played by Lee Tracy) solving the murder-mystery; Mervyn LeRoy's highly acclaimed newsroom drama *Five Star Final* (1931) had been a hit for Warner/First National the previous season.[129] Bryan Senn suggests that Warner were unconvinced of the "viability of the fledgling 'horror' genre"[130] and desired to soft peddle the horror angle. Certainly, emphasizing the murder-mystery element above the horror angle mollified the Hays Office at a time of concern about the possible "flood" of horror following the box office success of *Frankenstein*. In his weekly report to Hays, Jason Joy wrote on March 17, 1932: "Warner also has another story in process which is almost in the horror class. It is called DOCTOR X. Cannibalism is suggested, but it is being handled in such manner as to make it a murder mystery rather than a gruesome picture, and there is little cause for concern on our part that we will have another *Frankenstein* on our hands."[131]

As MacQueen has remarked, some aspects of *Doctor X*, including its theme of cannibalism and various grisly details such as the living heart on Dr. Wells' desk and his removal of his artificial arm, were "strong stuff for 1932,"[132] but the genre switch and emphasis on comedy made these elements altogether more palatable under the Production Code. On March 21, 1932, Joy wrote to Zanuck in reference to the script for *Doctor X*: "We have read the concluding pages of *Dr. X* and believe the picture will be satisfactory under the Code and free from any reasonable censorship difficulties providing the gruesome aspects are not too realistically developed. It is particularly important to handle carefully the scene in which Wells reveals himself as a monster with his human mask and his human arm."[133]

Joy went on in his letter to remark, "you know the situation in regards to the horror films," and advised Zanuck to protect himself "in those scenes which lend themselves to gruesomeness." Joy was, of course, referring in particular to the moment where the murderer, Dr. Wells, dons a hideously deformed mask of synthetic flesh: a scene that has been described by contemporary critics as "the closest thing to a clinical nightmare in the 1930s horror film."[134] The synthetic flesh scene had, in fact, appeared in the original adaptation written by George Rosenberg, a script which was otherwise completely reworked by Zanuck and his writers. Zanuck, it seems, made a considerable contribution to the script development. He, Tasker and Baldwin developed Rosenberg's idea of the killer fashioning an arm and mask from synthetic flesh, and turned it into a gruesome and surreal setpiece, describing the resulting monster as "large, horrible and bulging," with a "pig-like head and two cruel and fiery little eyes set on either side of a big snarling nose." Director Michael Curtiz filmed the sequence in graphic detail, showing each phase of the creature transformation from a variety of camera angles (perhaps to facilitate any shortening of the sequence required by state censors).

Dr. Wells (Preston Foster) dons his hideous mask of synthetic flesh in *Dr. X* (1932, First National/Warner Bros.) (courtesy of Ronald V. Borst/Hollywood Movie Posters).

As it was, Lamar Trotti, Joy's assistant at the Hays Office, wrote to Jack Warner on May 16, 1932, subsequent to a screening of *Doctor X*, pronouncing the film satisfactory under the Code: "While there has been a tendency on the part of the censors to do some cutting in pictures of this type where there is an element of the gruesome, there are no changes of this character which we suggest your making."[135] Zanuck's ploy to combine popular cycles (murder-mystery, newspaper and science-thriller), and to ensure a "final couple" ending (one that manages to be quite saucy) had paid off with the state censors, and with reviewers too, who praised its novelty and use of Technicolor. *Motion Picture Herald* advised exhibitors not to sell the picture as a "horror" film, as it was felt after the failure of *Freaks* that the horror cycle had about run its course, but instead to "bring out the idea that [the audience] will laugh until they cry and that they will be thrilled as they never have been before. Emphasize the Technicolor. Don't go in for that foolish line of having nurses in attendance and don't advise anyone to stay away if he has a weak heart."[136] Few critics objected to the gruesome scenes (although *Harrison's Reports* described the synthetic flesh sequence as "the most horrible thing seen in any horror picture, even worse than the transformation scene in *Dr. Jekyll and Mr. Hyde*"[137]).

The Film Daily reported on July 26, 1932, that *Doctor X* had been passed without eliminations by all censor boards in the United States, with the exception of Chicago, "where the censor board passed it after causing the elimination of one word"[138] However, *Doctor X* did not fare as well with the British Board of Film Censors, who demanded the synthetic flesh scene cut in its entirety. According to MacQueen, Will Hays persuaded the British censor instead to eliminate the words spoken by Wells, making it unclear that it was flesh that was being molded, and thereby managed to save the scene from total deletion.[139]

Doctor X went on to become one of Warner's top ten hits of the season, with exhibitors clamoring for the Technicolor version. However, it is telling that when Warner submitted the film for reissue to the Production Code Administration in 1937, MPPDA official Vincent G. Hart wrote Joseph Breen: "Governor Milliken and I looked at Warner Bros. reissue feature picture, *Doctor X*. Because of the gruesome theme, as we telegraphed you, we thought it was un–Codeable."[140] Warner was persuaded by Hart to quietly withdraw their application for Code Certificate of Approval, marking *Doctor X* significantly as one of the few pre–Code horror films to become effectively banned in the United States on the grounds of its gruesomeness after Breen took over the administration of the Production Code in 1934. Warner subsequently withdrew *Doctor X* from distribution; the Technicolor version was not to resurface until 1970 (along with *Mystery of the Wax Museum*, which had been considered lost), and later restored by the UCLA Film and Television Archive. *Doctor X* was rarely shown in TV revivals; many in the Monster Kid generation missing out on what critics now describe as "the greatest horror set piece of the thirties."[141]

"Pretty gruesome in spots": The Most Dangerous Game (RKO, 1932)

Needing a project during a long production hiatus on *King Kong*, producer/director team Merian C. Cooper and Ernest B. Schoedsack picked up Richard Connell's 1924 short story "The Most Dangerous Game" from the story department files at RKO. The tale of a big game hunter shipwrecked on an island where he is himself hunted by an insane Russian aristocrat, Count Zaroff, one previous (abortive) attempt had already been made to adapt the story into a film, by tyro screenwriter Harry Martin, who, circa 1930, tried to turn it into a zany comedy called *Who Zoo*.[142] A story editor's note attached to the unused treatment declared that it "does not make the most out of the situation that the story affords."[143] Cooper, Shoedsack and Selznick at RKO, however, immediately saw in the manhunt scenario the potential for a grisly "tropical thriller" (Hollywood was, at that time, "in thrall to jungle movies"[144] following the box office success of MGM's *Tarzan the Ape Man* [1932]). *King Kong* screenwriter James Ashmore Creelman was assigned to make the adaptation, and the result is a fascinating example of how studios were able to negotiate the level of brutal and gruesome screen content by ensuring that scripts also contained certain moral elements that would make them satisfactory under the Production Code.

A new synopsis was written, retaining the basics of Connell's short story but developing it in two significant areas. In Connell's story there are only two main characters: Zaroff (the hunter) and Rainsford (the hunted). Added to this was a love interest in the form of the female captive, Eve (played by Fay Wray in the film). "Thematically it is a sardonic tale of a hunter hunted—a man who is made to learn that to the sportsman's quarry, no odds are even, nor the game worth the stake," states the synopsis. "The love-story develops as the girl suspects the Russian's intentions, appeals to the boy, and in the end is saved by him."¹⁴⁵ Thus, screenwriter Creelman was able to build into his adaptation a moral "final couple" ending, and, unusually, one that retains story logic. Bryan Senn remarks: "the film's romance, what there is of it, is only implied (simply by the facts that the two protagonists are man and woman and that Rainsford is dedicated to protecting her)."¹⁴⁶ It is made clear in the synopsis that "Zaroff hunts *men*." As for the women survivors, "he saves them for those special occasions when a man-hunt has excited him emotionally. It is a symptom of his madness that his interest in women arouses him only after he has killed. Then he returns from the hunt to force the women to his will." We can see here RKO simultaneously injecting sexual sadism into the story while mitigating it as an abnormality: Zaroff's sadism is a portrayed quite clearly as clinical insanity triggered by "an injury to his head, caused while hunting," which has made Zaroff "quite mad."¹⁴⁷

Another mitigating factor as far as the Production Code was concerned, was the fact that gruesomeness in *The Most Dangerous Game* is restricted largely to one scene, albeit a shocking and memorable one. Zaroff's trophies, it is revealed, are the heads of men he has killed. This gruesome detail, already in the synopsis, was dramatized in the screenplay in the now-famous "trophy room" scene, although the number of heads on Zaroff's trophy wall would be reduced to one (again, by limiting the overall horror in their screenplays to individual scenes, producers were able to get away with a higher level of gruesomeness in those scenes). In the final script, dated May 5, 1932, screenwriter Creelman adds a further declamatory note, clearly wishing to assure the Hays Office that the trophy room scene would be filmed in a tasteful manner.

93. INT. TROPHY ROOM—NIGHT

MEDIUM SHOT. TRUCK moves with them as they approach stone shelf on the wall. What seemed to be a bust turns out to be a human head, preserved and mounted like the heads of animals.

(NOTE: throughout this sequence, room to be very dimly lit with all the heads etc., to be seen as shadowy, mummified, hardly discernible forms. Director is urged to avoid anything repulsive.)¹⁴⁸

In fact it is evident from the Hay's Office's response to the final screenplay that Selznick had previously submitted a treatment in order to obtain advice as to what would be acceptable under the Production Code. On May 9, 1932, Joy's assistant, Lamar Trotti, wrote to Selznick to advise him that the screenplay for *The Most Dangerous Game* was satisfactory under the Code and would be free from "any reasonable censorship difficulties": "As we suggested previously," Trotti added emphatically, "care should be taken in the trophy room scene to avoid gruesomeness."¹⁴⁹

But sensing further room for maneuver in terms of what might be acceptable under the Code, after submitting the final screenplay to the Hays Office, Selznick and his team prepared a "revised final draft," dated May 16, 1932 (possibly written by Edward Eliscu, after Creelman was reassigned by Selznick to adapt E. Arnot Robertson's 1929 Borneo-based novel *Three Came Unarmed*), which added more sensationalism to the trophy room scene: "A leather belt hangs on a hook. There is a stone pillar in which an iron ring is set. At one side are several instruments of torture—a wheel with spikes, a rack, iron pincers and screws etc. All these things, however, are so dimly lit as to be unnoticeable at this point."¹⁵⁰

Of course, the use of shadow and suggestion to mask intention within the screenplay– an ambiguity encouraged by the Production Code itself (as voiced by Jason Joy in his com-

"The Heads of Hunted Men in Zaroff's Trophy Room!" RKO used one of the film's most gruesome images in its advertising campaign for *The Most Dangerous Game* (1932, RKO).

ment that producers had to develop a system of representational conventions "from which conclusions might be drawn from the sophisticated mind, but which would mean nothing to the unsophisticated and inexperienced"[151]) could bring with it useful obfuscation of what would actually be shown on screen, as this continuity synopsis prepared by an RKO employee from the revised script suggests: "The trophy room presents a picture somewhat similar to the dungeons of the inquisitions. There are stone shelves, upon which are mounted shadowy, mummified heads of human beings!—a ferocious animal or two—and whole figures of men! There are instruments of torture—racks, screws, pillars of torture,—all cast in flickering shadows of the candle-light, to be less horrible but more foreboding."[152]

The scene was further modified by Schoedsack (and co-director Irving Pichel) in its filming, and a second gruesome jump scare introduced after Rainsford and Eve come across a mummified face on the wall. As written in the film's cutting continuity notes: "MEDIUM CLOSE UP—Head floating about in jar—Eve coming on at right foreground—backs into jar—turns—sees—gasps—horrified—."[153]

In a letter to Selznick dated July 22, 1932, following a preview screening of *The Most Dangerous Game* at the Ritz Theater the previous night, Joy remarked that although the film "seemed pretty gruesome in spots," it was "on the whole satisfactory as far as the Code is concerned." Indeed, Joy congratulated Selznick on "the beautiful photographic effects which add so much to the weird qualities of the picture," and adds that although he knew the story beforehand, he had "got a real thrill out of *The Most Dangerous Game.*"[154]

A More Gruesome *Game*?

Motion Picture Herald (July 30, 1932) reports that Selznick sent *The Most Dangerous Game* back into the cutting room after the July 21 preview screening "for working over before final presentation."[155] The preview running time is listed as 78 minutes, indicating that Selznick made substantial cuts, most likely for pace. Senn describes *The Most Dangerous Game* as a film in two parts: "The first half carefully builds the mood, creating a feeling of unease and dread, a feeling which is validated by the sheer fast-paced terror of the second half."[156] George E. Turner has also suggested that cuts were made to the trophy room sequence after the preview, removing further gruesome footage from the scene which to this day remains unrestored. According to Turner, there were deleted shots of a row of human heads, a full-figure man mauled by one of Zaroff's hounds, the mounted remains of two dogs, and an emaciated man pinned by an arrow to a tree trunk.[157] A production still does indeed exist of Zaroff surveying the full-figure corpse of a man being mauled by a (presumably taxidermied) hound. This gruesome trophy is in fact dimly visible in the movie print, seen in the background as Zaroff demonstrates the instruments of torture that "Ivan is such an artist with." Close examination of the scene reveals an awkward edit (at 35:10), slight discontinuity of eye-line in a close up of Rainsford (35:26) and use of a sound bridge taken from elsewhere in the scene ("The stupid fellow tried to escape, through the swamps of Fog Hollow," 33:50), suggesting that the trophy room scene has in fact been abbreviated as Turner claims, with these shots removed. However, Joy makes no comment of this gruesome footage in his letter to Selznick written the day after the preview, in which he specifies the gruesome details that might create difficulty with official censor boards: "[S]uch as the horrifying screams of the stokers as they are enveloped in the steam from the boilers, the shot of the human head bobbing in the alcoholic jar in the trophy room, the flash shot of one of the Count's men as he runs into the spear that McKenna [sic] has stuck in the ground, the sound of the crunching of the bones of one of the Count's men when McKenna breaks his back in the final struggle."[158]

Given the detail of Joy's notes, and the gruesomeness of the trophy room scene, it seems unlikely that Joy would *not* have included in his letter mention of the footage that Turner claims was eliminated only after the preview. Might it be, then, that Selznick—perhaps realizing that the trophy room scene was simply *too* gruesome in its full version—himself ordered it edited down *before* the preview took place? (Was this material even included in the "final draft" screenplay approved by the Hays Office?)

As Joy predicted, cuts were made to *The Most Dangerous Game* by censors. As Tom Johnson comments on the film's reception in Great Britain: "High on the lurid scale was a line delivered by Leslie Banks as the mad human-hunter, 'Kill, then love. When you have known that, you will have known ecstasy.' A close second must have been a severed head in a jar, or those mounted, like trophies, on Zaroff's wall."[159] These shots were deleted from British prints.

"The joys of fleshly love": The Old Dark House (Universal, 1932)

"Does any producer pay attention to the Hays Code?"[160] asked the *Hollywood Reporter* (June 25, 1931), quoting an anonymous screenwriter who declared "the Hays moral code is not even a joke anymore; it's just a memory."[161] Although studios—if not always the filmmakers themselves—needed to be seen to be observing the Production Code, incidents of spicing up scripts *after* the Hays Office gave its approval on a screenplay, as RKO did with *The Most Dangerous Game*, show that Heads of Production such as Selznick, willing to take their chances with state censors later on, were not above trying, on occasion, to pull the proverbial wool over the eyes of MPPDA officials in the bid for box office returns. Universal's *The Old Dark House* is another case in point where a studio attempted to slip material past the Studio Relations Committee without their noticing. It also provides further example of an important thirties horror film being buried in a studio vault for decades after its initial release, to resurface only in the late 1960s.

Venerated nowadays for its sardonic wit and frank sexuality (as in the oft-quoted speech by Eva Moore decrying "lustful red and white women" and accusing Gloria Stuart of reveling in "the joys of fleshly love"), the screenplay of *The Old Dark House* had been approved by Joy with the now familiar judgment that "it has elements in it which make it satisfactory under the code and free from reasonable censorship difficulties." However, Joy also noted a number of exceptions in the dialogue: "stray bits of profanity which now run through the script." In a letter to Junior Laemmle dated March 23, 1932, Joy itemized these with reference to the sequences in the screenplay, thus:

>"Hell"—A-3   "Damned fool"—H-28
>"Damn"—F-22   "Oh My God"—J-32[162]

Junior Laemmle duly replied to Joy on March 28, 1932, thanking him for noting the individual bits of profanity which, although not eliminated from the final script which Laemmle was sending that day, would be "taken out before the picture goes back into production."[163]

Rebecca Femm (Eva Moore) accuses Margaret Waverton (Gloria Stuart) of revelling in "the joys of fleshly love" in *The Old Dark House* (1932, Universal).

However, when Joy attended a screening of *The Old Dark House* at Universal on June 24, 1932, he was surprised to find that, despite Universal's assurances, not all the profanity seemed to have been removed. He wrote to Junior Laemmle the following day:

> We enjoyed very much seeing your picture, *The Old Dark House*, and in our opinion it seems satisfactory from the standpoint of the Code. It did, however, seem to us that the opening line of the picture sounded very much like the word "hell." Mr. Fithian informs us, however, that the word is instead "well." If this is the case we of course have no objection to the line. We believe, however, that you should be very careful in this instance to be sure that the sound in this particular line is distinct enough to carry the word which you intended to use.[164]

Perhaps the MPPDA in the early days of the Production Code were more concerned to enforce it than is often thought. Two days later, after a meeting of the MPPDA Board of Directors, Joy wrote to the New York offices of all of the Hollywood companies to politely inform them that a decision had been taken to write to them from then on regularly "giving you our opinion as to the probable censorship reception" of every picture in production. Joy presented this as a helpful step in trying to lessen mutilation of pictures by state censors. "It has been my experience that the censors are desirous of having advice," Joy wrote. "Of course I know that when you individually present your pictures to the Censor Board you are able to develop the arguments you need, but you can't be present personally at all of the presentations and for that reason you may find our letters helpful to your branch managers in other territories."¹⁶⁵

In seeking closer liaison with the front office, Joy was also trying to impress upon them the need to enforce the Production Code on the West Coast if they were to minimize censorship problems further down the line. Although *The Old Dark House*, as Joy wrote in his letter to Sydney Singerman at Universal's New York office, "ought to cause you no censorship difficulties," he added—rather presciently as it turned out—that "there will be pictures of yours that will require all the arguments and all the finesse we have to get them by in anything like their original shape."¹⁶⁶

The Old Dark House did have a few censorship difficulties of its own when Universal released it in October 1932. Ohio approved without eliminations, as did Kansas and New York, but these were the only state censors not to demand cuts. Massachusetts approved the picture without eliminations only after "hell" was removed. Pennsylvania, in addition to cutting "hell," ordered further eliminations of the more suggestive dialogue; also eliminated in Pennsylvania were some of the views of the fight between Brember Wills and Melvyn Douglas. Chicago, Alberta and Quebec eliminated much the same dialogue as Pennsylvania. As for the overseas territories, Australia cut the first part of Gloria Stuart's undressing scene as well as some of the racier dialogue; Latvia rejected the film altogether, considering it "empty, brutal and of inferior value as to contents."¹⁶⁷

When Universal submitted the film for reissue in 1936, Joseph Breen demanded the following dialogue cuts:

"...and of course ... he gives me money ... oh not very much ... just enough to keep me going."
"You probably won't believe me ... but.... Bill doesn't—he doesn't expect anything. Do you know what I mean by anything?"
"Yes, I know what you mean by anything..."¹⁶⁸

By then, studios were taking no chances with the Production Code. Universal even took the precaution of sending cutting continuities to the PCA rather than be "stuck" with the cost of prints if they did not secure the PCA certificate of approval for *The Old Dark House*. It was not, however, problems with the Production Code Administration that forced Universal to take *The Old Dark House* out of distribution but the lapse of their rights to J.B. Priestley's novel on which the film was based. Although the film had enjoyed theatrical re-releases until the early 1950s, after Universal pulled it from circulation in 1957 it became lost (it was not a part of Universal's *Shock! Theater* TV package) until director Curtis Harrington discovered a printable negative over ten years later.¹⁶⁹ Even after its revival in 1970, *The Old Dark House*, according to Greg Mank, only "tentatively made a limited comeback in archival showings in sad 16mm versions."¹⁷⁰ Further improvements were made in the mid–90s by the Library of Congress.¹⁷¹ James Whale's "lost masterpiece" was finally released on laserdisc in 1998 and VHS a year later.¹⁷² It was a long slow journey from obscurity to taking its rightful place, as Tom Weaver says, "among the best of the Universal horror films of the period."¹⁷³

"Lurid scenes of torture": The Mask of Fu Manchu (MGM, 1932)

In his DVD commentary to MGM's Boris Karloff vehicle Greg Mank describes *The Mask of Fu Manchu* as "the most gleefully sadistic, sexually delirious high camp horror movie of pre–Code Hollywood."[174] It is an apt description of a film that has become best known for its censorship cuts made to scenes of torture, sexual sadism and racism. *The Mask of Fu Manchu* also offers a fascinating study of Thalberg's preview-retake production system taken to chaotic (and costly) extremes. Reported to have gone into production without a finished script, only for production to have been halted mid-way, the director replaced, footage scrapped and filming begun again from scratch with a completely new screenplay (followed by weeks of retakes and additional scenes), *The Mask of Fu Manchu* has, in many ways, come to represent pre–Code Hollywood at its most "unbridled, salacious, subversive, and just plain bizarre."[175]

Certainly, MGM's intention, when it bought the rights to Sax Rohmer's 1932 novel, was to create a "*new* Fu Manchu ... not to be confused with the Fu Manchu of other pictures," distinct from the more sympathetic character of Paramount's The *Mysterious Fu Manchu* (1929) and sequel *The Return of Fu Manchu* (1930). MGM's version would follow the studio's vow to "go all out for sex" in its pictures, as announced in July 1932 by MGM's Head of Publicity, Howard Strickling[176]; a statement designed no doubt to grab trade headlines for the studio's new schedule. MGM already had hits in such Paul Bern-produced "sex fables" as *Susan Lenox* (1931), *As You Desire Me* and *Red-Headed Woman* (both 1932). Indeed, *Variety* estimated that during 1932–1933, no fewer than 352 of 440 pictures produced by Hollywood that year included "some sex slant."[177] "Sex pictures" were second only to "underworld crime" on the Hays Office's watch list of problematic cycles by October 1932 (with "horror-thrills" coming up third).[178] As Mank comments in *Hollywood Cauldron*, "sex would be a major spice of *The Mask of Fu Manchu*,"[179] adding a sado-erotic edge to the film's many torture sequences.

Thalberg did not supervise *Fu Manchu* himself; instead the assignment was given to Hunt Stromberg, the only producer at MGM who, by contract, could work without Thalberg's approval.[180] Even so MGM took the economy measure of capping the budget of *Fu Manchu* at $200K and limiting its shooting days to sixteen, as it did with two other films in production at that time: "Tin Foil," a romantic drama starring Robert Montgomery (released under the title *Faithless*[1932]), and *Kongo* (1932), the remake of Tod Browning's *West of Zanzibar* (1928), which was to be shot on the leftover sets of *Red Dust* (1932). As it turned out, all three films failed in that plan: *Kongo* suffered script difficulties which held it back (the screenwriter was Leon Gordon, who had co-written *Freaks*); "Tin Foil" was delayed due to Montgomery needing an emergency appendectomy, and *Fu Manchu* was held up by, as *Variety* (August 30, 1932) reports, "directorial disagreements, with Charles Brabin finally replacing Charles Vidor."[181]

Disagreements on *Fu Manchu* seem not to have been limited to the directorial department. In late July 1932, *Variety* had reported that scripting was "being done by Courtenay Terrett,"[182] an experienced screenwriter who specialized in adaptations. On August 3 and 4, Terrett turned in a total 37 pages of screenplay in sections to Stromberg,[183] and was quickly replaced by veteran playwright, screenwriter and film director Bayard Veiller, who fared little better. Veiller handed in 50 screenplay pages on August 19[184]; Stromberg duly replaced *him* with novice Irene Kuhn (although much of Veiller's dialogue and scenes, such as the bell torture sequence, seems to have made it into the final film) who, on August 23 and 24, presented Stromberg with a 16-page treatment and seven pages of screenplay.[185] Kuhn, at least, seemed to have done something right, despite her relative inexperience, as

Stromberg would retain her to co-write the complete screenplay with Edgar Allan Woolf and John Willard throughout the rest of the production.

What makes this quick procession of screenwriters all the more intriguing is that it appears to have been taking place *during* filming, which had started on August 6, without a script. According to Greg Mank, Stromberg "set the tone of the show": "dictating the storyline, scattershooting plots, tortures and melodrama" that the writers would try to turn into coherent screenplay pages during the two and a half months of production.[186] When MGM executives saw dailies mid–August they were said to be appalled. Production was halted while the writing team was sent off to work up a usable treatment (likely the August 23 one written by Kuhn). Heads would roll, but "box office producer" Stromberg's would not be one of them (Stromberg was also supervising *Red Dust*—another troubled production—concurrently). Instead, debuting director Charles Vidor was fired, and Charles Brabin was switched from *Rasputin and The Empress* (1932)—then shooting at MGM and having troubles of its own—as Vidor's replacement.

Some scholars have suggested that the MGM front office had taken exception to the sensationalism of the material that Vidor filmed—that the torture and sexual sadism in that early footage had been *too* extreme—and MGM ordered it to be scrapped. However, if the footage was indeed scrapped, this seems unlikely to be the reason why it would have been so. It is more likely perhaps that Vidor filmed Terrett's script pages, turned in before production started, and that this footage could not be used later, after the screenplay was rewritten, because it no longer fitted the story. On the other hand it is possible that some of it *was* used. In February 1933, *Movie Classic* wrote that "Charles Vidor had been given the first scenes ... to direct, while Charles Brabin was busy elsewhere"[187]; perhaps *Movie Classic* was just being discreet about Vidor having been fired, but it may also be that at least some of the existing footage in *Fu Manchu* was directed by Vidor.

As it was, a month of retakes and added scenes ensued, swelling the final budget to $327,627[188]; some of these added scenes were presumably the result of the film having gone into production without a complete screenplay. The practice of rewriting the screenplay during filming was fairly common; however, starting production without a full screenplay of *some* description was unusual in the high efficiency days of the Hollywood studio system of the 1930s and 1940s, going very much against the standardized mode of production. Another factor affecting the protracted schedule was that four of the players in the film—Karloff, Myrna Loy, Karen Morley, and Jean Hersholt were shooting other pictures at the same time for other studios (Karloff flitted between *Fu Manchu* and *The Mummy*, then in production at Universal).[189]

"Faster, faster, faster, faster!"

Stromberg ensured that a good number of sensational elements made it into the final version of *Fu Manchu*. As Bryan Senn details in his book, *Golden Horrors*:

> The film is filled with vicious tortures (Sir Lionel becoming "frantic with thirst [and] unspeakably foul" under the torture of The Bell; Nayland Smith strapped to one end of a monstrous teeter-totter with the sand running out the other end, lowering him head downwards into a pit of hungry alligators; Von Berg held between two walls of sharp spikes moving ever closer to his corpulent, sweating form) and shots of creeping spiders and slithering snakes. Couple this with the general air of sadism exuded by the laughing Fu Manchu and the wanton sado-eroticism of his wicked daughter, and *The Mask of Fu Manchu* contains enough horrific sensationalism to keep most viewers engrossed.[190]

Myrna Loy (who played Fu Manchu's daughter) described her character as a "sadistic nymphomaniac."[191] The film depicts her becoming sexually aroused as she orders the "not unhandsome" hero Terry (Charles Starrett) to be hung up and whipped: "Faster, faster, faster, faster!" she commands, before having the stripped and beaten man cut down from the rope from which he hangs, and taken to her boudoir where she joins him on the bed, only to be interrupted by her father. "May I suggest a slight delay in your customary procedure?" Fu Manchu (Karloff) intones. The sequence makes use of what Doherty terms "figurative literalness": "mental pictures of what lay just beyond the edges of the film frame … vividly outlined."[192] It does this primarily through the power of cinematography and editing to suggest off-screen action. Describing the sequence, Senn writes that Loy's character "trembles and cries out in almost orgasmic shudder … before finally grabbing the whip herself to apply it first-hand in an uncontrollable burst of frenzied sado-sexuality."[193] This action is, however, wholly implied. We see her step forward and out of shot, but we never actually see her take the whip, although the editing of the sequence plants this idea firmly in our minds. Likewise, in the boudoir, as Loy bends over Starrett to kiss him, we cut away just before the kiss to a shot of Karloff entering the room, and then cut back to Loy just *after* she has kissed her victim. Figurative literalness, thus, as Doherty explains, "could infuse the onscreen narrative with otherwise censorable material."[194] In the case of the thirties horror cycle, directors would increasingly use off-screen action to present gruesomeness, as I discuss later.

One might suppose that the sequence may have been cut at the behest of the Hays Office; however, this does not appear to have been the case. In a letter to Thalberg dated October 27, 1932, James Wingate, newly-installed at the SRC, detailed elements of the film that "seem questionable from standpoint of censorship." These included: cuts to dialogue in the scene where Barton is being tortured under the bell, i.e., "the reference to the physical filth attendant upon being confined in this particular situation"; the suggestion to be prepared with "protection shots to cover any or all of the snake sequences"; "ditto" the scene where the syringe is "sunk into the hero's neck"; in the scene where Fu Manchu incites the mob to "kill the white man and take his women," Wingate suggests a cover shot be used in case any censor boards delete the line "conquer and breed." In the lashing scene, Wingate merely advises Thalberg that "certain boards may delete one or more of the shots where the whip curls around the body of the victim."[195]

In truth, Wingate appeared not to be overly concerned about the sensationalism of *Fu Manchu*. In his weekly report to Hays covering cycles and individual pictures that were of censorship concern, Wingate wrote of *Mask of Fu Manchu*: "It is an expensive production, beautifully mounted, and in the version we saw a little long on horror elements. This is purely a censorship matter and we have written Mr. Thalberg in detail, pointing out the danger spots where we think he had better protect himself. I judge the studio is not over-enthusiastic about the picture in its present shape, and I think they will be inclined to take our suggestions and make the requisite changes."[196]

The Mask of Fu Manchu opened on May 5, 1932, to so-so reviews and equally average box office. *Variety* (December 6, 1932, 15) seemed to pick up on the muddled production and its impact on the resulting film and performances, which were uneven: "[E]verybody is handicapped by the story and its situations. It's strange how bad such troupers as [Lewis] Stone and Hersholt can look when up against an assignment as this. Miss Morley, miscast,

2. "Five reels of transgression followed by one reel of retribution" 77

The evil Fu Manchu (Boris Karloff) turns Terrence Granville (Charles Starrett) over to his "sadistic nymphomaniac" daughter, Fah Lo See (Myrna Loy), in *The Mask of Fu Manchu* **(1932, MGM).**

is never her sophisticated self, and disappointing." Seeing through MGM's and Stromberg's intentions to "go all out" for sensationalism, *Variety* goes on to claim that this approach had in fact misfired with the audience at the film's premiere: "The doc goes in for more cruelty than usual this trip through an obvious desire by producers to lessen the mysterious and embellish the horror aspects. On this occasion he specializes in torture instead of quick death. The diabolical stuff is piled on so thick at the finish, audiences are liable to laugh where they oughtn't. The audience at the Capitol did."[197]

Censors made cuts exactly as Wingate predicted. The New York State Censorship Board, for example, ordered deletions of dialogue in The Bell scene ("Just a bell ringing— You can't move. You can't sleep. You will be frantic with thirst. You will be unspeakably foul"). All views of the whip striking Terry's body were ordered eliminated. Cuts were ordered in the snake scenes and of close up views where Fu Manchu injects the syringe in Terry's neck. In addition, the New York censors ordered the elimination of all close views of Von Berg as spikes of the torture machine come close to him, allowing only a "flash as he is rescued."[198] In Britain, trade journal *Today's Cinema* deplored the film's "lurid scenes of torture ... and mental and physical degradation."[199] The *New York Times* was even more damning in its review, decrying that: "[A]nd still the cinema goes busily about its task of terrorizing the children."[200]

The most controversial element of *The Mask of Fu Manchu* today remains its racism, and it is for this aspect that the film has been censored in recent years. It is also the most probable reason for the film remaining unavailable on home video until 1992, and not being released in its fully restored original uncut version until as late as 2006—much later than most other classic horrors. When MGM/UK released the film on video in 1992 one minute five seconds of contentious footage was removed: eliminations were made to dialogue which was felt to be xenophobic.[201] Among the trims were some of Myrna Loy's lines, diminishing the sado-eroticism of her character. These were reinstated for the 2006 DVD release.[202] However, this places *Mask of Fu Manchu* as yet another thirties horror film not seen for many years in its full gruesomeness.

"Horrifying enough for the addicts, but subtly done": The Mummy (Universal, 1932)

By the time of *The Mummy*, Universal had begun to feel that, in the words of *Variety*, "the creepy cycle had exhausted its box office appeal." There was a definite sense, as scholar

Imhotep (Boris Karloff) retrieves the scroll of Thoth from a traumatized Ralph Norton (Bramwell Fletcher) in *The Mummy* (1932, Universal). Although this production still reveals Imhotep, in the film he remains off-screen.

Alison Peirse notes, that from late 1932 and early 1933, "distributors and exhibitors were shying away from the horror angle."[203] This in turn affected the studios, which became more cautious about making and promoting their movies as horror films. Properties such as *The Suicide Club*, which had been in development at the studio since Junior Laemmle purchased the rights in 1931, were given overhauls, removing much of the horror element, but retaining the novelty aspects. In response to rapidly changing audience tastes, the screenplays for *The Mummy* and *The Invisible Man*, in particular, would go through a series of rewrites, with a number of writers engaged to give a variety of approaches to the subject matter which were subsequently rejected by studio executives struggling to second guess where the marketplace was headed. This coincided with a policy change at Universal whereby associate producers were given more leeway to handle scripts, further freeing up Junior Laemmle to concentrate on his dual role as studio boss and production chief.[204] Thus, an element of indecision beset Universal for a time as the horror cycle stalled, with attempts made subsequently to move away from the horror picture to the "weird mystery." Tom Johnson writes: "It seems that [during this period] Universal was toning down its product, as witnessed by *The Mummy* and especially *The Invisible Man*, which generated as many giggles as gasps."[205] State censors demanding extensive cuts to *Frankenstein* and *Rue Morgue* may also have influenced Universal to develop material away from the graphic visual shock in favor of more subtle thrills.

In this way, *The Mummy* serves as an interesting case study of Thomas Doherty's "figurative literalness" in action, thanks largely, it can be argued, to director Karl Freund's cinematic treatment of the story which uses off screen space for psychological effect. As the *Hollywood Reporter* would say of *The Mummy* on its release in December 1932, "It has most of the thrills of the 'shock' picture without the gruesomeness of the cycle."[206] Sensation would still be a staple for the studios, and gruesomeness would in fact not go away, but, as we shall see, studios would make increasing use of oblique presentation in its various forms until after the reaffirmation of the Production Code in 1934 when the Breen Office began to clamp down on the screams, silhouettes and shadow-play being used to push gruesomeness and brutality past the censors and the reviewers in an indirect way.

Wanting a vehicle for Karloff, in early 1932 Junior Laemmle assigned Nina Wilcox Putnam to write a story based on the 1922 discovery of the ancient Egyptian tomb of Tutankhamen, and the supposed curse that struck down the archaeologists who entered the tomb, which had sparked great public interest. Putnam submitted, in February 1932, a nine-page synopsis entitled "Cagliostro," the tale of a spiritualist living in modern day San Francisco who calls himself Dr. Astro, but is, in fact, a 4000 year old Egyptian priest who has managed to preserve himself throughout the centuries with injections of nitrates. Putnam managed to tie in her story with that of the notorious eighteenth century occultist, Count Alessandro di Cagliostro, by revealing that Astro was, in fact, Cagliostro at that point in his history. Intrigued by the storyline, Junior Laemmle put Richard Schayer to work alongside Wilcox, and by February 19 they had written a full-length treatment of the idea, now called "The King of the Dead," which Junior Laemmle promptly rejected, feeling that it was "too science-fiction—no monsters in it." Laemmle then brought in John L. Balderston (who, as a journalist, had been present at the opening of Tutankhamen's tomb) to write the screenplay, with the instruction to relocate the action to Egypt and to focus on the "Curse of the Pharaohs." In March 1932, Balderston submitted his first incomplete script, which Junior Laemmle presumably okayed, as it was followed by a complete version on July 13. Balderston then wrote five more drafts between August and September.[207]

Balderston titled his initial screenplay *Undead*, and played up the mystical aspects of the storyline, rather than the science fiction and occult elements which underlay the Wilcox/Schayer treatment. It is unclear what, if any, further input Junior Laemmle or Schayer, or indeed associate producer Stanley Bergerman, had in the redrafts, although, as many scholars have noted, Balderston incorporated many story motifs from *Dracula* into his screenplay (now retitled *Im-Ho-Tep*), possibly at the behest of Junior Laemmle who wanted to repeat the box office success of that picture, something that David J. Skal cites as an example of the "creative conservatism"[208] fostered by the studio system. Another, lesser noted, influence is H. Rider Haggard's 1887 novel *She: A History of Adventure*, which Universal had commissioned Balderston to write at the same time as *The Mummy*, and which shared many of the same themes.[209] (Universal would sell the rights to the novel, along with Balderston's screenplay, to RKO; Merian C. Cooper produced the film in 1935 with a screenplay by Dudley Nichols and Ruth Rose.) The push towards "weird mysteries" at Universal might therefore be seen as having had a general effect on *The Mummy*'s development.

The Mummy and Questions of Authorship

There has been much debate as to the contribution that director Karl Freund made to the final screenplay. Mark Vieira, for example, claims that "assigned the job on a Saturday, Freund cast it on Sunday and started shooting on Monday."[210] Indeed, the general consensus seems to be that Freund, having been "hired to direct two days before filming began"[211] had no choice but to shoot the script as handed to him due to lack of time. However, in his 2002 DVD commentary to the film, Paul Jensen challenges this assumption that Freund had no input into the script of *The Mummy* due to time constraints. Jensen claims that, in fact, Universal had announced Freund as director of *The Mummy* on August 29, 1932, one week before Balderston completed his final draft of the screenplay, two weeks before the shooting script was written, and 21 days before shooting began. As Jensen points out, Freund had completed his previous assignment (as cinematographer of Universal's *Afraid to Talk*, AKA *Merry-Go-Round* [1932]) earlier in August, and therefore would have been free "for about one month" to help develop the script.[212]

In support of Jensen's claim, certainly the *Hollywood Filmograph* had reported as early as September 3, 1932, that Freund had been hired as director of "Imhotep."[213] *The Film Daily* later reported on November 7 that Freund was now "shooting added scenes,"[214] and *American Cinematographer* that month confirmed that *The Mummy* had taken "seven weeks of intensive filming."[215] Therefore, if shooting had commenced on Monday, September 19, as Jensen suggests, these trade journals would corroborate his timescale, suggesting that Freund had at least two weeks to work on the script and prepare for filming *The Mummy*.

The screenplay is credited solely to Balderston, of course, therefore any attempt to specify Freund's contribution requires some speculation, as Jensen readily concedes. However, a second consideration must be that the script includes detailed description of editing and camera movements which Freund followed closely in the filming. *American Cinematographer* (December 1932) in fact praised the direction of the camera in *The Mummy*, writing that the film's "cinematic treatment could not be improved upon; there are no superfluous scenes, nor angles, or any superfluous movement of the camera. [Freund] has utilized the moving camera strictly as means of story-telling; not ... as a bit of cheap directorial pyrotechnics."[216]

As Jensen points out, it is difficult to imagine that Balderston, a first time screenwriter, "possessed such a refined cinematic sense that all Freund had to do was follow his instructions." Furthermore, as Jensen surmises, it is hard to imagine that Freund, then a veteran cinematographer of over 100 films, including masterpieces by Murnau, Lang, Dupont and Dreyer, in his directorial debut "would have deferred so completely to a novice." Therefore, while one cannot be certain as to the exact nature or extent of Freund's contributions, it is, as Jensen argues, "more reasonable to assume that he participated than to assume that he patiently waited for the finished script and then modestly shot it as written."[217] Jensen's conclusion is supported too by extant script material for *Mad Love*, which evidences a significant (and credited) contribution by Freund to the development of the story and its cinematic treatment, as discussed later.

"He went for a little walk"

Jason Joy wrote to Junior Laemmle on July 28, 1932, declaring the script of "Im-Ho-Tep" satisfactory under the Code and free from reasonable censorship difficulties. He suggested the removal of some mild profanities, such as "for God's sake." "Also," he added, "I'm sure you will want to guard against the element of gruesomeness in the scenes in the embalming room at the museum where they are preparing to kill Helen."[218] Indeed, this scene in which we see a dagger pressed against the naked flesh of a woman's torso would be one of the few graphic images in the film. There is also a shot in the finished picture of a Nubian slave impaled by a spear; the rather more disturbing sight of a passive Karloff wrapped in bandages until his mouth and eyes are covered; and the final close up of Karloff as he decomposes in a brief series of lap dissolves at the end of the film (a sequence that shows signs of having been shortened by the studio prior to the film's release). There is also some gruesome dialogue at the opening of Imhotep's tomb, in which it is explained that the Mummy's "viscera was not removed" and that he was "buried alive."

Joy, however, makes no mention of what has become *The Mummy*'s most celebrated sequence, in which we see the mummified Karloff return to life and terrify an archaeologist into hysteria, before retrieving

A production still of Jack Pierce's make up for Boris Karloff in *The Mummy* (1932, Universal).

the sacred Scroll of Thoth, the parchment that holds Imhotep's power. Reviewers of the time warned audiences that this scene in particular was decidedly horrific: the archaeologist (played by Bramwell Fletcher) "going quite mad, laughs in a way that raises the hair on the scalp," wrote the *New York Times* critic (January 7, 1933)[219]; the *New York Daily News* confirmed, "The screams of Bramwell Fletcher ... will chill your blood."[220] The scene's horrific effect derives precisely from the decision to exclude the Mummy from the frame, with the camera instead dwelling on the victim's graphic response to the Mummy's having come to life; the source of the horror thus becomes Fletcher's shocking reaction to the revived Mummy rather than the sight of the Mummy itself. As Jensen comments of the screenplay, "the script's description of the Mummy's return to life includes all the subtle camera movements and the decision not to show the mummy move through the room."[221] Thus, the scene, because of its imaginative use of off-screen space to avoid showing the monster in all its gruesomeness, was considered satisfactory from the standpoint of the Production Code, while becoming, at the same time, more psychologically brutal to the viewer for having done so. As the *Manchester Guardian* (June 27, 1933) wrote of the Mummy's revivification, it is "ghastly" precisely because it is "presented by signs more horrible than a blunt statement."[222] In *After Dracula*, Alison Peirse reflects on the oral testimonies of British cinemagoers in the 1930s who watched *The Mummy*: "The awakening sequence is repeatedly identified as a particularly terrifying moment in the memories [of interviewees], many of whom were children at the time."[223] Key to the power of the scene is that, according to Paul Jensen, it "involves viewers by requiring attentiveness and imaginative collaboration [and] the result is both understated and intense."[224]

As Jensen has speculated, "what self-discipline it must have been to go for the implication and the suggestion and the hint rather than the blunt statement."[225] It seems, however, that the scene may have, in fact, caused considerable disagreement between Freund and Junior Laemmle. In *Universal Horrors*, Tom Weaver comments that "the Mummy's reawakening would have been presented differently had Carl Laemmle Jr. had his druthers."[226] As recounted to Weaver by film producer Richard Gordon (who claimed to have heard it from Karloff himself):

> Laemmle Jr. and (Freund) almost came to blows over the opening sequence. Laemmle wanted the Mummy to come to life and be introduced in a series of stylized close-ups like those that James Whale used in *Frankenstein*. Freund insisted that the Mummy should not be shown at all after its first stirrings of life in the sarcophagus and that audiences would be far more horrified by the specter of Fletcher's descent into madness, and his maniacal laughter, if they didn't see what drove him to it. Fortunately Freund prevailed and the sequence is one of the most revered in Universal's horror classics.[227]

Jensen maintains that there is a production still of the standing Karloff in his Mummy make-up reaching to take the Scroll of Thoth from the table (a shot that is not in the film).[228] Close examination of the scene suggests that reverse angle shots of Karloff may, in fact, have been taken (possibly on the orders of Junior Laemmle), but perhaps never edited into the film.

The Mummy received preview screenings in November 1932, after which six minutes were removed from the film in order to tighten up its pace.[229] These scenes were of Zita Johan's various incarnations throughout the ages recalled in flashback, and were considered extraneous to the main action. Removing them enabled Junior Laemmle to streamline the film and its climax.

Around the time of *The Mummy*'s release in December 1932, Universal announced a policy for only utilizing stories that would draw patronage from overseas as well as in the United States. At the heart of this plan was the belief in cinema as the "universal language," and the feeling that talkies had ushered in an era that was "too American for its own good." Junior Laemmle advocated a 25 percent reduction in dialogue for every new picture produced at Universal and emphasized the necessity of greater concentration on dramatic action, rather than on dialogue, to tell stories. "The future of talking pictures," Laemmle declared, "is to make them moving pictures of interest to all the world." From that point on, he stated, Universal was "only interested in plays, novels and stories that will be as interesting and entertaining to German, French, Australian and African audiences as in America. Foreign countries need this product and we need this market." Junior Laemmle went on to reveal that Universal had been working towards that goal for months and cited *Airmail* (1932) and *The Mummy* as examples of stories told in dramatic physical action with a minimum of dialogue. Both films, of course, showcased the cinematographic talents of Karl Freund. Moreover, in adopting as company policy "more painstaking direction and film editing," Junior Laemmle was leading the way for a subtler, more refined and more oblique but no less powerful treatment of screen horror that would reach its zenith in such films as *The Black Cat* and *Bride of Frankenstein*.[230] As Stephen Prince has noted, films like *The Black Cat* would present their gruesomeness more "discretely," veiled in shadow and suggestion, "in part because the idea of what is being depicted ... is more extreme and ghastly"[231] than it had been in previous films.

"The dangers of gruesomeness, brutality and the mistreatment of animals": Island of Lost Souls *(Paramount, 1932)*

While *The Mummy* led the way for a subtler more oblique approach to horror at Universal, other studios, meanwhile, continued to favor blunt statement, sensationalism and ballyhoo in their bid to win over audiences. Buoyed by the critical and financial success of *Dr. Jekyll and Mr. Hyde*, in the spring of 1932, Ben Schulberg at Paramount sent a copy of H.G. Wells' novel, *The Island of Dr. Moreau* to Jason Joy asking for his general opinion on the story's suitability for adaptation and its censorship angles. As Bryan Senn remarks, Wells' novel was rife with scenes with vivisection, sadism and implied bestiality[232]; factors which had no doubt aroused Paramount's interest in adapting it for the screen, but which might equally prove to be a no-no as far as the Production Code was concerned. Ultimately, the gruesomeness of the film's make-up effects, together with its blasphemy, and its vivisection and bestiality themes, would result in the film experiencing severe problems with state censors, and receiving bans in a number of territories, including in Britain, where its veto was to remain in place until 1958.

From Joy's fairly elaborate response to Schulberg's letter, we can see how studio heads in their dealings with MPPDA officials might seek to flatter the egos of these men and make appeals to their vanity by soliciting their artistic views as well as their official verdict on whether a story would be satisfactory or not under the Code (Joy would soon leave the Hays Office to take an administrative position in the script department at Fox). Thus Joy ventures his opinion on the artistic merits of the story. "I do not see in the story as it now stands, enough of the unusual or the plausible, to make it worthwhile," he opines, while, on the other hand, assuring Schulberg that "if you feel a treatment can be evolved which will be financially worthwhile, then of course, I think you should go ahead, for I haven't any doubt that a treatment could be found which would make the picture satisfactory under the Code and reasonably safe in censorship territory." Paramount was, at that time, considered the most prestigious of the studios, and this may also have influenced the sometimes sycophantic responses of MPPDA officials to pictures made by the studio: "I am sure that with your usual good taste and your ingenuity you can find a treatment which would be reasonably safe," writes Joy, "having in mind, of course, the dangers of gruesomeness, brutality and mistreatment of animals."

Joy did, however, see the need to caution Schulberg on one area of the story that he felt to be particularly censorious. "I assume that some thought has been given to the possibility of injecting the idea of crossing animals with humans. If this is the case it is my opinion that all such thought should be abandoned, for I am sure you would never be permitted to suggest that sort of thing on screen." Joy refers to Universal's *Murders in the Rue Morgue* as the nearest approach to such an idea: "of course, there was only a hint of blood transfusion," Joy writes, "but even so, wherever there was the slightest suspicion of such mating the idea was rejected." Joy mentions also *Ingagi* (1931) which "got into a lot of trouble, not only because it purported to be an authentic story, but because it suggested that a tribe of African women were mating with apes. It just couldn't be done."[233]

Referring to *Ingagi* in such a way underlines, in Thomas Doherty's words, the "convergence in space and time between the racial adventure film and horror film."[234] Both film cycles, which ran concurrently in the early 1930s, fixated on "gruesome imagery and sadistic scenarios built around creatures no longer fully human."[235] In both genres, "man, beast, and beast-man trace an evolutionary regression from the normal, to the stunted, to the mutated."[236] *Ingagi* and *Rue Morgue*, featuring at the heart of their narratives the mating of human with gorilla, symbolize the "racial paranoia and forbidden lure of miscegenation" of that era, while *King Kong* would later represent "the most gargantuan realization" of the "coded figure" of the gorilla.[237]

Paramount assigned Philip Wylie to adapt the Wells novel, and Waldemar Young to write the screenplay. Paramount contract director Norman Taurog was penciled in to direct, but later replaced by Erle C. Kenton due to his running behind on *The Phantom President* (1932), then shooting on the Paramount lot.[238] On September 21, Young delivered his first script to the studio which was duly sent to the SRC.[239] Joy wrote to associate producer Harold Hurley five days later declaring the *Island of Lost Souls*, as the story had been retitled, satisfactory under the Code, with one exception: "with regard to official censorship it is very likely that you will lose the line on page D-35 in which Moreau says: 'Do you know how it seems to feel like God?'" Joy remarked that "a similar line in a recent picture was eliminated by the majority of the boards," referring, of course, to *Frankenstein*.[240]

Shortly afterwards, the studio recalled Wylie for further dialogue work while Young went off to work with Taurog on the screenplay for the musical comedy *A Bedtime Story* (1933). Wylie handed in his revised script on September 30, 1932.[241] It seems that the studio was especially keen to retain the one line of dialogue that Joy had advised them would likely be a problem. Paramount's Head of Publicity, Tom Baily, wrote to Joy on October 3, asking if the SRC might suggest an alteration that would still retain the meaning of the line but pass the more critical boards: "It is necessary to the sense of the scene that Dr. Moreau, in his fanaticism, believe that he is the equal of the Creator Himself, inasmuch as the whole theme of the picture is that of the would-be Creator, who is himself destroyed by his fantastical creations. It is very important that we get the equivalent of our line in the picture."[242]

Assuring Joy that he wasn't trying to put him on the spot and that his plea was "a sincere one," Baily ventured that he phone Joy the next day to get his opinion. This Baily did, and after speaking with Geoffrey Shurlock in Joy's absence, came away with the suggestion he had surely been seeking from the SRC. In his note of the telephone conversation made for the Hays Office file, Shurlock wrote: "our suggestion was that they do not try to juggle words in this case, but use the line in question honestly and sincerely, and let it take its chances with the censor Boards."[243] Paramount would thus keep their sensational line of dialogue when the film was presented for Production Code approval in December.

Island of Lost Souls is, of course, famous for the publicity drive that Baily and the studio mounted even before the film went into production. Paramount undertook a nationwide search for an actress to play the Panther Woman, a campaign advertised as a national contest, in which 50,000 young women took part, before 19-year-old Kathleen Burke was cast in the role.[244] Publicity stunts such as this continued into the production itself. As David A. Kirby has pointed out, *Island of Lost Souls* was produced at a time when society was starting to address the concept of direct genetic manipulation. For Paramount, *Island of Lost Souls* therefore seemed an ideal way to capitalize on societal fears of a technologically driven eugenics. According to Kirby, the studio even invited the British eugenicist Sir Julian Huxley onto the set during filming, ostensibly to verify the accuracy of the film's science, and continued this line of publicity after the film's release.[245]

It seems that Joy at the SRC may genuinely have felt *Island of Lost Souls* "reasonably free from censorship difficulties" as he wrote in what must have been one of his final weekly reports to Hays in October 1932.[246] Harold Hurley presented the film to the newly-appointed James Wingate early in December. Wingate subsequently wrote him that in the SRC's opinion, it was satisfactory from the standpoint of the Code, reiterating that—as stated in their letter on the script—it was probable that state censors would make them lose Moreau's line about knowing how it seems to feel like God. "Aside from this we see nothing in the picture to which any objection could be made," Wingate states, before adding that he had enjoyed the picture thoroughly and hoped it would meet with the "success which it certainly deserves."[247] Perhaps wishing to ingratiate himself further with the studio, the newly-incumbent Wingate also wrote to John Hammell at the New York office to congrat-

An example of one of make-up artist Wally Westmore's gruesome designs for *Island of Lost Souls* (1933, Paramount) (courtesy Ronald V. Borst/Hollywood Movie Posters).

ulate Paramount on "a splendid job and one which should not only meet with a great deal of success, but which should also cause very little difficulty from a censorable standpoint."[248]

Island of Lost Souls was previewed at the Academy in Los Angeles during the second week of December—a month before its January 11, 1933, opening. It was then that reviewers first began to voice their concerns about the film. Movie journalist Maude Latham, for example, marveled at Wally Westmore's Beast Men make-up, "so gruesome [yet] so realistic at the moment, one feels almost like they are about to witness a human being created by the hand of man." However, she also worried that "there are people to whom this cinema will be ... offensive."[249] The *New York Times* (January 13, 1933) commented: "The attempt to horrify is not achieved with any marked degree of subtlety,"[250] while the *Los Angeles Times* (January 10, 1933) called it "horrible to the point of repugnance."[251]

LOST SOULS AND THE CENSORS

Latham was right. In terms of the overseas market, the reception of *Island of Lost Souls* was disastrous. It was banned in Singapore, New Zealand, Holland, Tasmania, Germany, India, Hungary, Italy, South Africa, The Netherlands, Sweden, Denmark and Latvia.[252] Domestically it fared little better, being rejected by 14 censor boards in total. Paramount found itself in much the same position as Universal had with *Frankenstein*. One of the first boards to reject the film as "too extreme" was Virginia. After the picture was turned down a second time by the board, Paramount threatened legal action, which Virginia said it would fight.[253] Both sides eventually backed down and *Island of Lost Souls* was passed in Virginia at the end of January 1933, with considerable cuts. "What's left of the picture is attracting eager business," reported *The Film Daily* (January 31, 1933) ironically[254]; an observation echoed by *Motion Picture Herald* which commented, "People knock it, then come back and bring others to see it."[255] Perhaps the most damage done was in Britain, where the new "H" certificate advisory system for horror films was about to come into operation. There, the President of the British Board of Film Censors, Edward Shortt, himself viewed the film, and subsequently rejected it on grounds of its blasphemy and its themes of animal cruelty. When Paramount resubmitted *Island of Lost Souls* to the British censor on July 6, 1951, even following the horrors of the Second World War it was again rejected. According to James C. Robertson, "The same fate befell it a third time on 29 October 1957, when the 'X' certificate had been firmly established." Finally, through Paramount's persistence, *Island of Lost Souls* was at last awarded an "X" certificate on July 9, 1958, but, as Robertson points out, was never shown on British television and remained "a very difficult production for British cinema-goers to see,"[256] until it was released on video in Britain in 1996.

The Breen Administration's own subsequent view of the film on reissue was very much colored by the censorship problems it had faced on its first release. When Paramount submitted it for a Production Code certificate of approval in 1935, it was flatly refused because of its "extreme horror."[257] In 1941 Paramount tried again to reissue the film. Breen wrote on March 4, informing the studio that *Island of Lost Souls* could not be approved by the Production Code as it stood, and respectfully suggested that Paramount withdraw their application "on this particular picture." Breen's tone in the letter could not be more different than that of his predecessors Joy and Wingate back in 1932, illustrating the contrast between the comparative laxness of pre–Code regulation and the rigor of Breen Office monitoring:

The general unacceptability of this picture is suggested by the blasphemous suggestion of the character, played by Charles Laughton, wherein he presumes to create human beings out of animals; the obnoxious suggestion of the attempt of these animals to mate with human beings, and the general flavor of excessive gruesomeness and horror.

In our judgment, all these tend to make the picture quite definitely repulsive and not suitable for screen entertainment in theaters before mixed audiences.[258]

Breen, however, had other reasons to refuse the Production Code seal beside his personal distaste for the film. He attached to the Paramount letter an excerpt from the notes of testimony on the hearing of the Neely Anti-Block Booking and Blind Bidding Bill that had gone before the Congressional Committee in Washington the previous spring. Although the Bill had died in the House of Representatives, as had been expected, the Roosevelt Administration had already started up anti-trust proceedings against Paramount by 1938. The excerpt from the testimony that Breen attached concerned the advertising campaign for Paramount's lurid adventure-thriller *Island of Lost Men* (1939), which was cited at the hearing as evidence of distributors peddling immoral pictures unwanted by the majority of American communities ("Murder.... Suicide.... Headhunters.... Jungle Fever.... They Never Come Back from the *Island of Lost Men*!").[259] "In our judgment [*Island of Lost Men*] is not nearly so definitely unacceptable as ISLAND OF LOST SOULS," Breen wrote. "Thus you will see how importantly the advertising for this kind of a picture impresses itself upon the Congressional Investigating Committee."[260]

Nevertheless, Paramount arranged a screening of the film for Breen, and set about making extensive cuts to dialogue which, in the studio's opinion, "eliminate from the picture the suggestion that Moreau considers himself on par with God as a creator, and reduces him to the status of a scientist conducting bio-anthropological [sic] experiments; remove any suggestion that Moreau attempts to mate the beast-girl with a human being; remove any suggestion that he encourages the mating of a beastman with a human being." The studio also shortened the undressing of Leila Hyams in Reel 7, and eliminated the close up of the beastman on the table, and the sound of his groans in Reel 4. Paramount made over 20 cuts in total—including the line, "Mr. Parker, do you know what it means to feel like God?"[261] Breen, despite misgivings, and still feeling the film contained no social significance, awarded the severely truncated reissue of *Island of Lost Souls* the Production Code seal two days after the screening, on March 17, 1941.[262]

This version of the film played on TV and in repertory screenings for decades, at least until the Production Code's dissolution in 1966.[263] However, cuts would not be restored to prints of *Island of Lost Souls* until the film was released on VHS by Universal in 1993, and the film did not appear uncut on DVD until 2011 when distributor Criterion finally produced a full picture/audio restoration (taken from existing 35mm prints and 16mm collectors' prints) for DVD/Blu-Ray release, with all censorship eliminations reinstated.

"Make ups are about the last words in gruesomeness": Mystery of the Wax Museum *(Warner Bros./ First National, 1932)*

On February 21, 1933, *Variety* reported, "Not so many months ago Warners' 'Dr. X.' ... with this same cast ... had to do with moulten [sic] wax masks, although the premise was different. 'Dr. X' was also in Technicolor, if memory serves, hence there may arise some vague recollections and comparisons among the observant fans."[264]

By the end of 1932 the Great Depression had begun to hit Warner Bros. hard. Corporate revenues tumbled from $130 million in 1930 to $72 million by the end of the fiscal year of 1933.[265] Warner sold assets, pared down its wages bill and trimmed expenses wherever it could. Production budgets were cut to the lowest of any of the five major studios; staff directors like Michael Curtiz were made to work fast, on short shooting schedules, delivering an average of two minutes and 30 seconds of finished film per day, driving cast and crew relentlessly in the process.[266]

At the height of the Depression, many movie theaters would close during the summer months—traditionally a time of low attendance—and reopen later in the year. Likewise, Warner would shut down operations for several weeks each summer, loaning out its talent to other studios in order to generate revenue; production would begin again at a frantic pace when the studio reopened each August. In 1932 early releases from Warner Bros./First National had been unusually successful, prompting the schedule to be resumed that year at "top speed with an average of five pictures in production most of the time," as reported *The International Photographer* in October 1932. One of those pictures would be Warner Bros.' follow-up to *Dr. X*, titled simply *The Wax Museum*: "So great has been the box office success of the Technicolor feature, 'Dr. X,' another has been launched in production at the Burbank plant."[267] *Mystery of the Wax Museum* would attempt to repeat the successful box office of *Dr. X* by utilizing the same cast, Curtiz as director and Ray Rennahan again providing Technicolor cinematography; it would combine horror and newspaper cycles in much the same way. And its gruesome set piece "unmasking" of Lionel Atwill as the disfigured mad sculptor who creates waxworks from human bodies would prove just as memorable—and gruesome—as its prototype: the synthetic flesh scene of *Dr. X*. Like its predecessor too, *Mystery of the Wax Museum*, would remain unavailable for many years after its first release. Indeed, prior to the discovery, in 1970, of a copy in the Warner archive in Burbank, *Wax Museum* would be considered lost. Although it would amass a cult reputation among horror fans through the decades it would remain unseen by many modern viewers until its eventual appearance on video in 1992 (it was released on DVD in 2003 as an extra on the disc of the 1953 remake *House of Wax*).

Warner Bros. had secured the rights to Charles Belden's unproduced play *The Wax Museum* (based on his own short story "The Wax Works") from Charles R. Rogers (who would take over from Junior Laemmle as studio chief at Universal after the studio was sold to Standard Capital Company in 1936). Rogers had recently left RKO and set up as an independent producer. After canvassing prominent movie exhibitors and the editors of popular magazines early in 1932, Rogers determined that the public was "keenest for stories containing high-class melodramatic situations." With that in mind he purchased the rights to a number of mystery stories, among them sports thriller *70,000 Witnesses* (1932) and *The Wax Museum*, both of which Rogers planned to produce independently at either Universal or Pathé.[268] When Rogers discovered that Warner Bros. had simultaneously bought the rights to Belden's short story, and a copyright suit was filed against him by a playwright who claimed *The Wax Museum* infringed upon his work, Rogers decided to cut his losses. He dropped his option on *The Wax Museum*, after which Warner Bros. stepped in to acquire the full rights.

"The Wax Museum is of the thriller-type," *The Film Daily* (September 9, 1932) reported, "with a fine love story running through the action ... it is a most unusual story, the details of which are being kept under cover for the present."[269] Indeed, Zanuck would ditch most of the details of Belden's original play, retaining only the title and the basic premise, which, according to Scott MacQueen was "pure Grand Guignol about the horribly disfigured survivor of a wax museum fire raging through London, abducting and killing, mounting the waxed corpses of his victims in a new museum."[270] Screenwriter Don Mullaly wrote an initial treatment in July 1932; Zanuck handed the treatment to one of his staff writers, Carl Erickson, from which to create an "optional outline"; Erickson added ideas and refinements of his own to Mullaly's scenario. Pleased with Mullaly and Erickson's work, Zanuck assigned both writers to continue on the screenplay as a team.[271]

In making the sculptor (played by Lionel Atwill) a sympathetic character hiding his mental and physical disfigurement behind a wax mask, Mullaly, according to MacQueen, had borrowed from *The Phantom of the Opera*, while Erickson added a revenge motif by giving the sculptor a villainous partner "whose greed precipitates the tragedy." However, as MacQueen points out, Zanuck held story conferences with the writers where he would "redirect their work," thereby imprinting the Warner house style on the screenplay, which was taken through four drafts: "The locale was switched to New York City and the narrative thread grafted onto a more typical Zanuck storyline of newsgathering in the big city."[272]

New "Angles" and "Slants"

Around the time the screenplay for *Mystery of the Wax Museum* was being finalized, *Variety* (September 27, 1932) published a news piece that revealed how the studios, including Warner Bros., were seeking at that time to reformulate cycles by injecting them with new "angles" and "slants":

> Film production in future, the trend indicates, is away from cycles.
>
> Majors are trying to lend stories different slants or inject atmosphere so that they will not appear strictly of the cycle on which mainly founded. Paramount did this with "70,000 Witnesses," a football story with a strong murder mystery angle. Warner Bros are varying the horror film thing [sic] "Wax Museum."
>
> Companies are of the opinion that if film cycles are to be followed, stories must possess a companion angle or combine two or more cycle elements. In the past it's been only the first or second picture of the newly developed cycles that did the business: those that followed meant little.[273]

By combining cycle elements in this way, producers were aware that they could also "do the business" with the Hays Office and state censors when it came to getting gruesome subject matter passed. The exact same day as *Variety* published the news piece, Jason Joy wrote to Zanuck regarding the script for "Wax Museum." Although he felt that the "one possible danger" was a "leaning toward too great gruesomeness in certain scenes," Joy was of the opinion that the script "seems to handle this element very successfully" and that it was in accordance with the Production Code. Indeed, Joy's notes with regard to details which "you may wish to change in order to avoid their loss" related not to gruesomeness, but to the mild profanities in the dialogue and the suggestion of police brutality: potentially censorable elements more typically associated with the newspaper picture, perhaps, than the horror film.[274] When the finished film was presented to the Hays Office late in December, James Wingate wrote to Zanuck with the verdict that *Wax Museum* was satisfactory under the Production Code and "free from elements to which official censorship could take serious objection."²⁷⁵ Writing also to the Warner front office in New York, Wingate added "it is an interesting story of the horror type ... and has been handled ... in such a manner as to be free from any serious censorship problems."²⁷⁶ Wingate highlighted the mitigating factors of *Wax Museum* in his report to Hays on December 30: "The gruesomeness of the story is lightened by the comedy element of a woman reporter and her editor; and, on the whole, the picture struck us as being very acceptable entertainment of this type."²⁷⁷

Thomas Schatz makes the point that distinctive in Warner Bros. pictures were the "lack of naïve optimism and a disdain for romantic love as either a motivating plot device or a means to a narrative resolution."²⁷⁸ Perhaps that is the reason why the final couple ending of *Mystery of the Wax Museum* seems so arbitrary (the editor isn't even given a name), such an obvious sop to the censors:

184   INT. EDITOR'S OFFICE
      He looks up as Florence enters room. She is gloating.

                    FLORENCE
            Well, Poison Ivy, how about it? Was that
            a story?

      He looks up sourly.

                    EDITOR
            Lousy! You had a million dollars' worth
            of luck.

      She looks at him indignantly.

                    FLORENCE
            Listen, stupid, could I do anything
            that would possibly meet with your
            approval?

                    EDITOR
            Yes, you could. Cut out this rotten
            business and act like a lady. Marry me.

      She hears the honking of an automobile in the street below and walks to the window, looks down for a moment.

185   SHOT FROM FLORENCE'S ANGLE WINTON IN CAR
      in front of the Express Building, honking impatiently.

186   INT. EDITOR'S OFFICE
      Florence turns back from window, grins at editor.

                    FLORENCE
            Marry you?
                    EDITOR
            That's what I said.
                    FLORENCE
            I'm going to get even with you, you dirty
            stiff! I'll do it!

      He rises and catches her in his arms. As they embrace, we hear the raucous "honk-honk" of the car in the street below.
                    FADE OUT²⁷⁹

Even so, the comedy element of the film and its entertainment were not seen by all viewers as sufficient mitigation for the gruesomeness of certain sequences. After a screening of *Wax Museum* at Warner Bros. on February 6, 1933 (ten days before its New York opening), Hays Office employee Vincent G. Hart wrote for the file: "This is a new type of horror picture, with the creeps. It contains many gruesome scenes, in particular, the close-ups of the burning wax figures.... Adults will find plenty of thrills and much excitement, but it is too strong for others than adult audiences. I am of the opinion that some censorable criticism will be had because of the gruesome sequences.... The stealing of the bodies from the morgue may also cause trouble because of the statutes forbidding the mutilation of bodies after death."[280]

Hart may have been right. Three days later, B.O. Skinner, director of education for the Ohio Division of Film Censorship, wrote a letter of complaint direct to Warner Bros. "Gentlemen ... we are, as you know, approving [*Mystery of the Wax Museum*] with eliminations. I wish, however to register a formal protest against the film. It contains so many elements we find objectionable..." Skinner itemized these elements as "setting fire to the museum to obtain insurance, naming a poison and telling how it could be taken to produce death, using of dope," and finally—and perhaps most objectionable of all—"the general theme of horror." Skinner ended his letter: "I feel it would be much better for all of us if the production of this type of film would be discontinued."[281]

Despite the objections of censors, there was every sign that *Mystery of the Wax Museum* would be a hit with the public. "It made quite an impression at the preview," *Motion Picture Herald* reported on January 7, 1933.[282] By early February *Wax Museum* had received 75 pre-release bookings in A-class picture houses nationally, a very respectable figure for a movie with a $297,000 budget.[283]

Reviews following the New York premiere on February 16, 1933, were, however, mixed. *Variety* (February 21, 1933) complained that loose ends never quite gelled, criticized the wise-cracking reporter angle ("like most newspaper stuff, the flippant, cynical and hard-boiled manifestations ... rarely convince"), and described the film on whole as "one of those artificial things whose sole retrospection will inspire an uncomfortable feeling of the physical misshapen and little else ... make ups are about the last words in gruesomeness."[284]

Mordaunt Hall of the *New York Times* (February 18, 1933) liked the reporter angle but thought the rest "too ghastly for comfort." "It is all very well in its way to have a mad scientist performing operations in well-told stories," he wrote, "but when a melodrama depends upon the glimpses of covered bodies in a morgue and the stealing of some of them by an insane modeler in wax, it is going too far." For Hall, the narrative was most of the time "much too intent on its extravagant blood-curdling ideas, which include the sudden revealing of Igor's frightfully disfigured countenance."[285] *The Film Daily*, however, described it as a "fantastic horror picture in Technicolor" that "should appeal to fans who like the bizarre," and again singled out the unmasking scene: "among the horror is the discovery that the doctor himself has a wax face, covering up a hideous deformation," but praised it as one of the "gruesome activities [that] sends chills through tender spines."[286]

Despite the combination of cycles, *Wax Museum* was perceived first and foremost as a picture of the "horror type," and the general wisdom, by the time *Wax Museum* played second run and rural theatres in July 1933, was that the horror cycle was over. Theatre managers in such places as Oxford, North Carolina, and Blackstone, Virginia, reported average or below-average business, with the verdict: "people fed up long ago on scare pictures."[287] Nevertheless, it became Warner Bros.' biggest overseas hit of 1933 after *42nd Street* (1933), and gained notoriety in Great Britain, whose censor described the monster make-up as "the most nauseating and by far the worst of its type."[288] The British public flocked to it, however; the advisory "H" (for "Horrific") certificate having been introduced in May of that year (although *Wax Museum* was not one of the films to be actually classified as "Horrific").

Why did *Mystery of the Wax Museum* become "lost"? It is generally thought that Warner Bros. never formally reissued *Wax Museum*, although the film was granted a Production Code certificate letter on September 3, 1936.[289] When Technicolor switched from two-color to three-color by 1936, rather than go to the expense of converting their old "obsolete" films to three-color Technicolor, the studios junked most of their two-color negatives. *Mystery of the Wax Museum* was therefore assumed lost for this reason. However, a 35mm nitrate print was found in the Warner archive in 1970. It had been sitting there all along: an example of Hollywood's general indifference to its own heritage. In the interim, *Wax Museum* remained unseen for over 30 years, and became the subject of much speculation among fans. After its rediscovery, *Wax Museum* received a limited airing on television, screened non-theatrically in 8mm and 16mm prints, and became a favorite among film collectors.[290] It remained a rare film until its release on videotape and laser disc in the early 1990s.

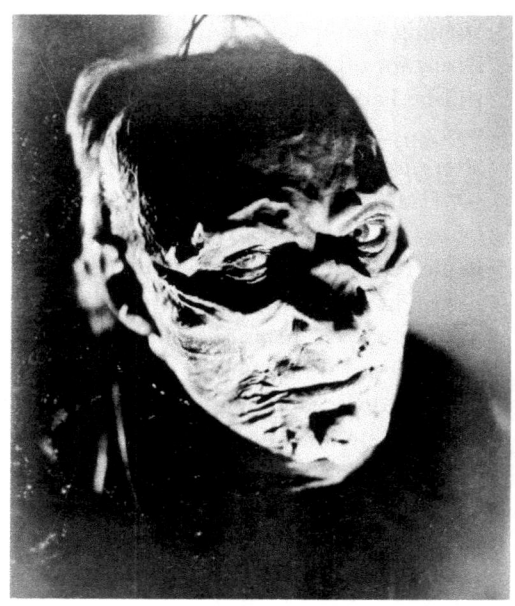

"The last words in gruesomeness": Lionel Atwill's burn make-up for *Mystery of the Wax Museum* (1932, First National/Warner Bros.) (courtesy of Ronald V. Borst/Hollywood Movie Posters).

"Gruesome gorilla": King Kong *(RKO, 1933)*

"It is said the basic theme of Cooper's original idea," wrote *Hollywood Reporter* in February 1933, "was a beast so large he could hold the beauty in the palm of his hand, pulling bits of her clothing from her body until she was denuded. Gentlemen, that's imagination."[291] That this single image which, according to Thomas Doherty, lies at the heart of *King Kong* ("intimating an unrequitable interspecies sexual liaison"[292]), was recognized from the moment the film appeared in 1933 is testament to its extraordinary potency—and to its limitless exploitation value. *King Kong*, may have become, as David Robinson wrote in 1979, "the most potent myth that the cinema has given the 20th century,"[293] but at the time of its release, RKO and its exhibitors feared that the film would be lost in the cycle of wild animal-adventure movies that followed in the wake of *Tarzan, the Ape Man*. Its sensational aspects were played up from the get-go, both by the studio in the film's conception and production, and by exhibitors in their ballyhoo. "With imagination running riot in the production of *King Kong*, so ought the exploitation ideas of exhibitors to run riot," advised

2. "Five reels of transgression followed by one reel of retribution"

The Hollywood Reporter. "It's that kind of a picture."[294] "KING KONG IS THE FREAKIEST OF FREAK PICTURES EVER MADE," headlined *The Hollywood Filmograph* (April 1, 1933). "BRUTAL ANIMAL FIGHTS AND GRUESOME GORILLA SHOULD PLEASE THE LOVERS OF HORROR PICTURES." "There is the worst brutality of animals fighting and tearing each other to pieces," *The Filmograph* detailed. "And if you like horror pictures and wish to see a monster gorilla with a beautiful girl in his clutches, and hear her screaming for reels, you can get all this and more in *King Kong*."[295] "Don't let them get ... the idea it's just another animal picture" concluded *Motion Picture Herald* (February 25, 1933). "There's only one way to understand *King Kong*: It's big!"[296]

At the time of *King Kong*'s release, RKO had gone into permanent receivership and was in desperate need of a box office hit of *Frankenstein* proportions. The studio's losses in 1932 had been huge: $4,075,834 from production and distribution; $3669,504 from theatre operations.[297] In short, RKO was on the verge of bankruptcy. David Selznick had brought Merian C. Cooper (with whom he had become associated on *The Four Feathers* [1929]) to RKO as his executive assistant in 1931, and had assigned him to find ways of cutting down the studio overhead. Cooper had already approached RKO prior to this with the idea for *King Kong*, but it had been turned down as too expensive (Cooper had originally envisaged it being filmed on location, and had wanted to buy the rights to *Tarzan* from MGM with the plan to film both productions back to back in Africa). When Cooper viewed a test reel made by Willis O'Brien for an unrealized project called "Creation," he saw in the stop-motion animation and back projection techniques a way to make *King Kong* cost-effectively and managed to secure Selznick's interest.[298]

In December 1931, British mystery novelist Edgar Wallace was hired to work on *Kong*, as well as a further horror picture for director Herbert Brenon, and several more projects besides, including a "sex play" for actress Constance Bennett. Wallace was duly installed in an office on the RKO lot, had screened for him *Dracula* and *Murder by the Clock*, and put to work. Selznick allowed Cooper the writer for his pet project, *Kong*, but the famous and prolific Wallace was seen as a studio commodity, and his services were called upon in between times, as a script doctor on the reshoots of *The Lost Squadron* (1932).[299]

While Wallace worked up a storyline for *Kong* under Cooper's close supervision, O'Brien created a new test reel showcasing the animated model of Kong himself. With Selznick now fully behind the project, the test reel was screened for the RKO front office in January 1932, and a budget of $500,000 approved—almost twice the average cost of an RKO "A" picture at that time (the final budget would, in fact, swell to $672,254).[300] Clearly RKO would have a lot riding on the success or failure of *King Kong*.

After Wallace's sudden, unexpected death in February 1932, Cooper brought in James Ashmore Creelman to write the treatment, after which Ruth Rose penned the full dialogue script and worked on revisions during the filming process. It is clear from Creelman's "revised treatment" (dated June 9, 1932) that Kong's licentious stripping of Ann, the brutal animal fights, and other sadistic aspects of the story (such as Kong's deliberately crushing natives underfoot) were already in place. For example, page 74 of the treatment details Kong's mauling of Ann:

INT. LAIR—FULL SHOT—NIGHT.
Kong, in side angle, begins to pick her clothes off, as a monkey might pick a rag doll to pieces.

INT. LAIR–MED. SHOT—NIGHT.
Ann shrinks and screams as her clothes are pulled off bit by bit.
EXT. TRAIL–FULL SHOT—NIGHT.
Driscoll comes up the trail. He can hear the girl's screams.
INT. LAIR—FULL SHOT—NIGHT.
The girl is almost naked. SIDE ANGLE. Kong is still picking at her when he turns startled.[301]

The story synopsis produced by RKO from the final screenplay describes Kong's actions in picking off Ann's clothes as "playful."[302] However, the rape threat scenario inherent in Creelman's treatment may have been ported over from the original Wallace storyline in which Ann (named Florence in the Wallace version) is threatened with rape by the ship's crew.[303] Interestingly, Creelman attributes this rape threat to Kong rather than the crew. However, the language Creelman uses serves both to desexualize Kong (perhaps as a strategy for getting the scene past the Hays Office)—thus he picks off Ann's clothes "as a monkey might pick a rag doll to pieces"—while at the same time providing a salacious angle from which the audience can view the scene—Ann shrinks and screams as her clothes are picked off "bit by bit" until she is "almost naked."

The essential ambiguity of the scene can be seen reflected in Fay Wray's own response to it. When, in 1970, she saw the "uncut" version of the film for the first time in decades she remarked:

> Last year I saw what is called the "uncensored" version; and I was very distressed by the scene where the monkey is ... pulling at the girl's clothes...
> Originally she was supposed to have fainted; and Kong held her in his hand, turned his head from side to side, looked at her and pulled at her like a little girl might pull at a flower petal. There was nothing sensual about it at all. But in this other version, the camera looks down on her as if from his viewpoint, and she is struggling a great deal and it seems as if a rectangular patch of cloth has been superimposed, so that the monkey can pull it away.... Now everyone I talk to about *King Kong* says, "Oh, the scene where he tries to undress you—that's back in." But no such scene was ever designed.[304]

In this way, we can see in *King Kong* a classic case of pre–Code thirties horror cinema being more lurid than is generally remembered—even by those involved in its making. The public's memory of *King Kong* is generally that of censored versions through the years, creating the misperception of the picture being "softer" than it actually is.

"No less than the sexual byplay," Doherty comments, "the level of gore and sadism stretched the limits of pre–Code license."[305] In *King Kong*, men are chewed up by a dinosaur; others fall screaming to their deaths as Kong shakes them from a log; blood oozes from the mouth of an Allosaurus whose jaws Kong prizes apart; the natives of Skull Island are crushed, eaten and terrorized; Radio City Music Hall patrons and the passengers of an elevated train are similarly mutilated and mangled; and Kong callously hurls a woman to her death from a skyscraper. The brutality of Kong is already highlighted in Creelman's early treatment, as can be seen in the detailing of the fight between Kong and the Allosaurus:

EXT. CLEARING—GENERAL VIEW—DAY.
The animals fight. Kong grabs the meat-eater's head, bites and twists. The meat-eater falls, then gets up. Kong leaps on his back, grabs his mouth, trying to pry open jaws. Ann under tree in foreground.

2. "Five reels of transgression followed by one reel of retribution" 95

Stripped by the gorilla: A lurid publicity shot of Fay Wray for the sensational advertising campaign of *King Kong* **(1933, RKO).**

EXT. CLEARING—MEDIUM SHOT—DAY.
Kong grabs the meat-eater's jaws, pries them open.

EXT. CLEARING—MEDIUM SHOT—DAY.
The girl under the tree, staring horrified. REVERSE ANGLE.

EXT. CLEARING—GENERAL VIEW—DAY.
Kong, on the meat-eater's back, pulls open its jaws. Girl in the foreground under tree.

Kong pulls back, so that he pulls the meat-eater over. He falls over with it, gets up, grabs his jaws again. The meat-eater lies prostrate as he works on it.

EXT. CLEARING—MEDIUM SHOT—DAY.
Kong's hands break the jaws. Ann under tree in the foreground.
EXT. CLEARING—GENERAL VIEW—DAY.
Kong sees he has broken the meat-eater's jaw. He gives it a waggle to make sure, sees he is dead, then rises and pounds his chest with a triumphant roar.[306]

Thus we can see how the cross cutting between Ann watching in horror and Kong's insistent attempts to pry open the meat-eater's jaw serves to emphasize the scene's brutality.

As previously mentioned, the PCA file for *King Kong* has gone missing; therefore it is not known how the Hays Office responded to the screenplay or the completed film. However, given that much of the gruesomeness and brutality of the screenplay made it into the final film (its subsequent censorship by state boards notwithstanding) it seems fairly safe to assume that the Hays Office found *Kong* generally satisfactory under the Production Code when it was presented in early 1933.

Censoring *Kong*

King Kong was previewed in San Bernadino in January 1933, and at least one scene was subsequently excised by Selznick and Cooper as a result of the preview screening: A sequence showing crew members being eaten by a giant spider-crab was cut because it was deemed to slow down the action. This footage is presumed destroyed. Cooper and RKO made further cuts between its New York premiere on March 7, 1933, its Los Angeles premiere on March 24, and its April 7, 1933, general release, reducing *Kong* from 14 reels to 11. These cuts appear to have been made to improve the pace of the film.[307] However, at least one state censor (and probably several) demanded cuts be made to lessen the film's brutality. The New York State Censor, for example, issued in March 1933 the following list of cuts:

REEL 8.—Eliminate all views of monster holding girl as he tears clothing from her body.

REEL 9.–Eliminate all views of views of monster with natives in his mouth as he tears them apart.

Eliminate all views of monster crushing natives with his foot.

REEL 10.—Eliminate all views of monster biting man whom he holds in his mouth.[308]

In England *King Kong* was one of the first films to be given the "Horrific" advisory classification (alongside *Vampyr* [1932], *The Ghoul*, *The Invisible Man*, and *The Vampire Bat* [all 1933]).[309] According to Tom Johnson, no mention was made in the British trade press of "negative reactions to the giant ape's slaughters" at the time of its UK release in April 1933,[310] although the British Board of Classification (nee British Board of Film Censors) lists on its website that cuts of 45 seconds were made to the film.[311]

Kong fared even worse with the Production Code Administration when RKO presented it for reissue in 1938. According to Senn, a number of damaging cuts were demanded including those already made by the New York state censor as itemized above and, in addition, Kong's "casual dropping of the 'wrong woman' in New York." Senn claims that Cooper was incensed by these deletions, and that it was this censored version which, for five decades, "played in movie houses and on television sets across the nation, with the missing footage considered lost."[312] (It may in fact be that *Kong* received further censorship cuts when it was released again in the forties and fifties; various scenes including Kong's fight with the Allosaurus were also darkened to minimize gruesomeness.)

RKO spent a great deal of money advertising *King Kong* prior to its 1933 New York engagement, using circus "sniping" on an unprecedented scale in a bid to draw patrons into theatres during the bank holidays that followed Roosevelt's inauguration. The studio mounted a wholesale billing campaign placing *King Kong* billposters and heralds across four territories, according to *Motion Picture Herald* (March 11, 1933): "invading the highways and byways all the way from New York to Albany, on both sides; throughout Long Island to Quogue; and cross-country to Riverhead; all of Staten Island and Westchester County, to Hartford, and along both railroad and automobile highways to Wilmington to catch the crowds going to and from the Washington inaugural." Besides being RKO's first participation in sniping activities it was said to be the widest poster billing ever given to a motion picture at a single theatre at that time.[313]

RKO had its reasons for mounting such a massive campaign. With the banks closed, patrons might not have the money to hand to actually go see the movie: potential disaster for any film that, like *King Kong*, was opening that month. RKO knew it had a prospective box office hit but realized too that without an advertising campaign to match (which also included a 30-minute radio teaser and a magazine serialization advertised as "the last and greatest creation of Edgar Wallace")[314] *Kong* might be seen as just another jungle movie of the type "occupying the attention of practically all major companies" at that time (*Motion Picture Herald*, March 4, 1933, listed at least eight major "animal adventure films" in production at the same time as *King Kong*, plus "numerous independent features and short subjects").[315] But *Kong* was an exploitation film designed to be exploited. Within a year of its release it had made $2,000,000 at the box office. Cooper's stock at RKO was such that, following Selznick's departure in 1933 to start his own production company, Cooper became, albeit temporarily, the new RKO production chief.[316]

In any event, *King Kong* would be shown in censored versions until 1969, when Janus Films restored the film to its original theatrical running time of 100 minutes using material taken from a 16mm print discovered in Philadelphia.[317] We can only assume that subsequent television airings in the seventies and early eighties were of this restored, uncut version. *King Kong* was released uncut on home video and laser disc in 1984, and thereafter in various restorations undertaken by Universal Studios. In 2005 Warner Bros. restored the film digitally from a dupe negative discovered in England and dating back to 1933. At the head of the film was the BBFC rating card declaring, rather aptly: "this film has been rated horrific."[318]

Ranked in the top 50 of the greatest American movies of all time by the American Film Institute,[319] *King Kong* is now one of the most beloved films in cinema history; it is also one of the most gruesome and brutal horror films of the classic era, a fact perhaps not fully appreciated because it was shown in censored form for so many years.

"A particularly gruesome specimen": Murders in the Zoo (Paramount, 1933)

Many contemporary scholars have cited the opening scene of *Murders in the Zoo*, in which a man's lips are sewn together as punishment for his having kissed the wife of the film's sadistic murderer (memorably played by Lionel Atwill), as an example of 1930s horror at its most gruesome. Tom Johnson, for example, describes this particular scene as "one of the most horrific scenes ever, one that was way over the line even in the pre-Code era."[320] Indeed, some critics of the time felt that the film had gone too far in terms of its gratuitous violence. Writing in the *New York Times*, Andre Sennwald declared: "[J]ust as it seemed that the cinema's experiments in sadism were ended for the season, Paramount disclosed a particularly gruesome specimen."[321] It is more accurate perhaps to describe Paramount's experiments as being in *marketing* sadism, as the opening scene in question—and much of the film that followed it—was designed to fit into the studio's drive for sensationalism following its hit with Cecil B. De Mille's biblical epic *The Sign of the Cross* (1932), a film that had exploited, in the words of screenwriter John Balderston, "the great box office values of torture and cruelty."[322]

Indeed, Paramount would use the opening scene as the basis of one of its lurid advertising campaigns for *Murders in the Zoo*, with the headline: "HE SEWED A MAN'S LIPS TOGETHER … for Daring to Look at Her With Eyes of Love!"[323] It may be that the scene itself was devised for the express purpose of creating a shocking talking point that would

Sadistic Eric Gorman (Lionel Atwill) molests his wife, Evelyn (Kathleen Burke) in *Murders in the Zoo* (1933, Paramount).

aid promotion of the film by word of mouth. *Murders in the Zoo* is one of the few 1930 horror films not based on a pre-existing property. Its story and screenplay were written from scratch by Philip Wylie and Seton I. Miller (with additional dialogue by Milton H. Gropper), and it is possible to see, from treatment to revised final script, how the writers tailored their screenplay to meet the demands of the studio's marketing strategy.

A synopsis of the final script describes Atwill's character Eric Gorman as "a peculiar man with a sadistic nature and a fiendish streak of jealousy so far as his wife, Evelyn, is concerned."[324] This aspect is, of course, considerably played up in the opening sequence in which the man has his mouth sewed shut by Gorman because "under the influence of liquor, he had the audacity to kiss Evelyn." The sequence is not present in Wylie and Miller's initial undated 23-page treatment. It is, however, present in the first draft script (dated December 22, 1932). A note attached to the aforementioned treatment states "to be discussed at the production staff meeting, November 2, 1932,"[325] and it is possible that the shocking opening scene was devised at that meeting, possibly by associate producer E. Lloyd Sheldon (himself a screenwriter with numerous credits) in conference with Wylie and Miller, and added to the screenplay after that. Certainly the writers would be aware, by studio dictate, of the current trend for combining cycle elements: Paramount had already done this with *70,000 Witnesses*. *Murders in the Zoo* also comprises into its "horror picture—animal picture" storyline a comedic angle involving a newspaper publicist with a drink problem (played by Charles Ruggles) hired by the zoo as a press agent. This comedy, as many modern commentators complain, seems grafted onto the story and ill-fitting. Thus, the opening scene as presented in the screenplay is similarly gratuitous:

FADE IN

A-1

INDIAN JUNGLE—CLOSE SHOT

We see a man lying on the ground. He is dressed in an explorer's costume, leather boots and a pith helmet at his side. He is being pinioned by two vicious faced Orientals in native costume who, by their sadistic grins, denote that they enjoy the man's agony.

We do not see the man's face because it is concealed by the figure of Eric Gorman, who is kneeling over him, BACK TO CAMERA. He is also dressed in explorer's costume.

(Sound: Man's agonized groans)

A-2

CLOSE-SHOT GORMAN

As he bends over the prostrate figure. His face is sober, tense, cruel, in sharp contrast with the natives'.

Into scene Gorman's hand comes up rhythmically holding a bloody needle to which is attached a catgut thong. As he reaches the top of each stitch he pulls it tight but we are unable to see what he is sewing.

The man's groans accompany this grisly act…

And later in the scene:

MEDIUM CLOSE UP TAYLOR

As he struggles to his feet and turns towards camera we see for the first time Gorman's horrible handiwork. His lips are sewn firmly together with catgut. Agonized sweat stands on his face. He is mute, but his eyes express vividly his anguish and desperation.[326]

Although the screenplay and film were considered satisfactory under the Production Code, this opening scene, unsurprisingly, would be eliminated by a number of censor boards, including New York, who in March 1933 ordered Paramount to remove "all close views of man where his mouth is shown sewn together."[327] Likewise when Paramount presented the film for reissue in September 1935, Joseph Breen ordered the elimination of "close-up of man's lips stitched together."[328] This was not the only elimination ordered by the New York State Censor, however: other aspects of the film's sensationalism were also cut; including much of the climax where Gorman gets his comeuppance and is crushed to death by a giant Mamba (another element of the story which featured heavily in the studio's advertising campaign for the film), and a graphic moment in an earlier scene where Gorman chokes his wife, Evelyn (played by Kathleen Burke), and throws her to the alligators, callously kicking her hand from a bridge as she tries to hang on for dear life.

Further scenes of sexual brutality and animal savagery tenuously grafted onto the slender murder plot betrayed the intentions of the studio to reviewers of the time. "There is little or no mystery about any of these murders," complained the *London Times* (June 12, 1933), "and the murderer is a plain, untarnished villain.... [T]he narrative is plain and workmanlike."[329] The plot of *Murders in the Zoo* may only be a device for a string of gruesome murders and scenes of sexual sadism à la *Dr. Jekyll and Mr. Hyde* (Paramount's previous horror hit) but that was clearly Paramount's objective: to boost the sensationalist angle for marketing purposes.

During the years of its publication from 1930 to 1972, the trade journal *Motion Picture Herald* ran within its pages a regular column called "Showmen's Review," written "from the point of view of the exhibitor." In its review of *Murders in the Zoo*, the *Herald* responds to the calculated gruesomeness of the film in terms of its exploitation possibilities for exhibitors:

> If your audiences are favorably inclined towards melodramatic horror pictures, *Murders in the Zoo*, should hit them in the right spot. It's an out and out shocker. There is little mystery. It stresses to the utmost every attempt to inspire fear, thrills and terror.... [N]o novel means of raising goose-flesh and providing shrieks has been overlooked apparently. Comedy relief is offered; romance and love interest are of secondary importance, serving principally as the basis for further shocks; sympathy for any of the characters is stimulated by audience anticipation as to whether, when and how they may be killed.... [I]t's pretty strong. There is no doubt it packs a certain entertainment punch.... [It may be] a little too brutal for feminine appreciation.... [E]mphasize the thrill, terror and melodrama ... you can count on capturing the interest of the thrill seekers... [A]mple opportunity for startling exploitation in which ideas based on snake and alligator angles can get you away from the lion-tiger exhibitions which may have become too common through their use in connection with other current animal pictures.[330]

The *Hollywood Reporter* similarly declared the story "fairly patchy and scrappy" but recognized that "there are several punch sequences that will chill the spectators' spines and make them feel they are getting their money's worth."[331]

"CALCULATED CALLOUSNESS":
MARKETING *MURDERS IN THE ZOO*

In late February 1933, Paramount took an eight page advert in several trade papers selling its forthcoming season of pictures in the wake of the "sensational box office records of *Sign of the Cross* and *She Done Him Wrong*": among its offerings, which included *Song of Songs, King of the Jungle,* and *Shame of Temple Drake*—all marketed by graphic sensationalism—was *Murders in the Zoo*, illustrated with a painting of a blood-soaked body lying on the ground by a row of tiger cages. The advert urged exhibitors to watch for "a smash [publicity] campaign" for *Murders in the Zoo* and *King of the Jungle* in particular.[332]

In April, the studio ballyhooed *Murders in the Zoo* for its New York opening, turning the lobby of the Paramount Theatre into a "combination sideshow and Midway," as *Hollywood Reporter* (April 4, 1933) described: "Outside has a giant and a midget, making announcements. The inner lobby has a snake exhibit and an illusion of a girl without a body. Just beyond them a six-day bike rider circles around, and there is also a Coney Island weight-guesser, a poet who composes any kind of ode for you, on any subject, in one minute, groups of wax models, a cigar store Indian and a singing parrot."[333] But despite all this novelty, *Hollywood Reporter* concluded: "still the picture is only doing fair business."

The New York reviews for *Murders in the Zoo* were mixed: *The American* declared it "a delightful whimsy," while *News* wrote, "If mystery dramas are to be measured in terms of goose pimples and crawling flesh, then this one is good." However, other publications were less convinced. *The Mirror* remarked that the inspiration of the director, the writers and the performers "appear to be at their lowest ebb," and the *World-Telegram* complained that in spite of its gruesome deaths, *Murders in the Zoo* "leaves the state of mystery films just about where it found it—considerably punch-drunk."[334] The calculated gruesomeness of *Murders in the Zoo* did not appeal to all audiences either, with some theatre owners in the smaller cities reporting that "people are fed up on murder pictures,"[335] and that "if Charles Ruggles had not been in the picture it would have failed to click."[336] One theatre owner in Vancouver adjudged the film "just a bit too gruesome" and reported several walkouts, "mostly women with kids."[337]

The film did "top business in London,"[338] however, where, according to Johnson, the opening scene appears to have been cut from all prints[339] (the British Board of Film Classification lists *Murders in the Zoo* as having been passed uncut on May 5, 1933, with an A certificate, at a running time of approx. 60 minutes).[340] The trade publications in England again seemed to see through the film's "calculated callousness" describing the plot development as proceeding on "shock lines," but adjudging the film's high level of incident as sufficiently entertaining to ward off any feelings of repulsion in the onlooker.[341] Not so in Australia, Sweden and Germany where the film was banned.[342]

As mentioned in my introduction, it was William K. Everson who put *Murders in the Zoo* on the map for many horror fans when he wrote about it in his 1974 *Classics of the Horror Film*; until then the film had become largely forgotten. He makes the point that the film, at that time, had received limited exposure on television, and was "usually cut." According to Everson, neither had *Murders in the Zoo* been revived theatrically.[343] Indeed, fans would have to wait until its release on VHS in 1995 to see it uncut. A Turner Classic Movies/Universal DVD release followed in 2010.

"A truly horrible and nauseating bit of extreme sadism": The Black Cat *(Universal, 1934)*

On March 4, 1933, *The Film Daily* announced Roosevelt's inauguration as the United States' president and with it the promise of a reconstructed prosperity for the film industry. Industry executives, including Will Hays, Adolph Zukor, Harry Warner, Nick Schenck and

Carl Laemmle, Sr., published welcome messages to the incoming president and his New Deal which promised relief, recovery and reform. "From the bottom of my heart I pledge Mr. Roosevelt and his administration the fullest support which the Universal Pictures Company and I can give," wrote Laemmle, adding that the new administration was about to tackle a herculean job that would require everyone to "put his shoulder to the wheel."[344]

"Leaders in the film industry see renewed hope for the speedy enactment of measures that will restore the country," announced *The Film Daily* editorial, "and motion picture business with it, to normal prosperity."[345] These measures, as briefly outlined in Chapter 1, would come to include direct subsidy of the major chains and permission, for the time being, to exercise monopolies, thus enabling the chains later to establish a "run zone clearance system" of exhibition that would ensure the Hollywood majors maximum profits. This was, of course, particularly beneficial to the "Big Five": Warner, RKO, Paramount, Fox and MGM, who owned the best first-run houses in metropolitan areas (accounting for 70 percent of the box office) but less so to Universal, which did not own a theatre chain. Thus, Junior Laemmle, in 1934, pushed on with his strategy to separate Universal's horror output into prestige and programmer units, reflecting his desire to maintain a first run presence with "A" pictures while also supplying low-budget programmers for neighborhood theatres, small-town exhibitors and rural markets. Many theatres outside first-run were by that time playing double-bills. Independent theatres had seen the double feature as a way to fight declining audience attendance and to compete with first-run theatres. MPPDA affiliated theatres eventually followed suit. As exhibitors could not afford to pay for two "A" picture rentals on one bill, all the major studios alongside Universal began to develop "B" picture production units to supply exhibitors with class-B pictures cheaply. Poverty Row studios like Monogram, Republic and Producers' Releasing Corporation got in on the act, grinding out small budget genre movies for the lower half of double bills in theatres often located "on the wrong side of the tracks." Although revenues from B pictures were usually small, they allowed studios to operate at full capacity and provide a training ground for new talent.[346]

And so it was that Junior Laemmle assigned Edgar George Ulmer to direct a low budget programmer based on Edgar Allan Poe's short story "The Black Cat." Ulmer had been involved with Universal since the early twenties, as an art director, and as a director of two-reel Westerns and shorts. He was able to work quickly and cheaply: two major prerequisites, as *The Black Cat* was to have a budget of $91,125, and a shooting schedule of 15 days—half the amount of money and time of the average Universal "A" picture.[347] By comparison, "The Return of Frankenstein," to be directed by James Whale, which Junior Laemmle was developing concurrently with *The Black Cat*, would be allocated a budget of $293,750 and a 36 day schedule.[348] Nevertheless, Universal had hopes that *The Black Cat* would prove a money-spinner due to the pairing of the studio's two horror stars, Karloff and Lugosi, a novel idea at the time.

The Invisible Man had been a hit for Universal, and had convinced Junior Laemmle that novelty was "in." Karloff was back under contract to Universal for "The Return of Frankenstein," and Junior Laemmle had the idea of pairing him with Bela Lugosi in an adaptation of Poe: a meeting of "Frankie," "Drac" and "Eddie," as *Universal Weekly* (March 31, 1934) put it in a manner evocative of Universal's later "monster rallies" of the 1940s.[349] As Kyle Edwards points out, the original Poe story of *The Black Cat* also offered a number of gruesome episodes that might create horrific effect, such as near decapitation by ax, and the gouging out of a cat's eye (which Dwain Esper staged in *Maniac* [1934] in a "borrowing" from Poe), but brought with it considerable problems for adaptation in terms of its almost non-existent plot.[350] Various attempts had already been made at Universal to adapt Poe's short story before Ulmer was brought in, including treatments by Stanley Bergerman (co-authored with Jack Cunningham), Richard Schayer, and Garrett Fort. All three had been rejected by Junior Laemmle. In February 1933, contract writer Tom Kilpatrick and producer Dale Van Every had submitted a synopsis which, according to Tom Weaver, contained a number of elements that Ulmer and co-writer Peter Ruric ultimately used in their story: including "a young couple trapped in a castle ruled by two madmen, the dread of cats, torture on the rack and insanity."[351]

Sadism in *The Black Cat*'s Screenplay

Ulmer evidently saw in this particular synopsis the bare bones of an idea that would lend itself to allegory. As he explained to Peter Bogdanovich in 1970: "I wanted to write a novel really, because I did not believe the literature after the war and during the war, on both sides. In Germany and in England, [war] was very much the heroic thing.... I couldn't believe that. Therefore I took two men who knew each other and who fought their private war during the time that capitalism flourished. I thought it was quite a story stylistically.... It was very much out of my Bauhaus period."[352]

Ulmer and Ruric drew on two further influences when writing their treatment of *The Black Cat*, and both can be seen in the sadism inherent in the film: the first was contemporary news reports of a couple who had supposedly encountered the black magic cult of English occultist Aleister Crowley[353]; the second was the historic French fort of Douaumont near Verdun, that had been captured by the German army in 1916 and retaken by the French nine months later at the cost of over 100,000 men: a stark illustration of the madness of warfare. Ulmer had been told about Douaumont in the 1920s by the novelist Gustav Meyrinck, who had considered writing a play about it. The merging of these disparate influences into *The Black Cat* resulted in a dreamlike, almost abstract narrative, one that Greg Mank describes as "the most perverse of Universal's horror tales, spiked with incest, necrophilia, sexual perversity and insanity."[354] Nevertheless, Junior Laemmle must have seen Ulmer's storyline as a suitable vehicle for the Karloff-Lugosi pairing and gave it the go-ahead.

The Black Cat was entrusted to E.M. "Eph" Asher while Junior Laemmle embarked on a visit to Europe to induct production units in London and Paris; a trip that would ultimately be cut short ostensibly due to illness.[355] He was still away on February 6, 1934, when Ruric and Ulmer presented their 44 page treatment to Asher. There is no evidence to suggest that Asher found the story anything other than "great" and left them to their own devices.[356] Indeed, it seems likely that Asher was preoccupied with another production that he had also been assigned to supervise at that time, a prestige costume drama called *Elizabeth and Mary* to star Margaret Sullavan as Mary Queen of Scots. Lowell Sherman had been slated to direct from a script by Arthur Caesar. However, Leslie Carter, who was to play Queen Elizabeth, had called for script changes that Asher and Universal would not agree to. Universal ended up shelving the film on February 12, after several weeks of preparation.[357]

Meanwhile Ruric completed the screenplay of *The Black Cat* on February 19. It was ripe with scenes of sexual perversion, black magic, animal cruelty and suggested necrophilia. Particularly gruesome was the final showdown between Poelzig (Karloff) and Werdergast (Lugosi) in which the former is skinned alive. The screenplay describes the scene thus:

J-19–The wall. The shadow of Werdegast and Poelzig. An effect as if Werdegast was splitting the scalp slowly, pulling the sheath of skin down over Poelzig's head and shoulders.

J-25–Poelzig, sans skin, is struggling on the rack. By superhuman effort he frees himself and falls to the floor.

J-30–Poelzig raises his hideous body—his eyes focused dully, expressionlessly, on Joan. He laboriously, painfully, crawls toward her.[358]

Much has been made by horror fans over the years as to supposedly deleted footage from this scene depicting a "bloodied, skin-shorn Poelzig crawling on the floor after enduring Werdegast's torture session."[359] However, no such footage has been found to exist. As Tom Weaver comments, despite the sequence appearing in the shooting script, no production reports have been found to indicate the scenes were actually shot, and no studio stills have materialized of the missing scenes.[360] It is therefore possible that shots J-25 and J-30 were never really intended to be included in the final film, and were therefore never shot, but were written into the screenplay so that their subsequent removal would allow other potentially censorious elements to stay during negotiations with the SRC: they could be used, if necessary, as a bargaining point.

"These scenes of skinning a man alive are too brutal and gruesome"

In March 1933, following widespread criticism over the levels of sex and violence in movies, the MPPDA's board of directors, at Hays' behest were asked to sign a "Reaffirmation of Objectives" of the Production Code.[361] On March, 8, Hays wrote to the heads of production at all of the studios—including Junior Laemmle—asking them to sign a "reaffirmation of adherence to the Production and Advertising codes."[362] James Wingate was tasked with the enforcement of "production standards." In this, he was to be assisted by Joseph Breen in the "execution of the Code and Resolution for Uniform Interpretation."[363] Although Breen had been involved with the MPPDA since 1932, this signaled a move toward a stricter enforcement of the Production Code in the face of growing calls for federal censorship; the first step toward widespread industry self-censorship (via the soon-to-be-formed Production Code Administration) that the studios, following the Legion of Decency's threats to mass boycott movie theatres mid-1934, would no longer resist.

Thus, on February 26, 1934, Asher, Ruric and Ulmer met with Breen for a conference regarding the screenplay of *The Black Cat*. In a follow up letter sent that afternoon to Harry Zehner at Universal, Breen outlined a number of details in the screenplay that he felt ought to be carefully handled to avoid the film being mutilated by censor boards. "The major difficulty on this score," Breen wrote, was predictably "the gruesomeness, suggested by the script, dealing with the scenes of the action of skinning a man alive." Breen confirmed that it was his understanding from the meeting that the scene was to be merely suggested by shadow or silhouette, but emphasized that "this particular phase of your production will have to be handled with great care, lest it become too gruesome or revolting."

In his detailed list of concerns, Breen itemized sequences J-16, 17, 18, 19, 26 and 30 in the screenplay with the note: "these scenes of skinning a man alive are too brutal and gruesome and some change could be made to bring them in conformance under the code. This entire sequence is a very dangerous one and it would be advisable for us to discuss them thoroughly before any further preparation is made."

Breen detailed a number of other concerns in the script which had been discussed in the meeting, and which "it was agreed that it would all be taken care of," including a further scene of gruesomeness depicting "the corpse of a young girl suspended in a glass coffin" which Breen felt was "open to serious objection." Also inadvisable due to likely problems with state censors were moments of sexual intimacy, animal cruelty, black magic ritual, suggested indecent exposure, a reference to Czechoslovakians as people who "devour their young," and Poelzig's keeping of an inverted cross.[364]

Two days after the meeting, Universal wrote to Breen to assure him that, as per his suggestions, Ulmer and Ruric had modified the script, and to inform him that production of *The Black Cat* would begin that day, February 28, 1934.[365] However, an SRC interoffice memo reveals that the "revised" script was little changed. "[T]he only changes I find," wrote Islin Auster, "is the elimination of the reference to Czech Slovakians, and the description of the inverted cross, although a cross of some type is still used. As far as the skinning alive scenes, they remain unchanged."[366]

As Stephen Prince has commented, the cases of *The Black Cat* and *Bride of Frankenstein* especially show the SRC/PCA's "limited ability to overrule filmmakers and studio executives when they were really determined to push screen violence past a point the PCA felt was safe."[367] Breen appears not to have followed up Auster's memo informing him that few of Breen's advisories had been followed by the studio.

Ulmer completed filming on March 17, 1934, one day over schedule and within budget. A rough cut was screened later that month. Some sources suggest that Universal executives, including Carl Laemmle, Sr., responded badly to the film, feeling that the nominal hero of the piece—Werdegast—had been portrayed unsympathetically. It may also be that Ulmer was ordered to remove some of the more objectionable material (including an "orgy" among the Satanists, that Breen had asked to be eliminated from the script) before screening the rough cut to the Hays Office, although it is impossible to confirm whether or not that this the case. What we do know for certain is that from March 25, Ulmer shot three days of additional scenes with Lugosi, David Manners, Lucille Lund, Jacqueline Wells, and others, intended to soften both Lund and Lugosi's characters, and to an extent, help to explain the mystifying plot. Among the list of requirements in the budget for these additional scenes are "6 girls [sic] extras."[368] They were needed for the scene of Poelzig in his cellars staring at embalmed corpses in vertical glass cases. As Mank notes, "the director gambled that Breen would let it pass."[369] Its inclusion suggests that Universal was willing to push the gruesomeness of *The Black Cat* if they could get away with it ("You will not soft-pedal on the ghoulishness of *The Black Cat*," Carl Laemmle urged exhibitors in *Universal Weekly*, "but you will capitalize it").[370]

On April 2, 1934, Breen saw a rough cut of *The Black Cat*, and wrote to Zehner that it was his judgment that the picture conformed to the Production Code and contained "little, if anything, that is reasonably censorable." Furthermore, Breen ended the letter, "[W]e are particularly pleased with the manner in which your studio and director have handled this subject and we congratulate you." Breen mentioned that "three or four scenes were missing from the print," which he assumed were process or stock shots.[371] Zehner wrote back to Breen to assure him that the missing shots would not in any way "ciolate censorship or the Code."[372]

A number of scholars have questioned why Breen raised so little objection to a film that in 1934 was "unprecedented in its perversity."[373] Did a later version of the film differ radically from the rough cut that was screened for the SRC? Or was Breen simply too preoccupied with other matters, such as the grassroots campaign that was now underway to impose a more stringent Code, to pay much attention to Ulmer's B movie? Indeed, in his report to Hays (April 10, 1934), Breen remarked almost off handedly that *The Black Cat*, "another one of their horror stories … seems to have been handled satisfactorily" by Universal, whereas *Tarzan and His Mate* at MGM warranted much more concern "on account of an underwater swimming sequence in which the girl was shown completely in the nude" that had prompted Breen to reject the picture, to which MGM had appealed to a jury of MPPDA members.[374] Breen's decision had been upheld by the jury (which had included Junior Laemmle), but clearly the case had been something of a test for Breen as the new director of public relations of the MPPDA. In May 1938 the PCA approved the reissue of *The Black Cat* without eliminations, presumably viewing a print that had been in circulation since 1934.[375] It seems unlikely therefore that Universal had released *The Black Cat* in 1934 in a radically altered version to the rough cut that the Hays Office had pronounced satisfactory under the Code. It may be, then, that Breen did not expect state and foreign censors to raise any serious objections to *The Black Cat*, as he stated in his April 2 letter to Zehner. Or, as his final comment suggests, Breen may have been genuinely pleased that Universal and Ulmer had toned down some of the screenplay's most graphic moments, in particular the skinning scene.

In any event, *The Black Cat* received its gala premiere at the Pantages Theatre in Hollywood on May 3, 1934.[376] The skinning scene immediately became a talking point of the film for some critics. *Time* revealed that the film climaxes with Lugosi "skinning Karloff alive with a scalpel" in their review of May 28, 1934.[377] *Variety* (May 22, 1934) proclaimed that "the skinning alive is not new. It was done in a Gouveneur [sic] Morris story, 'The Man Behind the Door,' filmed during the war." (Irvin Willat's film *Behind the Door* [1919], a revenge story set during World War 1, may well have been a further influence on Ulmer and/or Ruric.) Even so the reviewer, "Land," declared it "a truly horrible and nauseating bit of extreme sadism," adding that "its inclusion in a motion picture is dubious showmanship." The devil worshipping cult was also considered "close to the border." *Variety*'s reviewer lists the running time of *The Black Cat* as 70 minutes.[378] Whether Universal made cuts to the film before its general release on May 7, 1934, is unknown (the duration of the extant print is generally listed as 65 minutes).

Certainly state and overseas censors demanded extensive cuts in *The Black Cat*, more so than Breen seems to have anticipated. Unsurprisingly the skinning scene came under close scrutiny. Although New York, Massachusetts, Kansas, and Pennsylvania approved the film without deletions, Ohio, Ontario, Chicago, Maryland, Quebec and Sweden all demanded the skinning scene removed. Ohio and Maryland seem to have taken particular objection, demanding all reference to the skinning—including dialogue, sound effects and shadow and silhouette shots—eliminated. Australia deleted the shadow shots and insisted all publicity bear a warning that the picture was suitable only for adults. Ontario and Japan required further cuts in addition to the skinning. In Great Britain, the skinning remained but references to Satanism were removed; also cut in the United Kingdom (where the film was retitled *House of Doom*, possibly to avoid association with an earlier proposed stage adaptation of Poe's *The Black Cat* which had been banned by the Lord Chamberlain's Office in June 1932)[379] were the shots of the glass cased corpses that Ulmer had snuck past the Hays Office. The film was given an "H" advisory certificate. Austria, Finland, British Malaya, and Italy rejected the film completely: Austria on religious grounds and because of "offence to the national feeling of the people"; Italy because the film "could create horror."[380]

One might have imagined that *The Black Cat*, with its theme of Satanism, and general gruesomeness, would have raised the ire of the Roman Catholic Legion of Decency, which had been formed in April 1934 by the nation's bishops to combat "indecent and immoral pictures"[381]; however, that does not appear to have been the case. Had the Legion condemned *The Black Cat* it might have encouraged thousands of churchgoers to boycott the film—if they had felt any inclination to see it in the first place. But, according to Gary D. Rhodes, the critical reception of *The Black Cat* was accompanied by the feeling that the film's treatment of black magic was generally "silly" and therefore no such controversy ensued.[382]

Although *The Black Cat* was subsequently touted as one of Universal's big hits of 1934, its box office take, at $236,000 gross, was the sign of a modest success[383] (in comparison with, say, *The Invisible Man*'s record-breaking New York opening the previous season). Certainly profits were sufficient for Universal to release another Karloff-Lugosi-Poe picture, *The Raven* the following year (and the studio had originally planned to team them up in *The Suicide Club* and *The Return of Frankenstein* before that).[384] However, there was a national lack of faith with which exhibitors booked *The Black Cat* that belied Universal's predictions for the film's box office potential. As Rhodes points out, theatres did not prophesy major grosses for the film, and it was double-billed in numerous cities at a time when most films in those cities were not being paired.[385] Despite the novelty attraction of Karloff and Lugosi starring together, audiences did not flock to see it, although it undoubtedly drew in a niche of "thrill-hunters" who habitually attended horror films.

THE BLACK CAT'S TAG

Perhaps the "terrific air of weird unreality" that *The Black Cat* carried (*The Film Daily*, May 19, 1934) proved too esoteric for many.[386] (*The Billboard* described the film as a "gruesome mess of celluloid,"[387] while *Photoplay* adjudged its storyline "all too unconvincing."[388]) Kyle Edwards, drawing on Thomas Schatz's theory of genre development, suggests that *The Black Cat* signaled the 1930s horror cycle's entering a self-referential "late classical" stage of development: the late classical stage results when the aesthetic codes and narrative conventions of a genre become widely known to an audience; thereafter studios and filmmakers look for ways to "toy" with those familiar features, and their films "self-consciously gesture towards the genre itself."[389] We can see an increasing sense of self-parody in the later films of the thirties cycle: in *The Black Cat*, *The Bride of Frankenstein*, *The Raven* and *Mad Love*. In these films, among other self-conscious features such as increased theatricality or "campness," horror is piled upon horror until, as *Film Weekly* (March 15, 1935) said of *The Black Cat*, "it all becomes just silly"[390]; furthermore, the endings of these films become increasingly absurd, and often self-reflexive. A case in point is the original scripted ending of *The Black Cat*, which takes the form of an elaborate in-joke, as Mank describes in his book *Bela Lugosi and Boris Karloff*:

> The script originally offered a tag in which a bus—piloted by none other than Edgar G. Ulmer, in white beard and goggles—stops. Will you take us to Vizhegrad? Asks Peter (David Manners).
> "I'm not going to Vizhegrad," replies the disguised Ulmer. "I'm going to a sanitarium to rest up after making *The Black Cat* in fourteen days! However, it will be a long walk. For you, I shall make an exception."[391]

One can only assume that it was always the intention to replace this "tag" with something more suitable. However, its inclusion highlights a certain truth about the tag ending of thirties horror films: regardless of whether they are comic, or appear to restore normality and/or give closure, they are largely redundant to the narrative. *The Black Cat* concludes with the final conflagration of the fort, from which the newly-weds escape: "the end." One might argue that any further scene would be irrelevant. The ironic, self-reflexive coda as filmed (which I discuss in this book's introduction), by its very triteness (deliberately or not—but probably deliberately, given the inside joke tag that Ulmer and Ruric had previously written) invites audiences not to take the horrors of *The Black Cat* seriously, which may not have sat so well in pre-"meta-horror" 1934, given the allegations of silliness often directed towards the film by reviewers of the time.

The Black Cat's critical stature has, of course, grown in the intervening years and it is now considered a highly distinguished film by fans and scholars alike; justifiably so, as it is an important film in many ways, not least because it was one of the few notably gruesome entries in the thirties cycle that was reissued after 1934 without suffering further cuts under the PCA. In other words, whenever *The Black Cat* was reissued theatrically, or shown on television, it was the original 1934 version that viewers saw. *The Black Cat* thus offered a unique glimpse into the gruesomeness and brutality of the thirties cycle, when other horror films of the thirties were shorn of these elements, or remained unseen altogether.

"Excessive brutality and gruesomeness": The Bride of Frankenstein *(Universal, 1935)*

When Junior Laemmle returned from his Europe trip in early 1934, it was to a restructured Universal. His father Carl Laemmle, Sr., had himself taken control of production, with Henry Henigson as general manager supervising associate producers E.M. Asher, Dale Van Every and James E. Grainger. Producer Stanley Bergerman was away from the main production fold, answering only to Laemmle Sr. Likewise, Junior Laemmle was given his own independent unit, and in 1935, announced a slate of six prestige pictures, including "The Return of Frankenstein."[392] Plans for a sequel to *Frankenstein* had been in Junior Laemmle's mind for some time (altering the ending of the original *Frankenstein* may have been done in part to leave open the option for a sequel), and a script had been submitted by staff writer Tom Reed in July 1933, after a previous aborted attempt made by Robert Florey (who wrote a seven page outline as early as December 1931).[393]

James Whale had resisted pressure to direct the sequel for several years, and had, in fact, after *The Invisible Man* (which he had accepted as an assignment partly to get out of "The Return of Frankenstein") been looking to move to Paramount where he felt he would be afforded greater autonomy. However, by November 1933, Universal had offered Whale an improved contract whereby he would function as producer on his pictures, and for every horror picture he made at Universal he would be given the choice of one mainstream assignment.[394] This, he accepted. Junior Laemmle thus again pressed Whale to direct "The Return of Frankenstein" after his success with *The Invisible Man*. Whale, however, rejected Reed's screenplay as well as subsequent treatments by L.G. Blochman and Philip MacDonald, and meanwhile, stalled the project further by mounting an adaptation of John Galsworthy's novel, *One More River* (1934). Part of the problem for Whale was that he felt that he had "squeezed the idea dry on the original picture" and "never want[ed] to work on it again."[395]

Blochman's treatment attempted to incorporate elements of the "wild animal movie" popular at the time: In the early stages of the story it is revealed that the monster reappeared after its supposed death in the burning mill. Its continued terrorization of the countryside had "brought death to Baron Frankenstein, ruin to the Frankenstein fortune, and the enmity of the villagers towards Henry and his bride." Henry and Elizabeth escape by joining a travelling carnival, but they are pursued by the monster who demands a mate. The monster is eventually killed by an escaped lion. Blochman promises a "semblance of a happy ending in the knowledge that Henry and Elizabeth are at last free from the menace of the monster."[396]

MacDonald's storyline attempted greater topicality given Adolf Hitler's recent rise to power as chancellor of Germany. In MacDonald's version Henry is developing a death ray which he offers to the League of Nations as a weapon with which to prevent imminent war in Europe. When he tests the ray in the foothills of the village, Henry inadvertently revives the monster which goes on the rampage. Eventually Henry confronts the monster and both are killed by the ray. An interestingly blasé note written by McDonald at the end of the treatment illustrates just how casually screenwriters regarded the convention of the "tag" ending: "This is the real end. But a tag would probably be needed. If so nothing could be easier. A Fade-and then Victor and a convalescent Elizabeth. And Frankenstein's son. And a reference to Frankenstein and how, by bequeathing the Ray, he did in the end, after all benefit humanity..."[397]

One can see how in their treatments MacDonald and Blochman attempted to provide the studio with stories that held "a decidedly novel and shocking appeal": the type of screenplay Junior Laemmle adjudged the order of the day. "We have found that the theatre-going public like the unreal, the weird and the uncanny," he told *Universal Weekly* (December 30, 1933), "and we are preparing to cater to this great audience with colorful imaginative stories."[398] However, one can also see why Whale had rejected these treatments: behind the novelty neither significantly develops the Monster and its relationship with Henry, and, crucially, the Monster is treated unsympathetically. Ultimately both rehash the story of *Frankenstein* without moving it into new territory. Whale's fear of a redundant sequel was well-founded.

On the other hand, certain elements in the Reed and Blochman treatments made their way into John Balderston's subsequent screenplay; indeed Reed's story, in particular, contains the bare bones of many narrative aspects of *The Bride of Frankenstein*, plotlines that would be developed by Balderston and later by William Hurlbutt and Edmund Pearson—

who wrote the final shooting script. (*The Invisible Man* screenwriter R.C. Sherriff also prepared a version but, according to James Curtis, "nothing came of it.")[399] When Balderston subsequently contested his screenplay credit for *The Bride of Frankenstein*, studio employee Finlay McDermid made a written comparison of all the submitted versions. Interestingly, among McDermid's conclusions were that Reed originated the idea of the peasant family with whom the Monster hides and the blind hermit who takes him in, and that the central idea of the Monster wanting a mate existed in both the Blochman and the Reed treatments.[400] In short much of what became *Bride of Frankenstein* already existed in Tom Reed's original script. Many scholars credit the original source novel as Balderston's primary inspiration for the final screenplay. However, it is clear from McDermid's research that, when he finally accepted the assignment, Whale sent Balderston back to many of the ideas in Tom Reed's version almost a year after Reed's script had been written; another indication perhaps that Whale—resenting his label as the "Monster Man"—had sought to stall his involvement with *The Return of Frankenstein* for as long as possible by rejecting a script that at the time he had pronounced as "stinks to heaven" but later used elements of in the final screenplay.

Such were the exigencies of the studio system, of course, the practices of which might nowadays be called "development hell." What is clear throughout, however, and further evident in correspondence between the studio and the Production Code Administration, is that James Whale—rather than Junior Laemmle or an associate producer—took overall control of *Bride of Frankenstein*, at least during the script development stages and into the filming. Thus, the shooting script that was submitted to the PCA on November 30, 1934, was, as James Curtis notes, a cut and paste amalgam of the various drafts, a working script-in-progress.[401]

Brutality and the *Bride*

Breen wrote to Harry Zehner on December 5, advising him that "The Return of Frankenstein" basically seemed to meet the requirements of the Production Code. However, he noted that several things ought to be modified: these primarily to do with the brutality and gruesomeness of the script, which he considered excessive. In particular, Breen was concerned with the number of killings that took place in the story. "We counted ten separate scenes in which the monster either strangles or tramples people to death," Breen wrote, this in addition to some other murders by subsidiary characters. Breen was of the opinion that in a picture as "basically gruesome" as "The Return of Frankenstein," "such a great amount of slaughter is unwise, and we recommend very earnestly that you do something about toning this down." He also advised Universal that care would be needed with the details of the killings, in order to avoid making them "too realistic or gruesome." The other issue that concerned Breen was the "suggestion of irreverence, particularly with the use of the name of God," and he highlighted certain lines in the script that were "advisable for you to delete." These included, of course, Henry's reference to knowing what it was like to be God that had caused censorship problems in the original *Frankenstein*, a line which, as Breen pointed out had proven "offensive as somewhat blasphemous."

"Your studio is, of course, only too well aware of the difficulty which attended the release of the first FRANKENSTEIN picture in a great many parts of the world," Breen prompted. "The criticism at the time, directed at the picture, seemed to be based principally on the two elements of undue gruesomeness and an alleged irreverent attitude on the part of the characters, particularly wherever they even suggested that their actions were paralleling those of the Creator." Breen finished off his letter by conceding that the element of gruesomeness would "depend largely upon the way the picture is actually shot, but we urge you to use the utmost care and good taste, in order that your picture may meet with the widest possible favorable public reaction."[402]

Whale had, in fact, toned down the gruesomeness and brutality in Balderston's rough draft screenplay quite considerably. The British scriptwriter had approached the story as a straightforward morality play, with the Monster desperately seeking the love and acceptance of his human creator and the female "mate" that he forces Henry to make for him. When the Mate shuns him in favor of Henry, the Monster, in a fit of jealous rage, brutally kills Henry, Elizabeth and the Mate. He crushes the skulls of Henry and Elizabeth with a club "half the size of a young tree," and breaks the neck of his Mate, flinging her body across the floor. The brutality was not intended as gratuitous, but was used to heighten the sense of tragedy. Balderston refers several times to the Monster as being an outcast, and notes within the script: "We must make it clear throughout that his savagery and murder evolve from what people do to him, and not from an innate viciousness."[403] Balderston ended his version with the Monster struck down by lightning after praying for "peace and oblivion," the natural order being restored by the heavens above.

Whale too was against gruesomeness for its own sake, claiming in an interview with *Universal Weekly* (March 23, 1935) to have "no sympathy" for it, and differentiating his films from those in which gruesomeness featured merely to repulse though "blood horror." Gruesomeness and brutality were justified when they served a dramatic purpose, according to Whale, in the creation of pathos, say, or when used satirically in depicting Henry's ghoulish experiments, or in the depiction of the "fantastical imagination."[404]

Breen had worked closely with Whale and Universal on *One More River* in an attempt to eliminate elements of sexual sadism from the film. However, despite his best efforts, *One More River* had been condemned by the Legion of Decency on its release in 1934; a turn of events that had no doubt placed Breen in an awkward situation politically. His consternation at the *Frankenstein* sequel was, therefore, understandable. It was mitigated somewhat by the new ending that Whale had given his screenplay, which was as destructive as Balderston's, if somewhat less violent, and containing what Breen deemed to be "a sufficient moral lesson" to obviate any offence on grounds of blasphemy:

> The Bride recoils from the Monster into Henry's arms.
> Monster: "She is like the rest…"
> Monster advances on lever that will, according to Pretorius, "blow us all and the mountain itself into atoms." Elizabeth pounds on the laboratory door, come to save Henry.
> Monster swings the lever, "in his eyes the gleam of wild vengeance."
> With the lightning and thunder of the heavens for accompaniment—the structure that was the laboratory collapses into a burning heap—the cloud of smoke and dust disperses a little and settles down over the scene—the thunders of a jealous and triumphant Jehovah roll—for positively the FINAL FADE OUT.[405]

For Whale this ending provided a moral lesson that would hopefully satisfy the Breen Office and state censors, while also precluding the possibility of his being asked to make further sequels. The finality of this ending was to be accompanied by a lack of reassurance or reaffirmation of ideology. "Nothing will be resolved except the end destruction scene,"

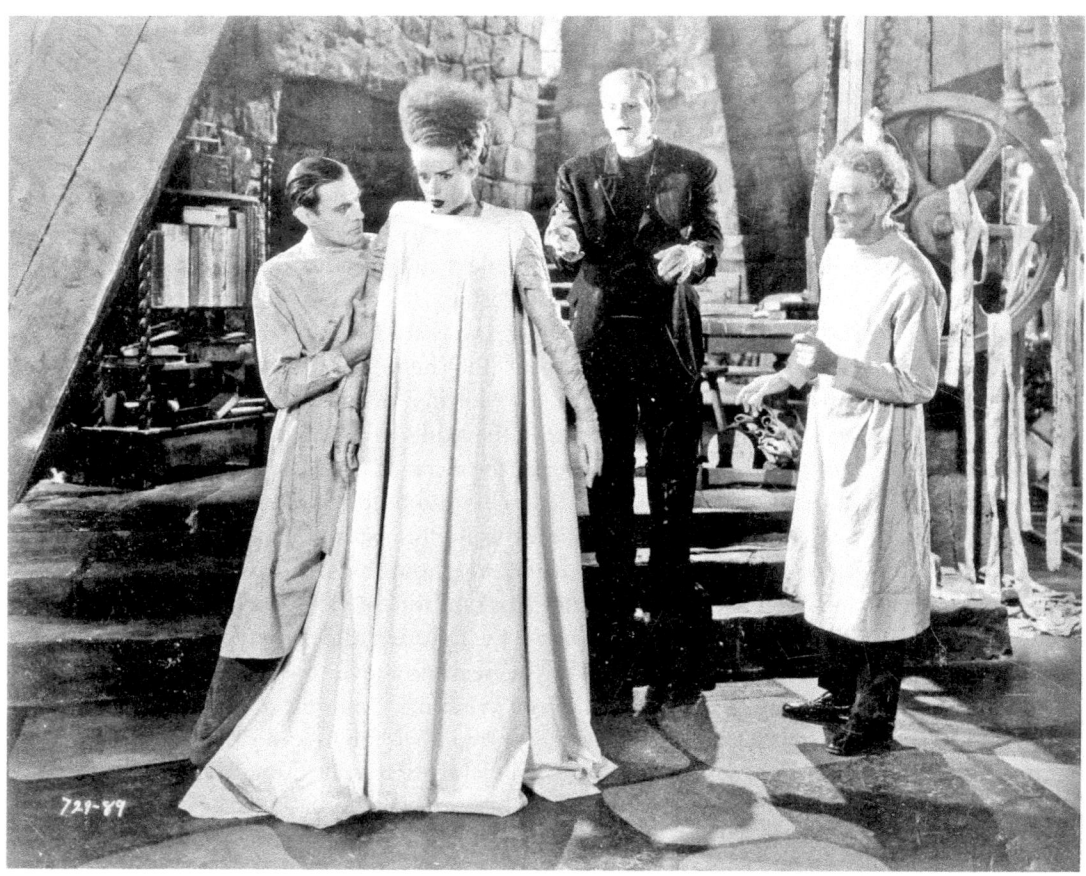

Elsa Lanchester as The Bride rejects The Monster (Boris Karloff) much to the dismay of Henry (Colin Clive) and Dr. Pretorius (Ernest Thesiger) in *The Bride of Frankenstein* (1935, Universal).

Whale told Franz Waxman, and he asked the composer if he would write an "unresolved" score.[406]

That Universal had set up an Office of the Censor, to liaise with the Production Code Administration shows that Universal had accepted the amplified authority of the Production Code as of July 1934, whereby MPPDA members had agreed not to produce or distribute any pictures which had not been given the Seal of approval.[407] Vested with the power to pass final judgment on the "fitness of all pictures for public showing" was Joseph Breen.

Script revisions for "The Return of Frankenstein" which would address the concerns of the Production Code Administration appear to have been assigned to staff writer Leonard Spigelgass, who suggested that, before work commenced on a new version, a conference be held between Whale and a PCA representative to "determine just how the several dangerous elements may best be handled."[408] Thus Whale met with Islin Auster and Geoffrey Shurlock on December 7 to discuss how Whale planned to film the screenplay. "It is our understanding," Breen wrote later, "that Mr. Whale intends to shoot the various killings ... in a decidedly impressionistic manner, without devoting much footage to them, and in such a way as to avoid gruesome details."[409] Indeed, Whale himself confirmed with Breen by letter his feeling that "we can evade any possible trouble" on the points that had caused Breen concern: "the killings will all be minimized in the photographing of the scenes, most of them being in one little Sequence to describe the reign of terror, and the whole of the film on this will be very short." In addition, Whale assured Breen that the potentially "offensive as somewhat blasphemous" dialogue would be changed. Breen had advised Whale to cut a scene in which the Monster, passing through a cemetery, mistakes the figure of Christ on the Cross as a real man suffering the same physical torment as it had itself been subjected to earlier in the story. In his letter, Whale was at pains to justify the scene's inclusion in the script, clearly hoping that Breen would relent from demanding this particular deletion: "Although the scene ... as I explained to Mr Sherlock [sic], was meant to be one of supreme sympathy on the part of the Monster as he tries to rescue what he thinks is a man being persecuted as he was himself some time ago in the wood, if you still find this objectionable I could easily change it to the figure of death."[410] In lieu of any further comment from Breen on this particular detail, Whale decided it best to make the change anyway, although in the scene as shot, he featured Christ on the Cross in the background, thereby allowing the association to be made between Christ's persecution and that of the Monster.

Whale exercised considerable diplomacy in his dealings with Breen, partly out of common courtesy and good manners, but also in the pursuit of his artistic aims for the picture. He understood the moral directive of the Code, and played up to it when it suited his needs. Thus, he reinforced in his letter to Breen that "The Return of Frankenstein" was intended as

The Monster (Boris Karloff) encounters the Christ figure in a churchyard in this controversial scene from *The Bride of Frankenstein* (1935, Universal).

a "moral lesson," and that "the destruction at the end is sufficient warning to anybody I should think." However, there is nothing in Whale's correspondence with Breen to suggest insincerity on Whale's part, or a desire to undermine the Production Code per se, which make the subsequent difficulties that Whale experienced with *Bride of Frankenstein* all the more intriguing.

Whale continued to revise the screenplay during production, adding new bits of business and incorporating ideas that arose during the filming process. At some point, Whale and his screenwriters came up with a gruesome plot twist that would see Elizabeth killed by the Monster and her heart transplanted into the body of the Mate. Lillian Russell, Universal's liaison in the Office of the Censor, was tasked with sounding out the idea with the PCA to see if it would be acceptable under the Code. Geoffrey Shurlock quickly vetoed it, as he recorded in a memorandum: "I suggested that the script was already top heavy with gruesome elements and expressed fear that any further exaggeration along this line might make the finished picture unacceptable screen fare." Russell indicated to Shurlock "that the studio was not at all committed to the idea themselves,"[411] which implies that Whale might already have encountered some resistance to the idea from the studio. Steven Prince suggests that the PCA may have taken the query as a warning sign that the filmmakers were contemplating additional horrific material beyond what was scripted, and that they might have looked upon the query as a test by filmmakers who wanted to see what they could get away with.[412] If this was indeed the case it would go towards explaining the PCA's reaction to the finished picture when it was screened for them on March 21, 1935.

"THE FINISHED PICTURE SEEMS TO US DEFINITELY TO BE A VIOLATION"

"As you know, we have given much serious thought to your production THE BRIDE OF FRANKENSTEIN," Breen wrote to Zehner two days later, "and as I have indicated to you, we are gravely concerned about it. The finished picture seems to us definitely to be a violation of our Production Code because of its excessive brutality and gruesomeness."[413] Was the picture that Whale shot significantly different to the screenplay that Breen had okayed after changes? It seems unlikely that Whale would have included new material that was unacceptable to the Code, considering that he had already broached the heart transplant idea with them, and then subsequently chosen not to film it after Shurlock's veto. Breen had emphasized to Whale that the element of gruesomeness would depend largely upon the way the picture was actually shot, and Whale had assured Breen that he would shoot it with "the utmost care and good taste."[414] This he undoubtedly did. What, then, had gone wrong?

The PCA's modus operandi was to focus its attention primarily on the script-review process, based on the rationale that censorship was best done in preproduction "to eliminate the need for costly reshooting and reediting" later on. As Thomas Doherty has remarked, it was the PCA's aim to ensure "all problem areas have been ironed out during the meticulous script-review phase."[415] However, the screenplay, no matter how detailed, is an evocative document rather than a blueprint, and the power of the final celluloid image and accompanying sound is not always fully apparent in the script, especially given the affective nature of screen horror. It may be then, that Whale's skills as a filmmaker had inadvertently served to amplify those areas of the screenplay that the PCA had considered problematic, such as the killings, despite his assurances to exercise discretion in their filming. It is also telling that, in his letter to the studio Breen pointedly directs his suggestions to "Mr. Laemmle" instead of to Whale; perhaps, after *One More River*, Breen had grown wary of the director's assurances. We might, on the other hand, see Breen's taking a harder line with *The Bride of Frankenstein* as part of a wider strategy in seeking to tighten up the Code in line with some of the tougher state censors such as Ohio and New York which at that time were eliminating material that had been passed under the Code. This involved minimizing suggestions of brutality and depictions of murder across all genres, including horror pictures. Certainly, *The Bride of Frankenstein* would come to mark the beginning of a clampdown by the PCA on gruesomeness in the horror film.

Thus, Breen indicated in his letter to Zehner that "careful and intelligent editing of the picture may remove the difficulties." Breen then went on to itemize his recommendations for cuts that would make the film acceptable under the Code:

1. Delete all the offensive "breast shots" in reel one.
2. Delete the shots of the monster in the pool actually drowning Hans.
3. Delete shot of the monster actually pushing Hans' wife into the cistern.
4. Delete the shots of the little girls coming out of the church in their white dresses and discovering the body of the little child lying on the ground.
5. Delete the shot of the mother carrying the child's dead body in her arms.
6. Delete the shot of the bloody hands of the monster in the hermit's hut.
7. Delete entirely the sequence of the idiot nephew strangling his uncle.
8. Delete the close up shot of the monster as he falls, crashing the lid of a coffin and later seems to fondle the head of a corpse.
9. Delete the footage showing the entrance of Dr. Pretorius into the vault accompanied by the two men and all their talk about the young girl, the action of opening the casket etc.
10. Cut the entire sequence of the deserted street and the murder of the woman by the half-wit.
11. Cut the shot of the heart being taken from a jar with the forceps
12. Cut the shot of the monster throwing the man over the roof.

The eliminations that Breen recommended were, excepting his objection to Elsa Lanchester's décolletage in the film's opening scene, indicative of his "seeking to lessen those phases of the picture which suggest excessive brutality and gruesomeness." Breen went on to assure the studio that he recognized that "in a story of this kind ... a certain amount of what might be called brutality and gruesomeness is necessary to the proper telling of the story," but he warned the studio that the picture as it then stood was "likely to be quite offensive, and to result in a very definite unfavorable audience reaction.... It is our thought that the recommendations made herein above will accomplish much by lessening the brutality and gruesomeness, and that your story will suffer little, if any, as a result," Breen concluded. "Indeed it is our considered unanimous judgment here that these eliminations will very materially help your picture from the general standpoint of entertainment."[416]

As Steven Prince has pointed out, several of the eliminations sought by Breen—such as the bloody hands of the Monster—followed the strict letter of the Code but were minor visual details in the film that may well have been allowable in other circumstances.[417] Breen's list of eliminations can therefore be seen as an opening gambit in negotiations that would inevitably follow: Neither party expected all the cuts to stand. On the other hand, the PCA were asking not just for individual shots but for *whole sequences* to be eliminated, surely a first under the Production Code for a horror picture, and an indicator of how things had changed since the PCA came into being.

On March 25, Whale, Zehner and Junior Laemmle himself met with Breen to thrash out the cuts. It was agreed that shots 1, 5 and 7 would be deleted as Breen had requested. Other sequences would be shortened as a compromise. These included: the drowning of Hans by the Monster, which would lose a section showing the bubbling of water and the Monster chortling as Hans drowns. Also the section where the "the little girls coming out of the church in their white dresses" was cut short so that the action switches to another scene just as the body is discovered; the murder of the woman by the "half-wit" was similarly abbreviated, as was the shot of the heart being taken from the jar with forceps, which now dissolves to the next scene just as the heart comes into frame.[418] Although Whale was able to keep a number of shots and sequences that Breen had originally asked deleted, the cuts ultimately made to the film in order to secure a Production Code seal, as Steven Prince points out, left the action in some sequences "choppy and unsatisfactorily enigmatic"[419]; one can see in the final print that material has been removed and the film's overall effect is damaged because of the deletions.

Whale Loses his Original Ending—Again

Universal previewed *The Bride of Frankenstein* on April 6. As a result of the audience reaction, Whale decided to take out further material that slowed the pace, including one entire sequence of the skeptical Burgomaster interrogating villagers who claim to have seen the Monster. With additional dialogue trims throughout, Whale removed almost ten minutes from the film after the preview. However, Whale also extended some sequences to boost suspense. One of these was the scene near the start of the film where the Monster pulls the girl out of the pool and is shot by the hunter after the rescue. Islin Auster of the PCA gave his approval for the scene to be changed on the strict proviso that the scene "will, in no sense, have a sexual connotation" (he was perhaps mindful that censor cuts to the drowning of the little girl in the original *Frankenstein* had created just that). The scene in the jail, where the Monster is chained to the chair, was also lengthened to show the Monster being roughly treated by the jailers. This the PCA allowed as long as there was no evidence of "excessive or gruesome brutality." Finally, Whale shot a new scene showing the Monster stalking Elizabeth before it kidnapped her.[420]

Universal screened the film again for the PCA on April 15, who finally adjudged the picture acceptable under the provisions of the Production Code. However, along with the seal, Joseph Breen issued a warning to Universal that the picture was likely to meet with considerable difficulty at the hands of the censor boards, both in America and abroad: "the very nature of the production is such as to invite very critical examination on the part of the censor boards, and you may well expect difficulty with it wherever the picture is shown." Breen closed by advising Universal to tell its New York office to be on the lookout for problems with the censors. *The Bride of Frankenstein*, Breen concluded, was the kind of picture that was "acceptable under the *letter* of Production Code, but very dangerous from the standpoint of political censorship."[421]

Zehner replied to Breen telling him that his letter had been passed on to New York and its contents "duly noted." "Whilst on the subject," Zehner informed him, "we have put a happy ending on this picture." At the last minute, Whale had—once again—lost his unresolved ending, and *Bride of Frankenstein* would, like the original *Frankenstein*, see its conclusion changed so that Henry and Elizabeth could live on as the "final couple." As Zehner enthusiastically told Breen: "At the moment where Frankenstein's bride (Valerie Hobson) comes to the window of the laboratory and tries to get in, Dr. Frankenstein motions her to go away. At that moment the monster sees this and says to Frankenstein, 'You—friend—go.' And Frankenstein rushes to the door, turns the key and escapes. The monster then pulls the lever and he, his mate and "Dr. Pretorius" are all killed in the ruins. The final shot being Dr. Frankenstein and his bride on the outside looking at the crumbling heap."[422]

Had Universal, with $397,023 of its shareholders' money invested (the picture came in ten days over schedule and $100,000 over budget),[423] and the prospect of censorship problems looming in key territories, pressured Whale at the final moment to change his cherished ending to one more audience-friendly? That seems the most likely scenario. After all, the film had already been granted its Production Code seal of approval, and the preview had been a great success (*Hollywood Reporter* had described it as "one of the finest productions that has come off the Universal lot in many a day").[424] However, Universal would have had its eye firmly on the bottom-line. A happy ending would maximize *The Bride of Frankenstein*'s appeal as popular entertainment, and perhaps help to minimize any costly censorship problems that might arise. Whale may have put up a protest against the change but would ultimately have been left with little choice. Better to shoot the new ending himself as he had done on *Frankenstein*. And so, cast members were recalled and Whale shot an ill-matching last minute reprieve for Henry and Elizabeth, finally completing *The Bride of Frankenstein*, according to James Curtis, with "literally just hours to spare"[425] before its April 19 opening in San Francisco.

Censor cuts did arise, but not to the extent warned of by Breen. Massachusetts, Kansas and New York approved the film without eliminations. Alberta demanded deletions to the scene of the Monster attacking the girl, and references to the fresh heart. Pennsylvania eliminated the line: "I have also created life in *God's own image*." Overseas, Sweden demanded extensive cuts. China eliminated scenes that showed violence towards women, such as the Monster's attack on the girl and Dr. Pretorious ordering his henchman to seize a woman. Hungary rejected the film because "picture portrayed crimes and acts of a monster called into being through scientific experiments." Palestine rejected the picture without explanation.[426] The major headache for Universal was Ohio, which demanded cuts that were, according to Paul Krieger, the Universal Branch Manager in Cincinnati, "drastic and harmful to the success of [the] picture." In Krieger's opinion, Universal had got a bad break in rushing the head censor B.O. Skinner to review the picture in time for impending cinema bookings in Cleveland.[427] Skinner, as we know, was unsympathetic to horror pictures generally, and had demanded the cuts to *Bride of Frankenstein* as a knee-jerk response.

Universal once again sought the MPPDA's help in trying to get some of the cuts reinstated, as it had done in 1931 when the Kansas state censor had sought to decimate the original *Frankenstein*. Breen did so, but ultimately used the problems that Universal encountered with Ohio over *The Bride of Frankenstein*, to lobby for greater power to veto horror and crime films, arguing that "matters which are so generally unacceptable to censor boards, ought to be unacceptable under the Code."[428]

Skinner did, however, agree to look at the film again, and reinstated most of the originally proposed cuts, eliminating only one scene in its entirety: "woman finding her little girl murdered."[429] Zehner sent Breen a grateful note advising him that in England *The Bride of Frankenstein* had "passed censorship with only one minor cut" (it had been given the advisory "H" certificate). "This shows you did an excellent job and Junior and everybody here is very happy about it," gushed Zehner, hoping that "Joe," who was vacationing at the time, was having a "pleasant trip over-seas and enjoying yourself at Karlsbad or some other Spa." The tone of Zehner's final letter to Breen on the subject of *Bride of Frankenstein* is familiar, even affectionate (Zehner would eventually join Breen's staff at the PCA). Zehner sent "love to you and Mary," and signed himself "your sincere friend." He even scrawled at the bottom of the letter by hand "Miss you!!!"[430] It is possible of course that Zehner and Breen had been friends, or become friends, during the course of their business together. Breen no doubt enjoyed the hospitality of the studios during screenings and in conferences with studio heads and producers. Perhaps Zehner had been sincerely grateful to Breen for his help in persuading Ohio to reconsider their cuts, unaware that Breen had recently written to Hays complaining that the situation had arisen because "Universal executives waved aside our decision in the matter [in earlier negotiations with the PCA] and told us they were willing to 'take a chance' on these eliminations."[431]

The Bride of Frankenstein, of course, went on to become a box office hit for Universal, and a classic of the horror genre. In *Golden Horrors*, Bryan Senn canvassed over 30 writers, editors, critics and filmmakers—some of classic horror's foremost scholars—for their top ten horror films of the 1930s: *The Bride of Frankenstein* came in at number one, ahead of even *King Kong*, as favorite thirties horror movie.[432] In 1998, it was added to the National Films Registry at the Library of Congress, for preservation.[433] Unfortunately it is unlikely that a restoration will ever take place of the material that the Production Code Administration requested eliminated due to its "excessive brutality and gruesomeness": that footage, together with the scenes that Whale took out after the preview, was likely destroyed by the studio shortly afterwards, as was common practice with excised celluloid. The best we can ask for in terms of an "uncut" *The Bride of Frankenstein* is the original shooting script, published in 1989 by Philip J. Riley.

"Cruelty for cruelty's sake": The Raven *(Universal, 1935)*

The commercial success of *The Bride of Frankenstein* rehabilitated Junior Laemmle's position at Universal, at least in the eyes of his father, Carl Sr. In April 1935, Stanley Bergerman resigned and Universal finally moved to a unit production system whereby a number of associate producers were responsible for between four and eight titles each. Junior Laemmle refused the general managership of the studio after Bergerman's departure, and instead chose to continue his own prestige unit with six to ten features slated for 1935[434] (one of which would be the financially disastrous *Show Boat* [1936], directed by James Whale). Junior Laemmle was still intent on the first run market, but *The Black Cat*'s modest success had also proven the lower budget programmer viable in relation to the horror market.

Universal had first announced *The Raven* among its forthcoming productions in June 1934[435]; The original plan had been for the scenario department to combine Poe's poem "The Raven" and short story "The Gold Bug" into one screenplay to be entitled *The Raven*. However in July that year, *Variety* reported that *The Raven* was on hold due to "need of a better script."[436] Indeed, during the months that followed, a number of writers attempted to fashion a script that Universal deemed a suitable vehicle for Karloff and Lugosi. Among them were Guy Endore, author of *The Werewolf of Paris*, who submitted a 19-page treatment in August 1934, and Michael Simmons and Clarence Marks, who in September 1934 collaborated on a longer treatment and full screenplay.[437] Apparently not satisfied with "the several treatments that had been made" by those and further writers, Universal, according to *The Film Daily* then engaged Dr. Jim Tully "to perform a major operation" on *The Raven*.[438] Tully submitted various synopses and typescript pages to associate producer B.F. Zeidman by the end of November. An abridgement of *The Raven*'s final screenplay published in the 1935 periodical *Romantic Movie Stories* credits the screenplay to David Boehm and Jim Tully, and so it may be possible that some of Tully's work found its way into the final product.[439] However, come February 1935, Zeidman had left Universal, to be replaced by first time producer, David Diamond, and a starting date announced of March 1. By now Universal had spent somewhere in the region of $10,000 on the screenplay of *The Raven*, a not-inconsiderable amount given the film's allocated budget of $109,750. The studio would invest a further $5,375 in commissioning Boehm to revise the screenplay; Boehm wrote three more complete drafts during February and March.[440] On March 7 *Motion Picture Daily* reported that director Louis Friedlander had been switched from Universal's serial department to *The Raven* which had been given the new start date of March 18.[441]

As Kyle Edwards has commented, *The Raven* contains "a meta-generic series of allusions"[442]: it references previous roles played by Karloff and Lugosi, and through familiar characters and plot devices establishes continuity with earlier Universal horror pictures (especially *The Black Cat*, which it partially remakes). Furthermore, *The Raven* presents in its dialogue and imagery a discourse on torture and sadism, ostensibly connecting to the works of Poe, but relating equally to the horror cycle itself, a further example of the tendency towards gruesome self-parody that marked the later films in the thirties cycle. Thus Boehm laces *The Raven*'s dialogue with self-referential sadism; such as in this exchange between Dr. Vollin and Bateman:

> Vollin: You shot your way out of San Quentin. Two guards are dead. In a bank in Arizona, a man's face was mutilated, burned, a cashier of the bank.
> Bateman: Well, he tried to get me into trouble. I told him to keep his mouth shut. He gets the gag out of his mouth and starts yellin' for the police. I had the acetylene torch in my hand—
> Vollin: So you put the burning torch into his face—into his *eyes*.
> Bateman: Well, sometimes you can't help things like that.

Much of *The Raven*'s torture chamber imagery would be taken directly from Poe's short-story "The Pit and the Pendulum," including the swinging pendulum itself and the room with walls that move inwards to crush its occupants. Other torture imagery was to be more realistic, such as the array of surgical instruments that Dr. Vollin uses to horrifically disfigure Bateman, externalizing the "monstrous ugliness" within him and turning it into "monstrous hate" that Dr. Vollin uses to wreak vengeance on his enemies.

"The risk of excessive horror"

On March 11, Breen wrote to Harry Zehner to inform him that the story seemed "fundamentally satisfactory" from the standpoint of the Production Code and censorship. However, he added that "as you know ... in this sort of story great care must be exercised concerning any evidence of excessive horror and brutality."[443] Since February, Breen had been seeking to tighten up policy on stories of crime and bloodshed. Although primarily directed at gangster pictures, Breen's stipulations that "there must be no suggestion, at any time, of excessive brutality" and that "action showing the taking of human life, even in the mystery stories, is to be cut to the minimum" was to impact on the horror picture, as we have seen in the case of *The Bride of Frankenstein*.[444] Hence Breen's warning against "excessive horror and brutality." Specifically Breen cautioned Zehner on four points in *The Raven*'s script: the operation upon Bateman; the presentation of various instruments of torture; exposing the bleeding head of one of the characters; showing the pendulum sweeping down on Vollin's victim near the end of the story.

Universal appeared to take Breen's caution seriously. A conference was held at the studio on March 14; in attendance were David Diamond, Louis Friedlander, Lillian Russell and Harry Zehner of Universal, and Karl Lischka and Arthur Houghton of the PCA. The agenda of the meeting was to discuss possible danger points in *The Raven*. However, it also served the purpose of satisfying the Production Code officials that the producer and director of *The Raven*—both new to feature films—were "disposed to exercise reasonable moderation and good taste" throughout the production. Thus it was agreed at the meeting that:

1. no detail of the actual operation upon Bateman will be shown. A knife may be flashed to indicate the impending operation.
2. Bateman's appearance will never be unhumanly repulsive.
3. the instruments of torture will be passed in review, as if in a museum.
4. blood will not be shown, except perhaps in a flash.
5. the pendulum knife will not touch Thatcher's body.
6. there will be no improper dress or contact in the bedroom scenes.[445]

The second point was open to further policing by the Production Code Administration, and can be seen as part of Breen's clamp-down on "excessive horror" (Universal's *Werewolf of London* [1935], had, two months earlier, met with similar objection from the PCA concerning its wolf-transformation make up). Boehm's screenplay had included a detailed description of Bateman's appearance after Dr. Vollin had operated on his face thereby transforming him into a monster: "Bateman turns so that his face is toward us. His face is a horror. Certain muscles have been paralyzed through cutting of the nerve ends. Certain others have been permitted to remain—giving life to the part of the face they control, so that here is a face—a crazy quilt of death and life. One part of the face remains fixed in a horrible dead grimace, while the other remains alive—side by side with the corpse. One eye remains open, unblinking—staring straight ahead."

A resume in *The Raven*'s Production Code Administration file dated March 16, reveals that Karl Lischka and Islin Auster of the PCA had been presented with various shots of Karloff in Jack Pierce's make-up for the production to "determine whether they are suitable for screen presentation."[446] As Universal had previously toned-down the wolf make up in

Werewolf of London in response to concerns raised by the PCA, it is possible that they did the same in *The Raven* with regard to Karloff's make up (Greg Mank describes Karloff's make-up as more comical than horrific),⁴⁴⁷ thereby minimising the "excessive horror" of Bateman's appearance as it was described in the screenplay, in direct response to Breen's tightening of the Production Code.

According to some sources, Dore Schary, later president of MGM, provided a last minute polish of *The Raven* screenplay, and it is possibly his "final white script" dated March 19, 1935, that Breen acknowledged in his letter of March 20, with the words: "[W]e can only refer you to our specific warnings issued in previous correspondence concerning this story." Despite Universal's compliance to the requirements of the Production Code Administration, it is clear that Breen had, by then, begun to discourage the studios from producing horror pictures, a campaign that would become more vociferous over the coming months. "We ... deem it necessary to remind you once more that

Boris Karloff's disfigurement make-up for *The Raven* was vetted by the Production Code Administration (1935, Universal) (courtesy Ronald V. Borst/Hollywood Movie Posters).

because of the stark realism of numerous elements in your story, you are running the risk of excessive horror," Breen concludes in his letter.⁴⁴⁸ Six days later, after receiving yet another draft of *The Raven*, Breen's discouragement continued, even increased: "Within the limits of the cautions given to you in former letter, *The Raven* is still acceptable under the Production Code," Breen informed Zehner on March 26. "However, the current accumulation of horror in motion pictures must of necessity cause continued concern."⁴⁴⁹

Tag Ending for *The Raven*

Friedlander and Diamond went into production with *The Raven* on March 20, and completed filming 16 days later on April 5; on schedule but $5,450 over budget (final cost $115,209.91) due to extra time in editing and synchronizing. The final version was viewed by the PCA on April 15 and awarded Production Code certificate no. 790, it seems without problem. Universal previewed *The Raven* in the last week of May.⁴⁵⁰ Reviews listed the film at 62 minutes. Greg Mank reports that two scenes were removed from the film prior to its July 8 general release. The shooting script began with Jean leaving a theatre after a dance recital while autograph hunters vie for her attention. This scene was filmed but later cut after the decision was made to start the picture instead with Jean's car crash: a more dramatic opening. Also shot but cut was an early scene showing the fugitive Bateman spying on Dr. Vollin at the hospital before trying unsuccessfully to approach him outside in the street. Instead, Karloff's character is given less of a preamble before he arrives at Vollin's house, having already obtained the address from a fellow criminal-type in a shady bar.

The biggest change, however, was the addition of the tag ending (discussed in my introduction). This did not feature in the shooting script but was added later during shooting. It is unclear who wrote it, or indeed, who decided the need for it. The shooting script had ended with two of Vollin's party guests awakening the next morning, unaware of the mayhem that has ensued while they soundly slept; "hasn't it been a wonderful night!" one of them proclaims.[451] The tag eventually used is equally inane, if more befitting in terms of convention: we see the final couple drive away from the house while discussing the previous night's horrors rather nonchalantly (it also provides plot symmetry on a superficial level similar to the tag of *The Black Cat*). This last minute change highlights how difficult it was for screenwriters to come up with tag endings that were logical and convincing. In this case, while the final couple is ostensibly preserved, their ready acceptance of the sadism and torture which has taken place in the Vollin house, which has included a shooting, attempted murder by pendulum, and themselves nearly being crushed to death (which seems to have left neither of them particularly phased), ironically, belies—even normalizes—the horror of it.

THE RAVEN AND CENSORSHIP BACKLASH

A number of scholars dwell on the poor reviews and box office performance of *The Raven*, as illustration of its unoriginality and as a symptom of the censorship backlash against it and other horror films. However, a number of reviews were enthusiastic: *The Film Daily* (June 4, 1934), for example, proclaimed it "FANTASTIC MELODRAMA THAT SHOULD CLICK WITH PATRONS WHO GO FOR THE BIZARRE STUFF,"[452] and its box office take in many territories was above-average. It opened very well at The Roxy in New York (on July 4), where, according to *Motion Picture Daily* (July 6, 1935), "it broke all holiday marks ... since the theatre went into receivership in 1932."[453] Despite soaring July-August temperatures it also did above average business in Cleveland, Oklahoma, Buffalo and Cincinnati.[454] It is, however, clear that a backlash against horror pictures was beginning to foment among the state and overseas censors that summer. Although Massachusetts and Kansas passed *The Raven* without cuts on July 12 and 31, respectively; earlier, in June, New York had ordered among the deletions "all views of Judge and torture machine, excepting final view where he is to be released"; Ohio the same; Virginia on July 10 requested to be cut all views of the swinging torture machine and the acetylene torch remark, while Pennsylvania and Quebec on July 17 and 22 ordered to be cut all torture room scenes and the acetylene torch remark.

On July 10 Ontario rejected the film with the comment, "features horror and shuddering melodrama. Full of fiendish and diabolical doings." British Columbia initially rejected the film but, on July 26, after the film had been "reconstructed" by the Canadian Film Exchange, passed it. Meanwhile, Alberta passed the film with the warning: "The Alberta Censor Board advises nervous and excitable people to avoid this picture as it is a HORROR PICTURE."[455]

In Britain the right-wing press seized upon the film as evidence of the need for tighter cinema censorship generally and of horror films in particular. It used *The Raven* as part of a campaign to pressure the British Board of Film Censors into introducing a stricter ratings system that would prevent children under the age of 16 from attending horror films (this eventually came to pass in 1937 with the introduction of the formal "H" certificate which replaced the Horrific advisory label). On August 2, the *London Daily Telegraph* published an article lambasting the British Board of Film Censors for passing *The Raven*, which the reviewer adjudged "quite the most unpleasant picture I have ever seen ... it exploited cruelty for cruelty's sake"[456]; two days later the *London Times* (August 4) used similar language to describe the film as one of "'horror' for 'horror's sake," that "exploits degrading abnormalities of human nature." Common to the argument of these social commentators was that horror films, such as *The Raven*, had a capacity for harm, not just to children, but to adults with "certain mentalities [that] are susceptible."[457] Therefore, while "intelligent people will find *The Raven* at once funny and unreal," pronounced the *Telegraph*, "all film fans are not intelligent and some are very impressionable." Such "an orgy of sadism" (as the *Telegraph* called *The Raven*) might, in other words, harm those who were less well-educated than the readers of those newspapers. *The Daily Express* (August 4) used even blunter rhetoric as part of what seems to have been a concerted effort in the right wing British newspapers to create a moral panic over *The Raven*: "Edgar Allan Poe ... was fond of graves but he would turn in his own if he could see this.... Its horror is revolting. I thought the censor had put his foot down on horror films of this kind?"[458]

By September, the trades in Hollywood were reporting that censor boards internationally had been going on a "vivisection spree" in their crack down on such horror "operas" as *The Raven*: "Rough treatment at the hands of the censors has given producers of so-called horror films a few shudders of their own. Echoes of wholesale snipping, and in some cases complete rejection, are rumbling through the cutting rooms and studios are hewing to the line rather than have outsiders wield the shears and possibly ruin continuity."[459]

This report in *Variety* (September 4, 1935) which detailed the responses of the censor boards in America and abroad to *The Raven* and *Werewolf of London*, as well as to MGM's *Mad Love* and *Mark of the Vampire*, raises some interesting questions with regard to the abrupt cessation of the horror cycle the following year. Historians have generally attributed the end of the 1930s horror cycle to three closely interconnected factors. First is the British so-called ban on the horror film which coincided with the arrival of the "H" certificate. Joseph Breen's tightening up of the Production Code and discouragement of "horror," as a result of the British ban, is the second factor. Third, is that after the acquisition of Universal by Standard Capital in March 1936, new studio head, Charles B. Rogers, took horror pictures off the production slate, and the other studios quickly followed suit, bringing the cycle to an end. Clearly the moral conservative campaign against the horror film played a part in halting horror production in 1936; however, the fact that Universal resumed the cycle with *Son of Frankenstein* in 1939, despite familiar warnings by the Production Code Administration, suggests that the financial imperative held greater sway over the studios than a potential ban in the United Kingdom. The 1938 reissues of *Dracula* and *Frankenstein* had convinced Universal that horror was profitable again. Ultimately, then, the decision to end the horror cycle in 1936 lay with the studios, not the PCA, the state censors or the British Censor despite their growing opposition to horror pictures. Why, then, did the studios—seemingly by general consensus—decide to cease production of horror in 1936?

The answer perhaps lies in how the industry perceived horror pictures in the 1930s. Censorship objections in the thirties were not to horror pictures per se, but to gruesomeness and brutality in any genre. Moreover, as we have seen, gruesomeness and brutality were perceived to be what attracted audiences to horror pictures in particular. As Doherty says, "gruesomeness was to the horror film what sex was to the vice film." Studios "hewing to the line" gruesomeness and brutality as a response, in 1935, to "wholesale snipping" by state and overseas censors, must have realized that by doing so, they were removing the raison d'etre of these pictures; taking out what audiences were coming to see them for in the first place. Hence, further production of horror pictures became pointless (in the same way that vice films petered out in the late thirties after the studios removed their suggestiveness). Of course, the studios came to see horror in a different light in the 1940s: Universal produced family-friendly pictures that emphasized spookiness in a way that was fun but safe, while RKO pioneered the psychological horror film with *Cat People* (1942). The identity of horror changed as studios found different ways to sell it based on less sensationalist elements that made the genre acceptable once again to the PCA and state censors.

The Raven was itself planned to be remade by Universal in 1938,[460] again pairing Karloff and Lugosi, according to Tom Weaver, but with a "fresh angle" for the story.[461] This did not transpire. Film Classics did, however, reissue *The Raven* in 1949 (tagged as "The Edgar Allan Poe Mystery Show!"). But the ad line used when *The Raven* was sold to television as part of the original Screen Gems *Shock* package in October 1957 seems more apt: "Sadist plots revenge with torture!"[462]

"Audience should be inclined to laugh": Mad Love *(MGM, 1935)*

In his excellent DVD commentary to *Mad Love*, film historian Steve Haberman comments that the early 1930s gave us a "surprising number of films that reveled in sadism" (citing *Dr. Jekyll and Mr. Hyde, Murders in the Rue Morgue, The Most Dangerous Game, Island of Lost Souls* and *The Raven* as examples) but according to Haberman "arguably none of them are quite as sick and disturbing as Karl Freund's ultimate offering in a career of horror, *Mad Love*."[463] Indeed, we might see *Mad Love* as an apotheosis of the 1931–1936 horror cycle in several ways. The film's self-reflexive discourse on sadism is similar to that of *The Raven* (made almost at the same time as *Mad Love*) except that its sexual element is greater. This becomes apparent in *Mad Love* from the outset, when Dr. Gogol derives voyeuristic sexual gratification from attending a Grand Guignol play in which the actress, Yvonne, with whom he is obsessed, is tortured as part of the scenario. As Haberman notes, Gogol closes his eyes "in orgasm at the very moment the hot poker is touched to Yvonne somewhere below her waist." In this way we can see *Mad Love* taking the sado-eroticism of *Murders in the Rue Morgue* and *Dr. Jekyll and Mr. Hyde* to a level of perversity that borders on parody. In satirizing the Grand Guignol "Theatre des Horreurs," *Mad Love* is also satirizing the 1930s horror film cycle itself and its gruesome attraction for audiences; in the words of Greg Mank, *Mad Love* plays "like a sassy in-joke for horror fans [of the era], paying mock homage to *Frankenstein, Freaks, Doctor X, The Mummy, Mystery of the Wax*

Museum and *The Black Cat*."[464] In fact the level of homage to those films is such that *Mad Love* at times resembles a compendium of 1930s horror scenes and tropes: the transplant scenes of *Frankenstein* and *Island of Lost Souls*, the newspaper reporter of *Dr. X*, the waxwork figures of *Mystery of the Wax Museum*, and so on. Dr. Gogol even plays a church organ like Lon Chaney in *The Phantom of the Opera*, Karloff in *The Black Cat*, Frederic March in *Dr. Jekyll and Mr. Hyde*, and Lugosi in *The Raven*. Colin Clive's appearance as the tormented Stephen Orlac completes this sense of obsessive generic referencing. Based on evidence of the screenplay drafts we can attribute *Mad Love*'s mix of sadism and satire primarily to John Balderston and Karl Freund, both of whom clearly enjoyed toying with the by-now familiar features of the horror film to make *Mad Love* "self-consciously gesture towards the genre itself," as Kyle Edwards puts it. Such intertexuality is more associated with the postmodern horror film than classical Hollywood cinema, and is yet another indication, perhaps, that the 1930s horror film has more in common with contemporary horror than is often thought. Certainly *Mad Love* brings with it the sense of reductio ad absurdum that frequently accompanies films that come at the end of a cycle, carrying, as it does, its genre tropes to extremes. Like other key horror films of the thirties it was also mutilated by studio and censors alike: MGM removed over 15 minutes of footage before its release, while the British censor, in the words of *Variety* (September 4, 1935), went after *Mad Love* "hot and heavy," making cuts in every reel but one.[465] *Mad Love*, like *Dr. Jekyll and Mr. Hyde*, *Island of Lost Souls*, *Freaks*, *The Old Dark House*, *Dr. X* and *Mystery of the Wax Museum* also remained unseen for many years having been shelved by MGM shortly after its 1935 release.

Karl Freund and the *Mad Love* Screenplay

Early in 1935, Karl Freund left Universal for MGM after directing a string of films for Junior Laemmle, the last of which had been the poorly received musical comedy *Gift of Gab* (1934). There he was attached to the unit of producer John W. Considine, Jr., where he would "specialize in unusual themes."[466] Considine himself had come to MGM from Fox in 1932, assigned to a Wallace Beery wrestling picture, *Flesh* (1932), directed by John Ford. It is unclear who at MGM first had the idea of adapting Maurice Renard's 1920 novel *The Hands of Orlac* (a film had already been made of it by Robert Wiene in 1925, starring Conrad Veidt). Greg Mank suggests that it was Considine who recognized in the central premise (in which the hands of a murderer are surgically grafted onto a concert pianist whose own hands have been severed in a train wreck) "two bastions for horror fans": the Grand Guignol theatre setting and the concept of medical transplants.[467] However, what is clear from the various script drafts is that Freund made a significant contribution to the screenplay of *Mad Love* both in terms of story development and cinematic treatment; indeed, close scrutiny of the various extant screenplay drafts of *Mad Love* reveal the film's guiding hand (no pun intended) from the outset to have been Freund's. (*The Film Daily* announced in April 1935 that Freund had left Universal to "direct a picture at MGM from his own scenario," and he may well have looked upon *Mad Love* as his own scenario.)[468]

Guy Endore was hired to write an outline based on Renard's novel. This he submitted as a 12-page document on February 22, 1935. Endore's storyline opens with Orlac at a concert. He phones his wife, Yvonne, who is in her dressing room backstage at the Grand Guignol theatre. Dr. Gogol (called Lebri in the outline) is briefly glimpsed in his box in the theatre. Then we focus on the train crash and its aftermath. Yvonne and Stephen's stories are foregrounded at this point, and Lebri as a character only comes into focus on page 6—halfway through the story—as he attends a guillotine execution. It is then revealed that Lebri has a wax statue of Yvonne—his obsession—in his house. Just as his "mad love" becomes clear to the reader the story ends at that point, as a wax Yvonne appears in a negligee in a "dainty rococo boudoir, discretely lit": "Doctor Lebri's eyes take in with evident joy this lovely scene. Overcome, he kneels beside the figure, speaks to her, kisses her hand."[469]

Here the outline comes to an abrupt halt, as though Endore was unsure where to take the storyline from there.

Freund and Endore collaborated on a longer treatment which they completed on March 13. This 61-page treatment is credited as "an original story by Karl Freund and Guy Endore," and it constitutes the entire story, as eventually appeared on screen, told in visual terms. As such, it demonstrates a cinematic sensibility that is almost entirely lacking in Endore's 12-page outline, and forms a remarkably close blueprint of the final film. Moreover, in the longer treatment Freund and Endore completely rework the source material, shifting the focus from Orlac to Lebri, the sexually obsessed surgeon who performs the transplant.

The treatment foregrounds Lebri as the central character. It opens as per the final film: at the Box Office of the Theatre des Horreurs with a man and frightened girl about to go in.

> Behind credit titles immense CLOSE UP of pair of eyes. CAMERA DRAWS BACK, wicked malicious face appears behind iron bars.
> MAN'S VOICE (Off-screen)
> There's nothing to be afraid of.
> As camera draws back further the face is seen to belong to a ticket seller at the box office of a theatre exclusively devoted to horror plays.
> GIRL'S VOICE (Off-screen)
> But you know I have a weak heart
> TICKET SELLER
> Madame, we have a trained nurse in attendance.
> A bearded man (type of Charles Laughton), in coat and soft fedora stands lost in thought before ghastly wax model in lobby, showing a beautiful girl (Yvonne) lying on rack in agony.[470]

The story then proceeds almost exactly as per the final film, focusing primarily on Lebri's obsession with Yvonne and his growing insanity, with the Orlac storyline as a secondary plot. New elements are added in the treatment to develop Lebri as a character, such as the introduction of Rollo, the murderer. With Freund's contribution as co-scenarist, Endore was thus able to fully develop the storyline, and give it a conclusion, which was, again, remarkably close to that of the final film:

INTERIOR LOCKED ROOM
Professor continues to prepare funeral pyre. But his body is wracked with great pain. Knife from Stephen has penetrated deep in to his body. As he is about to strike match, he collapses, dies.

CUT TO:
WAX FIGURE ON ROCKS

Water washes it into stream. With shattered visage—bedraggled clothes—it floats away into darkness.

FADE OUT:

FADE IN:
With piano music over shot of Stephen's hands, playing music. Applause, Yvonne etc.

As we can see Freund would eventually discard his rather poetic image of the wax figure on the rocks, a symbol of Lebri's "mad love"; less of a loss was the final couple tag perfunctorily sketched in here. The tag would be retained through the various screenplay drafts until Balderston came onto the project; one of his contributions was to remove the tag, allowing the film to end abruptly with Gogol's death (as touched upon in this book's introduction).

To write the screenplay, Considine first brought in MGM contract writer P. J. Wolfson, whose subsequent "temporary complete screenplay" dated April 6 follows the Freund and Endore treatment exactly, merely filling in missing dialogue.[471] Wolfson's 122-page screenplay (held in the Turner-MGM collection at the Margaret Herrick Library in Beverly Hills) is lightly annotated in German, presumably by Freund himself, indicating that Freund oversaw the subsequent script revisions made by Wolfson—which implemented Freund's corrections—and which were completed on April 8.[472]

Producer Considine appears to have had little input in the screenwriting process of *Mad Love*, at least from a story point of view. Notes from a script conference that took place between himself and Wolfson on April 9 reveal that he had suggestions concerning the screenplay's dialogue rather than its story or structure.[473] Wolfson's subsequent drafts (dated April 18 and 22) carry out Considine's suggested dialogue changes and other minor quibbles.[474] Although it has been suggested that Leon Gordon and John Balderston were subsequently brought in to polish the dialogue, Gordon's contribution was limited to revising the opening theatre scenes only. Balderston made more extensive revisions, changing Lebri's name to Gogol, and contributing a further dialogue polish. Balderston also stayed on three weeks into production making revisions to the first 50 or so pages of the script, tailoring it for Peter Lorre. In addition, a medical doctor, T.F. MacLaughlin, was brought in to cast an eye over the screenplay from a surgeon's perspective.[475] Throughout these revisions, however, *Mad Love*'s screenplay did not deviate from Freund and Endore's March 13 treatment in terms of story and basic characterization.

Mad Love's Gruesomeness and Sexual Suggestion

Wolfson's April 18 script was sent to the PCA. On April 22, Breen wrote to Louis B. Mayer to give his reaction. Breen considered the basic story acceptable under the Production Code but added a "general caution": "We should like to direct your attention to the imperative need for your exercising the utmost care throughout the shooting so that the finished picture will not offend by being too brutal or too shocking.... We also desire to call your attention specifically to the need at all times for observation of that provision of the Code with regard to costumes. The Code provides that 'the intimate parts of the body—male or female organs and the breasts of a woman—are to be fully covered at all times.'[476]

In three pages of notes, Breen outlined particular points of concern which related primarily to gruesomeness and sexual suggestion. First was the train wreck that formed the story's first major turning point. Breen warned that the detail of the railroad crash should be merely suggested and "handled to get away from any suggestive horror." In particular was a scene inside the train showing "the injured, the dead, and the dying lying about." Also of concern was the "laboratory business" in which the knife murderer Rollo's head is strapped back onto his body by Gogol. Breen warned that the scene would have to be handled with extreme care to prevent its becoming too gruesome, too shocking, and too horrifying (MGM would eventually cut the scene from prints after *Mad Love*'s preview). Finally Breen warned the studio to be careful in the final scene "with the shot showing the knife embedded in [Gogol's] body between the shoulder blades," adding, "[I]t should not be too shocking or horrifying."

These scenes, from the Production Code perspective, were relatively straight forward, invoking, as they did, the Code's provision for "extreme brutality" and, by now, gruesomeness. However, *Mad Love*'s sexual suggestion was trickier, and therefore, from Breen's point of view, more of a concern, and something to be nipped in the bud:

Yvonne Orlac (Frances Drake) is readied for torture in the opening Théâtre des Horreurs sequence of *Mad Love* (1935, MGM) (courtesy Ronald V. Borst/Hollywood Movie Posters).

2. "Five reels of transgression followed by one reel of retribution" 129

[I]n all the business between the professor and the wax figure which he has in his combination sitting room and boudoir, you will have to exercise great care so that there will not be the slightest suggestion of perversion. The professor should not at any time handle or fondle the figure, and it might be well, also, to cut down as much as possible the spraying of the perfume. This kind of action is dangerous material from the standpoint of public entertainment for mixed audiences, and the less suggested about it, the better all around.

When Balderston came to revise the opening, he clearly realized that the scene of torture in the Grand Guignol Theatre des Horreurs was equally risqué in terms of censorship. In the screenplay he added a disclaimer that appeared to be a note for the director, but was really there for the benefit of the Production Code Administration: "Little playlet that follows should not be played for gruesome or horrible values. Our audience should not be horrified, but should be inclined to laugh at the Paris audience for taking all this serious."[477] Thus, by pointing out the satirical nature of the scene Balderston was able to deflect attention away from its underlying sexual-sadism. However, just to be sure, Balderston himself sent an inter-office memo to Breen about the scene in question, assuring him that "the little horror playlet ... will be played for burlesque, not horror, as is indicated by the climax ... and direction will be careful to avoid making the scene on the stage seem real or showing anything offensive."[478]

The ploy seemed to work. Freund completed shooting on June 8, one week over schedule, and at a final cost of $257, 562: more than $40,000 over budget.[479] MGM previewed *Mad Love* in Hollywood at the end of June. The reviews were initially positive. "STRONG HORROR MELODRAMA HITS HIGH SPOT IN ITS CLASS WITH NEW TWISTS AND EXPERT PRODUCTION," headlined *The Film Daily* (July 1, 1935); *Variety* (June 27, 1935) adjudged it a "wildly fantastic horror offering, daring unusual limits in the gruesome, but cut to the taste of the confirmed gooseflesh addict." *The Hollywood Reporter* (June 27, 1935) was a little more reserved, praising the film as a "personal triumph for Peter Lorre" but otherwise writing off the picture as "neither important nor particularly compelling." *Motion Picture Daily* (June 29, 1935) noted the preview running time as 82 minutes but remarked that "the film will undoubtedly be trimmed."[480]

MGM seemed to take the reviewer's advice, removing 15 minutes in total from *Mad Love*. First to go was the "laboratory business" that Breen had flagged up as a concern during script review.[481] The picture previewed had been without a Production Code seal, and it is possible that MGM ordered this scene removed so as not to incur the wrath of the censor boards and to secure its PCA certificate of approval. Other cuts seem to have been in an attempt to speed up the film's pace. *The Hollywood Reporter*'s reviewer had written: "For all its potential dramatic value, the picture is heavy in both direction and writing, with heaviness that doesn't make for tenseness or thrill except in a few scenes that are far apart. It's turgid and falls right in the middle between Art and Box Office."

Motion Picture Daily had similarly pronounced the film "rather heavy" and Freund's direction, "brilliant, but arty." Clearly MGM wished to veer more toward "Box Office" than "Art," so cut from the release print was an encounter between Gogol and a blind man outside the Theatre des Horreurs; further scenes inside the theatre showing its backstage; and a moment where Yvonne shows Gogol a bust of her concert pianist husband's hands. A scene later in the story where Orlac's father, Henry, brings a street girl into his jewelry shop, unaware that she is a thief's accomplice planning to rob the shop, was probably cut because of Breen's advice during script review that the scene would "surely be deleted by censor boards everywhere because it shows in detail the activity of the crooks." The extant print picks up the action from the point where a mysterious figure enters the shop and throws a knife into Henry's back. Also to go was a subsequent scene with the street girl, having been caught pawning jewelry, protesting her innocence of the murder.[482]

MGM opened *Mad Love* at the Roxy in New York on August 2 (with a preview the night before). "[G]ets across solely on strength of its gruesomeness," was the verdict of the *Independent Exhibitors Film Bulletin* in a review published two days before.[483] As many scholars have noted, *Mad Love* was one of the few horror films of the cycle to have made a loss for its studio. MGM was down $39,000 on *Mad Love* by the end of the film's run. Although it did reasonably well in some cities and abroad, the picture was deplored in many places, especially, it seems, in small towns. This report to *Motion Picture Herald* (November 16, 1935) from Phil Billet, manager of the 600 seat Coliseum Theatre in Annawan, Illinois (a town with a population of approximately 530 people circa 1935) following its one night showing on October 30, 1935, seems representative of the reaction by many cinema patrons to the film: "Terrible—one of the worst pictures I have ever shown. Absolutely nothing to it. I had more walkouts on this picture than I ever had before on all the rest of the pictures I ever ran in the history of the theatre. The plot is impossible and there were altogether too many horror scenes."[484]

The *Herald*'s own review of *Mad Love* (July 6, 1935) had remarked that Gogol was "detestable ... to whom no sympathy can possibly accrue," and predicted that patrons might admire Lorre's performance, but would not like "the things he has to do" in the film.[485] By then, of course, *Mad Love* was caught up in the "vivisection spree" among state censors that had also affected *The Raven*, *Mark of the Vampire* and *Werewolf of London* that summer. *Mad Love* fared particularly badly with the British censor: according to *Variety* (September 4, 1935) "twenty scenes fell by the wayside [in England] and every reel but one felt the heavy touch of the morals squad."[486] There is some disagreement among scholars as to whether or not *Mad Love* was given a "Horrific" advisory in England (where it was released under the title *Hands of Orlac*). Tom Johnson writes: "[A]lthough not-by-definition a 'horror movie,' it could have received a horrific advisory. Instead the BBFC passed it, greatly cut, with an 'A.'"[487] However, James C. Robertson lists it as one of six films to be classified in 1935 as "Horrific" (alongside *Bride of Frankenstein*, *Mark of the Vampire*, *Night on Lonely Mountain*, *The Raven* and *Werewolf of London*).[488]

Many other questions remained unanswered in relation to *Mad Love*'s censorship history. One that scholars often ask is: how did a film as "perverse" as *Mad Love* manage to secure a Production Code seal? In the absence of an official letter from the Production Code Administration accompanying the certificate of approval (PCA#1034), one can only assume that the sado-sexual elements that remain in *Mad Love* were not perceived by Production Code officials as being gruesome, brutal or perverse under Code guidelines. This does, of course, seem difficult to believe. The waxwork figure of Yvonne that Breen warned against using suggestively as a fetish object during script review presented an obvious instance of potential perversity, but material that remains in the extant print (presumably passed by the PCA), such as the hot poker that is pressed "somewhere below Yvonne's waist" and Gogol's clearly sexual reaction to the torture, seems equally, if not more, censorable under the Production Code guidelines. Another possibility is that *Mad Love*'s undertones of sexual sadism were not fully grasped by Production Code officials. Steve Haberman illuminates these aspects of the film in his DVD commentary:

> [*Mad Love*] becomes the tale of a doomed, tragic and compulsive sexual obsession for an unattainable object of attraction. [The] addition of the sadomasochistic element makes this aspect all the more compelling, especially as Gogol first falls in love with Yvonne as a character in a play he attends every night, a character who is beautiful and bound and tortured. He seems to enjoy her performance the most at the moment of her greatest pain. Obviously, Gogol fantasizes himself as the torturer and Yvonne become attractive to him as the victim of his inflictions. As a surgeon, Gogol is used to pain. His compulsive attendance at the Grand Guignol, and at executions by "Madame Guillotine," leads us to believe that Gogol not-so-secretly enjoys the pain he inflicts in his quest to heal.[489]

Equally perplexing is that never in his correspondence with Mayer regarding *Mad Love* does Breen voice his concern about "the current accumulation of horror in motion pictures," as he had with *The Raven*. One might reason that Breen did not at that time look upon *Mad Love* as a "horror picture" (the *London Daily Telegraph* argued that *Mad Love* "does not, like *The Raven*, exploit cruelty for cruelty's sake, and is perhaps tolerable as a morbid but otherwise acceptable thriller"[490]). However, if this were indeed the case, by September 1935 Breen had changed his mind: an inter-office memo reveals that Breen had included *Mad Love* among his list of "horror pictures" released during 1934–35. (It is interesting to note that Breen had opened his April 22 letter to Mayer by saying that he had read the screenplay of *Mad Love* "with considerable pleasure.") We must conclude that Breen specifically targeted Universal, as the main producer of horror pictures, for particular pressure in the lead up to the removal of horror pictures from studio slates by late 1936.

Stung by the poor box office of *Mad Love* and its mauling by the censors, MGM withdrew the film from circulation after its initial release. There is no record of the studio reissuing the film theatrically or it playing on television prior to its rediscovery in the early 1970s. Thus the most "sick and disturbing" of the thirties horror cycle remained unseen for over 30 years. It was finally released on VHS by MGM in 1992.[491]

Peter Lorre himself reviled sensationalism in the horror pictures of the thirties. When interviewed for *Film Weekly* (December 14, 1935), Lorre said:

> I hold no brief for the purely horrific film. I agree, with its critics, that its appeal is essentially evil. The average horror film from Hollywood is either absolutely obvious and silly, or else it appeals to the sadistic emotions of the audience by showing scenes of torture, whippings, etc. It is not only the horror film which does this. Certain films purporting to be historically accurate make it their business to stress licentiousness and cruelty. Something should be done to prevent film producers from deliberately setting out to appeal to base instincts by glorifying depravity.[492]

"A tiny stumbling step beyond the usual thing": Dracula's Daughter *(Universal, 1936)*

Glorifying depravity certainly seemed to be high on screenwriter John Balderston's list of priorities when in January 1934 he adapted Bram Stoker's short story "Dracula's Guest" into an outline for David Selznick, who was then at MGM, as an intended sequel to Universal's *Dracula*. Balderston's original storyline was designed, as he himself stated in an introductory note to his 11-page treatment, to capitalize on the "great box office value of torture and cruelty."[493] Balderston's intention was not realized in the final film, which was not to emerge until two and a half years later; instead, what we have in *Dracula's Daugh-*

ter as produced by Universal in 1936, is a prototype for the female monster of the 1940s, a film anticipating the emergence of psychological horror during the war years. This can be seen largely as a response to the restrictions placed on gruesomeness and brutality by the Production Code Administration under Breen, and opposition to the horror film by state and overseas censors, which would force studios to rethink their approach to screen horror after the three year horror hiatus of 1936 to 1939.

"SEX AND CRUELTY":
THE BALDERSTON AND SHERRIFF DRAFTS

Dracula's Daughter originated with Selznick, who had acquired the rights to "Dracula's Guest" from Stoker's widow in September 1933, possibly already with the intention of selling them on to Universal.[494] Balderston was engaged to work up a scenario, given "Dracula's Daughter" as a title, and the brief of writing a sequel to the Universal film. In some ways Balderston's conception of "Dracula's Daughter," "the female vampire, who masquerades in London as the Transylvanian Countess Szekely," is reminiscent of Myrna Loy's sado-erotic daughter of Fu Manchu in MGM's *Mask of Fu Manchu*; certainly the studio's emphasis on going "all out for sex" that previous season seems to have influenced Balderston's thinking, as did the box office success for Paramount of Cecil B. De Mille's *Sign of the Cross*, which Balderston explicitly referenced in his note preceding the "Dracula's Daughter" treatment: "The use of a female Vampire instead of a male gives us the chance to play up SEX and CRUELTY legitimately. In *Dracula* these had to be almost eliminated, because too horrible and unpleasant if added to the blood-sucking of women by a male-monster."

Balderston's storyline would use the same general vampire formula of *Dracula* but would profit from making the female vampire "amorous of her victims." The seduction of young men would be tolerated, Balderston contended, simply because of the gender switch, "whereas, we had to eliminate seduction of young girls in the original as obviously censorable": "Moreover, and I stress this point because it's unusual and I think very good, why should Cecil B. De Mille have a monopoly of the great box office value of torture and cruelty in pictures of ancient Rome, etc? I want, especially in Part Two, to establish the fact that Dracula's Daughter enjoys torturing her male victims … and that these men under her spell rather like it."

As long as it was done by suggestion, Balderston argued, the censors would allow this element of sadomasochism in the film, and it would be justified dramatically by the fact that the female vampire needs blood, "but can get it in other ways than merely biting their necks": "I want to see for instance her loathsome, deaf-mute servants carry into her boudoir … savage looking whips, chains, straps, etc., and hear the cries of her victims without ever seeing exactly what happens. We had none of this sort of thing in the original DRACULA. I feel sure that so long as it is a woman torturing men the thing is not too unendurable, as it would have been had the man Dracula so treated his female victims."

Another new twist (and a further element to make such a story acceptable to the censors) was to have the female vampire "in her horrible way really in love with our hero"; the hero would initially return that passion, but in the end overcome it, of course, "through the holy and beautiful love of his virginal fiancée who triumphs at the final fade out." It would, in other words, truly be a case of five reels of transgression followed by one reel of retribution.

Balderston's treatment follows on immediately from the close of Universal's *Dracula*. After destroying Dracula, Van Helsing and Doctor Seward arrange to travel to Transylvania to find the tombs of the female vampires and to "end their existence before they make more victims who will join the vampire kind after death." Before their arrival in Transylvania, however, in a gruesome moment taken from Stoker's original novel, *Dracula*, the female vampires feed upon a baby taken from a nearby village, while Szekely herself sucks the blood of a "handsome strapping young peasant" whom she has kept in the castle dungeon. Van Helsing and Seward stake the vampire brides but Szekely has fled the castle for England where she entrances a young nobleman, Lord Wadhurst, with the promise of "strange delights such as can only come to men through her." On returning to England, the two vampire hunters learn of Szekely and her telepathic hold over their friend Lord Wadhurst who is "half a vampire already." Van Helsing assumes that Szekely is attempting to exact revenge on the group for their having destroyed her father, but also recognizes that she really loves Wadhurst, "in her own foul way." He manages to trace Szekely to her daylight resting place in a country churchyard and plans are laid to go there during the day and drive a stake through her heart. However, Wadhurst ventures to the churchyard to warn Szekely, and in a "strange and terrible love scene," the female vampire tells him that he is the only victim of hers she ever really loved; before escaping, she promises to make him "king of the undead as her father was." In the final act, Van Helsing et al. pursue Szekely back to Transylvania, where Van Helsing protects the others with the Host as they near Castle Dracula. In the final hours of daylight, they manage to locate Szekely in a hidden vault. Wadhurst himself drives a stake through her heart and is thus redeemed.

While Balderston's treatment reprised the basic plot of *Dracula*, the intended *frisson* of the proposed sequel essentially came out of portraying Szekely as a dominatrix. In one early scene we were to see Szekely "amusing herself with a young man": "In this scene she is playing cat and mouse fashion with a pallid young man, a wreck of his former manly self. He is her abject slave and crawls at her feet while she laughs at him. She sends him to her boudoir; perhaps we seen [sic] an evil-looking deaf mute carrying whips and straps in after him."[495]

These "horrors" were, of course, merely to be hinted at, as Balderston indicates in his notes, rather than actually seen: "They will thus seem more horrible and at the same time be more difficult to censor." Writing in January 1934, Balderston was unaware of the changes then about to take place vis-à-vis the Production Code: however, by the time Selznick had resold the rights to *Dracula's Daughter* to Universal in October 1934, the Production Code Administration under Breen had surely made Balderston's treatment of the material unviable.

Greg Mank attributes the protracted and expensive delays to the production of *Dracula's Daughter* to "the disorganization and waste of the doomed Laemmle regime" at Universal, and this may well have been the case, at least in part.[496] Junior Laemmle had originally planned to produce the film himself, as one of six prestige productions on the 1935–36 slate, with James Whale directing.[497] Whale used his involvement as leverage in persuading Junior Laemmle to buy the rights to Alan Hobhouse's novel *The Hangover Murders*, which Universal produced for Whale as *Remember Last Night?* (1935).[498] While Whale was busy on that film, Junior Laemmle engaged R.C. Sherriff, who had been under contract to Universal since *The Invisible Man*, to prepare the screenplay for *Dracula's Daughter*.[499] Sherriff substantially revised Balderston's story in the process.

Sherriff opened his scenario in fourteenth century Transylvania, with Dracula taking peasant women from the local village for the amusement of his nobleman friends. One of these women he keeps for himself as his "daughter." When the peasants attack the castle in a bid to free the captive women, Dracula defends himself with molten lead. A traveler passing through the village summons a wizard who turns Dracula into a bat, but not before the Count (in bat form) has infected his adopted daughter with the vampire bite. We cut to present day. Two young Americans, John Martin and David Hartly, visit the Transylvanian village as tourists, and enter Castle Dracula where they see the remains of the events from centuries ago. In a nightmarish scene John encounters the peasant girl, who is now a female vampire of terrible power and extraordinary beauty. She immediately enslaves John as her captive and her means of escape from the Castle to England. The action moves to London, where Van Helsing is called for assistance in locating the missing American. Dracula's daughter has meanwhile assumed the identity of Countess Szelenski, with an emaciated almost unrecognizable John in tow. After John's fiancée spots him in a restaurant with the Countess, Van Helsing tracks Szelenski down, only to discover that she has booked a passage on a steamer to the Far East, where she intends that she and John will be together for all eternity. Van Helsing boards the steamer, and during a violent storm, breaks open Szelenski's coffin and drives a stake into her, freeing John from her influence.

A provision in his contract with Universal allowed Sherriff to work on his scripts in London,[500] and, given the growing opposition in Britain to horror pictures by mid-1935, Universal prevailed upon the author to present his screenplay of *Dracula's Daughter* to the BBFC personally. This he did on August 28, 1935.[501] The response of the chief examiner, John Hanna, to Sherriff's script was condemnatory: "*Dracula* was ghoulish-weird-eerie and every other adjective in the language that expresses Horror, but *Dracula's Daughter* would require the resources of half a dozen more languages to adequately express its beastliness. I consider this absolutely unfit for exhibition as a film."[502]

Hanna seemed to take particular exception to the fourteenth century sequence that opened the script, which contained numerous gruesome details, such as this moment when Dracula fools the peasant girl into believing he is her young lover from the village come to rescue her: "Suddenly she looks up in amazement: the shrouded figure has drawn away from her and stands under a pool of light—the hood drops from the face, revealing the evil, smiling features of Count Dracula. The girl, as if fighting a terrible nightmare, gazes round. Her lover's severed arm still hangs over her shoulder—it drops down between her back and the cushion of the couch when she moves—and the hand sticks up like a drowning sailor's from the sea."[503]

Added to the screenplay's strong sense of horror was a sexual element carried within the dialogue, which alluded to the nature of the "entertainment" that the kidnapped peasant women were to provide Dracula and the noblemen:

DRACULA

I've prepared for each of you a little dish to round off your repast: a little dish gathered freshly from the fields this very evening.... Each dish, my friends, is a little different from the other: it's my earnest wish that each of you shall select the flavor you desire.... But we must be fair: an unseemly scramble might take place if we're not careful: more than one of you may relish the same dish—and I wouldn't like to see these delicate morsels damaged before they are eaten.[504]

Hanna's assistant at the BBFC, Nora Shortt, suggested that the screenplay might be made acceptable if Sherriff rewrote the entire fourteenth century sequence to eliminate the objectionable material. At a meeting on September 10, between Sherriff, S.F. Ditcham (Universal's London representative), Hanna and Joseph Brooke Wilkinson of the BBFC, Sherriff agreed to amend the script. Two days later, Sherriff delivered a revised version of the screenplay, which Hanna received rather more favorably: "I think the result is excellent. The background of the old vampire legend is maintained, but all the gruesome and horrific details have been entirely eliminated. I do not think there is anything now left in to which we are the least likely to take exception."[505]

Submitting screenplays to the British Censor for comment had, by 1935, become standard practice, especially at Universal, as the studio was concerned not to lose the English market for its horror pictures. However, Hanna's enthusiasm for Sherriff's rewritten screenplay of *Dracula's Daughter* was not shared by Joseph Breen at the PCA.

In a memorandum (September 13, 1935), Breen recorded his verdict on Sherriff's original screenplay which had been rejected by the BBFC:

> This story, which was submitted to us "off the record" by Junior Laemmle, contains countless offensive stuff which makes the picture utterly impossible for approval under the Production Code.
> Messrs. Shurlock and Breen talked with Junior Laemmle about the matter yesterday afternoon, and told him definitely, we could not approve the picture.
> We learned from him that it is his purpose to have Mr. Sherriff, the playwright, entirely rewrite the story, cutting out much of the dangerous material which it now contains.
> We have promised to suspend judgment in the matter until Mr. Laemmle submits a new script.[506]

Accordingly, in his October report to Hays, Breen wrote: "The script submitted seemed to us to be completely unacceptable, as it contained a very objectionable mixture of sex and horror."[507] On September 26, Sherriff arrived in Hollywood from London "to confer with Carl Laemmle Jr." on *Dracula's Daughter*.[508] Sherriff submitted a revised screenplay to the PCA towards the end of October: it is not clear whether the revised script was the same one that had already been "approved" by the British Censor; however, it was certainly considered unacceptable by Breen, who wrote Harry Zehner on October 23: "The story in its present form is not quite acceptable under the provisions of our Production Code and is, likewise, dangerous material from the standpoint of political censorship. This is because there still remains in the script a flavor suggestive of a combination of sex and horror."[509]

To bring the script within the provisions of the Code, and to escape mutilation at the hands of the censors, Breen suggested the removal of "those elements in scene, dialogue, or action, which tend to flavor the story with sex." Breen insisted in particular that it be made unequivocally clear within the script that the young peasant women had been abducted with the express purpose "to provide dancing partners for the Count's assembled guests at the banquet." To this end, Breen even suggested dialogue for the sequence: "Into the speech by Dracula, beginning with the words 'You will help me' we recommend that somewhere down towards the end of the speech you insert the words 'your partners for the dance'—possibly in the sentence: 'you shall choose *your partners for the dance* in order of your rank.'"

Breen's suggestions to help sanitize *Dracula's Daughter* and bring it within the provisions of the Code ran to a further five pages of detailed recommendations including another major concern: "[E]stablish it at the outset ... that the "beautiful girl" with whom John meets up is really a vampire bat.... The purpose here is to establish in the minds of the audience at the very outset that, despite the fact that the girl appears to be a beautiful creature, she is in reality a vampire bat who preys upon the world by night."

Further suggestions included the recommendation that Universal shoot a protection shot of the scene in which the severed arm of the peasant girl's husband is replaced by showing "merely the ring from the young man's finger"; also requested was the elimination of a shot showing Dracula in his chamber "crushing the limp figure of the girl in his arms" ("this is to get away from the definite sexual connotation"); two scenes showing rats were also asked to be eliminated, as apparently, the exhibition of rats on the screen was generally considered "bad theatre." All in all, Breen detailed over 40 points of concern in Sherriff's revised screenplay that would need to be addressed for *Dracula's Daughter* to be considered acceptable under the Production Code.

As the vast majority of Breen's objections related to the opening sequence of *Dracula's Daughter*, Universal eventually made the decision simply to cut that sequence entirely, removing Dracula (and Bela Lugosi) from the picture. However, Sherriff made another attempt at the screenplay before that. On October 31, Zehner wrote Breen: "I am sending you the script of 'Dracula's Daughter,' written by Bob Sherriff after his conference with you and me. He informs me that he has tried to comply with every possible stipulation in connection with this subject."[510] At the same time Breen reported back to Hays on November 1: "The studio rewrote the first script, and eliminated a great deal of the offensive material. We had a further conference with them; and believe that a further revision of the script will bring it into line with the Code."[511]

"Eliminating the purely supernatural": Removing Gruesomeness from Dracula's Daughter

Amid this kerfuffle with the screenplay, James Whale began preparations for *Show Boat*, and so, come November 1935, Junior Laemmle found himself looking for another director. He approached Hollywood veteran William K. Howard, but as *Variety* reported (November 13, 1935), they "couldn't get together after several weeks of dickering" over the terms of the deal.[512] A clause in the sale of the story to Universal had stipulated that *Dracula's Daughter* would have to start production by December 1, 1935, otherwise rights would revert to the Joyce-Selznick Agency which had brokered the deal on David Selznick's behalf.[513] The expiration date has originally been October 1, so Universal had already obtained a two month suspension on the clause. With time ticking away, on November 20, Junior Laemmle switched contract director Edward Sutherland from *Song of Joy*, for which the studio had originally signed him, to *Dracula's Daughter*, after Sutherland had fallen out with the film's associate producer, Paul Kohner.[514] On December 6, *Motion Picture Daily* reported that *Dracula's Daughter* had gotten underway four days previously on December 2, but this appears to have been a ruse on Universal's part to buy more time.[515] Further negotiations were made with Selznick to extend the option again—now until January 25, 1936.[516]

Of course, during this period, Universal was awaiting the final settlement of the purchase deal of the studio by Charles R. Rogers and Standard Capital Corp, which was to take place on February 1, 1936. Until this date, a great deal of uncertainty hung over the future of Universal. As a result, on January 8, 1936, the decision was made to "slow up" production at the studio, and 30 employees were axed.[517] At the same time, *Dracula's Daughter*

2. "Five reels of transgression followed by one reel of retribution" 137

was being readied to start within two weeks. However, Sutherland had pulled out of the film just four days before, on January 4, and Junior Laemmle subsequently turned the production over to E.M. Asher, who seemed to have been given the impossible task of handling a picture with an impending start date but continued script delays and no director. As *Variety* (January 8, 1936) commented, "there's doubt whether *Dracula's Daughter* will be produced at this time." A week later, however, the picture was on the schedules again, now under the direction of Lambert Hillyer. Garrett Fort was assigned at the last minute to prepare a new screenplay based on the formula of Universal's *The Invisible Ray* (1936). *Variety* (January 15, 1936) reported that a "similar scientific approach to horror and thrill elements is being incorporated, eliminating the purely supernatural."[518] Thus, it was hoped that with a completely fresh script any further problems with the PCA might be avoided.

Asher wrote Breen on January 14, 1936, informing him that he had "discarded the entire first script of 'Dracula's Daughter' and have written a new story."[519] The new script would have, as scholar Alex Naylor observes, "an entirely new plot which contained no explicit gruesomeness at all."[520] The revised storyline lent a new twist: the now-named Countess Zaleska (Gloria Holden) desperately wants to be free of the vampire curse and looks upon psychiatry as a possible cure. Universal sent the 24 page storyline to the PCA the same day. Breen's January 15 reply to Asher illustrates just how hostile state censors and the PCA itself had become towards horror pictures in the two month interim while *Dracula's Daughter* was being rethought. In his letter Breen warned Asher: "We again call your attention to the fact, of which we believe you are already well aware—that political censor boards generally, and very particularly in England, have expressed their intention of scrutinizing all horror pictures very closely in the future. In fact, a recent trade paper indicated that certain British local boards had banned this type of picture entirely."[521]

Breen went on to advise Asher to have the new storyline looked over by the BBFC to protect himself against the possible "total loss of your British release on this subject." Breen added an extra caution against "showing any gruesome or horrifying details" that might bring about adverse public reaction, and concluded his letter with a final warning, this one even stronger than the last, "we again warn you that the making of a horror picture at this time is a very hazardous undertaking from the standpoint of political censorship generally."

Despite this very clear attempt to dissuade Universal from making *Dracula's Daughter* (or any more horror pictures whatsoever), the studio pressed on with the new Garrett Fort version. Filming was completed on March 10, at a total cost of $278,000. Ten percent of the budget had been spent on unused screenplays, and in fees to Edward Sutherland and Bela Lugosi, neither of whom contributed to the film.[522]

Dracula's Daughter was released on May 11 to above-average box office and generally positive reviews. It was approved in most states, including in England, with few or no censor cuts. During the editing of the film, Asher and Hillyer had been careful to avoid any gruesomeness and "excessive horror": "Though production effects are being counted upon to provide the weird terror of inhuman practices," reported *Motion Picture Herald* (March 21, 1936), "it is acknowledged that the power of illusion is being counted upon to provoke reactions to incidents that are not actually seen."[523] A number of reviewers would, in fact, praise the film for its use of eerie atmosphere in place of visual explicitness. *Movie Classic* (July 1935), for example, called it "intelligently produced and fascinating in its sinister implications," and remarked, "[N]ot as gruesome as some of its predecessors, it suc-

KIDDING THE HORROR ANGLE. Deciding that the chill-stuff in Miami was not as boxoffice as it used to be, Hal Kopplin, ad chief Wometco Theatres, took the unusual slant of kidding the date at the local Capitol on "Dracula's Daughter" with copy such as is illustrated in the two-column ad above, blown up for space requirements.

Hollywood Opening Held in Vienna

What was reported by Michael Havas to be a regular Hollywood opening for "Top Hat" was put on by Siegfried Bernfield, advertising and publicity manager of the Apollo Theatre in Vienna. The "who's who" of Vienna's musical circles were present at the opening, outstanding among whom were Franz Lehar, Emmerich Kalman, Jan Kiepura and others. Notables were introduced over radio. Pictures were taken of celebrities as they arrived and later in the evening these shots were shown on screen, as were wires from Rogers and Astaire.

Girls in white dresses and top hats distributed to the ladies small toppers filled with candy, which were promoted from candy manufacturer. Large album for congratulatory signatures on the arrival of Astaire Junior was placed in lobby, book later mailed to the star.

"Have You Contributed Lately?"

60-Day Exploitation Drives Precede Japan First-Runs

To properly launch a picture in Japan, advertising and exploitation campaigns commence two months prior to the first release date, and continues until the picture goes into general distribution, reports Frank Kennedy, RKO Radio manager for Japan. Publicity is confined chiefly to trade papers and fan magazines. There are scores of fan magazines on the market, most of which enjoy splendid circulation for the Japanese as a class are perhaps the most "movie minded" in the world.

In this territory of approximately 93,000,000 people there are about 1,700 theatres, many of which cater exclusively to Jananese produced pictures. Pictures full of action, particularly those dealing with spectacular military events, and socalled "freak pictures" making a direct appeal to the imagination, find the widest market.

Downey Ties Zane Grey To "West of Pecos" Date

The fishing camp of Bermagui, south of Sydney, Australia, is a favorite of author Zane Grey and also part of the circuit supervised by L. A. Downey. So when the famed author made camp there to get some swordfish, Downey arranged for a special screening at King's Hall of "West of the Pecos," one of the Grey stories.

Part of the proceeds were donated to the local life saving club with Grey making the presentation during the program. The event broke in the Sydney papers.

"Have You Contributed Lately?"

Cooper Poses With "Deeds" Newspaper Ad

With "Mr. Deeds" running for seven consecutive weeks at the Liberty Theatre, Seattle, Leroy Johnson, general manager of the Jensen and von Herberg Theatres dispatched a copy of the newspaper carrying the ad to Hollywood and had special still posed with Gary Cooper looking it over (see photo). Still was prominently displayed in lobby and broke newspapers with story.

Cooper Interested in "Deeds"

Atlanta Theatremen Given Free Rein

(Continued from preceding page)

advance story of each theatre's coming picture the day before the opening date. In recognition of this liberality, each theatre, including most of the suburbans, advertises in the daily papers heavily each Sunday, and liberally during the week-days. Personal opinion of the writer is that the newspapers are more valuable in getting the attention of the Atlanta patrons than probably any other kind of publicity year in and year out. Ballyhoos with noisemakers on the streets are forbidden by city ordinance, hence ballyhoos have to be unusual and outstanding to attract any attention on the streets, except in the residential sections.

There is very little except spasmodic opposition for theatres here to contend with, except baseball in summer, when the Atlanta team plays two night games each week, resulting in from 8,000 to 12,000 fans attending. This is a distinct opposition for those nights, but many of the theatre managers are of the opinion that baseball fans attending these night games attend the theatres either on other than baseball nights or in the daytime. However, baseball is practically the only serious opposition to the theatres. There are no dog tracks, race horse tracks or other distractions existent in Atlanta to the extent of being serious opposition, but, like other large cities of like nature, it has its wrestling matches, its amateur baseball games, basketball games, softball games, etc., and these prove an opposition, but only such opposition as is contended with legitimately in other healthy American communities of large size.

Good Show Town for Good Shows

To summarize, Atlanta is a good show town. However, it is not a particularly outstanding show town. Good pictures will do good business; outstanding pictures will do outstanding business. It is conservative in that it will not go out to see just anything, but will crowd into theatres showing definitely outstanding pictures. One of the theatres—the Capitol—has a dual policy, offering stage show in connection with pictures, but does no more than average business week in and week out. It would not be true to say that Atlanta is not a good show town for all types of stage entertainment, for a show headed by Katherine Cornell here a year or more ago at the legitimate theatre (which opens only spasmodically) did turnaway business for four performances, as did Walter Huston in "Dodsworth" recently, but an average stock company folded up here late last summer after four weeks.

Atlanta is a good show town for good shows. And Atlanta's theatre patrons have an uncanny way of detecting good shows. And bad ones, too. Ask Atlanta managers.

"Have You Contributed Lately?"

Rutherford Personal

The personal appearance of Ann Rutherford garnered plenty of publicity for the world premiere of "The Harvester" at the Broadway, Portland, Ore. Broadcast was held in front of theatre with Mayor Carson making formal presentation to Miss Rutherford of Parent's Magazine Award given the picture.

Figuring that "chill-stuff" was no longer box-office by 1936, theatre chain Wometco used the sex angle as a way to sell *Dracula's Dracula* (1936, Universal) in Miami.

ceeds in creating an atmosphere of credibility which makes it even more chilling."[524] *The National Board of Review Magazine, 1936–1938*, seemed to appreciate the film's pseudo-scientific theme, and even suggested that *Dracula's Daughter* might point the way forward to a more psychological approach to horror in future productions: "Anything so deeply embedded in the superstitions of the race as vampirism is (and its hold on the imagination is still tremendous) must have in it the stuff for something much more important than pasteboard melodrama. *Dracula's Daughter* is a tiny stumbling step beyond the usual thing."[525]

* * *

We might see, then, *Dracula's Daughter* in its various script incarnations as veering away from the sadism and gruesomeness of the 1930s cycle, becoming in its final form a precursor of 1940s psychological horror. In this way it was very much a harbinger of things to come for horror cinema in the next decade. However, despite this, in the same month as *Dracula's Daughter* was released, the "new" Universal, led by production chief Charles R. Rogers, made the decision to take horror pictures off the schedules, largely in response to the political censorship that Breen had warned of. As *Variety* (May 6, 1936) reported:

> Universal is ringing curfew on horror picture production for at least a year, following release of "Dracula's Daughter," just completed. Latter will be released on current season's schedule, with no chiller pictures contemplated for 1936–1937 release.
> Reason attributed by U for abandonment of horror cycle is that European countries, especially England, are prejudiced against this type of product. Despite heavy local consumption of the chillers, U is taking heed to warning from abroad. Universal has for a long time held virtual monopoly on this type of production, with unusual success at box office.
> Studio's London rep has cautioned production exec to scrutinize carefully all so-called chiller productions, to avoid possible conflict with British censorship.[526]

The one-year curfew would, as we know, become a three-year hiatus: with Universal as the market leader of horror pictures, no attempt was made by any other studio to put a horror picture into production after Universal announced its curfew. As discussed in the following chapter, active dissuasion by the Production Code Administration also played a part in the three-year interregnum. Indeed, the PCA tried hard to discourage Universal from making *Son of Frankenstein* in 1939, having already advised them against a planned sequel to the *Invisible Man* the year before. Only the promise of big profits from a new sequel to *Frankenstein*, following the extraordinary box office success of the 1938 reissues of *Dracula* and *Frankenstein* as a dual feature persuaded the New Universal to ignore the warnings of the PCA. By then, however, as Alex Naylor has commented, "the Production Code censorship negotiation was fully integrated into Hollywood filmmaking."[527] Gruesomeness was expunged from the horror film, as was sex from the vice picture and brutality from the gangster movie. In the words of Thomas Schatz:

> The studios were (by 1937) meshing into a vast interlocking system, unified by standardized production and marketing, a code of acceptable content, and an increasingly stable system of narrow technical and narrative conventions. These manifested in a narrower sense of audience interest and public taste, which in turn limited what passed in Hollywood as a viable story property. The prospect of anything truly innovative or distinctive being produced in Hollywood was becoming more remote.[528]

At the same time reissues of movies from the early thirties were subject to the same Production Code censorship: Hollywood, in other words, was revising its own film history. As Greg Mank writes of the 1938 reissues of *Frankenstein* and *Dracula*:

> The new prints … had suffered a 1937 pruning by the Breen Office. *Dracula* lost various moans and screams, the sound of Renfield's backbreaking…. *Frankenstein* forfeited Colin Clive's rhapsodic "In the name of God! Now I know what it feels like to *be* God!" as well as certain shots of the fight of the Monster vs. Henry Frankenstein, Waldman and Fritz, close-ups in the Frye-tortures-Karloff-with-torch-scene and—most famously—the actual sight of Little Maria splashing into the lake, and the Monster's ensuing shame…. Thusly, did the pruned Frankenstein play in its various re-releases, *Shock! Theatre* TV debut in 1957, and original video release. It wasn't until 1986, almost 50 years after the cuts, that Universal finally and officially restored *Frankenstein*. (A restored *Dracula* emerged in 1988).[529]

Thereby, the PCA had erased gruesomeness from the horror film history books.

3

"Brutality, horror and gruesomeness"

Thirties Horror and the Hays Office

> Picture producers have discovered what is the first loophole in all forms of censorship as well as their own Hays Production Code. There is no provision, it is officially conceded, in any censor law which rules on the quality and extent of gruesomeness
>
> —*Variety*, November 17, 1931

> Scenes of excessive brutality and gruesomeness must be cut to an absolute minimum. Where such scenes, in the judgment of the Production Code Administration, are likely to prove seriously offensive, they will not be approved
>
> —Amendment to the Production Code (circa 1937)

One of the main factors to influence the development of the 1930s horror cycle in terms of the quality and extent of its gruesomeness and brutality was the industry's own Production Code and the increasing power of the Studio Relations Committee and later the PCA to administer the Code as the decade wore on. Although studios were quick to exploit gruesomeness as a marketable commodity in their films, it was the Studio Relations Committee which, in their negotiations with studios over acceptable screen content, first came to identify gruesomeness as a defining element of the burgeoning horror cycle: one for which the Production Code initially made no provision.

Although horror pictures (in contrast with sex pictures and underworld crime movies) were of only mild concern to the Hays Office at the start of the cycle, increasing opposition to gruesomeness in the horror film by state censors and civic groups eventually forced the SRC to play, in the words of scholar Kyle Edwards, "a key role in defining the boundaries for the genre."[1] The gradual tightening of the Production Code in relation to sex and violence, particularly under Joseph Breen and the PCA, saw horror pictures increasingly censored in terms of their gruesomeness and brutality to the point where, by 1936, the PCA had an overbearing influence on actual story content and plot construction—as can be seen in *Dracula's Daughter, The Walking Dead* and *The Devil Doll*. As Alex Naylor points out (and as we began to see in the last chapter) the PCA were at this time "openly discouraging studios from making horror films as part of their attempt to guide studios towards 'inoffensive' types of filmmaking."[2]

It is thus possible to chart an arc of trajectory from *Dracula* to *The Devil Doll* in terms of the changing ways in which the Hays Office responded to gruesomeness in the 1930s horror film: from relatively light interference in the early days of the cycle to heavily curtailing the allowable level of gruesomeness later on as the Production Code Administration grew in power and influence, with the effect of rounding off horror's jagged edges. Furthermore, the 1935 dictate that reissues as well as newly-produced films must receive PCA approval would have major implications for the pre–Code horror heritage. As Thomas Doherty puts it, "when Joseph Breen took the reins of the Production Code Administration, unsavory pre–Code films were pulled from circulation and not rereleased unless rendered moral."[3] After 1935, in the cases of *Dracula, Frankenstein, Dr. Jekyll, Rue Morgue, Old Dark House, Murders in the Zoo,* and *White Zombie*, censored versions of these films would become the "official" ones to be exhibited in theatrical reissues, on television and even in non-theatrical 8mm and 16mm versions, while a film denied PCA approval entirely, such as *Dr. X*, would, after completing its initial run, be consigned to the studio vaults to gather dust.

The Hays Production Code and Its "Gruesomeness" Loophole

Salacious content and Hollywood scandals (such as the infamous Roscoe Arbuckle affair) in the early 1920s, as well as federal charges against monopolies prompted, in 1922, the formation of the Motion Picture Producers and Distributors of America. As part of his public relations drive, the MPPDA's president Will H. Hays mollified reformers demanding increased censorship with the promise that the industry would regulate itself. In 1924 the Committee on Public Relations (SRC), headed by Jason Joy, studied the deletions and rejections of state censor boards, and established a mechanism for vetting movie source material called "The Formula"; in 1927 the MPPDA published a code for production entitled "Don'ts and Be Carefuls," compiled by a committee chaired by Irving Thalberg and incorporating the restrictions and eliminations of state and foreign censor boards. Compliance to The Formula by producers was voluntary, and the SRC's function at this point was purely advisory. The vagueness of this code, in 1929, spurred the prominent Chicago publisher and Catholic Martin Quigley, in association with Father Daniel Lord, to draft a more detailed document clarifying the moral principles underlying screen entertainment. Meanwhile, faced with a renewed moral campaign against the movies ushered in by the promise of talking pictures "to bring Broadway to Main Street," Hays initiated a revision of the "Don'ts and Be Carefuls" in 1930, synthesizing the revised Formula with Lord and Quigley's document to form *The Code of Ethics for the Production of Motion Pictures*, also known as The Production Code. At the same time, the SRC was empowered to work with producers to see that the Code was implemented.[4]

The Production Code comprised two parts: a set of General Principles and their Particular Applications. The General Principles underlined the fact that the Production Code was first and foremost a moralistic document designed largely in response to complaints against sexual permissiveness on the screen, and increasing concerns about public lawlessness in the wake of the 1929 Wall Street crash and subsequent economic depression. Hence, "the sympathy of the audience should never be thrown to the side of crime, wrong-doing, evil or sin," and "law, whether natural or human, shall not be ridiculed." The Code provided latitude for the presentation of evil in the second Principle: "Correct standards of life, subject to the requirements of drama and entertainment, shall be presented." This was, of course, subject to the provision that "the trend of every picture should uphold and condemn evil."[5] In the initial draft, Thalberg, as chair of the committee, had written, "In putting this rule into practice more weight should attach to the tone and effect of the picture as a whole than to episodes or incidents. It often happens that in the unfolding of the story of the most unquestionable moral worth that there may be phases in which evil is temporarily victorious."[6] The ending of the picture, then, would be decisive in ensuring that good would be upheld and evil condemned: A "happy ending" would be synonymous with a moral one.

The Particular Applications sought to prohibit specific content that had, in the past, caused problems for the industry. A number of things were strictly forbidden from being represented on screen. These included: profanity, nudity, drug trafficking, sex perversion, white slavery, miscegenation, venereal disease, scenes of actual child birth, children's sex organs, ridicule of the clergy, and the willful offense to any nation, race or creed. These instances excluded, the Code provided that no other material presented "with good taste shall be taboo." Hence, a number of "repellent subjects" were listed as acceptable under the Code if treated within "the careful limits of good taste," among them "brutality and possible gruesomeness." *Variety*'s claim that there was "no provision" in the Code for gruesomeness is, therefore, not strictly true. Granted, brutality and gruesomeness were not among the subjects forbidden from the screen by the Code, but there was a proviso for their being treated with "special care." In practice, this meant that the quality and extent of gruesomeness allowable on screen was subject to negotiation. This was the loophole that Joseph Breen, after 1934, sought to close by amending the Code so that the PCA had the final judgment in what was to be considered "excessively brutal and gruesome" and therefore censorable under the Code.

"Pre-Code" Horrors: The Studio Relations Committee and Early Pictures in the Thirties Cycle

"The most striking thing about the first wave of horror films in the early sound period," writes Steven Prince, "is that the SRC underestimated its impact on public sensibilities."[7] This is apparent in the cases of *Dracula* and *Frankenstein*, the scripts of which were given, according to Prince, "relatively cursory treatment and quick approval" by the SRC. Joy's general approach to the new Code was to try to negotiate with the studios and filmmakers a system of representational conventions whereby all movies could play to general audiences without objection but from which "conclusions might be drawn by the sophisticated mind, but which would mean nothing to the unsophisticated and inexperienced."[8] In other words sophisticated audiences would be able to read into the film "adult content" which would be imperceptible to more innocent viewers. Without a system of ratings to differentiate films for audiences, Joy saw this as important to the well-being of the industry as a whole and crucial to the successful implementation of the Code. However, taking this approach meant improvement to standards of content would be gradual, and Joy could not have foreseen the public relations disaster that was about to take place concerning gangster films, sex pictures and eventually horror films.

Although the SRC misjudged reactions to *Dracula* and *Frankenstein*, the process of working with Universal on these films enabled the SRC to identify within the burgeoning cycle possible objectionable material under the Code, even if at first they did not take a hard line on it. Although the fantastical nature of *Dracula* led SRC reviewer James Fisher to conclude that it contained "nothing to which the censors could possibly object" because "Dracula is not really a human being, so he cannot conceivably cause any trouble,"[9] Lamar Trotti (the SRC's junior executive in New York), on the other hand, declared the trailer of the film sufficiently "gruesome" to deter potential moviegoers.[10] The SRC subsequently canvassed the views of preview audiences for *Dracula*, a number of whom commented negatively on the film, calling it: "unwholesome and ghastly, morbid, inhuman and pointless," and "a gruesome, hideous [sic], ghastly, horrible nightmare." Among the audience was a PTA chairman, Marjorie Ross Davis, who left after the first 15 minutes, later declaring that the film "should be withdrawn from public showing."[11] As Richard Maltby notes, *Dracula* was "widely condemned"[12] as being unsuitable for children and received numerous complaints for that reason (James Fischer had categorized it as "a family picture"), something of which Joy was no doubt mindful when Universal sent him the script of *Frankenstein*.

"The only incidents in [*Frankenstein*] about which to really be concerned are those gruesome ones which will certainly bring an audience reaction of horror," wrote Joy to Junior Laemmle in August 1931. He went on to add: "keep thoroughly in mind ... that the telling of a story with a theme as gruesome as this will not permit the use of superlative incidents of the same character."[13] As Kyle Edwards has pointed out, Joy used the term "gruesome" twice in the letter; a word that would become more prominent in discussions relating to horror as the cycle progressed.[14] The potential effect of *Frankenstein* on a general audience, creating in them a feeling of terror, was clearly of concern to the SRC, following the barrage of criticism they had received over *Dracula*. Furthermore, Joy had already identified potential objections under the Code's Particular Application of "brutality and possible gruesomeness," pointing out the need for its careful treatment during production. Indeed, internal correspondence between Joy and Hays show that "gruesome pictures" was the generic descriptor adopted by the SRC before "horror pictures" came into general use within the industry: a clear reference to the term as used in the Production Code, and an indicator that gruesomeness was what the SRC considered to be of potential concern to state and foreign censors content-wise.

Hence Fred Beetson, in his letter to Universal adjudging *Frankenstein* satisfactory under the Code and likely "reasonably free from censorship action," included the caveat "unless some of the official censor boards consider it gruesome."[15] Of course, that proved to be another underestimation by the SRC, as *Frankenstein*'s subsequent problems with the state censors were considerable, causing further damage to public relations for the movie industry. By then the SRC was already on the back foot due to the PR calamity arising from the gangster cycle. The "gruesomeness" loophole article published in *Variety* on November 17, 1931, only added to a growing sense of concern with which the SRC began to regard horror pictures.

By December 1931, the SRC was already starting to take a more stringent approach. Two months previously, on October 8, the SRC had made submission of scripts compulsory, clearly aiming to work more closely with the studios to weed out before production material that was likely to run into trouble with the censors. Now, Joy was trying to anticipate new trends that might be controversial in a bid to head off any more problematic cycles before they took root. "We saw a preview of the Fox picture, ALMOST MARRIED," he wrote in a note to the New York office on December 4, "It is another 'gruesome' picture."[16] The next day he consulted Hays personally regarding the number of what he termed gruesome pictures already in the studio pipeline, which, in addition to *Almost Married*, included *Dr. Jekyll* and *Freaks*. Joy was of the view that the SRC should canvass audience reaction and critical opinion towards these pictures, and, if necessary, take action to "retard or kill" the cycle in order to avoid any further public relations problems.[17] It is also a measure of Joy's growing concern at the cycle that he frankly admitted, in a letter to Ben Schulberg (December, 1), that he was unable to estimate what the censors' reaction would be to *Dr. Jekyll* "or to the other horror pictures."[18] As we know, the SRC had been worried about the degree of brutality in Mamoulian's film, and also the "realism of the Hyde make-up" which might be considered too horrific by public and censors alike.[19] (The PCA would later seek to vet monster make ups "for excessive horror" in much the same way they would veto women's costumes for "indecent or undue exposure.") Joy might also have added *Rue Morgue* to his list of gruesome pictures then in production, as there was already some concern that censors would consider it "too gruesome and full of horrors."[20]

Joy and Joseph Breen were duty-bound to intercede when, on December 11, the Kansas State Censors demanded cuts to *Frankenstein* that would "destroy all the dramatic power of the picture"[21]; in some ways this intercession demonstrates, as Prince points out, that the SRC "worked for filmmakers and the industry, not the regional censors."[22] However, the required cuts effectively sought to eliminate the Monster from the picture almost entirely, as well as sights and sounds of cruelty inflicted on, and by, the Monster.[23] In other words, regional censors wished to eliminate "horror" itself from the film, and with it, attendant brutality and gruesomeness: something that Joy and Breen could hardly have failed to notice. Moreover, as Prince comments, the national release of a picture such as *Frankenstein* required "a terrific amount of work, time and money from the SRC to get the picture into badly needed markets that were often blocked by the decisions of local censors," fragmenting the very markets in which such a picture might be exhibited.[24] Such films could end up being more trouble than they were worth: to the SRC and to the industry as a whole. President of the Motion Picture Theater Owners of America M.A. Lightman voiced that very opinion at the end of December when he warned of the "drastic consequences" that would result to juvenile and family cinema attendance if a "flood of horror" was to result from the success of *Dracula* and *Frankenstein*.[25]

Thus, by January 1932, Joy was convinced that it would be better for everyone if the horror cycle, like the concurrent gangster cycle, was discontinued. He was in fact no fan of censor boards, whose rejection or mutilation of films which were "conscientiously and sincerely made within the Code" he felt would inevitably result in the "complete downfall of the Code."[26] However, when the censorship backlash against the brutality of gangster films like *Little Caesar* and *Public Enemy* (1931) became so great, the SRC had little choice but to crack down on gangster pictures, and persuaded the studios to curtail production of future gangster pictures. In the case of *Scarface*, the SRC worked with the filmmakers to recut the film to try to sell it as a movie with an "anti-gun" message. Predicting a similar backlash to gruesome pictures as to the gangster cycle, on January 11, Joy wrote to Hays that Universal had, at that point, two more horror pictures in the pipeline and that other studios, "intrigued by the fact that FRANKENSTEIN is ... taking in big money at theatres" were bound to follow suit. Reasoning that the supply of suitable literary and theatrical properties for horror pictures were limited Joy foresaw an inevitable "straining for more and more horror until the wave topples over and breaks." This would surely result in an accompanying surge of resentment from censors and public alike: "how could it be otherwise if children go to these pictures and have the jitters, followed by nightmares?" Joy urged Hays to bring the situation to the attention of the studio bosses "and see how they feel about it."[27]

In referring to the possible harmful effects of horror pictures on children, Joy was following a moral imperative as well as an economic one, and was no doubt mindful of the Payne Fund Studies, a series of "scientific" investigations into "the problems of child delinquency in relation to movie attendance."[28] The studies had been taking place since 1929, and threatened to provide fuel for moral reformers and campaigners for federal censorship, despite the fact that the studies had concentrated on films produced before the introduction of the Production Code. Blumer's *Movies and Conduct*, for example, referred to silent versions of *Phantom of the Opera*, *Dr. Jekyll and Mr. Hyde* and *The Gorilla* (1927) as films which had traumatized child viewers. One 20-year-old male recalled "with horror" the plot of First National's *Go and Get It* (1920), in which the brain of an executed convict is transplanted into a rampaging gorilla: "The whole episode was gruesome and blood-tingling and something I remember distinctly to this day."[29] Joy may well have read Blumer's findings as early as May 1931, in draft form, when Blumer's paper "Influences of Motion Pictures on Conduct and Delinquency" was presented alongside other Payne Fund Studies at a conference in Ohio that month. It was Blumer's opinion that mystery and "spooky" pictures were likely to result in the child losing self-control, which would have serious repercussions on the child's overall conduct.[30]

Joy finished his January 11 letter to Hays with a reference to *Rue Morgue*, describing "the idea of the ape pursuing the girl [as] sufficiently disturbing." What would make the finished film even more disturbing to the SRC—and another reason why the SRC initially underestimated the impact that the first wave of horror films in the sound period would have on censors and the public—was the aural accompaniment to the image which intensified the sense of brutality and gruesomeness with its heightened realism. Some of the deletions to *Frankenstein* demanded by Kansas, for example, had been to the soundtrack, specifically the "horrible animal sounds made by [the] creature" and the "dead screams by Fritz" in the scene where the Monster strangles the hunchback.[31] The sound, in particular, had distressed the censor in this sequence as it accentuated the cruelty and brutality of the on-screen action.

As Prince notes, "It is the sound of pain that takes the action in [*Rue Morgue*] to such heights of violence that [it] became quite dangerous in the eyes of censors."[32] As we know, Joy had written in his letter to Junior Laemmle after screening the rough cut of *Rue Morgue* that he felt the screaming of the female victim being subjected to the test by Dr. Mirakle had been "over stressed" not only from the standpoint of possible public reaction but also censorship objection. He warned Universal that the screaming of the woman was very likely to lead to censors making cuts in the film to reduce gruesomeness, and advised Universal to make a new soundtrack for the scene, "reducing the constant loud shrieking to lower moans and an occasional modified shriek."[33] Joy's predictions proved right as a number of censors, including New York, Pennsylvania and Chicago eliminated the scene, while others—Kansas, Massachusetts and Virginia—allowed only brief sections of it to remain in the film.[34] Although Ohio passed the film with no eliminations, its Director of Education B.O. Skinner wrote a strong letter to Joy noting "an increasing tendency in the past few weeks to include in pictures scenes of horror and realism which we have found to be offensive." He gave instances:

MURDERS IN THE RUE MORGUE—Universal—scenes where "Doctor Merkel" [sic] has woman tied with her hands above her head and is threatening and torturing her.

BEHIND THE MASK—Columbia- sequence where "Doctor" is threatening Jack Holt with death as he has him strapped to operating table.

THE IMPATIENT MAIDEN—Universal—where prolonged operation sequence is shown, including administering of ether and actual steps of operation.

ETHER TALKS—Warner Brothers—short subject—where administering ether to patient is shown.

PRESTIGE—RKO—sequence of beheading native.[35]

Skinner advised Joy that although he had permitted these sequences to be shown, the public had reacted unfavorably to such scenes of "horror and realism," and that he would be forced to take drastic action to remove such scenes from films if producers insisted on including them in future. Although the sequences had been considered acceptable under the Production Code, it was suddenly apparent that sound was capable of intensifying horror and gruesomeness to an unprecedented level. This was something that the SRC had not anticipated in its negotiations with Universal over *Dracula* and *Frankenstein*, but which gradually became clear as sound technology developed and filmmakers learned to use sound design more effectively. With this new realism accompanying synchronized sound, would come increasing action by censors to limit its effects on the unsuspecting viewer. As previously noted, in a memo dated February 26, MPPDA general counsel CC. Pettijohn informed Joy and Vincent G. Hart that the Seattle Censor Board had taken action because of the horror and realism of *Rue Morgue*—ordering approximately two minutes and 45 seconds cut from the film.[36]

As Kyle Edwards points out, *Rue Morgue* marked a change in the attitudes of the SRC towards horror films; realizing that horror pictures could be seen as realistic and censorable, the SRC "began to exercise its limited authority and develop a more proactive stance" in its review of scripts and completed films.[37] By June 1932, Joy was writing to each studio to give them the opinion of the SRC as to the "probable censorship reception" of every picture, "in the hope that ... we may be able to suggest certain arguments which will be helpful as to why the picture should be passed without mutilation."[38] Gangster pictures, sex pictures and horror films were scrutinized particularly closely. Cycles considered problematic from a Code and censorship standpoint were categorized and monitored in weekly reports sent by Joy to Hays surveying films currently in production. One of the categories, "Horror-Thrills," was a cross-genre categorization grouping together films considered to be potentially censorable because of their brutality, gruesomeness and depictions of cruelty. Thus, *Island of Lost Souls*, *The Mummy*, *Fu Manchu*, and *Wax Museum*, for example, were grouped with *King of the Jungle*, *Nagana*, *The Mail Goes Through*, *Kongo*, and *Six Hours to Live* (all 1932) as films that might be horrific and realistic.[39] When the SRC examined films in this category it was to try to ensure in particular that "brutality and possible gruesomeness" were being handled carefully and tastefully as per Code guidelines. In its advisory capacity, the SRC also sought to make studios aware when gruesome scenes might encounter problems with certain state censors, even in cases where it was generally felt the film was acceptable from the standpoint of the Code itself.

In the case of *Dr. X*, for example, Lamar Trotti wrote to Jack Warner in May 1932 to advise him that while it was not necessary for the studio to make changes to the film to bring it within Code guidelines, there was a tendency for censor boards to make cuts in films where there is an element of gruesomeness.[40] In previous correspondence Joy had advised Zanuck to protect himself in those scenes which lend themselves to gruesomeness.[41] In other words, the advice was for studios to make sure that directors were shooting coverage of those scenes so that if a censor demanded cuts, the scene might be truncated with minimal damage to the narrative flow of the film. Trotti had advised the same thing to Selznick over at RKO during production of *The Most Dangerous Game*, urging him to take care with the filming of the trophy room scene to avoid gruesomeness.[42] Thus the SRC would use the script review to try to negotiate strategies of representation that would avoid censorship later on. If a studio did not heed that advice, Joy, at least, would usually come down on the side of the filmmaker. He had, for example, adjudged *The Most Dangerous Game* "pretty gruesome in spots," but advised in a letter to Selznick:

> You may have some difficulty with official censor boards over some of the most gruesome details…
> However, I think it would be best to leave these in since they do much to add to the effect you want to create with the picture and it is always possible that the different boards will not be of the same opinion.[43]

Even those films in the cycle which turned out to be relatively innocuous were scrutinized closely during script review for possible instances where careful handling was advisable to avoid excessive brutality and possible gruesomeness. On April 16, 1932, Trotti wrote to Junior Laemmle after reading the first draft of *The Invisible Man*: "In showing a close up of Carpenter in his transformation scene you will of course want to avoid gruesomeness."[44] The SRC adjudged a later draft of the script "reasonably free of difficulty. However, it might be wise to avoid any action which may seem overly brutal in connection with the various killings."[45] And another draft of the screenplay submitted six months later by a new screenwriter received consistent advice: "With reference to official censorship, we assume you will handle the various murders in such a way as to keep them from being either brutal or gruesome as to cause them to be eliminated."[46]

Despite shooting continuities containing specific details of each shot allowing the filmmaker to visualize almost exactly how the screenplay will appear on screen, the SRC became adept at anticipating possible problem areas arising in the visualization that perhaps not even the studio could foresee. After reading the final screenplay of *The Mummy*, Joy wrote to Junior Laemmle: "you will want to guard against the element of gruesomeness in the scenes in the embalming room at the museum where they are preparing to kill Helen."[47] In those instances where studios took the SRC advice regarding the details of filming, Joy was quick to offer praise. Despite "leaning towards too great gruesomeness in certain scenes," Joy adjudged the screenplay of *Mystery of the Wax Museum* in the way it was written "to handle this element very successfully," and thus Joy "felt sure that [Zanuck's] good taste will take care [of any possible danger] in the actual shooting."[48] What is apparent from cor-

3. "Brutality, horror and gruesomeness" 149

Dr. Jack Griffin (Claude Rains) is about to reveal the truth behind the bandages in *The Invisible Man* (1933, Universal).

respondence between the SRC and the studios is that before July 1934 it was very rare that specific shots would be highlighted for deletion under the provisions of the Code for brutality and possible gruesomeness. More often the SRC would make general comments on instances of brutality and gruesomeness, whereby the studio would be urged to make their own modifications. However, this is not to suggest that the SRC did not itemize specific deletions under other provisions of the Code, in particular those pertaining to profanity, where very often specific words or phrases within the dialogue would be highlighted for removal. As the PCA grew in power and influence, however, Breen would operate like the state censors and detail specific shots, and even whole sequences, for removal. However, this was rarely seen as desirable: Much better, from the PCA's perspective, to take an active part in the screenwriting process in order to prevent questionable material from being included in the first place.

Despite the best efforts of the SRC, the moral conservative climate, manifest in the tightening standards of the state censors and the relentless zeal of the reformers, was not compatible with Joy's aim to establish a consensual Code. As Prince notes, "the first wave of horror films pointed to the region of crisis in which the SRC and the industry itself operated. The SRC was caught between the interests of the studios to exploit the box office potential of these films ... and the demands of regional and overseas censor boards opposed to this material." There was, as Prince remarks, "no easy resolution of these competing imperatives."[49] In October 1932, Jason Joy resigned as director of Studio Relations, and was replaced by former New York censor James Wingate. Richard Maltby comments that Wingate was unable to build rapport with the studio heads, and concentrated too much on the details of eliminations rather than tracking overall trends as Joy had attempted to do.[50] Certainly Wingate had sought to ingratiate himself with the studios early on, as his letters show. Writing to Paramount and Warner Bros regarding *Island of Lost Souls* and *Mystery of the Wax Museum* respectively, Wingate is fulsome in his praise of the films: "we enjoyed [*Island of Lost Souls*] thoroughly, and hope it will meet with the success which it certainly deserves," he wrote to Paramount's New York Office in December 1932, six weeks after taking over from Joy[51]; to Zanuck at First National/Warner Bros., he wrote, "we found [*Wax Museum*] a very interesting production and believe it should prove a good addition to the other successful pictures of this type which your company has produced."[52] Wingate made the point of sending complimentary letters of this type to both the Hollywood and New York offices of the companies, but despite Wingate's efforts to establish relations with the studios in this way, his genial assurances that *Lost Souls* and *Wax Museum* would cause "little difficulty" from censor boards proved to be incorrect in both cases, undermining his position from the outset. The studios would have little faith in him during his brief tenure as director of the SRC. Also, Wingate's watch on potentially problematic cycles, compared to Joy's, seems lax. In his December 30 report to Hays, Wingate stated: "most of the pictures reviewed ... present no particular censorship problems." Within his list of sex pictures, Wingate included *Baby Face*, a film that would in fact cause the SRC considerable problems late in its production which coincided with the reaffirmation of the Production Code in March 1933. Although Wingate adjudged *Baby Face* problematic from the censorship standpoint, with regard to the Code, he wrote, "there is nothing we can find in it which is a violation," and assured Hays, "we will do our best to clean it up as much as possible."[53] Indeed, *Baby Face* would need extensive revisions to bring it in line with the reaffirmed Code before its release in July 1933, illustrating how much tighter a rein the SRC would keep on controversial subject matter after Breen took up office as Wingate's assistant in March that year (Breen would later order *Baby Face* withdrawn from distribution as well as *Blondie Johnson* [1933], another Warner film that had been on Wingate's watch list).

In the "underworld-crime" category of Wingate's December 30 report to Hays is included *Mystery of the Wax Museum*, of which Wingate wrote: "It is a good horror story, done in Technicolor ... on the whole, the picture struck us as being very acceptable entertainment of this type and pretty well void of censorship difficulties."

Not everyone in the SRC agreed with Wingate's assessment, however. Vincent G. Hart of the East Coast office of the MPPDA adjudged it: "too strong for others than adult audiences," adding: "I am of the opinion that some censorable criticism will be had because of the gruesome sequences."[54] Nor did Wingate take note of the growing antagonism towards horror pictures in some overseas territories; which would shortly flare up in Great Britain with the banning of *Freaks* and *Island of Lost Souls* and the introduction of the advisory "Horrific" certificate.

The discrepancy between Hart's opinion and Wingate's may well have been symptomatic of internal battles over censorship between the SRC and the New York Board of the MPPDA where Hart was an executive, while Great Britain's stance on horror pictures was equally indicative of the external conflicts between the SRC and state and overseas censors over moral standards. (One of the most problematic state censors in this respect was Ohio, whose director of education, B.O. Skinner, had, as we know, written to Warner Bros in February 1933, to register a formal protest against *Wax Museum*.)

By spring 1934, the SRC would find itself under attack by the Motion Picture Research Council, the Roosevelt Administration's National Industrial Recovery Act and the Roman Catholic Church. This combined threat would prompt Hays to call for a Reaffirmation of the Production Code in March 1933, and would eventually lead, in July 1934, to the reformation of the SRC as the Production Code Administration under Joseph Breen. In amplifying and tightening the Production Code, Breen would effectively cut short the classic horror cycle by 1936, and ultimately eradicate gruesomeness from the later horror pictures produced during the war years and beyond.

From the SRC to the PCA

On March 6, 1933, the heads of the studios signed individual documents reaffirming their adherence to the Production Code and Resolution for its Uniform Interpretation. In so doing they agreed the following (stated in a letter from Hays to all MPPDA members written two days later on March 8): "If Code violations are not thus eliminated by the Studios themselves ... they shall be deleted here from the finished pictures and the responsibilities fixed."[55] In other words, studios thereon agreed to fully adhere to the Production Code, and if Code violations occurred, they also agreed to such violations being removed by the SRC. Thus Hays was urging the industry towards tighter self-censorship in efforts to maintain public sympathy and ward off ever increasing pressure for federal regulation. As Richard Maltby notes, by the end of 1932, nearly 40 religious and educational organizations "had passed resolutions calling for federal regulation of the industry."[56] This was in support of demands for federal regulation made by the Motion Picture Research Council whose Payne Fund Studies had—following the publication of its initial results in the sensationalized digest *Our Movie Made Children* (1933)—become a focus of concern about the cultural effects of Hollywood movies on children. With the movie business one of the industries scheduled for regulation and reorganization under the National Industrial Recovery Act, the board of the MPPDA had agreed to sign the Reaffirmation of the Code at Hays' behest, to forestall government censorship. Having thus secured the cooperation of the studios, Hays then set about reorganizing the SRC.

In a letter to Fred Beetson on March 8, two days after the Reaffirmation of the Code, Hays suggested Breen "assist Dr. Wingate in the execution of the Code and Resolution for Uniform Interpretation."[57] Breen thereafter took up full-time work at the MPPDA to concentrate on industry self-regulation. According to MPPDA files, Joy was employed for a temporary period from August 1933 to February 1934 as a consultant and advisor. Meanwhile, Breen, it was noted, "had been gradually lending his valuable aid to the Code enforcement machinery and at this time he was made responsible for the entire work of the department." In January 1934, during Wingate's visit to New York, Breen had signed all letters to the studios "and it was decided that this procedure would continue when Dr. Wingate returned."[58]

The newly instated Breen soon made his mark on movie content. In a report written for the Commission on Freedom of the Press in 1947, when the PCA was at the height of its power, Ruth Inglis accused the Hollywood film industry of hiding behind the Production Code to avoid trouble from pressure groups, making it impossible to treat sex honestly, while independent producers wanting to tackle important social issues such as race relations or radical politics could be kept out of the market entirely. "Motion pictures do not deal in honest fashion with the pressing concerns of an enlightened citizenry," she asserted, "instead, prodded by the Catholic Legion of Decency, Hollywood directs its powers of persuasion to preserving traditional concepts of morality."[59]

The screen homosexual, "the most scandalous vice element"[60] of pre–Code cinema, was Breen's first target. In March 1934, Breen instructed Vincent Hart that all "effeminate" men were to be eliminated from the screen under the Code. "In this office," Breen wrote, "we insist that any reference whatever to effeminate types be taken out."[61] According to Richard Maltby, Breen was in almost constant conspiratorial correspondence with Martin Quigley and other prominent Catholics, "attempting to involve Church hierarchy in a demonstration of Catholic cultural assertiveness."[62] Maltby argues convincingly that the Roman Catholic Legion of Decency was largely stage managed to intimidate the studios into accepting the effective enforcement of the Production Code under Breen, a tactic designed to outmaneuver all "those still demanding federal regulation of the industry." In April 1934, the Episcopal Committee on Motion Pictures, established by Roman Catholic Bishops at the suggestion of Breen and Quigley the previous November, formed the Legion "to combat indecent and immoral pictures, and those which glorify crime or criminals."[63] Members were asked to sign a pledge which promised not only to boycott these types of films but also the theatres that screened them. Eleven million church members signed.

On July 1, 1934, Hays issued a press release announcing that there was to be "amplified authority" for the PCA, effective July 15, and that all MPPDA members—which included the studios and distributors alike—were to "approve, endorse and be held responsible for all productions under the guidance of new powers invested in the administrators" of the Code (distributors had already been requested in March that year to include in their distribution contracts "the requirement that all pictures produced by unit producers conform to Code").

Under the new authority, Hays announced, "Joseph I. Breen will be vested with orders to pass final judgment on the fitness of all pictures for public showing." In addition, the producer's jury of appeal, which had operated under the SRC, was removed, leaving only the MPPDA Board in New York with the power to override Breen's decision on a picture's "fitness" for the screen. A PCA seal of approval, to be displayed at the front of each print, would show that the film had been passed. Member distributers and theatres agreed not to distribute or show a film without a certificate, enforceable by a $25,000 fine.[64]

Fox, Universal, Columbia and RKO had quickly conformed to the amplified authority of the PCA; Paramount and 20th Century took a little more persuading. There were dissenting voices: Tom Baily, Head of Publicity at Paramount, initially fought against the tightening of the Advertising Code, while Warner Bros.' employees loudly jeered the sight of the Production Code seal during preview screenings.[65]

Undeterred, Breen embarked on a number of new measures to clean up the movies. By February 1935, a list had been drawn up of "various films currently in circulation that are not considered appropriate under the Production Code."[66] A number of such films (including *Baby Face* and Tod Browning's Depression-set drama *Fast Workers* [1933]) were immediately and permanently taken out of distribution, while others considered inappropriate but less objectionable (such as Mae West's *I'm No Angel*) were allowed to complete their runs before being withdrawn. Breen also broadened the interpretation of the Particular Applications of the Code to make prohibitions more wide-reaching: adultery, for example, which the Code adjured "must not be explicitly treated, or justified, or presented attractively," was interpreted by Breen as covering "any loose sex-relationship," not just adultery in the legal sense.[67] In the same way, prohibitions on crime and bloodshed were tightened, ostensibly to curfew gangster pictures, but these could also be applied to films in the horror cycle to curb "excessive brutality and gruesomeness."[68] However, it was not simply by applying a "formula for bloodshed" that Breen managed to bring about the discontinuance of the horror cycle; active dissuasion by the PCA also played a large part in the new Universal's decision in 1936 to take horror pictures off production rosters. Moreover, the PCA's appropriation of a lengthy and meticulous script-review process as a means to shape the moral content of Hollywood cinema in effect served to strip horror pictures of much of their power by the end of the cycle.

Horror Pictures and the Production Code Administration: 1934–1936

According to scholar Alex Naylor, the PCA approached horror films with a two-prong attack. Using the growing antipathy towards the cycle shown by state censors and in particular the BBFC as leverage, Breen launched a campaign of increasingly harsh "warnings" to studios submitting horror scenarios trying to persuade them that horror films were unduly problematic in terms of censorship and damaging to the market. Alongside this, the PCA started to challenge every element in horror scripts that might be considered objectionable under the Code (especially to scenes of "excessive brutality and gruesomeness"), and subjected scripts and films to lengthy and troublesome negotiations. By 1936, this approach had become hard line policy: studios were being told that horror films were "a very hazardous undertaking" in terms of political censorship and potential loss of revenue as a result of possible bans, and the interventions made by the PCA during script-review stage was to the extent of completely remodeling plot and content. "The policy had an arguably deliberate filibustering effect," contends Naylor, "making production of a horror film contingent on time-consuming and obstructive negotiations and renegotiations over every aspect of production, from script to make-up."[69]

Largely the PCA brought this policy into play in an attempt to discourage consistently problematic film cycles. Thus, in 1935, Breen closely tied in the PCA's treatment of horror pictures with that of gangster films. In February 1935, Breen wrote to Vincent Hart that as a response to concerns over the recent increase of films involving crime and bloodshed he had sought to "evolve a formula" for guidance when handling those "potentially dangerous themes." Among the formula two directives appear to have been designed as a catch all that could be applied equally to horror pictures as to crime films: "there must no suggestion, at any time, of excessive brutality ... action showing the taking of human life, even in the mystery stories, is to be cut to the minimum."[70]

The tying together of crime and horror pictures by the PCA for "careful handling" became more apparent in April 1935. Wingate, on the East Coast, was using his influence there to discourage further production of crime pictures, an activity that Breen found "very helpful, indeed, to us here in the office," adding, in a letter to Wingate written on April 6: "there will be, too, a half dozen horror pictures. These, too, will have to be carefully handled."[71]

Among them Breen included *Bride of Frankenstein*, which "is now being recut. We saw the picture twice and asked for a number of eliminations, which the studio is now making." By September that year, however, when it came to problematic cycles, "compensating moral values" in the scenario and eliminations of excessive brutality in the finished film were not, in themselves, enough to make the PCA happy. In a report to Hays, dated September 5, Breen urged "united action be taken by our Board here to curtail the production of gangster films." Breen had it in mind to declare a moratorium on "films showing the activities of American gangsters," and clearly wanted to do the same to horror pictures.[72]

The depraved Baron Gregor (Boris Karloff) with his peasant servant Mashka (Katherine DeMille) in *The Black Room* (1935, Universal). The Production Code Administration ordered the script rewritten to avoid any indication of a "sex affair" between them.

3. "Brutality, horror and gruesomeness"   155

As we have seen, Breen's campaign of discouragement began in earnest with *Bride of Frankenstein* and *The Raven*, both of which underwent long negotiations on every aspect of production, from script to (in case of *The Raven*) make-up; *Bride of Frankenstein*, in particular, suffered major eliminations before it was awarded the PCA seal. Furthermore, at each stage in the review process Breen had issued warnings to Universal that "the current accumulation of horror in motion pictures must of necessity cause continued concern"[73] (*The Raven*) and "this picture will meet with considerable difficulty at the hands of political censors, both in this country and abroad"[74] (*Bride of Frankenstein*). Although Breen's campaign against the continuation of the horror cycle focused most intensely on Universal as the most prolific producer of such films, other studios felt the PCA's clampdown on horror production almost as keenly.

On March 27, 1935, Breen wrote to Harry Cohn at Columbia regarding the script "The Black Room Mystery" (released as *The Black Room* [1935]): "Great care should be exercised not to over-do (the horror sequences), or to emphasize the gruesome elements to the point which they might become questionable, from the standpoint either of the code or of general audience reaction."[75]

But it wasn't only brutality and gruesomeness that the PCA objected to in horror pictures, of course: the suggestion of sex also had to be quelled. Thus Breen stipulated that dialogue in "The Black Room Mystery" be rewritten to remove the "definite indication of a sex affair" between characters. In total, four drafts of "The Black Room Mystery" were produced to satisfy the demands of the PCA, including the removal of lines like "I'll tell her about us. Her future husband and her own servant," and "I'm just something you don't want any more."

The crackdown on horror by the PCA may also have led studios to take an overly cautious approach to some subject matter. The screenplay of MGM's *Vampires of Prague*, for example, seems to have raised no objection from the Breen office aside from a few minor suggestions concerning dialogue (e.g,. "page 21—Delete the word 'digitalis' from Dr. Doskil's line"; "page 66—in the Baron's line substitute the word 'Heaven' for the word 'Lord'"). Breen wrote to Louis B. Mayer of the rather anodyne script: "we find it fundamentally

Carol Borland and Bela Lugosi in *Mark of the Vampire* (1935, MGM). The anodyne script posed little problem under the Production Code.

satisfactory from the standpoint of the Production Code. We presume the ghost and horror sequences will be done with due delicacy"[76]; this proved to be the case, and on March 27, 1935 (the same day he had urged Harry Cohn not to overdo the horror of "The Black Room Mystery") Breen awarded *Mark of the Vampire*, as the film was retitled, the PCA certificate of approval without fuss.[77]

Independent producers, too, were understandably anxious to curry favor with Breen as they also needed the PCA seal before their films could be shown in MPPDA affiliated theatres. Victor Halperin sent a copy of the script for *Revolt of the Zombies* (1936) to Breen in January 1936, seeking his advice on the likelihood of the British Censor objecting to any "horror" element of the scenario. Halperin also wondered if the French and Japanese would object to aspects of the story in which French native soldiers are "zombeized," and suggestions in the scenario that the Orient might discover the zombie secret and use it to conquer Western civilization. Despite the fantastical nature of the plot, Halperin was clearly concerned by the political censorship of horror pictures which by 1936 threatened to jeopardize his film in overseas markets.[78] Securing the PCA seal for domestic territories was the nearest thing to an insurance policy for independents fearing potentially disastrous censorship problems abroad.

As Naylor points out, three horror films in particular suffered, in 1936, major changes to plot and content following script-review negotiations with the PCA. *Dracula's Daughter*, as examined in detail in the previous chapter of this book, was completely remodeled by Universal in order to render it acceptable to the PCA and the British Censor. Similar fates also befell Warner Bros.' *The Walking Dead* and MGM's *The Devil Doll*, the final films of the 1930s horror cycle.[79]

In September 1935, Breen had prefaced script negotiations with Warner Bros. for *The Walking Dead* with clear attempts to dissuade the studio from embarking on a horror picture: "Horror stories of all kinds are a precarious undertaking these days," he warned. "I think you know that the British Board in London has indicated a disposition not to approve out-and-out horror stories; and a number of boards in this country, and in Canada, have already demonstrated their dislike for this type of story by mutilating a number of 'horror pictures' which have been released in recent months."[80] Writing to Hays earlier that month, Breen had remarked that no horror scripts had been submitted recently, "but the trade press reports that Universal is planning two pictures of this type, THE INVISIBLE RAY and DRACULA'S DAUGHTER."[81] Breen may have been hoping that the horror cycle was coming to an end, which would explain why *Dracula's Daughter*, *The Walking Dead* and *The Devil Doll* in particular were given a hard time by the PCA.

The Walking Dead underwent similar extensive rewriting to *Dracula's Daughter*, at the behest of the PCA. As Naylor recounts:

> After viewing a treatment and meeting with the producer, Breen warned Warner to "exercise the utmost care" in toning down those potentially horrific aspects of the film "which are likely to give serious offense." The removal of explicit detail from both the revival of the dead and the murders which make up the bulk of the action, necessitated that the studio rewrite their story entirely. Over the course of several rewrites, the PCA repeatedly asked for the script to be further toned down, concentrating their attention on the revival of the dead, the murders and the appearance of Karloff's character, which must not "overdo the gruesomeness."[82]

Lengthy negotiations over the scenario, which took place between September 26, 1935, and January 20, 1936, meant that the production of *The Walking Dead* suffered script delays

3. "Brutality, horror and gruesomeness" 157

Marguerite Churchill and Boris Karloff in a noir-ish production still from *The Walking Dead* (1936, First National/Warner Bros.).

as a result. The PCA caused even greater obstruction to *The Devil Doll*, which underwent six months of rewrites before the PCA's demands were met. This proved costly to MGM, who had to engage a succession of writers—including Guy Endore, Tod Browning, Garrett Fort, Robert Chapin, Erich Von Stroheim and Richard Schayer—to produce the various drafts. Based on the novel *Burn Witch Burn*, the original treatment (by Endore and Browning) had been for a supernatural horror film, and given the title "The Witch of Timbuctoo." MGM sent Fort's temporary screenplay to the PCA in August 1935. Breen replied with a letter to Carl Mayer on September 13, stating:

> We find in it one element which is basically objective from the point of view of the Production Code. We refer to the fact that in the present treatment Duval, after effecting his revenge through the murder of several characters, commits suicide and thereby escapes due legal apprehension, trial and punishment. Such a solution to this present story is, of course, not acceptable. It would be most advisable to indicate that Duval is captured and does, or is to suffer, the penalties of the proper legal trial. We also suggest that in attempting to fight off the police and escape, he is killed.[83]

Thus, to give the story "compensating moral values" Breen actually suggests ways that MGM should revise their script, remodeling the narrative in the process. However, changes to the storyline made at the suggestion of the censors did not stop there. The British Censor also gave ideas during the script stage that changed not only the narrative but also the genre of the final film. On November 11, 1935, MGM's London representative, Dave Blum, sent a telegram to Sam Marx at MGM's New York office informing him: "Had a quiet talk with [British] Censor who confirms that Black Magic associated with Religious Rites definitely prohibited stop censor agreed without committing himself that converting human beings to size of dolls is legitimate drama therefore this helps a lot." Later in the telegram Blum reveals "[censor] suggested Duval meets scientist or Doctor at Devil's Island instead Black Man and believe this is solution."[84] Thus Blum's "quiet word" with the British censor resulted in Browning's film being radically rewritten to reflect its change of genre from supernatural horror to, as written in the press book, "a thriller, a melodrama, a punch, sock, dynamic story that is real entertainment ... but most of all it has novelty.... IT IS NOT A HORROR PICTURE ... in any sense of the word."[85]

Rewrites of "The Witch of Timbuctu" continued through to April 1936 with the PCA advising MGM on how "care should be taken to avoid a brutal or gruesome effect." However, even the final extensively rewritten script received Breen's now obligatory warning that the film was likely to meet with censorship objections: "There should be considered the dangers of political censorship ... we call your attention to the cablegram from Dave Blum, dated November 11, 1935, a copy of which you were kind enough to send to us. It would appear from this that the English censors are prepared to view this picture with a most critical eye."[86]

"The 'Svengali woman,' shrunken to doll's size, sets out on her master's errand of vengeance!" Lobby card for *The Devil Doll* (1936, MGM).

In any event, *Dracula's Daughter*, *The Walking Dead* and *The Devil Doll* met with little censorship difficulty, partly as a result of the extensive revisions made at the requests of the PCA and (in the cases of *Dracula's Daughter* and *The Devil Doll*) the British Board of Film Censorship. The studios had also attempted to play down the horror angles of the films in their marketing. *The Walking Dead* and *The Devil Doll* were sold as novelty thrillers, while Universal, as we know, emphasized the "science" elements of *Dracula's Daughter*.

As Naylor rightly comments, direct pressure on the studios from the Production Code Administration played a much greater role in ending the thirties horror cycle than "trouble and loss of profit from British censorship itself"; however, in discouraging the studios from making horror films as part of their attempts to curtail controversial cycles, the PCA played up the threat of an impending British ban as part of their strategy. As Naylor observes, several studios (including Universal) actually attempted to put horror films onto their production schedules between 1936 and 1938 but were persuaded not to by the PCA, which continued to emphasize the likely rejection by the British Censor of any film in the horror category. In March 1938, Universal sounded out the PCA on the Code certificate prospects of a proposed sequel to *The Invisible Man*. The PCA advised the studio to go ahead on the understanding that the film would "play the story for broad comedy" and avoid "subjects which are forbidden under the Code as excessively brutal or gruesome" causing Universal to temporarily shelf the script.[87] When Universal embarked upon *Son of Frankenstein* the following year, the PCA, in an attempt to dissuade the studio from going ahead with the film, contacted the British Censor who responded negatively to the proposition of a new horror production. This time, though, Universal would not be deterred and *Son of Frankenstein* spearheaded a second horror cycle that would continue until the late 1940s. However, while the PCA may have lost this particular battle, it arguably won the war in terms of curtailing gruesomeness and brutality in the horror film. As Steven Prince writes:

> [I]t should not surprise us that the genre, as practiced by Universal and other majors, would eventually devolve into safe adolescent programming (e.g., *Frankenstein Meets the Wolf Man*, *House of Frankenstein*, *House of Dracula*). This devolution is usually attributed to an exhaustion of the genre's classical monsters and narrative formulae. But it also stems at least in part from the suppression of violence, instigated by the reactions of regional censors to the (thirties) horror pictures and the PCA's increased scrutiny of the genre.[88]

To this end, by 1937, the "gruesomeness" loophole in the Production Code had been successfully closed, and an addendum made to the Code stipulating that scenes of excessive brutality and gruesomeness "must be cut to an absolute minimum." Otherwise films would not be approved.

Reissues of Horror Pictures: 1935–1938

In January 1935 the Board of Directors of the MPPDA voted unanimously that movie reissues should be submitted to the PCA for approval under the same processes as for new productions. The decision came as a response to the possibility of "many reissues or the renewed distribution of old pictures not entirely through ... growing out of the double-billing epidemic."[89] The demand by theaters for second features by 1935 was such that it could not be met by B-picture production alone, and so studios were looking to dust off their back catalogues in an effort to supply much needed product. In a letter to Milliken dated January 5, Will Hays wrote, "It is clear that such old pictures ought to be considered carefully before they are reissued," and that "we expect to get some old ones entirely withdrawn."⁹⁰ This was seen, then, as an opportunity to further clean up the industry by ensuring that controversial films of the past did not have their contracts renewed for distribution, and that old pictures would be subjected to the closer scrutiny of the PCA, and, if necessary, further cuts made before reissue. In the case of horror pictures, reissues would generally be shorn of brutality and gruesomeness in addition to sexual content that was now considered objectionable under the reaffirmed Production Code.

One of the first classic horror films of the thirties to be reissued was *Dr. Jekyll and Mr. Hyde*, which Paramount submitted to the PCA in June 1935. As we know, one of the bugbears of the SRC with this film, aside from the brutality of the Hyde character, was the scene in which Ivy strips in front of Jekyll. The SRC requested the striptease be cut short but Paramount had, in fact, gone against Joy's wishes, releasing the film with this "inimical" material still intact. When it came to the reissue, however, Breen, by comparison, stood firm in his demand for the deletion of the striptease scene in its entirety as a condition of the film being awarded the PCA seal. "We requested the deletion of the undressing scene," Breen wrote to Hays on June 21, "and the studio is now making the changes."⁹¹ With the additional elimination of the striptease scene thus "agreed upon," Breen awarded *Dr. Jekyll* the PCA certificate of approval (no. 1002) on June 22, 1935.⁹² It is worth reiterating that it was this reissued version that played until 1941 when MGM withdrew the film from circulation having acquired the rights for Paramount, and that the PCA cuts would not be reinstated until *Dr. Jekyll* was fully restored for release on home video in 1989.

Three months later, in September 1935, Paramount submitted *Murders in the Zoo* to the PCA, who duly eliminated the "close-up of man's lips stitched together" before approving the film for reissue on September 18, thus robbing the film of its single most sensational moment.⁹³ Once again, it would have been this PCA censored version that played in cinemas and on television until the offending shot was restored to the film for its home video release in 1995.

Universal, had in fact, long operated a policy of keeping films in almost constant reissue, but when the studio sought a PCA seal for *The Old Dark House* in January 1936, Harry Zehner, as we know, took the precaution of sending cutting continuities to Breen rather than "be stuck with the cost of prints" if the film did not secure the Production Code certificate. Breen trimmed a number of sexually suggestive lines from the film (as detailed in chapter 2) before awarding it PCA approval on January 29. It was this version that played in cinemas for the next two decades until Universal withdrew the film from circulation in 1957.

Despite his solicitation of the PCA's advice on the script of *Revolt of the Zombies*, Victor Halperin suffered a number of eliminations to *White Zombie* when he submitted it for a reissue certificate in June 1936. Vincent G. Hart wrote to S.S. Krellberg of Regal Distributing Corp on June 4, specifying the following eliminations:

1. Close-up of tyrant "grave man" with camera panning from feet to hairy chest.
2. All shots of girl in step-ins.
3. All shots of girl in coffin exposed to view
4. Close-up of body of Lugusi [sic] showing bullet hole in chest.
5. Close-up of enlarged eyes of Lugusi [sic] focused on the screen.⁹⁴

3. "Brutality, horror and gruesomeness" 161

We can perhaps see coming into effect in this list of deletions the PCA's policy to remove scenes of excessive horror, brutality and gruesomeness. More severe still were the PCA's demands for eliminations to the reissue of *Murders in the Rue Morgue*, which clearly reflect the clampdown on horror pictures in 1936. On October 2, Breen wrote to Zehner:

> We shall be glad to formally approve this picture, if, and when, the following eliminations are made:
> eliminate all views whatsoever, in silhouette or otherwise, of girl tied to crossed timbers, of her writhing, twisting and moaning in agony, of Dr. Mirakle coming to her, talking to her, stabbing her in the arm with lance, of her screaming, twisting and straining away from him, of Dr. Mirakle getting angry and holding her arm while he tortures her, of camera panning and bringing the laboratory apparatus into view, of him leaving girl and going to work table, of him sitting at work table, of girl crying and moaning and of him turning to her and raving at her, of him arranging microscope and looking through it, showing displeasure as he looks, of him knocking his microscope and other things off the table in his fury, raving at girl, of girl becoming more quiet, close-up views of girl dead—of axe cutting ropes, of girl's feet standing on trapdoor—of Dr. Mirakle's foot pushing lever, of trap door opening and girl falling through, with accompanying dialogue as follows:
>
> Dr. Mirakle: "Be patient. Are you in pain, Mademoiselle? It will only last a little longer."
> Girl: "Oh! Oh!"
> Dr. Mirakle: "Ah, you are so stubborn! Hush! It will only last one more minute and we shall see. We shall know if you are to be the bride of science."
> Dr. Mirakle: "Oh, hush! Hush! No, Mademoiselle, now. The clots—the black spots—Rotten Blood! You!"
>
> This allows scenes from where Dr. Mirakle is standing in front of the girl and says "Your blood is rotten! Black as your sins! You cheated me—your beauty was a lie!" —until Janos starts to cut ropes.
>
> If you will advise us when these eliminations have been made, we shall be glad to issue the formal Certificate of Approval.[95]

Remarkable here is the level of detail with which Breen specifies the action cut; there appears to be no room for negotiation in what must be eliminated in order for the PCA to issue the Certificate of Approval. The establishment of the PCA did not abate the process of negotiation over what constituted satisfactory material in new films, as Richard Maltby rightly contends. Studios often left in material that they knew would be eliminated in scripts as a negotiating ploy for other contentious material that they hoped to get through, and, as Maltby says, "frequently shots or sequences that the PCA initially objected to, survived into the final film."[96] However, when it came to reissues, there seemed to be much less chance of negotiating contentious material past the PCA in the same way. The closer scrutiny and further censorship of reissues was a way for the PCA to demonstrate that "self-regulation" had finally become effective.

Although *Rue Morgue* lost its most striking sequence of horror and gruesomeness when it was cut for reissue in 1936 (and the scene would not be reinstated until the film's release on VHS in 1998) perhaps the most significant single elimination made to a horror film of the thirties was to the reissue of *Frankenstein* in 1937. In a letter to Zehner on June 9, Breen again advised that the PCA's approval was subject to non-negotiable cuts. In *Frankenstein*'s case, these included the excision of Henry's dialogue "In the name of God. Now I know what it feels like to be God," shortening, as much as possible, "the views of Fritz with the lighted torch, rousing the fear and fury of the creature," and removing the shot of "Doctor jabbing hypodermic into back of the creature." These eliminations were clearly responses to concerns of offense caused by blasphemy and brutality. However, it was the final elimination that was to have the greatest ideological impact: "Reel 6—Eliminate scene in which the creature throws the child into the water."[97]

Whale had, as we know, fought for the retention of the scene when the film was first released, and for good reason, as deleting it in part or whole left the suggestion that the Monster had raped and murdered the child. This particular elimination, as historian Scott MacQueen remarks, "perverted the poignant encounter with the little girl into an act of paedophilic depravity,"[98] but it was this censored version of *Frankenstein* that was to play in theatres and on television in the United States for the next 48 years until the excised scenes were restored to the film in 1985.

The reissued *Dracula* did not suffer as greatly when it was submitted for PCA approval in March 1938, although a number of eliminations were requested. "You will, of course, have in mind that this is a horror picture, and will probably need some careful watching and attention in careful cutting before we can approve it under the Code, as now administrated," Breen advised his New York associate, F.S. Harmon, who was liaising with the East Coast office of Universal regarding *Dracula*'s reissue.[99] Accordingly, Harmon wrote to Universal on March 17: "there are two sequences in which it seems to us deletions from the soundtrack are desirable in order to avoid a violation of that section of the Code which forbids excessive gruesomeness." Of the section where Dracula attempts to kill the lawyer Renfield, Harmon wrote: "It seems to us that the lawyer's groans and moans are excessive. Kindly shorten this on the soundtrack so as to leave only one or two moans." The second elimination to the soundtrack was to "delete the groans of [Dracula] as the stake is driven through his heart" at the film's climax.

Dr. Moreau (Charles Laughton) cracks the whip on his man-beasts in *Island of Lost Souls* (1932, Paramount) (courtesy Ronald V. Borst/Hollywood Movie Posters).

"You realize, of course, that there has been a growing volume of protests against the so-called 'horror' pictures," Harmon concluded. "The deletions above are designed to tone down aspects of this film which might otherwise add to your difficulties."[100]

Dracula would remain in constant circulation in the United States throughout the thirties and forties, playing in this "toned down" version. It played on television from 1957 onwards, again in the version sanctioned by the PCA in 1938. Indeed, the audio of Renfield's scream and Dracula's moans would not be restored to the film until 1988, for a laser disc release in 1991, followed by VHS release the next year.[101]

The above films, despite eliminations, did at least meet approval for reissue. In the case of *Dr. X*, which Warner Bros. had put forward for approval in August 1937, Vincent Hart wrote to Breen with the view that the film was "un–Codeable": "We discussed the matter with [Warner Bros.] and suggested they withdraw their application for Code Certificate of Approval and they have agreed to do so."[102] *Dr. X*, as we know, would remain withdrawn from circulation until 1970. *Island of Lost Souls* almost met a similar fate; when Paramount submitted it for reissue in 1935 it was refused. Paramount tried again to gain approval for reissue in 1941. As recorded in the PCA file: "Picture at first rejected for reissue because of blasphemous suggestion of the character, played by Charles Laughton, wherein he presumes to create human beings out of animals; 'the obnoxious suggestion of the attempt of these animals to mate with human beings, and the general flavour of excessive gruesomeness and horror'; but later approved, in view of deletions made in picture."[103]

As detailed in Chapter 2, *Island of Lost Souls* was severely cut for the 1941 reissue, and these cuts not restored until 1993 for the VHS rerelease, making *Island of the Lost Souls* one of the most mutilated by the Production Code Administration of the thirties horror films.

* * *

The reissue of *Frankenstein* and *Dracula* et al. in expurgated form did not, ironically, prevent the films from causing controversy. In November 1938, the MPPDA received a letter from Katherine Vandervoort, Director of Attendance of White Plains schools in Westchester County, complaining that *Dracula* and *Frankenstein*, showing in a double-bill, had traumatized a number of children in her care. Breen's sympathetic response is illuminative of his personal feelings about horror films: "Personally, I dislike these pictures very much," he wrote. "Like yourself, I can hardly sit through them, but, like the popular novels of this same 'horror' category, there seems to be a very substantial market for these films, both in this country and abroad." Later in the letter he reassures her that while "the Universal Company" had in production now "a horror picture of the *Frankenstein* type," "this, I think, is much less horrifying than either of the two pictures exhibited at your local theatre."[104]

The effects of the SRC and the PCA served, perhaps to make horror pictures "much less horrifying," however, the processes by which they did so conversely enabled filmmakers to develop strategies of representation that would be applied to screen horror. The next chapter investigates the various ways in which filmmakers responded to and circumvented objections to gruesomeness raised by the Hays Office and state censors, in their deployment of mise-en-scène, cinematography, editing and sound.

4

"Why should Cecil B. De Mille have a monopoly on torture and cruelty?"
Thirties Horror and the Filmmaker

Although the strategies of representation of screen horror in the thirties were, as we have seen, formulated by filmmakers and studios partly in response to state censorship and as ways to circumvent the Production Code (with off-screen space just one of several methods by which directors tried to evade objections to gruesomeness) the appeal of gruesomeness to filmmakers is as old as the medium itself. Primitive American silent cinema contains some shockingly graphic case studies, such as the Edison Company's *Electrocuting an Elephant* (1903), for example, that constitute early attempts to use film aesthetics to horrify audiences. As Stephen Prince notes, filmmakers, then as now, have demonstrated a clear desire "to explore the capability of cinema for depicting gore and grotesquerie,"[1] and this is particularly evident in the thirties when the addition of sound gave directors a new element of filmic expression which they were quick to exploit in relation to the horror picture. "It is striking how quickly violence in early thirties horror films moved toward extreme forms of physical assault and violation," writes Prince, "and how essential sound was in the evocation of these portraits of atrocity."[2]

Directors such as Browning, Whale, Ulmer and Mamoulian, who were open to the expressive possibilities of this new medium early on, showed a particular affinity for the horror film, and, in interviews, expressed strong personal opinions regarding the dramatic, aesthetic and allegorical values of screen gruesomeness. Studios may have seized upon the sensational aspects of the horror film in their bid to maximize profits, but these key filmmakers saw gruesomeness and brutality, cruelty and sadism as legitimate theatre, and sought to push the horror film further in this respect. This chapter examines the ways in which these and other filmmakers in the thirties horror cycle deployed gruesomeness and brutality cinematically.

Filmmakers and Philosophies

"Ninety percent of the people are morbidly minded," Tod Browning has said. "I am not sure that the average should go higher. O. Henry once remarked that more people would gather to look at a dead horse in the street than would assemble to watch the finest coach go by, and this homely observation comes very close to representing the actual fact."[3] This comment, attributed to Browning (although possibly written by Universal's publicity department), expresses the filmmaker's apparent desire to tap into the morbid curiosity of the average cinemagoer, a condition, according to Browning, "responsible for the success of so-called yellow journalism, which features the morbid and the grewsome [sic] and which has been instrumental in bringing to such newspapers their enormous circulations." Browning's filmography is largely based on this fascination with the macabre. Whether this was due to personal preoccupation, or an ex-carnival man's sense of what appeals to the general public, is open to debate. Moreover, studios were not averse to typecasting their filmmakers much as they did their stars, and using the public personas of their top directors to help sell their films. It is difficult, therefore, to say for certain how much of the "auteurist tendency" of a director like Browning is manufactured by the studio system itself, especially when it comes to how the director is represented in industry publications, such as, in this case, the *Dracula* pressbook. Nevertheless, whether by natural inclination or not, Browning remained associated with morbid subject matter throughout his career; and, in 1931, adjudged *Dracula*: "The strangest, most morbid motion picture I have ever directed," based primarily on the character of *Dracula* himself, described by Browning as "undoubtedly the weirdest character in fiction," whom, "the audience watches frozen with horror, but so fascinated that even those who faint insist on returning to the auditorium to see the conclusion of the picture."

Other directors may not have shared Browning's—in the words of Elliot Stein—"unrelieved claustrophilia,"[4] but certainly responded to the horror film's corporeality. James Whale, as we have seen, claimed to have no sympathy with gruesomeness for its own sake, or when used to repulse; he was, however, very much intrigued by the dramatic possibilities of brutality in his horror films, especially in terms of the powerful effect it could have on the viewer. James Curtis describes Whale's excitement during an early screening of *Frankenstein*'s drowning scene:

> Jack Latham, who was in the projection room when Whale first ran a rough cut of the scene, could remember bubbles morbidly rising to the surface of the water. "It was pretty awful," he said, "and he made the decision to cut it down before the preview." The scene nonetheless seemed to amuse Whale, who had the habit of clenching his fists while watching something with which he was pleased. "I can see him with his fists clenched, rubbing the tips of his fingers and his hands down by his side, seeing a screening of that and going, "Oh, that's lovely.""[5]

It is perhaps no coincidence that Whale and his collaborators, John L. Balderston and R.C. Sherriff, came from the British theatre after serving in World War I. The three shared an understanding of the horrors of war—of man's brutality to man—and an appreciation of the Greek tragedy. Balderston's suggestion, written in his unused treatment, to "play up SEX and CRUELTY" in the scenario of *Dracula's Daughter*, stems as much from a dramatist's appreciation of the need to "rack the nerves of our audiences more than in previous horror films," as it does from crass commercialism. "If this picture is to top the original DRACULA, the tempo must grow faster, the excitement and tension increase," Balderston wrote. The mix of sex and cruelty was dramatically justified, as it "sets the horror theme, raises gooseflesh, makes the audience believe in the Female Monster."[6] Moreover, Balderston's screenplays, particularly the unproduced *The Return of Frankenstein*, contained elements of Greek tragedy: The Monster's clubbing to death of Henry and Elizabeth, before itself being struck by lightning, might find its antecedent in Romulus bludgeoning to death his brother Remus in his bid to establish the site for ancient Rome, or in any number of Greek tragedies in which family members kill each other. By the same token Sherriff's unproduced screenplay of *Dracula's Daughter* follows very much in the tradition of Greek mythology, telling the story of a sorceress, an enchantress, the daughter of a "King," who, *Medea*-like, is driven to murdering innocents. The extraordinary brutality of these unproduced screenplays derives from this mythical sense of gruesomeness, which Whale, Balderston and Sherriff saw as a legitimate part of the Western dramatic tradition dating back to ancient Greek theatre. Arguably, both screenplays contained a level of gruesomeness and brutality that would not be permissible in American horror cinema until *Psycho*.

While these British dramatists reaped the benefits of a classical education in their horror adaptations, Rouben Mamoulian brought to the horror film the aesthetics of the Moscow theatre. Revered as a visual stylist, Mamoulian nevertheless, in conversation with scholars, emphasized the psychological undercurrents of his work. Interviewed by Thomas Atkins in 1972, Mamoulian declared his belief that "everything on the screen and on the stage must be controlled by a dramatic point of view rather than by pure aesthetics."[7] In the case of *Dr. Jekyll and Mr. Hyde*, Mamoulian's aim was to dramatize the theme of sexual repression at the heart of Stevenson's novella: "[T]he original impulse of Jekyll is a noble one. He starts out by rightly rebelling against the narrow conventions of the Victorian period and especially against the sexual repression.... Jekyll's idea is that, if he can somehow separate the animalistic from this nature, he will become all one—totally spiritual and good."[8]

Hyde thus becomes the animal side of Jekyll set loose in the world. However, Hyde is not only animal; he is partly a human being, "and a human being—let's face it—is a very perverse creature. So because he is part human and possesses a human brain, he gradually begins to lose his animal innocence; and through that human brain, which on one hand reaches heaven and on the other wallows in depravity, he begins to refine his unorthodox pleasures—cruelty, sadism, and murder."

Mamoulian's depictions of Hyde and his cruelty, sadism and murder thus serve the purpose of expressing the return of the repressed in degen-

Dr. Jekyll and Mr. Hyde (1931, Paramount). Frederic March in full Hyde make-up poses for this gruesome publicity still.

erate form: the brutal sequences—such as Hyde's psychological sadism towards Ivy—are dramatically justified; furthermore the gruesomeness of Hyde's appearance fulfills a similar dramatic function: "Gradually Hyde changes from an innocent animal into a vicious ... human monster, a monster that is part of us but which we usually keep under control. Throughout the film you see Hyde getting worse, both physically and psychologically; and you also see Jekyll, instead of becoming liberated as he had hoped, deteriorating with Hyde."

Underlying Mamoulian's approach to *Dr. Jekyll and Mr. Hyde* (and arguably most, if not all, of his other films,) is a feeling for metaphor. Mamoulian comments: "The destiny of mankind lies in our ability to control certain basic elements in our nature. We seem to succeed in all sorts of miraculous achievements, but we fail to dominate ourselves—which is why we have murders and war—because it's difficult to control the primitive elements in ourselves. Any ideal that a man may have about achieving this control is noble."[9]

Allegory also underlies Edgar G. Ulmer's approach in *The Black Cat*, as we have seen. Indeed, perhaps the only way one can make sense of its extreme sadism (used in conjunction with its modernist design, and its symbolic setting of a World War I fort built literally on the bodies of war dead) is on the level of political allegory. In his analysis of the film, Herbert Schwaab, links *The Black Cat* to Pasolini's *Salo, or the 120 Days of Sodom* (1975) as a parable of "the horror of moral decay and fascism,"[10] and we might equally see Ulmer's film as a precursor to the horror excess of *A Serbian Film* (2010) in the way that it conflates political allegory and atrocity. These three films, at the very least, share a sense of outrage at man's inhumanity, vented in images of extreme torture and sadism, that transcends genre and, arguably, time of production.

Likewise, expressionism and the avant-garde have informed Robert Florey's work as can be seen in his use of the camera, lighting and set design in *Murders in the Rue Morgue*. Indeed, Florey's biographer, Brian Taves, notes the marked influence of *The Cabinet of Dr. Caligari* (1919) on *Rue Morgue* not only in terms of its expressionist visual style but also in its plot.[11] However, an equally significant influence on Florey (and arguably on the horror genre as a whole) was one that originated in his native France: that of the Théâtre du Grand Guignol du Paris.

Thirties Horror and the Théâtre du Grand Guignol

In *Robert Florey: The French Expressionist*, Taves recounts the story of a chance meeting that took place in March 1931 between Universal's Richard Schayer and Florey in Musso and Frank's Grill in Hollywood. Schayer told Florey that the studio was looking for ideas for a new horror film to follow *Dracula*. At a later meeting, Schayer and Florey discussed several possibilities for adaptations before settling on *Frankenstein,* including *The Invisible Man, Murders in the Rue Morgue*, and plays presented by the Théâtre du Grand Guignol de Paris.[12] Florey had associations with the Théâtre du Grand Guignol, having organized a roadshow of its plays in 1917.[13] According to Taves, Florey was engaged to script *Frankenstein* primarily because of his links to the Grand Guignol.

The Théâtre du Grand Guignol began in 1887 as the Théâtre Libre, founded by André Antoine and Oscar Méténier to stage *comédies rosses*—short dramatic pieces about the lives of the Parisian underclass. After the Libre collapsed due to bankruptcy in 1896, Méténier opened the Grand Guignol the following year as a theatre that "challenged moral orthodoxy." When Max Maurey took over as director in 1899, it was not, according to Richard J. Hand and Michael Wilson, "a theatre of horror per se but a successful house of naturalism, dedicated to the true to life representation of a society dehumanized by capitalism and bourgeois morality."[14]

During Maurey's 15-year tenure, the Grand Guignol was established as a popular theatre with distinctive programming, acting and production style. In its opening year, the Grand Guignol staged *Mademoiselle Fifi*, adapted from a short story by Maupassant, and *Lui*, written by Méténier. Both were about prostitution and murder, establishing the Grand Guignol formula: a combination of the erotic and the violent. A typical night's programming at the Théâtre du Grand Guignol might consist of four or five short plays—*la douche ecossaise* (a "hot and cold shower") of dramatic pieces interspersed with comedies.[15]

Grand Guignol translates as "big puppets," and the plays were thought of as visceral puppet shows for adults. According to Hand and Wilson, it was Maurey who established the Grand Guignol in terms of its use of stage trickery and special effects, establishing the Grand Guignol as the "theatre of horror." Although many sensationalist myths have arisen about the theatre in terms of its onstage gore and sex, and the effects of these on audiences (who were said to be fainting, vomiting or copulating at what they saw), horrific episodes did take place on stage: "A woman's face smokes and melts as it is covered in vitriol. A man amputates his own hand with an axe. A woman is skinned alive while another watches in sexual ecstasy."[16]

Indeed publicity shots exist of scenes involving eye gouging, bodily dismemberment, impalement with sharp objects, and, perhaps most memorably of all, a woman's face being pressed into a hot stove until it sears the flesh (*Un Crime dans une Maison de Fous* [1947]). Given these highly realistic gruesome set pieces, the emphasis of the plays of the Grand Guignol was firmly on terror and madness. It was Maurey who engaged the theatre's most celebrated playwright, André de Lorde, who, with the psychologist Alfred Binet, developed insanity as the prevalent theme. Maurey's successor, Camille Choisy, ushered the Grand Guignol through its most popular years from 1915 to 1927, developing the lighting and sound effects, and promoting staging over text as a means to create horror. According to Agnès Pierron, Choisy once "even bought a fully equipped operating room as a pretext for a new play."[17]

When Jack Jouvin took over from Choisy in 1930, the emphasis changed again from gory horror to psychological drama. After World War II the Théâtre du Grand Guignol went into gradual decline until its eventual closure in 1962. According to Hand and Wilson, the most likely reason for its losing popularity in the late 50s and early 60s is that it could not compete with cinema: with the likes of Hammer horror films and such thrillers as *Les Diaboliques* (1954), *Les Yeux Sans Visage* (1959) and *Psycho*[18]—films which, ironically, owe a debt of gratitude to the Grand Guignol.

In London, during the 1920s, José Levy staged Grand Guignol plays written by De Lorde and others at The Little Theatre in John Street. These were immensely popular and starred such notables as Sybil and Russell Thorndike and Lewis Casson. Levy had "zeitgeist on his side": a post-war public that was "eager for thrills and excitement—the artificial high theatricality of on-stage horror, rather than the devastating reality of the horror that had so recently taken place on the battlefields"[19] (significantly the Paris Théâtre du Grand Guignol also enjoyed its golden period in the years following World War I). London's Grand Guignol was more genteel than its Parisian counterpart, with sex suggested rather than enacted and strangulations and poisonings generally replacing bloody stabbings and dismemberment. Several of De Lorde's plays suffered censorship in England by the Lord Chamberlain's Office. Important to note is that, as an actor in the 1920s, James Whale had roles in two Levy productions at The Little Theatre: an adaptation of Hugh Walpole's *Portrait of a Man with Red Hair* and a revival of five Grand Guignol short plays. The former included graphic torture and the latter a head severed by guillotine.[20] Thus Whale, like Florey, was au fait with Grand Guignol long before making Universal horror pictures.

In terms of stage craft, the Grand Guignol tradition was a specialist form, created through a particular use of lighting, make up, sound effects and performance style. As Hand and Wilson write in *The Grand-Guignol: Aspects of Theory and Practice*, the theatre's location in l'impasse Chaptal in the red light district of Paris itself represented "a journey into forbidden territory, into the underbelly of Paris with its promise and danger of sex and violence."[21] The Théâtre du Grand Guignol was small, with approximately 200 seats (and boxes for the wealthy patrons) and a small proscenium stage. This helped to create an atmosphere of intimacy, even claustrophobia. The limitations of the performance space dictated the settings of the plays, which were usually interiors: prison cells, operating theatres, drug dens, brothels, asylums. Sets were naturalistic, in contrast to the make-up and performances, which were bold and exaggerated, and "reminiscent of German expressionism"[22] (indeed, De Lorde and Henri Bauche staged an adaptation of *The Cabinet of Dr. Caligari* in 1925).

Effects often relied on sleight-of-hand by the performers themselves, using fake knives fitted with blood syringes and the like. Devices for the more elaborate effects, such as amputations, included hidden bladders and tubes, and latex props. Stage lighting was important both to enhance effects and conceal their (usually simple) method of execution. Sound effects heightened atmosphere, and were "often used as far away as possible from the audience (possibly even behind the audience)," serving to make effects more chilling.

Although Théâtre du Grand Guignol was famous for its gruesome props and trickery, it was, as Hand and Wilson point out, "far from the gore-fest splatter show" of legend. Playwrights such as De Lorde sought to create an almost unbearable sense of expectation in the audience that made the climactic murders and mutilations, when they came, seem especially horrific. "The author should strive to create an atmosphere, an ambience, to suggest to the audience, little by little, that something dreadful is going to happen," De Lorde once wrote. "Murder, suicide and torment seen on the stage are less frightening than the anticipation of that torture, suicide, or murder."[23] In this way, Grand Guignol used a mix of suggestion and anticipation, capitalizing both on the unseen action and what an audience thinks it is seeing. The audience willingly "participates in the illusion"[24] with the depiction of gruesomeness on stage being furthered by the audience's own imagination.

Despite Grand Guignol's express aim to horrify, like the thirties horror film it rarely explored the supernatural: "its horror never strays far from a grounding in Zola-inspired naturalism," claim Hand and Wilson, "and therefore presents an unremittingly realistic depiction of the worst excesses of the human animal."[25]

Undoubtedly then, the Grand Guignol was an influence on Robert Florey when he came to write the initial screenplay of *Frankenstein* and subsequently co-write and direct

Murders in the Rue Morgue (Florey's later *The Beast with Five Fingers* [1946] also contains Guignol elements). As Taves remarks, the stylistic traits of Grand Guignol are evident in these films in "the make-up of the performers ... combining with dramatic lighting and close ups, to delineate character. The sound effects, musical scores, and vocal intonation all played crucial roles in generating a feeling of dramatic intensity." Moreover, Florey's horror films are "marked by some grisly occurrence, a type of mutilation which puts the plot in motion."[26] In *Rue Morgue*, this occurrence is, of course, the scene between Dr. Mirakle and the crucified prostitute, from whom he extracts her "rotten blood," a set piece that may well have been conceived in tribute to the plays of Théâtre du Grand Guignol, just as the many gruesome elements of James Whale's *Frankenstein* are clearly inspired by the beheadings, tortures and surgical dissections of Grand Guignol. In some ways we might see this as an indication that Universal (through Schayer, Whale, Florey, Browning, etc.) sought to follow the traditions of Grand Guignol even while it used the more respectable Gothic heritage for source material.

Certainly, there are direct homages to the Théâtre du Grand Guignol in several thirties horror films. Tod Browning cast former Grand Guignol actress Rafaela Ottiano in *The Devil Doll*, for example. *Mad Love* might be seen as a kind of love letter to the Grand Guignol: not only does much of the action take place in a *theatre des horreurs* but the character of Yvonne, the film's fictional Grand Guignol actress and object of sado-sexual obsession, seems to have been based on Paula Maxa, the real life star of the Paris Théâtre du Grand Guignol. Maxa has been described as both "the Sarah Bernhardt of the impasse Chaptal," and "the most assassinated woman in the world," the fetishized victim of, according to Pierron, "a range of tortures unique in theatrical history: she was shot with a rifle and with a revolver, scalped, strangled, disemboweled, raped, guillotined, hanged, quartered, burned, cut apart with surgical tools and lancets, cut into eighty-three pieces by an invisible Spanish dagger, stung by a scorpion, poisoned with arsenic, devoured by a puma, strangled by a pearl necklace, and whipped."[27]

Whether in terms of explicit homage, or with regard to particular aspects of style or theme, the influence of the Théâtre du Grand Guignol on American horror films—in the thirties and beyond—is undeniable.

Gruesomeness in Thirties Horror Cinema: Mise-en-Scène, Cinematography, Editing and Sound

Gruesomeness in the thirties horror cycle was largely a continuation of the Grand Guignol tradition, then, with filmmakers utilizing many of the technical codes and narrative conventions (and some of the stage trickery) of Grand Guignol plays in their movies. The ways in which they did so, however, was subject to the Production Code and state censorship which limited how graphic and frequent these depictions could be. This in turn forced the directors to develop strategies of representation that would simultaneously render the material acceptable to censors while at the same time deliver the gruesome goods to audiences. Working as they did within the classical narrative system, with its emphasis on continuity in time, space and narrative, filmmakers developed a set of representational codes in mise-en-scène, cinematography, editing and sound that would allow them to achieve these seemingly conflicting objectives. In the process, a set of genre-related cinematic codes and conventions were formulated which we still associate with the horror film today. These codes and motifs include: as previously discussed, the use of off-screen space to suggest gruesomeness or brutality that could not, for censorship reasons, be actually shown; the use of a shot-reverse shot syntax to "suture" the viewer into scenes of gruesomeness or brutality thereby intensifying the experience for the viewer while showing little actual violence; the use of sound to replace on screen brutality or, conversely, to amplify it; and the use of shadow play as a means to evoke what is too graphic to present explicitly.

In terms of visual motifs are scenes of "transvection" depicting the physical transformation from person to animal, monster, werewolf or vampire; in relation to this is the monster make up which has become iconic to the thirties horror film, but was increasingly subject to censorship under the Production Code towards the end of the cycle. Perhaps the most significant and recurring element of mise-en-scène in thirties horror, however, is the torture chamber or dungeon (or surgical theater), a feature of most films in the cycle, while its attendant theme of sadism is present in the myriad of knives, pendulums, whips, chains and other assorted devices of torture that pervade thirties horror.

Off-Screen Space

At first it might seem as though the use of off-screen space might be antithetical to gruesomeness in the horror film. However, as the Grand Guignol has shown, having gruesomeness occur out of sight of the audience can serve to enhance its dramatic power as much as obscure it. In many of the classic plays of the Grand Guignol, the horror is offstage, as Hand and Wilson observe: "Absent horrors may be recounted to the audience in the style of classic Greek drama, such as in *La Dernière Torture* when Bornin gives an eyewitness account of the sadistic tortures of the Boxers. In *Au téléphone* (1901) all the violence occurs at the other end of a telephone line."[28]

In *Dracula* Tod Browning relies on off-screen space to avoid depicting scenes of graphic horror; none of the film's deaths occur on screen.[29] However, it can be argued that this enhances, rather than diminishes, the film's sense of the macabre. For example, Browning uses off-screen space to suggest, rather than actually show, Dracula rising from his coffin. In an early scene, we see Dracula's hand opening his coffin lid; Browning then cuts to a shot of a possum scurrying around another coffin; another coffin lid opens, this time by a woman's hand; then a shot of an insect emerging from a small box; back to Dracula's wife sitting upright in her coffin; and finally to Dracula, now out of his coffin, standing upright. This elision preserves the macabre atmosphere of the scene, removing action that would inevitably have been awkward. (In *Nosferatu* [1922] F.W. Murnau emphasized the fantastical nature of the vampire by depicting his rising from the coffin as an act of levitation; however, most future filmmakers would go the Browning route and avoid showing the vampire actually getting out of the coffin.)

Browning repeats this strategy later in the film: we see Dracula's coffin in Carfax Abbey; the camera pans to the window as a wolf howls outside, and we hear also the creak of the coffin lid; the camera pans back to the coffin and Dracula is again standing upright having already fully emerged. Sound is used here to replace the image (in this case of the coffin lid opening) as it is in other scenes. The killing of the flower girl also takes place off-screen: Dracula embraces her and moves her behind a wall and out of our view; we hear her cry as he bites her. As we have already seen, the final staking of the Count is presented in an equally oblique manner, taking place out of view in the background behind Harker and Mina. The action is indicated only by the sounds of the hammering of the wooden stake and (prior to 1938 reissue) the vampire's groan. This final off-screen act of violence has been much criticized for its reticence, which as Ivan Butler claims, leaves the viewer "unsure of what is happening at all"[30]; and may be one instance where the strategy of presenting key plot information indirectly through off-screen action is ineffective.

The decision to stage the deaths in *Dracula* off-screen was, of course, partly in response to the Production Code edict that "brutal killings are not to be presented in detail." In *Dr. Jekyll and Mr. Hyde* Ivy's murder also takes place off-screen, again, in accordance with the Production Code; however, Mamoulian uses the strategy to brutal—and poetic—effect, as a culmination of Hyde's sadism towards the girl. In a wide shot Hyde seizes Ivy by her bed, his hands around her neck; we cut to a closer shot as Hyde moves the girl downwards, out of frame. The camera holds on a statuette of Canova's *Psyche Revived by Cupid's Kiss* (1793), a clearly ironic commentary on the action. We hear the sound of Ivy's last gasps, and Hyde's line of dialogue "Isn't Hyde a lover after your own heart?" followed by silence. Mamoulian holds the shot as Hyde moves back up into the frame, having strangled Ivy. We then cut back to the wide angle, and Ivy's body is hidden by the bed; Hyde quickly composes himself and hurries to leave before he can be caught. As in the scenes of *Dracula* and his brides rising from their coffins, what the camera focuses on *instead* of the gruesome action has symbolic value. The substituted image not only stands in for the gruesome action, but offers a metaphorical allusion that serves to make the off-screen horror more grotesque.

Thus, off-screen space, when used to its fullest effect, can capitalize on the unseen action and the power of suggestion to create gruesomeness in the mind of the viewer. In other words gruesomeness is not necessarily about what is depicted explicitly and bluntly on screen, but what *becomes* graphic in the mind's eye.

Suture

Hand and Wilson comment that the small size of the auditorium of the Théâtre Du Grand Guignol in Paris, whereby it was said that it was possible for the actors on the stage to shake hands with members of the audience sitting in the front seats, promoted a sense of intimacy between performer and observer: "No member of the audience felt far from the performers, and vice-versa. This level of intimacy exerted a major influence on the performance itself producing a focus and intensity that came to characterize the style that evolved."[31] Closely aligned to this in filmic terms is the concept of *suture*: the means by which the spectator is placed inside screen action through the use of shot-reverse shot syntax. The effect of suture on the viewer emotionally is to increase the sense of involvement in the action. Like the close proximity of performer and spectator in theatre, cinematic suture creates intimacy between viewer and the screen, and, in horror films, can serve to intensify scenes of gruesomeness and brutality. In *Frankenstein*, for example, James Whale sutures us into the scene where Fritz tortures the Monster with a flaming torch. By intercutting tight close ups of Fritz and the Monster in a series of shot-reverse shots we are drawn into the sadistic action. As Stephen Prince comments: "Had Whale filmed all of the action using the camera set-up that opens and closes the scene—the long shot framing—the violence would have had minimal stylistic amplitude.... Whale and Edeson, by contrast, have put the viewer inside the action, inside the violence—and placed the pain of the monster at the center of the design."[32]

Because it invites us to see from the point of view of the characters—the classic shot-reverse shot syntax first shows us someone looking, and then shows us what they are looking at—suture has ideological connotations. In this case the pain of the Monster, in contrast to Fritz's sadistic pleasure at inflicting that pain, invites our sympathy. However, the effect of the suture means that we are also invited to share Fritz's sadistic glee at torturing the Monster. Suture can, in other words, be used to create a complex set of sympathies, and a further example of this can be found in the opening scene of *Freaks*, where Freda watches jealously as Cleopatra playfully flirts with little Hans.

The sequence is built almost entirely on looks and gazes, established through a series of shot/reverse shots and matching eye-lines. Hans gazes at Cleopatra, the object of his desire; Cleopatra enjoys his attention but gently mocks him; Frieda sees all of this; Cleopatra, likewise, is aware of Frieda's gaze. The audience is drawn into the perspectives both of the "little people," Hans and Freda, and the "big woman," Cleopatra, creating a powerful attraction-repulsion in terms of conflicting sympathies with the three characters. This sequence finds its corollary in the penultimate scene whereby the freaks exact their gruesome revenge on the normals during a storm. Again, Browning sutures us into the action: we see the murderous freaks crawl through the mud towards a helpless Cleopatra and Hercules in a series of shot-reverse shots that intensify the action for the viewer, creating a palpable claustrophobia and further complicating our sympathies for the characters as the power relationships between the little people and the big people are violently reversed.[33]

In *Frankenstein*, James Whale also uses suture to powerful effect in the scene where the Monster drowns Little Maria. In this scene, Whale places his camera close to the girl, positioning it almost at her eye level. In the reverse shots of the Monster, we are therefore invited to take her perspective. The childlike connection between them is emphasized in the reverse shot of Maria pressing a flower into the Monster's hand; the camera moves up to the Monster's face, and he smiles at the scent of the flower. As the Monster and Maria kneel at the edge of the lake to throw their flowers into the water, Whale tracks his camera forward toward them, gently moving us into the action, again inviting intimacy through the close proximity of the camera to the performers. Another series of shot-reverse shots between Maria and the Monster sutures us into their shared game of floating the flowers and the Monster's childlike reaction of delight. As we know, Whale truncated the scene after the Monster throws Maria into the water; what we have left (in the fullest restored version) is a series of shots taken from behind the Monster as Maria drowns in the lake. However, the indications are that Whale originally included shots of bubbles in the water, indicating Maria's death, and possible further close ups of the Monster watching with growing dismay before fleeing the scene. The power of suture in creating such a gruesome and heart-breaking scene led Whale himself to realize that the scene's intensity was too great for him to elaborate on it further. However, even in its truncated form Whale's intentions dramatically and thematically are expressed perfectly in terms of the editing and the use of camera position and camera movement.

A final significant use of suturing occurs in the climactic scene of *Frankenstein* where Henry confronts the Monster in the burning windmill. Here, there is a clearly symbolic use of shot-reverse shot that further demonstrates Whale's ability to use the technique to express complex ideological ideas in filmic terms. As Henry tries to escape the clutches of the Monster he peers through the turning wooden cog of the mill at The Monster. Whale frames Henry through the cog as he looks directly at the camera; we then cut to the reverse shot of the Monster framed exactly the same way—a mirror image of his creator. However, it is as though we too are seeing ourselves mirrored in the Monster, such is the effect of the suture here. The ideological implication being, of course, that the Monster is a part of Henry and a part of us all. This combined breaking of the fourth wall and use of suture creates a space between the viewer and filmmaker in which deeper meaning can be negotiated.

In the thirties horror film, then, the power of suture allowed the filmmaker to create a visceral and meaningful scene for the viewer while showing little in the way of actual violence. Moreover, the implications of the cinematic gaze enabled directors such as Browning and Whale to create extraordinarily rich sequences that went beyond the visceral into the ideological.

Sound

Of all of the techniques used in the representation of screen horror and gruesomeness, sound particularly seems to have intrigued the filmmakers in this study, and for obvious reasons: Whale and Mamoulian commenced their screen careers during Hollywood's transition from silent to sound cinema; Browning, after a lengthy filmography in the silent era welcomed the introduction of sound; and Michael Curtiz, whose career as a director began in Hungary in 1912, made the transition to sound with great success.

Certainly, one of the major factors that these directors responded to in terms of the coming of sound was how it heightens the realistic or naturalistic quality of the image. As early as 1928 Browning enthused about the potential of sound, remarking in *The Film Daily* (August 26) that it would "greatly heighten the illusion of screen drama."[34] Correspondingly, Browning and other directors of the thirties cycle would explore the use of sound to heighten screen horror. In terms of gruesomeness, these filmmakers would use sound in a similar way to how they used shadow play and off-screen space: to both conceal it *and* amplify it.

Two early examples of sound being used to avoid showing explicit and censorable gruesomeness occur in *Dracula*. When the Vesta crashes onto the rocks in Whitby, its crew having been vampirized by the Count during a storm at sea, Browning shows the gruesome aftermath in the form of shadow play, with an off-screen voice relaying the action: we see the shadow of a man tied to the ship's wheel, and the voice informs us that this is the dead captain. The camera tracks across the deck revealing what seem to be broken and torn sails but which could easily be mistaken for human limbs bloody and torn asunder ("Horrible tragedy," the voice intones, "they must have come through a terrible storm").

As previously mentioned, sound was also used to replace image in the final scene where Van Helsing drives a stake into Dracula. Again this was designed simply to avoid showing the gruesome act at the behest of state censors; soon, however, filmmakers (and censors) began to realize the powerful effect that sound could have on the spectator in terms of amplifying pain and brutality. The PCA, as we have seen, in 1938 ordered Dracula's groan removed for the film's reissue, by then adjudging it excessively gruesome on the basis of the sound effect alone. Likewise, when the Kansas censor raised objections to *Frankenstein* in 1932, a number of the eliminations that the censor demanded were at least partly in response to the film's use of sound, among them "the entire episode of burning of mill in which monster is destroyed"; here the censor demanded all views of the monster removed and the "sounds he makes as he tries to escape the flames and as he is pinned down in the flames by [the] falling beam."[35] What the censor objected to in this particular sequence was the depiction of killing and death, and how the Monster's pain and suffering was heightened by the sound of its cries. The realism that the sound added to the scene was found by the censors to be too disturbing. Whale, in fact, uses sound to similar effect throughout the film: in the early grave robbing scene where the body is cut down from the gibbet, and later, when the Monster kills Fritz and strangles Dr. Waldon, the sound is such that it amplifies the gruesomeness of the action to the point that it becomes grotesque.

In *Freaks*, Browning eschews the use of a music score and instead relies on naturalistic sound effects to lend the final storm sequence starkness. As the freaks close in on Hercules and Cleopatra, they do so to the aural accompaniment of thunder and driving rain, rendering the gruesome revenge all the more nightmarish.

Certain sound effects originating from the thirties cycle (such as thundercracks) would, of course, become emblematic of the horror film, and perhaps none more so than the female scream. In many ways the female scream embodies the genre's most fundamental affects: pain, fear, anguish, revulsion. In *Murders in the Rue Morgue*, the screams of the crucified prostitute were found by the SRC to be excessive and Universal modified the sound mix to reduce the constant loud shrieking but, as Kyle Edwards remarks, censorship of this component "could not suppress its influence on the genre, where the female scream represents an indispensable feature of nearly all subsequent horror films."[36] Like the groans in *Dracula*, the screams in *Rue Morgue* demonstrated to censors, filmmakers and the public that sounds themselves, like images, can possess the quality of gruesomeness. Indeed reviewers of horror pictures in the thirties would regularly refer to screams on the soundtrack as an indicator of a film's promise of gruesome thrills and chills.

Moreover, the female scream in thirties horror, as well as being gruesome in and of itself, was also used by filmmakers as a way to register gruesomeness that is visually concealed, as, for example, when Werdegast flays Poelzig in *The Black Cat*. Here, the torture takes place off-screen and in shadow form; however, the horrified scream of Jacqueline Wells as witness to the gruesome event, provokes a similar response in the audience in lieu of the act's explicit depiction. The sound of the scream therefore heightens the gruesomeness of the skinning, despite standing in for the image, working in conjunction with the use of off-screen space and shadow views.

As Edwards notes, by the time of *The Raven* in 1935, "frightening frequent ... noises and piercing female screams" had become standard elements in the horror film formula.[37] We might add to that the maniacal laughter of the sadistic doctors and mad scientists whose tortures embody the transgressive appeal of the horror film to audiences eager for the vicarious thrills of screen gruesomeness.

Shadow Play

The use of shadow play in horror films, of course, dates back to the German Expressionist films of the early 1920s; with its influence, particularly on Universal, becoming apparent in American silent cinema later that decade as the émigrés brought cinematic techniques with them from Ufa to Hollywood. Universal's *Phantom of the Opera* (1925), for example, includes several scenes where action is seen only in shadow projections on walls. Stephen Prince describes shadow play as a form of "indexical pointing": a visual code that "refers back to imagery and action that is occurring beyond the frame line or behind some obstruction on-screen."[38] Because shadow play is a more direct form of representation than the visual strategies outlined above—it shows the action in silhouette or shadow form—it is more strongly suggestive of the explicit action itself, leaving less to the imagination. Not surprisingly, shadow play came into its own in pre–Code cinema, especially in the gangster picture and the horror film, because it allowed filmmakers to flout the Production Code in terms of acceptable levels of violence, brutality and gruesomeness. In the horror cycle, it was, as previously stated, already established as a code or convention, especially in the mystery plays. However, thirties horror directors quickly realized that it could be used to show "more" and suggest "less" in terms of horror's graphic presentation, and not merely as a device for creating mystery. Accordingly, the SRC recognized this strategy as generally acceptable under the Code until 1935 when Breen began the clampdown on horror pictures; after that the PCA began to take exception to the "undue repetition" of shadow play in horror films, an indication of the technique's power in depicting gruesomeness.

Examples of shadow play can be found in *Dracula*, *Dr. X*, *Mystery of the Wax Museum* and *The Most Dangerous Game*, among others. However, one of the most significant early uses of the technique in the thirties cycle occurs in *Rue Morgue*, at the start of the "rotten blood" scene. The scene opens with the shadow of the prostitute tied to the cross. We hear her screams as she struggles to free herself. We see the shadow of Lugosi enter the frame, and he sadistically asks her if she is in pain. The camera then pans around to reveal the full scene (which plays for the most part in one long uninterrupted take, adding immeasurably to the scene's intensity). Florey's decision to use shadow play at the start of the scene is partly a throwback to the twenties: the shadow is used to create mystery as a way of drawing us into the action. We want to know what is taking place that is being partly concealed from us. However, there is also the lurid use of the female scream and the titillating silhouette of the prostitute struggling with her bonds, which squarely places *Rue Morgue* in the Grand Guignol tradition. If we take a comparable scene in *The Black Cat*, when Werdegast skins Poelzig, we find that—correspondingly—the construction of the scene is reversed. The flaying scene of *The Black Cat* begins in full view but then moves into shadow play towards the end as Werdegast begins the gruesome skinning. As Prince points out in a comparison of the two scenes: "The trajectory of the visual design of violence in the Mirakle scene moves from the oblique to the explicit, whereas in *The Black Cat* it moves from explicit to oblique."[39]

4. "Why should Cecil B. De Mille have a monopoly on torture and cruelty?"   177

Prince attributes this reversal of emphasis to the changed political situation of the horror film by 1934, when the PCA was attempting to move filmmakers toward a more conservative presentation of gruesome material. Crucially, however, Prince also argues that compared to the scene in *Rue Morgue*, the flaying scene in *The Black Cat* is handled more discretely partly

The gruesome skinning of Poelzig (Boris Karloff) by Werdegast (Bela Lugosi) presented in shadow in *The Black Cat* (1934, Universal) (courtesy Ronald V. Borst/Hollywood Movie Posters).

because "the idea of what is being depicted (flaying alive as opposed to forcible injection) is more extreme and ghastly."[40] Indeed, the shadow play in *The Black Cat* is entirely in the services of Grand Guignol; no traces of the mystery play tradition remain.

In 1931, the SRC had already expressed concern about the scene in the script of *Rue Morgue* "especially shadows of her apparently strapped to a cross,"[41] but the explicit screaming in the final film had proved more problematic. Although the PCA adjudged the entire skinning sequence of *The Black Cat* to be "a very dangerous one," they also considered Ulmer's proposal "to suggest this merely by shadow or silhouette" of some mitigation.[42] By 1934, filmmakers like Ulmer were, however, using shadow play ever more gratuitously in scenes of brutality and gruesomeness. The PCA was beginning to have concerns about "the serious effect upon impressionable audiences of screen-sized shadows of horrors and their undue repetition."[43] The frequent (and flagrant) use of shadow play to depict brutality and gruesomeness was subsequently curtailed by the PCA. The technique would continue to be used in horror films of the forties, but never to the same gruesome effect as it was in *Rue Morgue* or *The Black Cat*.

Filmmakers very quickly learned to combine these various strategies to create a syntax that not only made for powerful horror cinema but also enabled a screen treatment of dubious subject matter that was less objectionable to censors. As James Wingate remarked of Warner Bros. gangster picture *Blondie Johnson* (1933) "the script presents a peculiar conglomeration of fundamentally questionable material, and very shrewd and censor-wise treatment."[44] Likewise, the filmmakers of the thirties horror cycle developed shrewd and censor-wise methods for presenting fundamentally gruesome horror.

Themes and Motifs

Our discussion so far has concentrated on the technical codes associated with early thirties horror cinema; alongside these, however, emerged certain themes and motifs which also help us to define the American horror film 1931–1936 in terms of its gruesomeness.

Transvection

In 1935, the PCA objected to what they termed a "transvection shot" in the script of *Werewolf of London*. Their concern centered on the transformation—or "transvection"—from man to wolf of the Henry Hull character, and the means by which it would be represented on screen. By the mid-thirties the transvection scene—by which a human being transforms into a monster or animal of some kind—had become a staple of the horror film. It had its theatrical origins, of course, in *Dr. Jekyll and Mr. Hyde*, and the performances of Richard Mansfield, in which the actor achieved a convincing physical transformation from the urbane Dr. Jekyll into the bestial Mr. Hyde. In the theatre (and in the 1920 screen adaptation starring John Barrymore) this was done primarily through physical performance and stage make up. However, it is fair to say that the trick photography and sophisticated make up effects of Mamoulian's 1931 film of *Dr. Jekyll and Mr. Hyde* took the transvection scenes to new levels of technical innovation and screen realism. It is, in fact, a testimony to the power of those scenes that Mamoulian for many years refused to reveal how they had been achieved.

There are three notable transformations in the film, each becoming more visually explicit. The first takes place in a continuous subjective shot as Jekyll observes himself in front of a mirror having taken the potion. A combination of polarizing filters and facial make-up give the impression of Frederic March's features changing, darkening and becoming mask-like: the early stages of Jekyll's transvection into Hyde. The subjective camera then whip-pans away from the mirror, and goes into a spinning motion, representing Jekyll's internal sensory perception of the transformation (a kind of drug-induced hallucination), with flashbacks of earlier scenes bespeaking Jekyll's sexual frustrations. The spinning camera slows, and returns to the mirror—still in point of view mode—where we now see Frederic March in full Hyde make up. By deploying the subjective perspective of Jekyll throughout the first sequence, Mamoulian thereby conceals, for the most part, the physical details of Jekyll's transformation into Hyde.

In the second transformation, Mamoulian takes a slightly more direct approach. Jekyll is sitting on a bench in the park and witnesses a nightingale caught and eaten by a cat, provoking him to change involuntarily into Hyde. We again see the early stages of the transformation as Frederic March's face begins to distort as in the previous scene; however, the camera once again quickly moves away from this, tilting down to his hands which are shockingly changed; the camera follows his hands back upwards as he covers his face in apparent pain. He lowers them to suddenly reveal that he has transformed into Hyde. Although the unexpectedness of the transformation gives the viewer a jolt—and the scene overall feels more graphic than the first transformation—the actual facial transvection shot is once again avoided (Mamoulian had originally included another transformation that came before this one in the film but which followed the same basic visual design; it was among the scenes cut by Paramount).

However, it is the next of the transformations in *Dr. Jekyll and Mr. Hyde* that is of the most interest here. In this version we see the full facial transvection (achieved through stop motion effects) in a single uninterrupted close up, depicting the various stages of the transformation of Hyde back into Jekyll, as witnessed by a disbelieving Lanyon. Undoubtedly this is the most explicit transvection shot in the film, as it takes place in full view of the camera (a reaction shot of Lanyon serves to amplify the horror of the transformation rather than conceal any part of it). It is the least artful of the three scenes perhaps, but easily the most confrontational to the spectator, who is aware that everything is on display and nothing has been left unseen. Certainly, the SRC, as we know, had its reservations about these transvection scenes and whether the public and censors would overlook their horrors.

Regarding *Werewolf of London*, the PCA wrote to Universal "we understand that you will not show the actual transvection from man to wolf, and that repulsive or horrifying physical details will not be used."[45] Because of its potentially graphic nature, the PCA sought assurances from Universal that the transformation scenes of *Werewolf of London* would not be "unduly terrifying to women and children." Ultimately it was agreed that "the transvection shot would merely mean a change of make-up for Henry Hull, such as increasing his growth of hair, lengthening nose, ears, teeth, etc., to make him a wolf-like man."[46]

Negotiations were thus made to limit the horrifying physical details of the transvection shots in *Werewolf of London*: If Henry Hull's werewolf seems particularly tame today it is more likely for this reason than because of the actor's aversion to heavy make up as is so often written.

Of course, the transvection shot continued to be emblematic of the horror film in the forties and beyond, whether suggested off-screen, as in *Cat People* (1942), or shown directly: *The Wolfman* (1941) and its sequels, for example, make extensive use of the stop motion techniques of *Dr. Jekyll*, but the effect is milder—less repulsive and horrifying.

The masking/unmasking of the monsters in *Dr. X* and *Mystery of the Wax Museum* can be seen as the transvection shot in another form. In both films the physical transformation of the human face to that of a hideous, deformed being is shown in graphic manner. The "synthetic flesh" scene of *Dr. X*, like the transvections of *Dr. Jekyll*, takes place in a continuous extended sequence in full close up. The unmasking of Lionel Barrymore's disfigured sculptor in *Wax Museum*, by contrast, is sudden, unexpected and shocking, and the horror of it compounded by Fay Wray's piercing scream.

In transvection scenes, hands are a dominant motif: Wray's fists beat against Barrymore's face, breaking it, to reveal the horrible deformity behind the wax visage; Dr. Wells begins his transformation into the Moonkiller by replacing his artificial hand with a gnarled claw; the first physical sign of Jekyll's transvection is the sudden growth of hair on his hands: a terrifying signal that he is about to change into Hyde. These transformations, despite their realistic presentations, carry strong elements of the fantastic.

Henry Hull's make-up for *Werewolf of London* (1935, Universal) was subject to the approval of the Production Code Administration (courtesy Ronald V. Borst/Hollywood Movie Posters).

Scientific and surgical transvections featuring medical transplants and vivisection occur in *Island of Lost Souls* and *Mad Love*. These transformations key into what Angela M. Smith describes as "eugenic narratives and icons" rendering in visceral form cultural anxieties of the thirties concerning the transformation of the human body through medical means.[47] Particularly disturbing is the scene in *Lost Souls* where Moreau performs surgical experiments on a man-beast he holds in captivity. Such scenes would resonate particularly with British audiences, and continue to do so for decades (a similarly gruesome human-animal experiment—whereby a man's head is transplanted onto the body of a beast—occurs in Lindsay Anderson's British black comedy satire *Britannia Hospital* [1982]).

Monster Make-Up

The transvection shot is, of course, a showcase for the ever advancing realism of special effects and monster make up, and in designing their screen monsters, Jack Pierce at Universal and Wally Westmore at Paramount (*Dr. Jekyll, Lost Souls*) moved away from simple stage make up to sophisticated prosthetic appliances, paving the way for the "gorehounds" (Dick Smith, Rick Baker, Tom Savini, etc.) of the seventies and eighties. Pierce's most iconic make-up, of course, is the Monster in *Frankenstein*, and it is instructive that Pierce approached this design from the standpoint of gruesome realism: bolts in the neck to conduct electricity; clamps in the forehead to secure the top of the skull which had been sawn open to allow the replacement of the brain; stitches around the wrists where new hands had been sewn on to the arms and so on. As Stephen Prince comments, there are within *Frankenstein*, implicit references to the "desecration of the dead ... the violation of corpses,"[48] and this motif is embodied in Pierce's make-up design of the Monster itself.

The crucial function of the make-up designer is to physicalize the monster to the fullest extent possible; to externalize the "horror" of the monster in its most vivid form. As George Ochoa writes, "the primary purpose of the horror film is to make the audience know the monster."[49] The most vivid form of the screen monster is, not surprisingly, usually a gruesome and repulsive one.

Certainly, the gruesome realism of monster make-ups in the thirties was of concern to censors, as we know. Jack Pierce's make-up design for Boris Karloff as the surgically deformed convict in *The Raven* would be toned down at the behest of the PCA, to ensure that it was not "unhumanly repulsive"[50] and "suitable for screen treatment."[51] And while the modern viewer may find it disconcerting to see the name of Max Factor in the credits of *Dr. X*, given his subsequent association with beauty cosmetics (he designed the make-up effects of the film), the contribution of the make-up artist to gruesomeness in the American horror film of the thirties should not be underestimated.

Torture Chambers

As outlined in my introduction, the torture chamber is a prominent visual and narrative motif of the thirties horror cycle. *Frankenstein, Murders in the Rue Morgue, The Most Dangerous Game, Island of Lost Souls, The Black Cat, The Raven* and *Mad Love* all feature torture chambers of some description. In general keeping with the presentation of gruesomeness in the cycle, there is a trajectory from the oblique to the explicit: the dungeon of *Frankenstein* in which torture just happens to take place, gives way to the all-electric torture chamber of *The Raven* especially designed and constructed with torture in mind. Likewise, the medieval whips, chains, torches and racks of *Frankenstein* and *Rue Morgue* are superseded by the delicate surgical instruments, pendulums and other ingenious purpose-made torture devices by the end of the cycle. The emphasis of thirties horror cinema thus becomes more explicitly on deliberate and sadistic acts of cruelty as the cycle progresses. In other words the filmmakers seem to adopt the motif more consciously as they go on.

The torture chamber—an insistent and recurring motif in thirties horror—invites metaphorical, even allegorical, readings: the shift towards a seemingly more conscious incorporation of torture chambers into the narrative by filmmakers in the mid-thirties (i.e., torture chambers that are specifically designed by characters in the film to function as such) becomes symbolic when considered in this context. It is significant that the torture chambers of Dr. Vollin, Poelzig, and Dr. Gogol (whose operating room is really a torture chamber in another guise) are all located in the houses of these characters; sadistic cruelty being literally close to home. (Not surprisingly, by the time of *The Raven*, the PCA cautioned filmmakers in their presentation of torture devices, demanding an almost historical distance: "instruments of torture [must] be passed in review, as if in a museum."[52])

Sadism

The torture chamber, of course, ties in to the themes of madness and sadism that are central to the thirties horror film as derived from the Grand Guignol play. As Andrew Tudor points out, "the classic period is overwhelmingly dominated by external threats derived from the actions of human beings."[53] The supernatural, as a threat, becomes increasingly rare in thirties horror; instead it is madness that threatens. This is also true of the Grand Guignol: "Only very rarely does the Grand-Guignol explore the supernatural ... even the comedies work with the same material as the horror plays: death, insanity, sex. In this way both genres inhabit the same universe, sharing an obsession with the excesses of the human animal and its potential: a veritable extrapolation of la bête humaine."[54]

As Tudor notes, the madness presented in thirties horror is distinct to the portrayal of insanity in later horror films like *Psycho* which make at least some kind of attempt at psychiatric plausibility. In thirties horror, according to Tudor, "madness is simply a bucket from which to pour strange and dangerous actions, and it is only in *The Black Cat*, *The Raven* and [*Mad Love*] that we can glimpse anything more."[55]

Gogol's character, in *Mad Love*, especially evokes insanity with a certain directness, and encapsulates a madness emblematic of the thirties cycle as a whole (as we know *Mad Love* was intended as a sort of parody of the thirties horror film). Gogol's first appearance—watching Yvonne being "tortured" as part of her performance at the Théâtre des Horreurs is—as Tudor points out—key to our understanding Gogol's insanity. The camera tracks into his face as the torture commences, his eyes focused intently on Yvonne. We cut to the red-hot poker pressed into her skin out of frame; Yvonne screams. The next shot presents Gogol's reaction to the torture: his eyes close in "a kind of orgasmic satisfaction as her screams of pain reverberate around the theatre."[56] Bracketing the staged torture tableau with these two shots of Gogol—his anticipation and his pleasure—the scene invokes, in Tudor's words, "a complex of interlinked references to violence, obsession, voyeurism,

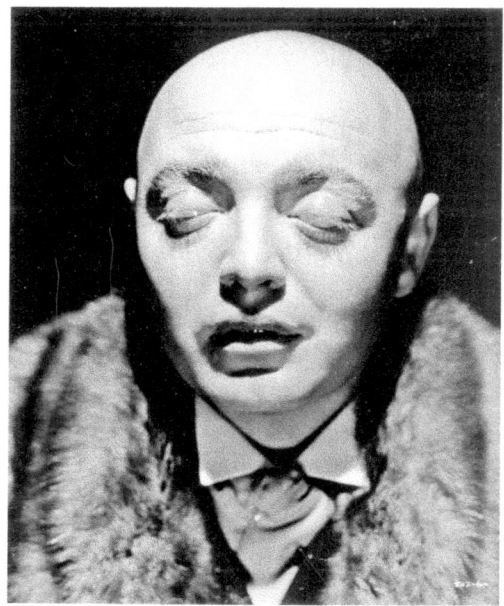

Witnessing scenes of torture sends Dr. Gogol (Peter Lorre) into the throes of ecstasy in *Mad Love* (1935, MGM).

eroticism and torture." Tudor rightly describes it as a "genuinely disturbing moment, the like of which would not be found again ... until films like *Psycho* and *Peeping Tom*." I would go further to say it is representative of the thirties cycle, and indicative of the link between classic and modern horror.

The nature of Gogol's insanity is, of course, sadism, "the tendency to derive pleasure, especially sexual gratification, from inflicting pain, suffering, or humiliation on others."[57] The term, as we know, is derived from the life and works of the Marquis de Sade. On the subject of Sade's influence on the cinema (in this particular case horror films which center on monstrous humans) Lindsay Anne Hallam writes:

> Like the monster, the monstrous human is both threatening and impure, but it hides its monstrous behavior behind a face that is undeniably, and unexceptionably, human. Because it perpetrates violence and sexual transgression in order to satisfy its own selfish desires, the monstrous human has no consideration for the law or the wellbeing of others. Sade's writing suggests that such behavior causes a cycle of transgression to be put into effect, one transgression always leading into another: transgression of body leads to transgression of behavior and transgression of societal law.[58]

If we allow that philosophically a horror film such as *Mad Love*, in its fascination with the urge to transgress and violate bodily taboos, is "Sadean" (as opposed to merely sadistic), we might also see the possibility of it exploring "precisely the limits between the normative and the transgressive."[59] In the next chapter I look at how critics have traditionally interpreted the thirties horror film as reinforcing normative values, and how it is only relatively recently that such transgression has been identified as inherent to thirties horror cinema.

5

"A secure universe"?
Thirties Horror and the Critics

As I stated in my introduction, much critical writing on modern/postmodern horror argues that classic horror films of the thirties and forties seek within the social-political contexts of the Great Depression and World War II to reaffirm dominant ideologies, as evidenced by their happy endings which typically restore normative values. Andrew Tudor, for example, has spoken of the classic period horror films creating a "secure universe," one in which the threat posed by the monster is external and therefore easily vanquished, with no ambiguity about the "fundamental stability of humanity itself." According to Tudor, this contrasts with the "paranoid" horror film of the seventies and eighties with its internal threats posed by the disturbed human psyche.[1] Isabel Pinedo has claimed that classic horror narratives, in comparison to postmodern narratives are characterized by narrative closure, in which the "human agency prevails and normative order is restored."[2] Even Robin Wood, in arguing the progressive potential of the modern seventies horror film in 1979, characterized the classic horror film by way of contrast, in terms of its narrative closure typically signifying the restoration of repression.[3]

However, as this study serves to illustrate, critics who lump together all pre-1960s American horror films as conservative miss important historical and industry factors: the restorative endings of the thirties films, although formulaic, must be understood in the context of censorship under the Hays Code and studio practices. Moreover, critics who stress the paranoia in modern horror as distinct to the safety and reassurance of classic horror are in danger of missing the gruesomeness and brutality of the thirties horror film. It could be counter-argued that in terms of its transgression, the thirties horror film, to a degree, challenged the increasingly conservative values seizing America during the Great Depression and in the lead up to World War II, and, as Thomas Doherty and others have suggested, reflected class conflict arising from the Hoover Doctrines and anxiety following the rise of Fascism in Europe.[4] We might therefore see these films working *similarly* to modern horror: proffering genre innovation, challenging censorship, reflecting historical trauma, and pushing boundaries.

So far in this book I have presented the four perspectives of industry, studio, censorship and artistic practices in order to highlight gruesomeness as a primary characteristic of the thirties horror cycle: a distinguishing mark that—I would argue—is at least equal to that of the "happy ending" as defining factor. This chapter looks at how critics have thus far read the thirties cycle. As previously stated, much critical opinion of thirties horror is based on simple misperception: its graphic explicitness has been undervalued and too much importance attached to the "happy ending" as an ideological indicator.

These misconceptions can be seen in the argument that the classic horror film (in comparison to the modern or postmodern horror film) is—based largely on the ending in which normative order is restored—inherently conservative or reactionary, or at best (and perhaps more accurately) ideologically "duplicitous" (to coin Gad Horowitz's term[5]): existing in a contradictory state as both progressive *and* regressive. In fact, as I have said in my preface and go on to explore in this chapter, it is only more recently that scholars have started to question the nature of the restorative ending in thirties horror films, and begun to investigate the impact of censorship and other industrial practices on the films and how we might read them.

Extreme Aversions: From Hitchcock to Everson

The underestimation of gruesomeness in the thirties horror film arguably originated with a group of film historians whose reference books in the early seventies informed the theoretical writings of a number of influential critics, including Robin Wood, later that decade. These historians—among them William K. Everson, Ivan Butler and Denis Gifford—shared an aversion to the increasing trend of graphic violence in cinema arising from the relaxation of censorship laws in Britain and America in the late sixties.[6] Their books, in reflecting the aesthetic tastes of the authors, championed suggestion rather than graphic explicitness in the presentation of screen horror, and pointed to the classic horror films of the thirties and forties as examples of the former; downplaying the gruesomeness of the thirties cycle in the process. This misrepresentation of thirties horror cinema, whether willful or not, was seemingly supported by the films themselves which were, as we have seen, in many cases shorn of their gruesomeness by the PCA and generally known to the public only in censored forms made suitable for family audiences. It would be wrong to blame these historians entirely for this misconception, however, as their nostalgia for family-friendly "old horror" has roots in horror fandom in the 1950s, and prior to that in the general turn towards the conservative in Hollywood itself from the mid-thirties onwards.

One of the first to write negatively about the gruesomeness of thirties horror was—surprisingly enough—Alfred Hitchcock. In January 1936, the future director of *Psycho* wrote a piece for *Picturegoer* extolling the virtues of the thriller while disparaging the then-recent cycle of horror pictures which at the time were facing censorial backlash. "The audience thrives on thrills, the cinema thrives on the audience, the director thrives on the cinema, and everybody is happy," he writes. "But the so-called "horror" film—that's an entirely different matter." Hitchcock goes on to explain:

> The term, meaning originally "extreme aversion," has been loosely applied to films which, to supply the desired emotional jolt, exploit sadism, perversion, bestiality, and deformity. This is utterly wrong, being vicious and dangerous. It is permissible for a film to be horrific, but not horrible; and between the two there is a dividing line which is apparent to all thinking people. The forerunner of the cycle of "horror" pictures which is now drawing to a close was the stage "Grand Guignol," and that was merely a "stunt," calculated to attract a neurotic section of the public. There is a growing body of opinion, inside as well as outside the film industry, against such films, which are successful in direct ratio to their power to create *unnatural* excitement. As a matter of fact, they are bound to fail, because the public is, as a rule, healthy-minded. Producers of "horrible" films realize this, and consequently "tone down" their product to make it acceptable. But in doing so

they tacitly acknowledge its basic fallacy; imagine a man hitting you on the head with a hammer with one hand to impress you, and with the other holding it back for fear it offends you![7]

What is remarkable in this attack on thirties horror—apart from these statements being made by the director of arguably cinema's greatest Grand Guignol of all—is that Hitchcock explicitly acknowledges the fundamental influence of stage Grand Guignol on the thirties cycle—something that critics would not again do for decades. Hitchcock's apparent (and I say apparent as he clearly changed his opinion in the intervening years between writing this and making *Rope, Psycho, The Birds, Frenzy* et al) distaste for the "horrible" nevertheless belies his clear and deep understanding of the thirties cycle, its appeal to "sadism, perversion, bestiality, and deformity," and its creation of "unnatural excitement." And while his seeming repudiation of horror pictures in the thirties may, of course, ultimately arise from a desire to align himself with industry opinion (in the knowledge that the horror cycle was coming to an end) Hitchcock still manages in just a few words to define the basic tenets of thirties horror with extraordinary accuracy.

Central to Hitchcock's argument is his assertion that the audience is, on whole "healthy-minded," and therefore more open to "secure" thrills than "neurotic" ones which undermine the public's basic feeling of security. Therefore, the kinds of thrillers that Hitchcock sought to make in 1936, so reasons the director, "leave the spectator with a subconscious assurance of absolute safety." Underlying his attack on the horror cycle, however, is the moral judgment that such films are wrong: "vicious and dangerous." Again, this may seem strange coming from the director who would spearhead horror-without-a-safety-net with *Psycho* 24 years later (prefigured by his psychological murder-thrillers in the fifties). Hitchcock, of course, would reason by 1960 that audience tastes had changed (and call *Psycho* a "shocker," as a means to distance himself from the horror film genre). We might, however, see his comments in the *Picturegoer* in 1936 as a disavowal of the transgressive; a psychical need to hide the Grand Guignol horror picture in the deeper recesses. Arguably, that is what happened to the thirties horror cycle, critically as well as censorially. After 1936, it was buried in the national psyche—or at least crucial parts of it were—and remained so for at least 20 years (we might also see this as coinciding with a general decline in intellectual engagement with the cinema on aesthetic terms during the mid-thirties. Maltby contends that the critical consensus of the time was that the advent of sound had diminished the film medium as an art form[8]).

Famous Monsters and Ivan Butler's The Horror Film

Famous Monsters of Filmland—launched in 1958 in the wake of the *Shock Theatre* TV horror revival—sparked a resurgence of interest in horror films among the youth of the fifties and sixties. Aimed squarely at a teenage and pre-teen readership, *Famous Monsters* and its legion of spin-offs and imitators fostered nostalgia for the Universal films as well as an enduring sense of traditionalism in much fan discourse concerning classic horror cinema (this is in no way intended to denigrate the invaluable scholarship undertaken by the historians writing in these magazines). As critic and fanzine editor David Flint comments: "Traditional horror magazines had tended to a somewhat moralistic and snobbish approach to low budget, gory, sleazy movies—that argument that what you DON'T see is more effective than what you DO see held sway. Modern horror was generally seen as inferior, tasteless and crude."⁹

It was precisely this approach that characterized the first horror film reference books, written in the late sixties and early seventies. One of the earliest to be published was Ivan Butler's *The Horror Film* in 1967. Butler's central discourse throughout is to separate the "continuing stream of poorly made, dully directed, often clumsily dubbed pictures with numerous shoddily sadistic and/or erotic scenes" that according to him have "given the genre a reputation for cheap sensationalism," from the classics of the genre that are "skillfully directed and played" and which stand up well "to any standard of criticism except the very highest."¹⁰ Butler's wider project is to rehabilitate the genre's reputation critically, and in an attempt to do this he frequently points to classic horror as an example of what can be achieved in the genre artistically, while often conveniently overlooking the very same sensationalism in the thirties cycle that he deplores in the modern horror film. In praising *Mystery of the Wax Museum* as superior to its 1953 remake, *House of Wax*, for example, Butler cites the final unmasking of Lionel Atwill as creating profound shock precisely because "there is not a great deal of the horrific" in the film otherwise; whereas, *House of Wax*, according to Butler, is "more contrivedly repulsive but actually less fearsome."¹¹ In other words, Butler commends the earlier film for its comparative restraint without fully acknowledging the graphic nature of the scene itself. Similarly, on the drowning scene of *Frankenstein*, Butler writes that it is "all the more effective in that we are not invited to watch the child's death struggles, water bubbling from her lips, eyes glazing, and all the rest of the latter-day stock-in-trade."¹² Butler's comparison of Browning's *Dracula* with its 1958 Hammer remake is equally revealing of his agenda: "It is a pity ... that [Terence] Fisher's usual determination to be horrid at all costs was allowed such free rein. Any suggestion of dark Gothic mystery—the saving grace of the old version—was satisfied to an orgy of blood-letting, stake-driving and general mayhem. Where originally the horrors were passed over with such restraint as at times to become unintelligible, here they were dwelt upon ... lovingly."¹³

To be fair to Butler, and those writers who followed, his hyperbolic commentary can partly be seen as a defense of the genre against the moral watchdogs of the day. Hammer films, of course, had met with considerable problems at the British Board of Film Censors in the late fifties; *Psycho* (and its slew of imitators) posed equal challenges to the Production Code Administration in the early sixties; sex, violence and nudity had become more explicit in cinema generally as the decade wore on and would reach a watershed by the early seventies, prompting a backlash against the cinema by civic and church pressure groups in both countries. In other ways, however, Butler's comments can themselves be taken as morally prescriptive and are at times reminiscent of Hitchcock's statement that Grand Guignol horror films are bound to fail because of the audience's distaste for them:

> Almost any degree of horror will prove acceptable to an audience provided it appears to fit into the context and not be gratuitously thrown in to satisfy their own presumed taste for violence. When a spectator of normal sensibility revolts it is invariably because the film seems to be indulging in beastliness for its own sake, to be enjoying cruelty. It is a mistaken idea, in the cinema at any rate (though not always, apparently, in the realm of pornographic or sadistic literature) that the lower the instincts appealed to, the wider the audience.¹⁴

William K. Everson's Classics of the Horror Film

Following the Butler and Gifford monographs, and taking the same basically conservative approach to screen horror, but perhaps more influential as a book, was William K. Everson's *Classics of the Horror Film* in 1974. Everson, of course, was a highly respected professor, collector and historian (deservedly so) and as a reference guide to the genre his book is considered a landmark. As a historical account it is not, however, free from bias.

Like Butler, Everson is an advocate of the "less is more" school of screen horror. In his introduction Everson states his aesthetic preference for "suggestion rather than outright statement" in the presentation of screen horror, and qualifies this with a detailed and convincing analysis of a scene from *Isle of the Dead* (1945) to illustrate how an audience can be manipulated to experience horror through sensitive editing rather than "an undisciplined charge through a series of shock close ups and brutalities."[15] At first it seems that Everson's argument, given the scene he uses as illustration (in which Katherine Emery has been buried alive and revives to find herself entombed in her coffin) does not necessarily preclude gruesomeness from the horror scenario, merely advocating that it be suggested rather than explicitly shown. (Indeed, it is difficult to disagree with his citing the off-screen child murder of Fritz Lang's *M* [1931] as a further example that "no director could ever come up with a scene to equal what the individual human mind can conceive. All he can do is plant the suggestion—and rely on the individual viewer to create what to him, personally, is the most horrifying visualization of that suggestion.")[16] It nevertheless becomes increasingly clear throughout the book that Everson had a deep aversion to on-screen gruesomeness in almost any form, which at times becomes quite rabid:

> Today, any child can switch channels on television and see not only the great horror films of the past and the increasingly gory and brutal horror films of more recent years, but also the real undiluted newsreel horror of warfare and mob violence. In theatres, where movies have become ever more competitive, the horror film has been diverted to one of two tangents. First, it is lampooned and ridiculed; secondly, it attempts to outdo its predecessors in the only way it knows, by adding grisly shock upon repugnant sensation. It is no trick to revolt and nauseate an audience via blood, decapitation, detailed killings, close-ups of floating hearts and eyeballs. It is the easiest, laziest trick in the world. And it proves over and over again, that the most effective screen horror is still the least detailed screen horror.[17]

Everson's evident despair at the state of horror cinema in the early seventies inevitably leads to a nostalgia for the old horrors, and quite an underestimation of the power of the thirties horror film to shock audiences.

> In terms of the content, the stylish Gothic horror films of the early 30s may seem mild indeed by today's standards, but they were simpler times. The horror film was new, talkies were new. Censorship (official and parental) was stricter, and children certainly had less easy access to horror films. Films designed and sold then for adult consumption, are now standard fare on kiddie matinees and on television. Audiences in the 30s were generally tense and more vulnerable to movie shocks—the depression, after all, affected almost everybody—but we were far less inured to horror in our daily lives.[18]

We can already see in Everson's comments the tendency to polarize horror into explicit modern horror and suggestive classic horror, and this is apparent throughout the book. Everson, was, of course, too conscientious a scholar to deny completely the gruesomeness of the thirties cycle (he does refer to the films as Grand Guignol, for example), but he continually de-emphasizes it in the way he details the individual films, in the way the book is organized (grouping together the thirties and forties cycles) and in his targeting of modern horror as deplorably graphic while constantly reinforcing the idea that classic horror films are mild in comparison.

In terms of specific examples, Everson describes *Dr. Jekyll and Mr. Hyde* as "ultra-stylish Grand Guignol" and defends its transformation scenes in terms of convincing techniques; nowhere, however, does he refer to the effectiveness of the make-up itself in creating horror in the viewer, and instead dismisses the effect merely as "grotesque." And while he admires the "sensual and erotic intensity" of the scenes between March and Hopkins, there is no mention of the brutality that caused such concern to the SRC.[19] He describes the cuts made to *King Kong* of the ape trampling the natives under foot as dramatically sound in that "they lost him a great deal of audience sympathy," but fails to detail other cuts made to the film to lessen its brutality.[20] Like Butler, he compares *Mystery of the Wax Museum* with the 1953 remake, praising the former for its restraint which made the classic unmasking both a shock and a surprise, whereas in the remake it was "handled much too abruptly and casually." Here Everson slips in the sly comment: "Horror films still had not reached the deplorable stage where they relied for much of their effect on physical repulsion."[21]

On other occasions his comments are similarly divisive: Of *Dr. X*, for example, he makes no direct mention of the prolonged synthetic flesh sequence, except to say: "While it doesn't pull any punches in the strong laboratory and Monster scenes, there's no sick emphasis on gore and blood."[22] More pointedly, he describes *White Zombie* as silly "through trying too hard to horrify its audience," and conflates the imagery of *White Zombie* with that of *Plague of the Zombies* (1966) and *Night of the Living Dead* (1968) as a way of attacking the latter films for their explicitness: "At a time when horror films were generally restrained, it anticipated the Hammer *modus operandi* of physical shock and repugnance via its closeups of repellent Zombies and their bullet-ridden torsos."[23]

He further downplays the potency of the thirties cycle by referring to its sadism in a facetious manner; thus he brushes off the skinning scene of *The Black Cat* as "medically drastic."[24] Similarly, in his analysis of *Mad Love*, he again comments, tongue-in-cheek: "[T]here's rather contemptuous humor in starting the whole film off in the framework of a grisly *Grand Guignol* performance of a play dealing with the torture-chamber branding of an unfaithful wife. Not only does it establish Dr. Gogol ... as a distinctly unhealthy personality, fascinated by both pain and sadism, and the sexual coveter of the star of the show ... but it also maliciously tweaks the noses of the audiences that dote on gruesome horror—namely, the audiences that have paid to see *Mad Love*."[25]

Everson takes a more serious view of *Island of Lost Souls* which he partially dismisses (again likening it to Hammer) as lurid and therefore less effective than others in the cycle: "[O]ne is often repelled by the film, but rarely convinced by it—even within the limited powers of conviction of most horror films—and thus, one is never really frightened by it."[26] Thus, the film is seen as something of an anomaly, and easily disregarded. *Freaks*, Everson admires greatly, but is again considered unrepresentative of the cycle; only its climactic final reel justifies its classification as a horror film.

Interestingly, *The Raven* is not discussed in detail, while *Murders in the Rue Morgue* is hardly mentioned at all except just to say that it owed more to *Cabinet of Dr. Caligari* than it did to Poe. There is, perhaps unsurprisingly, no reference made to the "rotten blood" scene. Indeed Everson writes the Universal Poe films off as "so played for comedy that Poe's association with them was virtually an insult."²⁷ It is perhaps inevitable that Everson sidelines the films in this way.

"A secure universe": From Wood to Pinedo

The subsequent division of the American horror film into two distinct periods, classical (conservative, secure, upholding the status quo) and modern (paranoid, ambivalent, suspicious of dominant ideology), while partly deriving from the historical accounts of authors such as Everson, moreover reflects post–Comolli/Narboni approaches to film criticism (as I discuss later). As Richard Maltby writes in *Hollywood Cinema*, evaluative paradigms initially adopted from F.R. Leavis' methods of literary studies in the early sixties ultimately proved insufficient in themselves when applied to modern cinema; the radical political orientation of *Cahiers du Cinema* post–1968 provided a solution, influencing a number of British and American critics. These included Robin Wood, and others, who, drawing on New Left theorists such as Herbert Marcuse, championed the modern "progressive text," while periodically returning to classic Hollywood cinema for critical reassessment under the broad critical framework of auteur-structuralism.²⁸

In terms of the American horror film, the opening up of film exhibition in the late sixties and seventies to a counterculture audience, led not only to a glut of independently made product and imported European films, but also to what film critics like Wood believed was a fundamental shift in the horror film paradigm, as filmmakers sought to appeal to progressive youth:

"CLASSIC" HORROR (1930s/1940s)	MODERN HORROR (1960s/1970s)
Foreign Monster	Indigenous monster
Monster is a supernatural being	Monster is psychopath/cannibal
Equilibrium is restored—good triumphs	The horror never ends—nihilism pervades
Society, i.e., religion, science, family is "good"	Society is to blame—family is seen as instrument of repression
The horror is suggested off-screen	Graphic on-screen horror
Reactionary	Progressive

This paradigm shift was partly attributed to changes in industry practices as well as changes in audience expectations. The thirties and forties horror films, for example, were studio-produced. The horror films of the seventies, by comparison, were typically produced independently, often outside of Hollywood (such as *Night of The Living Dead*—filmed in Pittsburgh) for very low budgets, shot on location with unknown actors. Whereas the directors of the classic era were predominantly inspired by expressionism, from the sixties onwards directors adopted the stylistic conventions of documentary realism. In the thirties and forties shadows and suggestion were thought to predominate, whereas from the sixties onwards, in the time of Vietnam, cinema generally, and the horror film in particular, was perceived as becoming increasingly graphic in its depiction of violence and bloodshed.

The broader purpose of this comparison between classic and modern horror, as made by Wood and later critics, is to emphasize the progressive aspects of the modern horror film, which, according to Wood, arose from the shared ideological "disturbance" of filmmaker and audience, and spoke for the "quandary of a civilization" in the seventies. Wood termed this new Golden Age of seventies horror cinema, "The American Nightmare," an allusion to the apocalyptic outlook of the films which was itself a reflection of the sociopolitical disillusionment of the era.

The American Nightmare

Drawing on Marxist-Freudian theory, in his highly influential essay, *The American Nightmare* (1979), Wood described the horror film as depicting in its monsters a "return of the repressed": a violent eruption of those aspects of the self that each of us represses (and that are oppressed by society as a whole) in order that we function as "bourgeois monogamous heterosexual capitalists." The conflict, therefore, between the monster and bourgeois capitalist "normality" in a horror film, and, crucially, how this conflict is resolved, reveals its ideological orientation: "One might say that the true subject of the horror genre is the struggle for recognition of all that our civilization represses or oppresses, its re-emergence dramatized, as in our nightmares, as an object of horror, a matter for terror, and the happy ending (when it exists) typically signifying the restoration of repression."[29]

Wood detected in the modern horror film a tendency towards apocalypse: an unrestorability of normality, which, by virtue, gave the modern horror film a subversive orientation. He termed the modern horror film progressive "in so far as its negativity is not recuperable into the dominant ideology, but constitutes, on the contrary, the recognition of that ideology's disintegration and its untenability."[30]

Wood compared the modern seventies horror film with the classical one, which, according to him, revealed a crucial difference between the two: "The typical ending of the (classical horror film) has the monster destroyed, the young lovers (sometimes the established family) united and safe; the typical ending of the (modern horror film) insists that the monster cannot be destroyed, that the repressed can never be annihilated."[31]

For Wood, distinguishing the reactionary from the progressive does not *necessarily* entail an assumption that all pre–1960 horror films are reactionary; rather it is those films that follow the classic horror paradigm (regardless of when they were made) that may be thought of as such (Wood, for example, places Val Lewton's horror films of the forties outside of the genre's mainstream development in this respect; likewise, he describes *The Omen*, made in 1976, as following the conservative traditions of classic horror). However, in drawing other divisions between the thirties and forties films, where "horror is always foreign," and the post–*Psycho* horror film where horror is implicitly recognized "as American and familial," Wood creates a framework where such an interpretation can be made.

Tudor's Monsters and Mad Scientists

Although Andrew Tudor rejects Wood's psychoanalytical approach to horror in favor of a prosaic one borne of a background in sociology, in *Monsters and Mad Scientists* (1989), he, like Wood, separates the genre's history into "two worlds of horror." Tudor describes these worlds as "secure" and "paranoid." The former type is characterized by a threat that is external to the protagonists (i.e. monsters, vampires, werewolves, space invaders); the former by a threat that is internal and psychological (spirit possession, psychosis). In secure horror, the narrative is invariably closed, the threat vanquished, and order restored; "human beings possess significant volition," according to Tudor, "while authorities and institutions generally remain credible protectors of social order."[32] In paranoid horror, by contrast, the threat is outside of human control, and in some cases, arises from *within* humans to cause disruption to the social order. "Lacking control of our inner selves," writes Tudor, "we have no means of resisting, and there is a certain inevitability to man's defeat."[33]

For Tudor, in the world of secure horror, traditional distinctions hold sway between life/death, secular/supernatural, normal/abnormal physical matter, and human/alien. Therefore, the line of defense against the unknown is easily distinguished. In paranoid horror, however, because the source of the threat is internal, this line between the known and unknown is easily blurred—conscious/unconscious, normal/abnormal sexuality, social order/social disorder, sanity/insanity and health/disease—presenting threats of "a rather different kind" that cannot be resolved by restoring normality.

Although Tudor points out that throughout the genre's history there have always been instances both of secure and paranoid horror, he claims that, historically, one has succeeded the other as the genre's dominant form. Like Wood, he sees this as an evolution of the genre that begins in the sixties and comes into fruition in the seventies and eighties. In other words, pre-sixties horror is, generally speaking, secure, whereas horror from the sixties onwards is predominantly paranoid.

Culturally, Tudor attributes this gradual shift to a change in social relations across the decades. Secure horror is characterized by the fear of social change; paranoid horror by personal and social confusions that follow in the wake of change. In pre-sixties horror films, there is no ambiguity about the nature of the threat to "normality," and about society's ability to defend against it: the pre-sixties films are implicitly conservative in their reflection of a world where tradition is valued for its own sake and where social change is resisted. In the secure horror world, deviation from normative values is presumed to be easily recognized and contained; in paranoid horror, by comparison, this sense of "the distinctiveness of deviance" and its potential for containment is undermined. Tudor's definition of "normality" invokes that of Wood: a hierarchical class society that marginalizes women, restricts sexuality, punishes social deviance and espouses bourgeois, patriarchal values. For Tudor the paranoid horror film reflects the "fearful prospect of unpredictable social relations in a world now open to the possibility of escalating chaos," but at the same time anticipates the possibility of a future free of restriction, oppression and orthodoxy, and therefore has progressive potential.[34]

Although Tudor maintains that the fear of social change is a prominent feature of the thirties horror film, he recognizes that its implicit conservatism is tempered by underlying anti-authoritarianism. "After all," he writes, "some part of our involvement in classic secure horror is grounded in the pleasures of witnessing authority flouted and rendered fragile, a feature often reinforced by making the threat itself attractive or sympathetic."[35] However, Tudor goes on to reinforce that authority ultimately triumphs in the thirties cycle, and "preservation of the status quo is axiomatic in the system of preconceptions within which secure horror functions." Finally, for Tudor, although classic secure horror may at some level seek to exploit a tacit antipathy to social authority, it never does so to the degree that the legitimacy of that authority is genuinely questioned. "The threat to prevailing social order," Tudor concludes, "is always finally conceived as more disturbing than is the constraint imposed by that order."

Tudor is not the only writer to have commented on the anti-authoritarianism of the thirties cycle. Writing in 1979 (at the same time as Wood, ten years before Tudor), Tom Milne asserted that the mythical status of the thirties horror film arose from its underlying appeal to post–Depression dissatisfaction with authority. "Many of these films," writes Milne, "implied a desire to rise up against the authoritarian regimes that callously curtailed man's inalienable freedom to pursue happiness."[36] Later scholars would further investigate anti-authoritarianism in the thirties cycle, and come to question Tudor's assertion that social authority prevails in classic horror narratives, as we shall see.

After Wood and Tudor

In 2004 Peter Hutchings remarked that much critical writing on modern horror argues that classic horror narratives are characterized by closure and reassurance, with the monster ultimately destroyed and the audience feeling that all is well with the world.[37] This now-embedded argument stems from a reductionist approach to the paradigm put forward by Wood and Tudor. Isabel Pinedo, for example, drawing primarily on Tudor, posits two historical periods of the genre: the classic horror film (1931–1960) and the postmodern horror film (1960-present). Although both periods share some of the same characteristics general to the horror film (violent disruption of the everyday world, transgression and violation of boundaries, questioning rationality) Pinedo claims that they differ in two important respects: the nature of their moral universe and resolution of conflict.

> The classical paradigm draws relatively clear boundaries between the contending camps of good and evil, normal and abnormal, and the outcome of the struggle almost invariably entails the destruction of the monster. Although boundary violations are at issue in classical horror, repairs can be effected. Good triumphs over evil; the social order is restored. In contrast, the postmodern paradigm blurs the boundary between good and evil, normal and abnormal, and the outcome of the struggle is at best ambiguous.[38]

Although Pinedo, like Tudor, is at pains to emphasize that the shift from classical to postmodern does not entail "a clean, historically definable break,"[39] and that there is historical overlap between the two paradigms, the separation of the two into essentially bipolar positions based on their morality and resolution of conflict seems overly schematic. Pinedo was writing in 1997, and since then, this absolutist moral designation given to classic horror by Pinedo, et al,, has prevailed.

In 2004, Harry M. Benshoff and Sean Griffin, in discussing the wider tendency of Hollywood genre to reaffirm the dominant ideology, cite the classic horror film as a case in point. According to them the horror film's emphasis on the threat posed to "normality" by the monstrous reinforces social ideas about what is considered normal. "Not surprisingly," they go on to comment, "in classical Hollywood horror films, 'normality' is conventionally represented by middle-to-upper-class, white, heterosexual couples and patriarchal institutions. Monsters and villains, on the other hand, are coded as non-white, non-patriarchal, and/or non-capitalist."[40] However, Benshoff and Griffin later contradict this statement, writing of the pre–Code era: "Gangster films, horror films, and stories of 'fallen women' proliferated, providing not only large doses of sex and violence, but also a cynical, pessimistic view of America and, to some degree, a critique of capitalist ideology."[41] But which is it to be? In some ways we might read this apparent contradiction as an indication of the classic horror film's resistance to pat ideological distinctions; in other ways it can be seen as a disconnect between two separated discourses in film studies, that relating to the Horror Film and that of Pre-Code Cinema, as I discuss later. The notion of closure and reassurance defining the classic horror film continues to predominate, however. As late as 2012, for example, Angela Ndalianis, in discussing the post-millennial "New Horror" of films like *Hostel* (2005) (which she describes as a "ritualistic violation of taboos ... that often threaten 'normal' society and its onscreen ideologies: murder and displays of sado-masochistic violence, perverted sexual acts, incest and interbreeding, the return of the dead, cannibalism—these themes are at the core of New Horror") defined the classic horror film by its restorative ending; simultaneously denying it those very same themes attributed by her to New Horror that, it may be argued, are equally "at the core" of the thirties horror film: "Whereas horror cinema –pre–*Psycho* unleashed horror in order to test the borders that demarcate society, order and normality from the anti-social, chaotic and abnormal, the social status quo was reinstated at the end. Horror cinema post–*Psycho* has demanded intellectual engagement of its audience, whether on the level of social critique presented by the film narrative or in the intertextual games that demand to be deciphered by the spectator."[42]

The Progressive Text vs. the Classical Text

As mentioned earlier, notions of the progressive text and counter-cinema arose from a post–May 1968 concern with cinema and ideology. In 1969, Jean-Louis Comolli and Paul Narboni published an editorial in *Cahiers du Cinéma* called "Cinema/Ideology/Criticism," which proposed a methodology by which cinema might be evaluated ideologically. This consisted of a set of cinematic categories into which individual films might be placed ideologically, based on the premise that "because every film is part of the economic system it is also a part of the ideological system" and therefore "every film is political, in as much as it is determined by the ideology which produces it."[43] The vast majority of movies, Comolli and Narboni argued, "are imbued through and through with the dominant ideology in pure and unadulterated form, and give no indication that their makers were even aware of the fact."[44] At the other end of the spectrum, according to Comolli and Narboni, were explicitly political films that deal with a directly political subject and use it to attack dominant ideology; other films, they argued might go "against the grain" insofar as they break down traditional ways of depicting reality and therefore become political, or, conversely, remain apolitical despite their apparently political subject matter through an adherence to classical form and its adherence to "bourgeois realism." Although Comolli and Narboni refer to a number of contemporary European New Wave films in relation to these first four categories, the fifth and most complex category, relates primarily to "many Hollywood films ... which while being completely integrated in the system and the ideology end up partially dismantling the system from within." These are films which

> seem at first sight to belong firmly within the ideology and to be completely under its sway, but which turn out to be so only in an ambiguous manner. For though they start from a nonprogressive standpoint, ranging

from the frankly reactionary through the conciliatory to the mildly, critical, they have been worked upon, and work, in such a real way that there is a noticeable gap, a dislocation between starting point and the finished product.... The films we are talking about throw up obstacles in the way of ideology, causing it to sway and go off course. The cinematic framework lets us see it, but also shows it up and denounces it.[45]

Critics like Wood used auteur-structuralism to untangle the ideological ambiguities of Hollywood films, arguing that "it is only through the medium of the individual that ideological tensions come into particular focus."[46] Hence, post–Comolli and Narboni scholars were able to champion certain directors—Ford, Hawks, Hitchcock—as progressive, despite their integration into the Hollywood system, their films constituting "rebel texts" within the mainstream. Barbara Klinger, however, writing in 1984, questioned the relational distinction, implicit in Comolli and Narboni, between counter-cinema and classical Hollywood, arguing that the bedrock proposition that the progressive must exhibit "textual characteristics which are strategically reactive to commonplace classicism" entails a "staunch conception of classic textuality against which progressive practice relies for its very definition."[47] Instead, Klinger posits that the differences to classical form that the progressive or counter-cinema text displays might be seen—not as partisan components of a "subversive text"-but as essential functioning elements of a system that thrives on a play of variation and regulation. In other words, the "disruptions" that Comolli and Narboni saw as indications of ideological contradictions in classic Hollywood films, were, on the contrary, "the modifications necessary to the maintenance and persistence" of the Hollywood system, rather than attempts to dismantle the system from within. "Critical assumptions which so measure the subversiveness of a film, based on its anti-classical formal attributes," writes Klinger, "underestimate the means through which supervising systems negotiate a normative function for even the most excessive, foregrounded, deformative textual tendencies."[48]

It is telling that in delineating the typical characteristics of the Hollywood progressive text, Klinger cites the seventies horror film, the film noir, the woman's film, the fifties melodrama, and the exploitation "B" picture as types of films usually accorded a "radical valence" by post–Comolli and Narboni critics, indicating that, by 1984, certain film genres/periods were (and still continue to be) championed over others in this respect. We might, of course, equally attribute the traits of the progressive text as outlined by Klinger to the thirties horror film. As Klinger remarks, these traits display in schematic form the consistent means through which the "progressive" is critically constructed.

Thus, a pessimistic world view is central to the progressive Hollywood text, in direct contrast to the optimism that characterizes the "typically celebratory" view of the American way of life in classical texts. The overall atmosphere is bleak, cynical, apocalyptic and/or highly ironic. Associated with this world-view are themes which dramatize, as Klinger puts it, the "demolition of dominant values"—including, the inviolability of the law and the family as an institution of social and sexual salvation (especially for women). "The center of hope in most narrative," writes Klinger, "the romantic couple, is shown as either cloyingly insipid or deranged," exploding the myth of the happy, unproblematic founding unit of the family.[49]

The overall narrative structure of the Hollywood progressive text is refined towards an exposure, rather than (as in the classical text) a suppression of ideological contradictions and tensions. Parallels are created between good and evil creating ambiguity and precluding easy identification and segregation of moral systems. And while classical texts promote the invisibility of the cause-and-effect mechanisms at work within the narrative, the progressive film departs from the classical system by either paring it down to its barest essentials so that the acknowledgement of that system is at its most minimized (for example, the exploitation film) or by exaggerating its principles to the point of stretching credibility and legibility.[50]

As Klinger points out, the issue of closure is crucial. "The progressive film must escape the compromising forces inherent in the conventional procedure of closure." Whereas closure usually signals the ultimate containment of matters brought out in the narrative, progressive films end in such a way as to refuse containment of the "excessive" narrative problems produced in the course of the film: The network of cause-and-effect remains unresolved, and the narrative is not returned to a final state of equilibrium. In film noir and the seventies horror film, as Klinger notes, narrative resolutions cannot recuperate their subversive significance, or provide redemption: "the amount of violence and destructiveness centered upon the social institutions is not adequately resolved through the conventional device of closure." Instead the usual process is circumvented through the use of certain textual strategies which undercut the affirmative ending: the "generic happy ending" brings with it a sense not of victory but of desolation, "the veneer of optimism not only unconvincing" but countered by unmistakable irony.[51]

As Klinger concludes, the cinema/ideology problematic cannot ultimately rely upon textual readings alone. "Industrial practices of exhibition and distribution, including promotional advertising"—extrinsic factors that are often expunged from the serious textual analysis—need to be incorporated into such readings, representing as they do the text "in practice": an "intersection at which multiple and 'extra-textual' practices of signification circulate." Furthermore, "the proliferation of diverse and co-existing representations at any given conjuncture," Klinger writes, "would suggest the pliability, rather than the rigidity of ideology." In other words, ideology allows for variety and for regulated forms of excess in the interests of its own continuity. The progressive Hollywood text may in fact be part of the "economy of variation, rather than rupture."[52] The politics of a genre, therefore, are by no means fixed.

Klinger's questioning of the easy distinctions made by critics between the progressive and the classical—based on a staunch conception of the latter—calls into question some of the common assumptions made about genre filmmaking. Movie genres are often described as evolving over time, forming a pattern of change through various phases of development: from an early experimental stage where the various generic signifiers are formulated, to a classical archetypal 'golden age,' to a demythologizing revisionist period, and finally into self-referential parody or pastiche. However, as we have seen in films like *Mad Love*, the horror film was already parodied long before the genre entered its revisionist period in the seventies. Indeed, what Tag Gallagher has said about the western arguably holds true for the horror film: cyclicism rather than evolution may be a more authentic hallmark of genre, generic codes and conventions merely being repeated, rather than elaborated upon or revised, throughout the decades. As Gallagher points out, directors continue to use the same generic devices nowadays that they used in early silent cinema, and critics continue to dismiss such devices as "old hat" now, as they did then.[53]

Toward Recovering Thirties Horror Cinema

It is tempting to say that all this has somewhat wiped the slate clean as far as the thirties horror film is concerned, making way for a reinterpretation of the cycle that dispenses with the usual attributions made to it in terms of its classicism and its ideology. Indeed, as Richard Maltby has said of recent film criticism, movie analysis has moved away from totalizing theories towards "a plurality of methods" with less grandiose ambitions.[54] This has led to an emphasis on historical study, involving a commitment to archival research and factual accuracy. More recent historical studies of thirties horror cinema have based their conclusions on such "hard evidence." These works—by Berenstein (1996), Doherty (1999), Prince (2003), Hutchings (2004) and Humphries (2006)—have gone some way towards making a recovery of the thirties horror film possible.

Interestingly, the only of these to recognize gruesomeness in the thirties horror film as key to its success with audiences is not a study of the horror film per se but an exploration of pre–Code cinema from 1930 to 1934, another indication, perhaps, of the disconnect that exists between Horror Film discourse and pre–Code Hollywood debate. In *Pre-Code Hollywood: Sex, Immorality, and Insurrection in American Cinema 1930–1934*, Thomas Doherty equates gruesomeness in the horror film with sex in the vice film as a taboo factor used by producers to attract cinemagoers into theatres during the Depression. Although Doherty does not explore the attraction of gruesomeness in detail, he does emphasize the social aspects of the thirties horror film, attributing its audience appeal to its venting of insurrectionist impulses. The monster, according to Doherty, embodies threat to the social order. That threat may be singular (as in Dracula, Frankenstein's Monster, Mr. Hyde and Dr. Mirakle's ape) or collective (as in the creatures of *Island of Lost Souls* and *Freaks*). According to Doherty, the singular threats were more readily subjugated, repressed and thus enjoyed by audiences than the collective dangers posed by mobs of monsters. "Certain kinds of revolutionary monstrosities," writes Doherty, "were too horrible to contemplate"; that is why *Island of Lost Souls* and *Freaks* failed at the box office.[55]

In many ways, then, Doherty's view of classical Hollywood coincides with Klinger's: the cultural work performed by and enforced upon Hollywood cinema, including its 'excesses,' served as a panacea during the Great Depression. Doherty links audience behavior in theaters where "movie goers reacted with audible expressions of ... discontent.... They hissed at images of Hoover ... and sneered at experts from government," with the actual images on the screen which "entertained, even embraced, visions of immorality and insurrection"; and thus by helping audiences vent their feelings in this way, these films played a crucial part in averting the threat of a radical overthrow of capitalism and constitutionalism during a time of great disillusionment and social upheaval.[56]

Doherty's study is invaluable in that it attributes many characteristics normally associated with the seventies horror film to the thirties cycle: it emphasizes that the horror is "personal and psychological," for example, and places it within a comparable socio-political context to seventies horror. "Nurtured by the incipient sense of disorder and disintegration in American culture," writes Doherty "the horror film blossomed in the early 1930s ... and gave freer rein to psychic turmoil and social disorientation."[57] Such assertions are often made about the modern horror film, but rarely about the classic one. Doherty also avoids much of the hyperbole often found in writing about pre–Code Hollywood, especially recent work which seeks to capitalize on the repackaging of Hollywood product in the age of DVD and *Turner Classic Movies*. Promoting pre–Code Hollywood as "unbridled, salacious, subversive" is as damaging, perhaps, as the misconception that classic horror is inherently conservative; scholars should, I suggest, work instead to connect pre–Code Hollywood and classic horror discourses more closely.

Stephen Prince does exactly this in *Classical Film Violence: Designing and Regulating Brutality in Hollywood Cinema, 1930-1968*. Neither a study of pre–Code Hollywood nor a historical account of horror cinema, this is instead a detailed account of how the SRC/PCA negotiated violence with filmmakers during 38 years of the Production Code. It is an important foundational work to this present study as Prince cites thirties horror cinema as a category of film that was especially rife with instances of brutality and violence. Indeed, Prince claims that the horror genre (along with the gangster film) was considered a "problem genre" by censors for this reason. Throughout, Prince emphasizes the "real hardness and brutality" of the thirties horror film, a characteristic that may be less apparent to desensitized contemporary viewers, but which is, nonetheless, a fact. As Prince writes, "[T]he modern viewer who believes there isn't much violence in the old Hollywood films, or much cruelty or sadism, needs to take a closer look." Itemizing some of the key scenes of thirties horror in terms of their atrocity ("a woman kidnapped, tortured, and executed"; "characters skinned alive, burned alive, murdered and their hearts ripped from their bodies, and the killing of children") Prince concludes that this is, indeed, "a remarkable amount of brutality" underlining the fact that, in their day, horror pictures were "dangerous for the industry to make."[58]

The value, then, of Prince's work in terms of horror film study, is that Prince is able to question certain assumptions about the nature of the classic horror film and his claims are supported by the "hard evidence." In the same way, a select few scholars working inside the horror field have begun to do the same. In *The Horror Film*, Peter Hutchings refutes Andrew Tudor's theory of secure and paranoid horror and the way they are mapped on to a classic/modern horror distinction; in so doing he questions the extent to which classic horror narratives are *actually* characterized by closure, reassurance and reinstatement of social authority. "A survey of them reveals that it is often quite hard to find many straightforwardly attractive authority figures," Hutchings writes, citing Van Helsing in *Dracula* (1931), Karl Brettschneider in *The Vampire Bat* (1933) and Dr. Garth in *Dracula's Daughter* as examples of authority figures undermined or compromised in some way. "[A]nd even when they either kill the monster or are involved in its defeat, this is rarely figured as a triumphant victory." Hutchings goes on to consider the "often sometimes arbitrary" conclusions of classic horror films, observing that endings have the sense of being merely tacked-on "once the film's running time has been reached."[59] He relates this to the very loose-structured narratives that often feature in horror cinema:

> In other words, while successful human intervention was usually present within a classic horror narrative, it is not clear that the fact of that intervention was in itself significant so far as an audience's response to the film was concerned. Certainly the films themselves often seemed more concerned with producing suspense, terror and pathos than they were with choreographing scenes of reassurance. It follows that perhaps classic horror cinema was not as obsessed with the protection of social authority as sometimes believed.[60]

So where does this leave the concept of modern horror vs. classic horror? "Inasmuch as it is predicated on a clear-cut distinction ... it becomes decidedly problematic," Hutchings concludes. "Clearly both 'classic' and 'modern' function as abstractions that do not do full justice to the variety of horror production apparent at any given moment in genre history."

Writing at the same time as Hutchings, Kendall Phillips conflates elements of the classic and modern horror film in *Projected Fears: Horror Films and American Culture*. Tracing the production and reception histories of ten key horror films from 1931 to 1999, Phillips, like Hutchings, questions the classical/modern horror distinction, in this case, with specific reference to Browning's *Dracula*, the film generally considered as the foundational text of classical horror. Again, Phillips questions the extent to which the classic horror film achieves closure and reassurance, and a reaffirmation of dominant values. At one level, Phillips notes, *Dracula* does achieve a degree of resolution: the threat is (we are told) vanquished; the bourgeois protagonists are protected through their use of traditional religious tools, and the "sanctity of normal sexuality is reestablished." However, on closer inspection, a number of elements undermine this sense of closure: Apart from the camera dwelling on Mina's "almost erotic reaction to the vampire's death moans rather than the act itself," Dracula's off-screen death robs the audience of the certainty that Dracula is definitely dead and undermines their sense of catharsis. This feeling would have been exacerbated in audiences who went to see the film in its first release as a final curtain speech made by Van Helsing (cut from later prints) suggested that "the threatening chaos of the vampire was not ended but only held off for the moment." The ending of *Dracula*, as Phillips concludes, thus provided no clear return to normalcy and rationality for audiences of its time. "Rather, as audience members filed out of the auditorium, the threatening chaos embodied by the vampire lingered behind the curtains—both the curtains of the theater palace and of their own homes."[61]

Instead of the usual approach to horror history that divides genre into classic and modern periods, the work of scholars such as Phillips and Hutchings advocates a critical approach that draws on micro-histories to give us a greater sense of the "ebb and flow of the genre as it adapts in various ways to shifts in the industrial and social circumstances of its production."[62] The growing perception of thirties horror cinema being more varied than previously thought can also be seen in the widening of classic horror discourse to include feminist studies. Here, particularly, classic horror has been celebrated in terms of its potential transgression of cultural norms.

In her 1983 essay, "When the Woman Looks," Linda Williams paralleled the roles of the monster with that of the female characters in horror films, as linked together through the woman's gaze. When the woman looks at the monster in a horror film, she shares the male's fear of the monster's freakishness, but crucially, also recognizes "the sense in which this freakishness is similar to her own difference" within the dominant culture. This leads to the "strange sympathy and affinity that often develops between the monster and the girl" (and, by extension, the spectator) in horror films.[63]

Rhona J. Berenstein further interrogated gender and spectatorship with respect to classic horror films in *Attack of the Leading Ladies*, published in 1996. Drawing on production histories, censorship files, and publicity material of the time, Berenstein uses this research to support a psychoanalytical re-reading of classic horror that refutes the oft-held assumption that horror spectatorship is typically gendered, predominantly male and sado-voyeuristic in nature. Instead, as Berenstein argues, gender in the horror film is a "permeable membrane" through which gender identifications can easily shift and switch.

Heightened gender performances in classic horror are ultimately an exaggerated form of role play: specific gender traits are made so extreme as to buffer "the genre's depiction of behaviors that push the parameters of patriarchal culture—such as female independence, a will to power and monstrosity, male fear and effeminacy, and male and female homosexuality."[64] In this way, gender representations in the classic horror film maintain the genre's dual relationship with society at large: "to destroy the status quo on the one hand, to confirm it on the other." In terms of gender, race and sexuality, the thirties horror film also provides a generic space in which human characters, male and female, behave monstrously and transgress the social rules and roles that usually confine them. However, as Berenstein also points out, that they do so for only 90 minutes or however long it takes for normality to be resumed is both "the promise and the letdown of horror's narrative contract."[65] In this way, Berenstein, like Klinger, believes classic textuality to be ultimately committed to the maintenance of the cultural status quo, but is at the same time more open to the transgression of boundaries than is often thought. Thus, Berenstein writes of narrative closure in the classic horror film: "Classic horror films may close with the reunion of the heterosexual couple, but that conclusion is usually forced and inadequate, Narrative threads are left hanging, and the promise of a sequel, which means the return of the monster or its brood, guarantees that happy endings and the stable gender roles they imply are temporary at best."[66]

For Berenstein, then, to designate horror as *either* politically reactionary or progressive, is to miss one of horror's most important qualities: its function as a "site of ideological contradiction and negotiation."

Reynold Humphries reaches a similar conclusion in his 2004 study, *The Hollywood Horror Film, 1931–1941: Madness in a Social Landscape*. Like Berenstein, Humphries draws on historical evidence to support his Marxist-Freudian readings of classic horror films. His stated aim is, indeed, to "turn the clock back to the days—not that long ago—before the notions of 'the end of history' and 'post-theory' had been concocted by those anxious to ensure that certain questions would never be asked again."[67] Those questions are, of course, what Marxism asks of class, economics and history. Humphries' analytical methods are those deployed by Freudo-Lacanian psychoanalysis, but are also informed by a close study of the industrial practices of marketing and distribution and, most crucially, censorship. In short, Humphries subjects the classic horror film to a level of serious social and cultural analysis usually only afforded the seventies or postmodern horror film. In taking this combined approach Humphries offers some penetrating insights.

Discussing the PCA's treatment of *Dracula's Daughter*, for example, Humphries refers to Breen's request that Universal omit from the script a specific line of dialogue that suggested a possible sex relationship between the Countess Zaleska and her manservant Sandor, having previously also requested the removal of any suggestion of lesbianism between Zaleska and the street girl, Lili. "Clearly the possibility of sex between a female aristocrat and her male servant is out of the question," Humphries remarks, "although this would just as clearly help hide the fact that the countess is sexually attracted to Lili." As Humphries then goes on to conclude, class, politics, and history are "far more massively repressed within horror and critical discourse thereon than sexuality of whatever persuasion."[68]

As Humphries comments in his introduction, his Freudo-Lacanian methodology "may not be to everyone's liking," and at times produces analysis that is arguably tenuous, as in this extract from his reading of the Théâtre Du Horreurs scene of *Mad Love*:

We can interpret the sequence as a beating fantasy and as the primal scene. In this case, Gogol simultaneously experiences orgasm in the imaginary position of the father, identifies with the position of the victim as mother figure ... and identifies with the sadistic husband deriving intense pleasure from having his unfaithful wife branded. Thus, Gogol derives simultaneously from the torture sequence the pleasure of not having to decide whether he is a man or woman, the masochistic pleasure of being punished for his own guilty

Arlene Francis and Bela Lugosi take a break from filming the "rotten blood" scene of *Murders in the Rue Morgue* (1932, Universal).

incestuous desire, and the sadistic pleasure of punishing the person "responsible" for the existence of this desire and whom he resents for being inaccessible. At the same time he can also occupy the absent place of the wife's lover, thus enabling him to fulfill a socially normally heterosexual function and behave in an active fashion.[69]

This is not, however, to detract from a study that is invaluable in its retrojecting Freudian-Marxist methodologies usually reserved for analysis of the modern horror film into classical horror cinema. Especially relevant to this present study is the focus on the sadism of the thirties horror film, which Humphries sees as a representation of the unconscious desire for mastery and control in a society divided by class and economics. (In some ways, we can draw parallels between this and Hand and Wilson's conclusion that ideologically the Grand Guignol is both "post–Nietzschean" and under the "shadows of the Marquis de Sade and Octave Mirbeau."[70]) Like Berenstein, Humphries ultimately views classic horror as a site of (fruitful) ideological contradiction and negotiation. In his conclusion he writes:

> The very themes and concerns of horror, touching as they do on forbidden and repressed desires, produces excesses of meaning which can never be reduced to a simple signified, such as "progressive" or "reactionary." The way class persists in making its presence felt is a factor that I have stressed again and again. Contradictions are rife and exist in the conflict between the individual and the collective, between ideology as the way subjects live out in the Imaginary their real social relations and conditions and some more human alternative, long repressed but capable of finding textual form in ways it is the critic's task to pinpoint, explain, and analyze.[71]

* * *

To conclude, in polarizing classic horror as typically restrained and modern horror as typically sensationalist, as authors such as Everson sought to do in the early seventies, we can already see in their writings, in nascent form, the concept of classic horror and modern horror as binary opposites: "mild" suggestive classic horror vs. "strong" explicitly graphic modern horror. This is the basis of the model that would be used by a number of critics and academics subsequent to these historians, informing their ideological readings of these films. Wood and Tudor further divided classic from modern horror in terms of their endings; and this tendency to polarize the two historical periods ideologically continued in horror studies until relatively recently. However, a movement towards microhistorical studies emphasizing archival research and factual accuracy has led recent scholars such as Berenstein, Hutchings and Humphries to start questioning easy distinctions made by critics between the progressive text and the classical text in terms of the horror film. It remains to be seen whether this new trend is set to continue.

Afterword

In the introduction to this book, I challenged critical opinion that 1930s horror is inherently conservative as defined by endings which typically restore normative order; I argued instead that its defining characteristics are gruesomeness and brutality, and that "happy endings" were often a sop to censorship and thus lacking ideological conviction.

I began in "'Nightmare pictures'" by charting the emergence of the 1930s cycle in an industrial context, showing how various stresses during the Great Depression, such as censorship controversy over sex and crime films, declining audiences and growing opposition to unfair business practices, formed a backdrop of ideological rupture and contradiction during horror's first golden age.

I went on to show how cash-strapped studios pushed for increasingly gruesome and sensational screen content to attract audiences, while simultaneously placating the Hays Office with moral endings; and how the production practices pioneered by Irving Thalberg—such as audience previews and retakes—also helped shape the form of the 1930s cycle as we know it. Critics of the genre at the time called such studio tactics "Five reels of transgression followed by one reel of retribution."

In "Brutality, horror and gruesomeness: Thirties Horror and the Hays Office," I documented the changing ways in which the Hays Office responded to gruesomeness in the 1930s cycle, from relatively light interference in the early days to heavily influencing the allowable level of gruesomeness from July 1934. I examined how even pre–Code horror films were subsequently censored for reissue and how these versions went into circulation and became the "known versions" until relatively recently, influencing a whole generation of critics in terms of what they perceived as horror's defining characteristics.

I then went on in "Why should Cecil B. DeMille have a monopoly on torture and cruelty?" to further explore links between producer, audience and censor. In this chapter I examined how screenwriters and directors deployed gruesomeness and brutality in the mise-en-scène through off-screen space, special make-up effects and the use of shadow play. I explored how Grand Guignol theatre had a pervasive influence on the thirties cycle in terms of its themes and use of gruesomeness.

Finally, in "'A secure universe'?" I discussed how and why critics have misread the 1930s cycle as conservative, and looked at how a recovery of thirties horror has started to take place among a select few scholars based on a micro-historical approach and archival research.

It is now time to return to the initial questions I raised in my preface: *How safe and reassuring were the thirties films really? And is the thirties horror film more akin to graphic modern horror than is often thought?*

It is difficult to argue against the view of classic horror cinema (and the genre in general) being, in the words of Rhona J. Berenstein, a site of "ideological contradiction and negotiation." However, that very quality of negotiation allows for revision of what is understood by "classic horror." One really does wonder how things might have been had, for example, James Whale been allowed to retain his original endings of *Frankenstein* and *Bride of Frankenstein* (where, in Whale's words, "nothing is resolved") or if Tod Browning had been granted release of his original cut of *Freaks* with little in the way of recuperation into the dominant order for the characters. Likewise, how might horror history have been different had Universal produced John Balderston's brutal and tragic "Return of Frankenstein" or R.C. Sherriff's uncanny, sexually transgressive and "excessively horrific" draft of *Dracula's Daughter*, screenplays that now seem extraordinarily ahead of their time (more befitting, in fact, of modern horror films)? Of course, in a sense, it is wrong to advocate a revision of history: we cannot deny the existence of the Production Code, for example, and its pervasive influence on the form and content of the horror film (especially as we have seen, in the revising of pre–Code horror films for reissue). On the other hand, to what extent can films ever be considered "fixed" texts? In a world of "extended editions," "director's cuts," "uncensored versions" and "alternate endings," can films ever be said to have a single definitive text? Consider *Bride of Frankenstein*. The film exists in a 75-minute official release version. (In reality, of course, the film existed in numerous versions depending upon the censorship demands of any given territory.) However, we know that a longer more brutal cut was originally prepared and later modified following negotiations with the PCA. We also know that the shooting script exists with a radically different ending. And then there is the myriad of screenplay drafts by different writers. All of these scripts and transcripts are cultural artifacts that *in their totality* constitute the text of *Bride of Frankenstein*; therefore all should be considered alongside the film as signifiers of the genre and its ideologies.

How has studying (even in script form) the original versions of thirties horror films, their original endings, and how and why these were changed by regulation and censorship, contributed to (or perhaps even changed) our understanding of what defines the classic horror film? Might the gap between modern horror and classic horror now be finally closed, or at least, narrowed, as Peter Hutchings suggests? Might it be possible to argue that classic horror is more akin to the modern horror film than some critics think?

The apocalyptic horror film of the sixties and seventies can perhaps be seen in embryonic form in the thirties horror film. The "apocalypse" as depicted in thirties horror is perhaps not fully acknowledged or fully expressed (the collapse of society in the thirties film is threatened rather than actual and typically contained within a family or small community, but the potential for collapse is always present) but is nonetheless portrayed in these films as an "endemic madness" (to borrow Andrew Tudor's phrase)—a world at odds with itself. The universe as presented in the horror films of the thirties is, as we have seen, far from secure. The thirties horror film is comparable to the modern horror film in many ways, not least in its presentation—despite the prevalence of "tacked-on" endings—of an irresolvable ideological crisis, an on-going (if not yet fully acknowledged and expressed) apocalypse. I suggest that the conservative/progressive distinction of the horror film is thus not definable by historic means as many theorists and academics have proposed. Instead I would argue that many of the elements usually attributed to the modern horror film can be seen in the classic period of 1931–1936, in its presentation of gruesomeness and brutality, sadism and madness.

This book should not, of course, be seen as the final word on the subject. There is more work that needs to be done to link modern horror theory to thirties horror cinema. However, if there is one thing that I hope this book has determined, it is that gruesomeness is a key factor of the American horror film 1931–1936. The full implications of this have, however, yet to be considered.

Chapter Notes

Introduction

1. Tom Johnson, *Censored Screams: The British Ban on Hollywood Horror in the Thirties* (Jefferson, NC: McFarland, 1997), 22–23.
2. Source: Andrew Tudor, *Monsters and Mad Scientists: A Cultural History of the Horror Film* (Oxford: Basil Blackwell Ltd, 1989), 27.
3. Thomas Schatz, *The Genius of the System: Hollywood Film-Making in the Studio Era* (London: Faber, 1998), 88.
4. Joseph Maddrey, *Nightmares in Red, White and Blue: The Evolution of the American Horror Film* (Jefferson, NC: McFarland, 2004), 3–4.
5. Rhona J. Berenstein, *Attack of the Leading Ladies: Gender, Sexuality, and Spectatorship in Classic Horror Cinema* (New York: Columbia University Press, 1996), 14, 16.
6. Stephen Prince, *Classical Film Violence: Designing and Regulating Brutality in Hollywood Cinema, 1930–1968* (New Brunswick, NJ: Rutgers University Press, 2003), 67, 72.
7. "Cycles and Other Things," *The Film Daily*, April, 3, 1932, 2.
8. Berenstein, *Attack of the Leading Ladies: Gender, Sexuality, and Spectatorship in Classic Horror Cinema*, 15.
9. Thomas Doherty, *Pre-Code Hollywood: Sex, Immorality, and Insurrection in American Cinema, 1930–1934* (New York: Columbia University Press, 1999), 16–17.
10. Ibid., 297.
11. Ibid., 365.
12. David J. Skal, *The Monster Show: A Cultural History of Horror* (London: Plexus, 1993), 189.
13. Douglas Gomery, *The Hollywood Studio System: A History* (London: British Film Institute, 2005), 159.
14. Mark Jancovich, "Hot Profits Out of Cold Shivers!": Horror, the First-run Market, and the Hollywood Studios, 1938 to 1942 in Richard Nowell, ed., *Merchants of Menace: The Business of Horror Cinema* (New York: Bloomsbury, 2014), 165.
15. Richard Maltby, "More Sinned Against than Sinning: The Fabrications of 'Pre-Code Cinema,'" *Senses of Cinema*, Issue 29 (December 2003), accessed October, 22, 2014. http://sensesofcinema.com/2003/feature-articles/pre_code_cinema/
16. Donato Totaro, "Monsters, Mad Scientists and Cultural Contexts of Horror," *Offscreen*, Vol. 17, Issue 6–7 (July 2013), accessed November, 20, 2013. http://offscreen.com/view/monsters_mad_scientists.
17. W.R. Garside, *British Unemployment 1919–1939: A Study in Public Policy* (Cambridge: Cambridge University Press, 1990), 261.
18. Alex Naylor, "'A Horror Picture at This Time Is a Very Hazardous Undertaking': Did British or American Censorship End the 1930s Horror Cycle?" *The Irish Journal of Gothic and Horror Studies*, Issue 9 (February 2011), accessed November, 20, 2013, http://irishgothichorrorjournal.homestead.com/1930shorrorbanprinter.html.
19. Johnson, *Censored Screams: The British Ban on Hollywood Horror in the Thirties*, 116–117.
20. Tudor, *Monsters and Mad Scientists: A Cultural History of the Horror Film*, 189.
21. Isabel Cristina Pinedo, *Recreational Terror: Women and the Pleasures of Horror Film Viewing* (Albany: State University of New York, 1997), 29.
22. Schatz, *The Genius of the System: Hollywood Film-Making in the Studio Era*, 94.
23. Page Cook, "Franz Waxman," *Films in Review*, Vol. 19, no. 7 (August-September 1968), 417.
24. David Bordwell, *The Classical Hollywood Cinema: Film Style & Mode of Production to 1960* (London: Routledge, 1985), 83.
25. Rick Worland, *The Horror Film: An Introduction* (Oxford: Blackwell Publishing, 2007), 21.
26. Bordwell, *The Classical Hollywood Cinema: Film Style & Mode of Production to 1960*, 83.
27. Ibid.
28. Robin Wood, "Prologue," *Hollywood from Vietnam to Reagan … and Beyond* (New York: Columbia University Press, 2003), xiv.
29. Carlos Clarens, *Horror Movies: An Illustrated Survey* (London: Panther Books, 1971), 90–154.
30. William K. Everson, *Classics of the Horror Film* (Secaucus, New Jersey: The Citadel Press, 1974), 3.
31. Ibid., 113.
32. John M. Miller, "Murders in the Zoo," *Turner Classic Movies*, accessed 18 August 2015, http://www.tcm.com/this-month/article/253085%7C0/Murders-in-the-Zoo.html.
33. Wood, "The American Nightmare: Hollywood in the 70s," *Hollywood from Vietnam to Reagan … And Beyond*, 63.
34. Tom Weaver, "Foreword," Johnson, *Censored Screams: The British Ban on Hollywood Horror in the Thirties*, x–xi.
35. Ibid., xi.

Chapter 1

1. "U Has Horror Cycle All to Self," *Variety*, April 8, 1931, 2.

2. Tino Balio, ed., *The American Film Industry* (revised edition) (Madison: The University of Wisconsin Press, 1985), 253–255.
3. Steffen Hantke, "Capitalist Horrors," *Other Voices: The Ejournal of Cultural Criticism*, Vol. 3, no. 1 (May, 2007), accessed November 22, 2014, http://www.othervoices.org/3.1/shantke/index.php.
4. Balio, *The American Film Industry*, 226.
5. *Ibid.*, 259.
6. Schatz, *The Genius of the System: Hollywood Film-Making in the Studio Era*, 203.
7. "Cycle on Wane?," *The Film Daily*, February, 26, 1932, 11.
8. Balio, *The American Film Industry*, 256.
9. Gomery, *The Hollywood Studio System: A History*, 75–77.
10. Balio, *The American Film Industry*, 256.
11. Gomery, *The Hollywood Studio System: A History*, 158.
12. See Maltby, "More Sinned Against than Sinning: The Fabrications of 'Pre-Code Cinema,'" *Senses of Cinema*.
13. See Kyle Edwards, "'House of Horrors': Corporate Strategy at Universal Pictures in the 1930s" in Richard Nowell, ed., *Merchants of Menace: The Business of Horror Cinema* (London: Bloomsbury, 2014), 16; see also, Schatz, *The Genius of the System: Hollywood Film-Making in the Studio Era*, 86–88.
14. "Memories of Carl Laemmle Jnr." in Philip J. Riley (ed.), *James Whale's Dracula's Daughter: An Alternative History for Classic Film Monsters* (Albany, GA: BearManor Media, 2009), 10.
15. Annette Kuhn, "History of the Cinema: American Film Industry" in Pam Cook ed., *The Cinema Book* (London: British Film Institute, 1985), 24.
16. Gregory D. Black, *Hollywood Censored: Morality Codes, Catholics, and the Movies*. (Cambridge: Cambridge University Press, 1996), 131.
17. Gary D. Rhodes, *Tod Browning's Dracula* (Sheffield: Tomahawk Press, 2014), 232.
18. *Ibid.*, 44.
19. Edwards, "'House of Horrors': Corporate Strategy at Universal Pictures in the 1930s," 16–17.
20. *Ibid.*
21. Schatz, *The Genius of the System: Hollywood Film-Making in the Studio Era*, 89.
22. Kyle Edwards, "Morals, Markets and 'Horror Pictures': The Rise of Universal Pictures and the Hollywood Production Code," *Film & History: An Interdisciplinary Journal* 42, no. 2 (Fall 2012): 27.
23. "Universal's 'Dracula' to Have Romance and Thrills," *Exhibitors Herald-World*, October 4, 1930, 58.
24. Advertisement. *The Film Daily*, February 16, 1931, 3.
25. Advertisement. *The Film Daily*, February 18, 1931, 5.
26. "U Has Horror Cycle All to Self," *Variety*.
27. "Over Saturation in Gang Films Is Feared by M.A Lightman," *The Film Daily*, March 9, 1931, 1.
28. "Hays' Office Checking If Films Foster Crime," *The Film Daily*, March 16, 1931, 1, 8.
29. Black, *Hollywood Censored: Morality Codes, Catholics, and the Movies*, 123–124.
30. "Virginia Censor Clips 14 Pictures in a Month," *The Film Daily*, March 17, 1931, 2.
31. "Anti-Gang Film Bill Defeated," *The Film Daily*, April 10, 1931, 1.
32. "Rochester Theater Heads See Humor in Gang Film Ban," *Syracuse Herald*, July 6, 1931, 4.
33. "Crime and Sex Film Output Dropping," *The Film Daily*, April 12, 1931, 1, 26.
34. Rhodes, *Tod Browning's Dracula*, 258.
35. Edwards, "'House of Horrors': Corporate Strategy at Universal Pictures in the 1930s," 18.
36. Rhodes, *Tod Browning's Dracula*, 257.
37. "Universal's 1931–32 Program Aimed at First-Run Houses," *The Film Daily*, May 11, 1931, 1, 3; also, "26 on Universal's New Season Schedule," *Motion Picture Herald*, May 16, 1931, 44.
38. "Censorship Activities Scored by Religious Body," *The Film Daily*, June 29, 1931, 1, 4.
39. "RKO Houses Bar Kids from Frankenstein," *The Film Daily*, November 12, 1931, 1, 4.
40. "U's Own Little Cycle Interferes with Self," *Variety*, November 17, 1931, 10.
41. "Last of U Horror Cycle," *The Film Daily*, November 19, 1931, 2.
42. "Universal Discards Two Gangster Films," *The Film Daily*, November 25, 1931, 1.
43. Advertisement. *The Film Daily*, November 21, 1931, 5.
44. "Thanksgiving Cheers for the B.O.," *The Film Daily*, November 30, 1931, 1.
45. "Frankenstein Clicks," *The Film Daily*, November 27, 1931, 8.
46. "Frankenstein," *New York Times*, December 5, 1931, accessed November 26, 2014, http://www.nytimes.com/movie/review?res=9901E5D6143DEE32A25756C0A9649D946094D6CF.
47. "Frankenstein," *Motion Picture Herald*, November 14, 1931, 40.
48. "Frankenstein," *Variety*, December 8, 1931, 14.
49. Quoted in Edwards, "'House of Horrors': Corporate Strategy at Universal Pictures in the 1930s," 19.
50. Advertisement. *The Film Daily*, December 2, 1931, 3.
51. "Along the Rialto with Phil M. Daly," *The Film Daily*, December 2, 1931, 8.
52. Advertisment. *The Film Daily*, November 30, 1931, 3.
53. "Novelty Next," *The Film Daily*, December 7, 1931, 1.
54. *Ibid.*
55. "The Laemmle-Universal Jubilee," *Motion Picture Herald*, February 6, 1932, 45.
56. "Abolition of Picture Cycles Being Considered by Studios," *The Film Daily*, December 1, 1931, 1, 8.
57. Letter, Beetson to Laemmle Jnr., November 2, 1931, Production Code Administration File, Special Collections, Motion Picture Academy of Arts & Sciences, Margaret Herrick Library, Beverly Hills (collection referred to hereafter as PCA file), *Frankenstein* (Universal, 1931).
58. "Inside Stuff—Pictures," *Variety*, November 17, 1931, 49.
59. Resume, December 4, 1931, PCA file, *Frankenstein* (Universal, 1931).
60. Letter, Joy to Hays, December 5, 1931, PCA file, *Frankenstein* (Universal, 1931).
61. Letter, Joy to Hays, January 11, 1932, PCA file, *Frankenstein* (Universal, 1931).
62. "Frankenstein ... A Picture and a Thought," *The Film Daily*, December 9, 1931, 1.

63. "Advertisement," *The Film Daily*, December 14, 1931, 7.
64. "Kans. Women Censors Ruin Frankenstein," *Variety*, December 15, 1931, 4.
65. Letter, Fithian to Joy, December 10, 1931, PCA file, *Frankenstein* (Universal, 1931).
66. "'Frankenstein' Is Passed by Kansas Censor After Protest," *Motion Picture Herald*, December 26, 1931, 25.
67. Resume, December 17, 1931, PCA file, *Frankenstein* (Universal, 1931).
68. "'Frankenstein' Is Passed by Kansas Censor After Protest," *Motion Picture Herald*, 25.
69. "Kansas in Arms as 'Frankenstein' Is Barred," *Motion Picture Herald*, December 19, 1931, 13.
70. "Film Critic Re-Edits 'Frankenstein' and Kans. Board Ok's It.," *Variety*, December 22, 1931, 7.
71. "Adhere to Code, Chief Censor of New York Urges Producers," *Motion Picture Herald*, December 19, 1931, 13.
72. "Hollywood Tries to Turn Horror into Monotony," *Variety*, December 22, 1931, 3.
73. "Warning Is Issued by Lightman Against Too Many Horror Films," *The Film Daily*, December 28, 1931, 1, 8.
74. "Snubbing Kids Until Spring," *Variety* January 19, 1932, 5.
75. Memo, Joy to Hays, January 11, 1932, PCA file, *Frankenstein* (Universal, 1931).
76. Clipping from *The New York Times*, February 14, 1932, PCA File, *Frankenstein* (Universal, 1931).
77. "Horror Cycle Seems on the Wane," *Variety*, February 16, 1932, 9.
78. "Cycle on Wane?," *The Film Daily*, February 26, 1932, 11.
79. Elias Savada, "The Making of Freaks," Reprinted from *Photon* 23 (Published 1973), accessed November 30, 2014, http://www.olgabaclanova.com/the_making_of_freaks.htm.
80. "On 'Horror Pictures,'" *Motion Picture Herald*, March 5, 1932, 92.
81. Balio, *The American Film Industry*, 226.
82. "Murdered Alive," *Variety*, April 12, 1932, 52.
83. "Wide Gap Between Average and Good Film Grosses Becomes Studio Ogre," *Variety*, April 19, 1932, 4.
84. Letter, Skinner to Joy, February 20, 1932, PCA file, *Murders in the Rue Morgue* (Universal, 1932).
85. "Mothers Should Be Their Own Censors," *Screenland*, June 1932, 98.
86. Doherty, *Pre-Code Hollywood: Sex, Immorality, and Insurrection in American Cinema, 1930–1934*, 156.
87. "Moving Movie Throng," *Hollywood Filmograph*, August 6, 1932, 9.
88. "Timeliness Is New Studio Motto," *Motion Picture Herald*, June 11, 1932, 16.
89. "Schedules Show Cycle of 'Horror' Pictures Continuing," *The Film Daily*, August 1, 1932, 1, 7.
90. "Picture Grosses," *Variety*, September 6, 1932, 9.
91. "Celluloiding London Wax Musee as Wb Pic," *Variety*, September 6, 1932, 4.
92. "Inside Stuff—Legit," *Variety*, November 8, 1932, 42.
93. "The Old Dark House," *Hollywood Filmograph*, July 9, 1932, 2.
94. "The Most Dangerous Game," *Variety*, November 22, 1932, 16.
95. "U Revives 'Suicide Club' Shelved Six Months Ago," *Variety*, December 6, 1932, 8.
96. "May Take the Censor to Court on 'Isle of Lost Souls,'" *The Film Daily*, January 9, 1933, 1, 3.
97. Letter, Joy to Schulberg, June 3, 1932, PCA file, *Island of Lost Souls* (Paramount, 1932).
98. Letter, Wingate to Hammell, December 8, 1932, PCA file, *Island of Lost Souls* (Paramount, 1932).
99. "Preview by Maude Latham—12/15/32," PCA file, *Island of Lost Souls* (Paramount, 1932).
100. "Island of Lost Souls," *The Film Daily*, January 12, 1933, 6.
101. "'The Island of Lost Souls' Out-Frankensteins 'Frankenstein,'" *Hollywood Filmograph*, December 10, 1932, 14.
102. "Island of Lost Souls," *Variety*, Jan 17, 1933, 15.
103. "What Will Happen to Movies in 1933?" *The New Movie Magazine*, January 1933, 70.
104. "The Vampire Bat," *Variety*, Jan 24, 1933, 19.
105. "King Kong," *The Film Daily*, February 25, 1933, 4.
106. Schatz, *The Genius of the System: Hollywood Film-Making in the Studio Era*, 167.
107. "Industry Set for 'New Deal' Under Roosevelt," *The Film Daily*, March 4, 1933, 1.
108. Advertisment, *The Film Daily*, March 4, 1933, 9.
109. Advertisment, *The Film Daily*. March 10, 1933, 3.
110. Advertisment, *The Film Daily*, March 20, 1933, 3.
111. "The Invisible Man," *Movie Classic*, January, 1934, 70.
112. "The Invisible Man," *Motion Picture Herald*, January 6, 1934, 53.
113. "The Black Cat," *The Film Daily*, May 19, 1934, 3.
114. Edwards, "'House of Horrors': Corporate Strategy at Universal Pictures in the 1930s," 22–23.
115. Schatz, *The Genius of the System: Hollywood Film-Making in the Studio Era*, 203–204.

Chapter 2

1. "Virtue in Cans," *The Nation*, April 16, 1930, 441.
2. Doherty, *Pre-Code Hollywood: Sex, Immorality, and Insurrection in American Cinema, 1930–1934*, 297.
3. *What Shocked the Censors! A Complete Record of Cuts in Motion Picture Films Ordered by the New York State Censors from January, 1932 to March 1933* (New York: The National Council of Freedom from Censorship, 1933), 15.
4. Schatz, *The Genius of the System: Hollywood Film-Making in the Studio Era*, 36.
5. Ibid., 22.
6. Balio, *The American Film Industry*, 264.
7. Schatz, *The Genius of the System: Hollywood Film-Making in the Studio Era*, 46.
8. Rhodes, *Tod Browning's Dracula*, 45.
9. Quoted in Stephen Jacobs, *Boris Karloff: More than a Monster—The Authorised Biography* (Sheffield: Tomahawk Press, 2010), 86.
10. Quoted in David J. Skal, *Hollywood Gothic: The Tangled Web of Dracula from Novel to Stage to Screen* (London: Andre Deutsch Ltd., 1992), 107.
11. Rhodes, *Tod Browning's Dracula*, 121.
12. *Dracula* Pressbook, Universal Studio Collection, Doheny Memorial Library, University of Southern Cali-

fornia (collection referred to hereafter as Universal Studio Collection, USC)

13. Rhodes, *Tod Browning's Dracula*, 135.

14. Philip J. Riley, Ed., *Dracula: The Original 1931 Shooting Script* (Absecon, NJ: MagicImage, 1990), 56.

15. Rhodes, *Tod Browning's Dracula*, 135.

16. Quoted in *Ibid.*, 141.

17. Riley, *Dracula: The Original 1931 Shooting Script*, 56.

18. Arthur Lennig, *The Immortal Count: The Life and Films of Bela Lugosi* (Lexington: The University of Kentucky, 2003) 112.

19. Elliot Stein, "Tod Browning" in Richard Roud (ed.), *Cinema: A Critical Dictionary* (London: Secker & Warburg, 1980), 162.

20. Rhodes, *Tod Browning's Dracula*, 166.

21. *Ibid.*, 170.

22. See Rhodes, *Tod Browning's Dracula*, 178–179; 203–205.

23. "Universal Adopts 'Overhaul' System," *Motion Picture News*, September 20, 1930, 57.

24. *Dracula* Shooting Schedule, Universal Studio Collection, USC.

25. Quoted in Skal, *Hollywood Gothic: The Tangled Web of Dracula from Novel to Stage to Screen*, 139.

26. Mark A. Vieira, *Hollywood Horror: From Gothic to Cosmic* (New York: Harry N. Abrams, Inc., 2003), 35.

27. See Rhodes, *Tod Browning's Dracula*, 195–208.

28. *Dracula* Pressbook, Universal Studio Collection, USC.

29. Rhodes, *Tod Browning's Dracula*, 203.

30. See Lennig, *The Immortal Count: The Life and Films of Bela Lugosi*, 121.

31. See, for example, John L. Flynn, *Cinematic Vampires: The Living Dead on Film and Television, from the Devil's Castle (1896) to Bram Stoker's Dracula* (Jefferson, NC: McFarland, 1992), 39.

32. Kendall R. Phillips, *Projected Fears: Horror Films and American Culture* (Westport, CT: Praeger Publishers, 2005) 32.

33. Rhodes, *Tod Browning's Dracula*, 273.

34. Gomery, *The Hollywood Studio System: A History*, 158.

35. Schatz, *The Genius of the System: Hollywood Film-Making in the Studio Era*, 86.

36. Quoted in James Curtis, *James Whale: A New World of Gods and Monsters* (London: Faber, 1998), 151.

37. Rudy Behlmer, DVD commentary, *Frankenstein*, Universal, 1999.

38. Schatz, *The Genius of the System: Hollywood Film-Making in the Studio Era*, 86.

39. "E. Richard Schayer," BFI, accessed January 8, 2015, https://explore.bfi.org.uk/4ce2ba8264ba4.

40. Behlmer, DVD commentary, *Frankenstein*.

41. Curtis, *James Whale: A New World of Gods and Monsters*, 128.

42. John Balderston and Garrett Fort, *Frankenstein—A Play* (ed.), Philip J. Riley (Albany, GA: Bear Manor Media, 2010).

43. Robert Florey and Garrett Fort, "Frankenstein" screenplay, in Philip J. Riley (ed.), *Robert Florey's Frankenstein Starring Bela Lugosi* (Albany, GA: Bear Manor Media, 2010).

44. Memo, Fort to Schayer, "Reactions to Mr. Henigson's Reactions to 'Frankenstein,'" June 13, 1931, Reproduced in Riley (ed.), *Robert Florey's Frankenstein Starring Bela Lugosi*.

45. Letter, Joy to Laemmle Jr., August 18, 1931, PCA file, *Frankenstein* (Universal, 1931).

46. Schatz, *The Genius of the System: Hollywood Film-Making in the Studio Era*, 94.

47. Curtis, *James Whale: A New World of Gods and Monsters*, 129.

48. Schatz, *The Genius of the System: Hollywood Film-Making in the Studio Era*, 94–95.

49. Quoted in Curtis, *James Whale: A New World of Gods and Monsters*, 154.

50. Reported by David Lewis, quoted in *Ibid.*, 152.

51. Quoted in Bryan Senn, *Golden Horrors: An Illustrated Critical Filmography of Terror Cinema, 1931–1939* (Jefferson, NC: McFarland, 1996), 29.

52. Curtis, *James Whale: A New World of Gods and Monsters*, 154.

53. Worland, *The Horror Film: An Introduction*, 174.

54. Letter, Beetson to Laemmle Jr., November 2, 1931, PCA file, *Frankenstein* (Universal, 1931).

55. "Along the Rialto with Phil M. Daly," *The Film Daily*, December 2, 1931, 8.

56. "Frankenstein," *Motion Picture Herald*, November 14, 1931, 40–41.

57. Balio, *The American Film Industry*, 256.

58. Enid Hibbard, Karl O. Tunberg, "Synopses," Sept 1930 and undated, Paramount Pictures Scripts, Special Collections, Motion Picture Academy of Arts & Sciences, Margaret Herrick Library, Beverly Hills (collection referred to hereafter as Paramount Pictures Scripts), *Dr. Jekyll and Mr. Hyde* (Paramount Pictures, 1931).

59. Schatz, *The Genius of the System: Hollywood Film-Making in the Studio Era*, 75.

60. Tom Milne, *Rouben Mamoulian* [Cinema One series] (London: BFI/Thames and Hudson, 1969), 39.

61. Vieira, *Hollywood Horror: From Gothic to Cosmic*, 41.

62. Johnson, *Censored Screams: The British Ban on Hollywood Horror in the Thirties*, 52.

63. Skal, *The Monster Show: A Cultural History of Horror*, 140.

64. Russ Hunter, "Gothic Horror," in Philip Kemp (ed.), *Cinema: The Whole Story* (London: Thames and Hudson, 2011), 90.

65. Percy Heath, "Treatment," June 11, 1931, Paramount Pictures Scripts, *Dr. Jekyll and Mr. Hyde* (Paramount Pictures, 1931), 2.

66. Percy Heath and Samuel Hoffenstein, "First Draft Script," June 23, 1931, Paramount Pictures Scripts, *Dr. Jekyll and Mr. Hyde* (Paramount Pictures, 1931).

67. "Memorandum for the Files," James B. Fisher, July 27, 1931, PCA file, *Dr. Jekyll and Mr. Hyde* (Paramount Pictures, 1931).

68. Letter, Wilson to Schulberg, August 10, 1931, PCA file *Dr. Jekyll and Mr. Hyde* (Paramount Pictures, 1931).

69. Percy Heath and Samuel Hoffenstein, "Second White Script," August 7, 1931, Paramount Pictures Scripts, *Dr. Jekyll and Mr. Hyde* (Paramount Pictures, 1931).

70. Prince, *Classical Film Violence: Designing and Regulating Brutality in Hollywood Cinema, 1930–1968*, 22.

71. Letter, Joy to Schulberg, December 1, 1931, PCA file, *Dr. Jekyll and Mr. Hyde*.

72. Greg Mank, DVD commentary, *Dr. Jekyll and Mr. Hyde*, Warner Bros/Turner Entertainment Co., 2004.
73. Joy and Fisher, "Resume," December 11, 1931, PCA file, *Dr. Jekyll and Mr. Hyde* (Paramount Pictures, 1931).
74. Mank, DVD commentary, *Dr. Jekyll and Mr. Hyde*.
75. "Miniature Review," *Variety*, January 5, 1932, 19.
76. "Jekyll and Hyde," *Variety*, January 5, 1932, 19.
77. "The Woman's Angle," *Variety*, January 5, 1932, 19.
78. See Gregory William Mank, *Hollywood Cauldron: Thirteen Horror Films from the Genre's Golden Age* (Jefferson, NC: McFarland, 1994), 28.
79. See Lennig, *The Immortal Count: The Life and Films of Bela Lugosi*, 141; Jacobs, *Boris Karloff: More than a Monster—The Authorised Biography*, 83.
80. Curtis, *James Whale: A New World of Gods and Monsters*, 132.
81. Lennig, *The Immortal Count: The Life and Films of Bela Lugosi*, 140.
82. Kyle Dawson Edwards, *Corporate Fictions: Film Adaptation and Authorship in the Classical Hollywood Era* (Austin: University of Texas, 2006), unpublished PhD. Thesis, 202.
83. Letter, Beetson to Laemmle Jr., October 13, 1931, PCA file, *Murders in the Rue Morgue* (Universal, 1931).
84. Prince, *Classical Film Violence: Designing and Regulating Brutality in Hollywood Cinema, 1930–1968*, 70.
85. "U Puffs 'Morgue,'" *Variety*, December 8, 1931, 6.
86. "Retakes for Two," *Variety*, December 22, 1931, 15.
87. "Murders in the Rue Morgue," Shooting Schedule, Universal Studio Collection, USC
88. J.V. Wilson, "Synopsis," Jan 11, 1932, PCA file, *Murders in the Rue Morgue* (Universal, 1931).
89. See Gregory William Mank, *Bela Lugosi and Boris Karloff, the Expanded Story of a Haunting Collaboration* (Jefferson, N.C. McFarland, 2009), 104.
90. Senn, *Golden Horrors: An Illustrated Critical Filmography of Terror Cinema, 1931–1939*, 51.
91. Letter, Joy to Laemmle Jr., January 8, 1932, PCA file, *Murders in the Rue Morgue* (Universal, 1931).
92. Prince, *Classical Film Violence: Designing and Regulating Brutality in Hollywood Cinema, 1930–1968*, 69.
93. Edwards, *Corporate Fictions: Film Adaptation and Authorship in the Classical Hollywood Era*, 209.
94. Letter, Fithian to Joy, April 21, 1932, PCA file, *Murders in the Rue Morgue* (Universal, 1931).
95. Letter, Fithian to Joy, April 12, 1932, PCA file, *Frankenstein* (Universal, 1931).
96. *What Shocked the Censors! A Complete Record of Cuts in Motion Picture Films Ordered by the New York State Censors from January, 1932 to March 1933*, 60.
97. "Office Memo," from Pettijohn to Hart & Joy, February 26, 1932, PCA file, *Murders in the Rue Morgue* (Universal, 1931).
98. Letter, Skinner to Joy, February 20, 1932, PCA file, *Murders in the Rue Morgue* (Universal, 1931).
99. "A Chat with Laemmle Jr," *New York Times*, April 3, 1932, accessed January 29, 2015, http://timesmachine.nytimes.com/timesmachine/1932/04/03/100708691.html.
100. Gomery, *The Hollywood Studio System: A History*, 99–104.
101. Balio, *The American Film Industry*, 256.
102. "Spurs" (story + synopsis), Turner/MGM Scripts, Special Collections, Motion Picture Academy of Arts & Sciences, Margaret Herrick Library, Beverly Hills (collection referred to hereafter as Turner/MGM Scripts), *Freaks* (MGM, 1932).
103. See, for example, Johnson, *Censored Screams: The British Ban on Hollywood Horror in the Thirties*, 68.
104. "Hollywood Tries to Turn Horror into Monotony," *Variety*, December, 22, 1931, 3.
105. Savada, "The Making of Freaks."
106. Quoted in David J. Skal and Elias Savada, *Dark Carnival: The Secret World of Tod Browning, Hollywood's Master of the Macabre* (New York: Anchor Books, 1995), 100.
107. "The Lowdown," *Hollywood Reporter*, March, 26, 1931, 2. Quoted in Rhodes, *Tod Browning's Dracula*, 190.
108. Quoted in Melvin E. Matthews Jnr., *Fear Itself: Horror on Screen and in Reality During the Depression and World War 2* (Jefferson, N.C.: McFarland, 2009), 52.
109. See, for example, Senn, *Golden Horrors: An Illustrated Critical Filmography of Terror Cinema, 1931–1939*, 61; Skal, *The Monster Show*, 153.
110. Gomery, *The Hollywood Studio System: A History*, 104.
111. "Complete Ok Screenplay," October 29, 1931, Turner/MGM Scripts, *Freaks* (MGM, 1932).
112. Senn, *Golden Horrors: An Illustrated Critical Filmography of Terror Cinema, 1931–1939*, 58.
113. "Letter from Elizabeth Conner," *Photoplay*, May 1932, 6.
114. Senn, *Golden Horrors: An Illustrated Critical Filmography of Terror Cinema, 1931–1939*, 58.
115. "Dialogue Cutting Continuity," January 29, 1932, Turner/MGM Scripts, *Freaks* (MGM, 1932).
116. "Freaks," *Motion Picture Herald*, January 23, 1932, 46.
117. Gomery, *The Hollywood Studio System: A History*, 104.
118. David Gasten, "*Freaks* Script Synopsis and Footnotes," *Olga Baclanova: The Ultimate Cinemantrap*, accessed September 8, 2015, http://www.olgabaclanova.com/freaks_script_synopsis.htm.
119. "*Freaks* Advertisement," reproduced in Senn, *Golden Horrors: An Illustrated Critical Filmography of Terror Cinema, 1931–1939*, 59.
120. "*Freaks*—Case Study," *British Board of Film Classification*, accessed September 8, 2015, http://www.bbfc.co.uk/case-studies/freaks.
121. Doherty, *Pre-Code Hollywood: Sex, Immorality, and Insurrection in American Cinema, 1930–1934*, 154.
122. Eric Schaefer, *Bold! Daring! Shocking! True! A History of Exploitation Films 1919–1959* (Durham, N.C: Duke University Press, 1999), 157.
123. Letter, Harmon to Breen, March 1, 1938, PCA file, *Angkor* (Road Show Attractions, 1937).
124. Letter, Breen to Wingate, May 9, 1938, PCA file, *Polygamy* (State Rights, 1937).
125. Schaefer, *Bold! Daring! Shocking! True! A History of Exploitation Films 1919–1959*, 156.
126. James MacDowell, *Happy Endings in Hollywood Cinema: Cliché, Convention and the Final Couple* (Edinburgh: Edinburgh University Press, 2013), 150.
127. Mank, *Bela Lugosi and Boris Karloff, the Expanded Story of a Haunting Collaboration*, 113.

128. Scott MacQueen, *Doctor X*, DVD commentary, Turner Entertainment/Warner Brothers, 2006.
129. *Ibid.*
130. Senn, *Golden Horrors: An Illustrated Critical Filmography of Terror Cinema, 1931–1939*, 101.
131. Report, Joy to Hays, March 17, 1932, PCA file, *Doctor X* (Warner Bros/First National, 1932).
132. MacQueen, *Doctor X*, DVD commentary.
133. Letter, Joy to Zanuck, March 21, 1932, PCA file, *Doctor X* (Warner Bros/First National, 1932).
134. MacQueen, *Doctor X*, DVD commentary.
135. Letter, Trotti to Warner, May 16, 1932, PCA file, *Doctor X* (Warner Bros/First National, 1932).
136. "Doctor X," *Motion Picture Herald*, June 11, 1932, 29–30.
137. Cited in MacQueen, *Doctor X*, DVD commentary.
138. "Doctor X Passed," *The Film Daily*, July 26, 1932, 5.
139. MacQueen, *Doctor X*, DVD commentary.
140. Letter, Hart to Breen, August 24, 1937, PCA file, *Doctor X* (Warner Bros/First National, 1932).
141. MacQueen, *Doctor X*, DVD commentary.
142. Harry Martin, "Synopsis -'Who's Zoo—A Comedy Adaptation of Richard Connell's the Most Dangerous Game,'" (undated), RKO Radio Pictures Studio Records (Collection PASC3) UCLA Library Special Collections, Charles E. Young Research Library, UCLA (referred to hereafter as RKO Studio Records), *The Most Dangerous Game* (RKO, 1932).
143. Harry Martin, "Treatment—'Who Zoo,'" (undated), RKO Studio Records, *The Most Dangerous Game* (RKO, 1932).
144. Vieira, *Hollywood Horror: From Gothic to Cosmic*, 59.
145. "Synopsis," (undated, no author given), RKO Studio Records, *The Most Dangerous Game* (RKO, 1932).
146. Bryan Senn, *The Most Dangerous Cinema: People Hunting People on Film* (Jefferson, N.C: McFarland, 2013), 16.
147. "Synopsis," (undated, no author given), RKO Studio Records, *The Most Dangerous Game* (RKO, 1932).
148. James Ashmore Creelman, "Final Script," May 5, 1932, RKO Studio Records, *The Most Dangerous Game* (RKO, 1932).
149. Letter, Trotti to Selznick, May 9, 1932, PCA file, *The Most Dangerous Game* (RKO, 1932).
150. James Ashmore Creelman, "Revised Final Draft," May 13, 1932, RKO Studio Records, *The Most Dangerous Game* (RKO, 1932).
151. Quoted in Maltby, "More Sinned Against than Sinning: The Fabrications of 'Pre-Code Cinema,'" *Senses of Cinema*.
152. Marjorie Dudley, "Continuity Synopsis," May 16, 1932, RKO Studio Records, *The Most Dangerous Game* (RKO, 1932).
153. "Cutting Continuity," undated & no author, RKO Studio Records, *The Most Dangerous Game* (RKO, 1932).
154. Letter, Joy to Selznick, July 22, 1932, RKO Studio Records, *The Most Dangerous Game* (RKO, 1932).
155. "Hollywood Openings," the *Motion Picture Herald*, July 30, 1932, 30.
156. Bryan Senn, *The Most Dangerous Cinema: People Hunting People on Film* (Jefferson, N.C: McFarland, 2013), 15.
157. George E. Turner, "What Is the Most Dangerous Game," *The Most Dangerous Game* (Laserdisc Edition), Roan Group, 1995.
158. Letter, Joy to Selznick, July 22, 1932, RKO Studio Records, *The Most Dangerous Game* (RKO, 1932).
159. Johnson, *Censored Screams: The British Ban on Hollywood Horror in the Thirties*, 61, 63.
160. "Producers Brew Wars," *Hollywood Reporter*, June 25, 1931, 1, 2.
161. "Writers War on Filth," *Hollywood Reporter*, February 27, 1933, 2.
162. Letter, Joy to Laemmle, March 23, 1932, PCA file, *The Old Dark House* (Universal, 1932).
163. Letter, Laemmle to Joy, March 28, 1932, PCA file, *The Old Dark House* (Universal, 1932).
164. Letter, Joy to Laemmle, June 25, 1932, PCA file, *The Old Dark House* (Universal, 1932).
165. Letter, Joy to Singerman, June 27, 1932, PCA file, *The Old Dark House* (Universal, 1932).
166. *Ibid.*
167. "Censor Reports," PCA file, *The Old Dark House* (Universal, 1932).
168. Letter, Breen to Zehner, January 29, 1936, PCA file, *The Old Dark House* (Universal, 1932).
169. See Mank, *Hollywood Cauldron: Thirteen Horror Films from the Genre's Golden Age*, 48.
170. *Ibid.*, 50.
171. See Tom Weaver, Michael Brunas and John Brunas, *Universal Horrors: The Studio's Classic Horror Films, 1931-1946 (Second Edition)* (Jefferson, NC: McFarland, 2007), 58.
172. "The Old Dark House," *Internet Movie Database*, accessed September 17, 2015, http://www.imdb.com/title/tt0023293/releaseinfo?ref_=tt_dt_dt.
173. Weaver, Brunas and Brunas, *Universal Horrors: The Studio's Classic Horror Films, 1931–1946*, 58.
174. Greg Mank, *Mask of Fu Manchu*, DVD commentary, Turner Entertainment/Warner Bros, 2006.
175. Doherty, *Pre-Code Hollywood: Sex, Immorality, and Insurrection in American Cinema, 1930-1934*, 2.
176. Mank, *Hollywood Cauldron: Thirteen Horror Films from the Genre's Golden Age*, 63.
177. Cited in Doherty, *Pre-Code Hollywood: Sex, Immorality, and Insurrection in American Cinema, 1930–1934*, 104.
178. Letter, Wingate to Hays, October 28, 1932, PCA file, *Mask of Fu Manchu* (MGM, 1932).
179. Mank, *Hollywood Cauldron: Thirteen Horror Films from the Genre's Golden Age*, 63.
180. Balio, *The American Film Industry*, 316.
181. "Metro Gets Tough Break on Planned 3 $200,000 Budgets," *Variety*, August 30, 1932, 5.
182. "Metro's Fu Manchu," *Variety*, July 26, 1932, 32.
183. Courtenay Terrett, "Screenplay Sections," August 3 & August 4, 1932, Turner/MGM Scripts, *Mask of Fu Manchu* (MGM, 1932).
184. Bayard Veiller, "Temporary Incomplete Screenplay," August 19, 1932, Turner/MGM Scripts, *Mask of Fu Manchu* (MGM, 1932).
185. Irene Kuhn, "Treatment and Screenplay Section," August 23 & August 24, 1932, Turner/MGM Scripts, *Mask of Fu Manchu* (MGM, 1932).
186. Samuel Marx, "Screenwriters: The Hacks, Wordsmiths and Literary Giants Who Invaded the New Sound-

stages of Hollywood," *The Movie: The Illustrated History of the Cinema*, Vol. 1, no. 8, 1979, 158.

187. Mank, *Hollywood Cauldron: Thirteen Horror Films from the Genre's Golden Age*, 64–65.

188. Jerry Bannon, "Karen Morley Weds Director Secretly," *Movie Classic*, February 1933, 31.

189. Cited by Mank, *Hollywood Cauldron: Thirteen Horror Films from the Genre's Golden Age*, 81.

190. "Metro Has 'Em Jumping Between Lots for 'Fu,'" *Variety*, October 4, 1932, 6.

191. Senn, *Golden Horrors: An Illustrated Critical Filmography of Terror Cinema, 1931–1939*, 132–133.

192. Quoted in Johnson, *Censored Screams: The British Ban on Hollywood Horror in the Thirties*, 65.

193. Doherty, *Pre-Code Hollywood: Sex, Immorality, and Insurrection in American Cinema, 1930–1934*, 119.

194. Senn, *Golden Horrors: An Illustrated Critical Filmography of Terror Cinema, 1931–1939*, 131.

195. Doherty, *Pre-Code Hollywood: Sex, Immorality, and Insurrection in American Cinema, 1930–1934*, 119.

196. Letter, Wingate to Thalberg, October 27, 1932, PCA file, *Mask of Fu Manchu* (MGM, 1932).

197. Letter, Wingate to Hays, October 28, 1932, PCA file, *Mask of Fu Manchu* (MGM, 1932).

198. "Mask of Fu Manchu," *Variety*, December 6, 1932, 15.

199. *What Shocked the Censors! A Complete Record of Cuts in Motion Picture Films Ordered by the New York State Censors from January, 1932 to March 1933*, 56.

200. Cited in Johnson, *Censored Screams: The British Ban on Hollywood Horror in the Thirties*, 65.

201. "Mask of Fu Manchu," *New York Times*, December 3, 1932, accessed September 21, 2015, http://www.nytimes.com/movie/review?res=9801E1DE1F31E333A25750C0A9649D946394D6CF

202. Mank, *Hollywood Cauldron: Thirteen Horror Films from the Genre's Golden Age*, 86–87.

203. Mank, *Bela Lugosi and Boris Karloff, the Expanded Story of a Haunting Collaboration*, 122.

204. Alison Peirse, *After Dracula: The 1930s Horror Film* (London: I.B. Taurus, 2013), 46.

205. "More Story Say-So by Associates at U," *Variety*, December 6, 1932, 19.

206. Johnson, *Censored Screams: The British Ban on Hollywood Horror in the Thirties*, 59.

207. Cited in *Ibid.*, 77.

208. See Senn, *Golden Horrors: An Illustrated Critical Filmography of Terror Cinema, 1931–1939*, 142–144; Weaver, Brunas and Brunas, *Universal Horrors: The Studio's Classic Horror Films, 1931–1946*, 64–72; Paul Jensen, *The Mummy*, DVD Commentary, Universal Studios, 2002; Nina Wilcox Putnam, *Cagliostro: The Great Imposter* (ed.), Philip J. Riley (Albany, G.A: BearManor Media, 2009).

209. Skal, *The Monster Show: A Cultural History of Horror*, 168.

210. Jensen, *The Mummy*, DVD Commentary.

211. Vieira, *Hollywood Horror: From Gothic to Cosmic*, 56.

212. For example, https://en.wikipedia.org/wiki/The_Mummy_(1932_film).

213. Jensen, *The Mummy*, DVD Commentary.

214. "Karl Freund to Direct 'Imhotep' for Universal," *Hollywood Filmograph*, September 3, 1932, 1.

215. "A Little from the Lots," *The Film Daily*, November 7, 1932, 8.

216. "Freund Finishes First as Director," *American Cinematographer*, November, 1932, 40.

217. "Thru the Lens of a Critic," *American Cinematographer*, December, 1932, 8, 50.

218. Jensen, *The Mummy*, DVD Commentary.

219. Letter, Joy to Laemmle, July 28, 1932, PCA file, *The Mummy* (Universal, 1932).

220. Cited in Senn, *Golden Horrors: An Illustrated Critical Filmography of Terror Cinema, 1931–1939*, 142.

221. Cited in Weaver, Brunas and Brunas, *Universal Horrors: The Studio's Classic Horror Films, 1931–1946*, 72.

222. Jensen, *The Mummy*, DVD Commentary.

223. "Picture Theatres," *Manchester Guardian*, June 27, 1933, 13.

224. Peirse, *After Dracula: The 1930s Horror Film*, 18.

225. Jensen, *The Mummy*, DVD Commentary.

226. Interview with Paul Jensen, *Mummy Dearest*, DVD feature, *The Mummy*, Universal Studios, 2002.

227. Weaver, Brunas and Brunas, *Universal Horrors: The Studio's Classic Horror Films, 1931–1946*, 68.

228. Quoted in *Ibid.*, 69.

229. Interview with Paul Jensen, *Mummy Dearest*, DVD feature, *The Mummy*.

230. Mank, *Bela Lugosi and Boris Karloff, the Expanded Story of a Haunting Collaboration*, 133.

231. "25 Per Cent Dialogue Reduction Ordered for Universal Pictures," *Motion Picture Herald*, October 29, 1932, 12.

232. Prince, *Classical Film Violence: Designing and Regulating Brutality in Hollywood Cinema, 1930–1968*, 74.

233. Senn, *Golden Horrors: An Illustrated Critical Filmography of Terror Cinema, 1931–1939*, 149.

234. Letter, Joy to Schulberg, June 3, 1932, PCA file, *Island of Lost Souls* (Paramount, 1932).

235. Doherty, *Pre-Code Hollywood: Sex, Immorality, and Insurrection in American Cinema, 1930–1934*, 295.

236. *Ibid.*, 298.

237. *Ibid.*, 295.

238. *Ibid.*, 289.

239. Gary Don Rhodes, *Lugosi, His Life in Films, on Stage, and in the Hearts of Horror Lovers* (Jefferson, N.C: McFarland, 1997), 96.

240. Waldemar Young (adapted by Philip Wylie from a novel by H. G. Wells), "Screenplay" September 21, 1932, Paramount Pictures Scripts, *Island of Lost Souls* (Paramount, 1932).

241. Letter, Joy to Hurley, September 26, 1932, PCA file, *Island of Lost Souls* (Paramount, 1932).

242. Waldemar Young (adapted by Philip Wylie from a novel by H. G. Wells), "Final Script," September 30, 1932, Paramount Pictures Scripts, *Island of Lost Souls* (Paramount, 1932).

243. Letter, Baily to Joy, October 3, 1932, PCA file, *Island of Lost Souls* (Paramount, 1932).

244. Geoffrey Shurlock, "Note," October 5, 1932, PCA file, *Island of Lost Souls* (Paramount, 1932).

245. See Peirse, *After Dracula: The 1930s Horror Film*, 37.

246. David A. Kirby, "The Devil in Our Dna: A Brief History of Eugenics in Science Fiction Films," *Literature and Medicine*, Vol. 26 No. 1 (Spring, 2007): 88.

247. Letter, Joy to Hays, October, 1932, PCA file, *Island of Lost Souls* (Paramount, 1932).
248. Letter, Wingate to Hurley, December 8, 1932, PCA file, *Island of Lost Souls* (Paramount, 1932).
249. Letter, Wingate to Hammell, December 8, 1932, PCA file, *Island of Lost Souls* (Paramount, 1932).
250. "Preview by Maude Latham—12/15/32," PCA file, *Island of Lost Souls* (Paramount, 1932).
251. Mordaunt Hall, "Island of Lost Souls," *New York Times*, January 13, 1933, accessed October 3, 2015, http://www.nytimes.com/movie/review?res=9D04E1DD1738E333A25750C1A9679C946294D6CF
252. Philip K. Scheuer, "Eerie Cinema Proffered," *Los Angeles Times*, January 10, 1933, 7.
253. "Censor Reports," PCA file, *Island of Lost Souls* (Paramount, 1932).
254. "May Take Censor to Court on 'Isle of Lost Souls,'" *Film Daily*, January 9, 1933, 1, 3.
255. "Passed After Slashes," *Film Daily*, January 31, 1932, 2.
256. "Island of Lost Souls," *Motion Picture Herald*, June 17, 1933, 47.
257. See James C. Robertson, *The Hidden Cinema: British Film Censorship in Action, 1913- 1975* (London: Routledge, 1989, reprint 1993), 55–57.
258. Letter, Breen to Hammell, September 18, 1935, PCA file, *Island of Lost Souls* (Paramount, 1932).
259. Letter, Breen to Luraschi, March 4, 1941, PCA file, *Island of Lost Souls* (Paramount, 1932).
260. Committee on Interstate and Foreign Commerce, House of Representatives, *Motion-Picture Films (Compulsory Block and Blind Selling): Hearing, Seventy-Sixth Congress, Third Session on S. 280, a Bill to Prohibit and to Prevent the Trade Practices Known as Compulsory Block Booking and Blind Selling in the Leasing of Motion-Picture Films in Interstate and Foreign Commerce, Part 1* (U.S. Government Printing Office, 1940), 544.
261. Letter, Breen to Luraschi, March 4, 1941.
262. Letter, Luraschi to Breen, March 15, 1941, PCA file, *Island of Lost Souls* (Paramount, 1932).
263. Letter and attached Certificate of Approval no. 7210-R, PCA to Luraschi, March 17, 1941, PCA file, *Island of Lost Souls* (Paramount, 1932).
264. "Wax Museum," *Variety*, February 21, 1933, 14.
265. Gomery, *The Hollywood Studio System: A History*, 132.
266. Schatz, *The Genius of the System: Hollywood Film-Making in the Studio Era*, 141.
267. "Burbank Buzzing," *The International Photographer*, October 1932, 25.
268. "Charles R. Rogers Plans 12 Mystery Thrillers," *Film Daily*, February 5, 1932, 1, 4.
269. "Warner Studio Preparing 15 Stories, All Different," *Film Daily*, September 9, 1932, 6.
270. Scott MacQueen, "The Mystery of the Wax Museum," *American Cinematographer*, 71, no. 4 (April 1990): 42.
271. Senn, *Golden Horrors: An Illustrated Critical Filmography of Terror Cinema, 1931–1939*, 167.
272. Scott MacQueen, "The Mystery of the Wax Museum," 42.
273. "Prod. Veers from Cycles," *Variety*, September 27, 1932, 25.
274. Letter, Joy to Zanuck, September 27, 1932, PCA file, *Mystery of the Wax Museum* (Warner Bros/First National, 1933).
275. Letter, Wingate to Zanuck, December 28, 1932, PCA file, *Mystery of the Wax Museum* (Warner Bros/First National, 1933).
276. Letter, Wingate to Howson, December 28, 1932, PCA file, *Mystery of the Wax Museum* (Warner Bros/First National, 1933).
277. Letter, Wingate to Hays, December 30, 1932, PCA file, *Mystery of the Wax Museum* (Warner Bros/First National, 1933).
278. Schatz, *The Genius of the System: Hollywood Film-Making in the Studio Era*, 136.
279. Richard Koszarski (ed.), *Mystery of the Wax Museum* (Madison, Wisconsin: University of Wisconsin Press, 1979), 169.
280. "Review by V.G. Hart," February 6, 1933, PCA file, *Mystery of the Wax Museum* (Warner Bros/First National, 1933).
281. Letter, Skinner to Howson, February 9, 1933, PCA file, *Mystery of the Wax Museum* (Warner Bros/First National, 1933).
282. "Wax Museum," *Motion Picture Herald*, January 7, 1933, 23.
283. "75 Museum Pre-Releases," *Film Daily*, February 8, 1933, 6.
284. "Wax Museum (In Technicolor)," *Variety*, February 21, 1933, 14.
285. Mordaunt Hall, "The Mystery of the Wax Museum," *New York Times*, February 18, 1933, accessed October 9, 2015, http://www.nytimes.com/movie/review?res=9E03E0DF173BEF3ABC4052DFB4668388629EDE
286. "The Mystery of the Wax Museum," *Film Daily*, February 18, 1933, 3.
287. "What the Picture Did for Me," *Motion Picture Herald*, July 8, 1933, 49.
288. Quoted in Skal, *The Monster Show: A Cultural History of Horror*, 174.
289. MPAA certificate letter, September 3, 1936, PCA file, *Mystery of the Wax Museum* (Warner Bros/First National, 1933).
290. See John McElwee, "Pre-Code Horror—Mystery of the Wax Museum," *Greenbriar Picture Shows*, April 12, 2008, accessed October 9, 2015, http://greenbriarpictureshows.blogspot.co.uk/2008/04/pre-code-horror-mystery-of-wax-museum.html.
291. "Imagination Inspired Kong," *Hollywood Reporter*, February 15, 1933, 6.
292. Doherty, *Pre-Code Hollywood: Sex, Immorality, and Insurrection in American Cinema, 1930–1934*, 290.
293. David Robinson, "King Kong," *The Movie: The Illustrated History of the Cinema*, Vol. 1, no. 6, 1979, 114.
294. "Imagination Inspired Kong," *Hollywood Reporter*, February 15, 1933, 6.
295. "King Kong," *Hollywood Filmograph*, April 1, 1933, 3.
296. "King Kong," *Motion Picture Herald*, February 25, 1933, 40.
297. "Permanent Rko Receiver Named," *Motion Picture Herald*, February 25, 1933, 36, 46.
298. "King Kong," *AFI Catalogue of Feature Films*, accessed October 22, 2015, http://www.afi.com/members/catalog/DetailView.aspx?s=&Movie=4005.

299. Edgar Wallace, *My Hollywood Diary* (London: Hutchinson & Co, 1932), 62–132.
300. "King Kong," *AFI Catalogue of Feature Films*.
301. James Ashmore Creelman, "Revised Treatment," June 9, 1932, RKO Studio Records, *King Kong* (RKO, 1933).
302. "Story Synopsis," undated and no author, RKO Studio Records, *King Kong* (RKO, 1933).
303. See Donald F. Glut, *Classic Movie Monsters* (Lanham, MD: Scarecrow, 1978), 297.
304. Fay Wray, "King Kong's Girl," *The Movie: The Illustrated History of the Cinema*, Vol. 1, no. 6, 1979, 116.
305. Doherty, *Pre-Code Hollywood: Sex, Immorality, and Insurrection in American Cinema, 1930–1934*, 292.
306. James Ashmore Creelman, "Revised Treatment," June 9, 1932, RKO Studio Records, *King Kong* (RKO, 1933).
307. "King Kong," *AFI Catalogue of Feature Films*.
308. *What Shocked the Censors! A Complete Record of Cuts in Motion Picture Films Ordered by the New York State Censors from January, 1932 to March 1933*, 47.
309. James C. Robertson, *The British Board of Film Censors: Film Censorship in Britain, 1896–1950* (London: Croom Helm, 1985), 183.
310. Johnson, *Censored Screams: The British Ban on Hollywood Horror in the Thirties*, 84.
311. "King Kong," *British Board of Film Classification*, accessed October 22, 2015, http://www.bbfc.co.uk/releases/king-kong-1970-5.
312. Senn, *Golden Horrors: An Illustrated Critical Filmography of Terror Cinema, 1931–1939*, 180.
313. "Rko Breaks Rule Sniping Kong," *Motion Picture Herald*, March 11, 1933, 53.
314. "King Kong," *AFI Catalogue of Feature Films*.
315. "Animal Pictures a Current Cycle," *Motion Picture Herald*, March 4, 1933, 57.
316. "Merian C. Cooper New Rko Production Chief," *Hollywood Filmograph*, February 11, 1933, 10.
317. "King Kong," *AFI Catalogue of Feature Films*.
318. Robert A. Harris, "RAH on King Kong," *The Digital Bits: Celebrating Film in the Digital Age*, October 25, 2005, accessed October 22, 2015, http://www.thedigitalbits.com/site_archive/articles/robertharris/harris102505.html.
319. *Afi's 100 Years ... The Complete Lists*, accessed October 24, 2015, http://www.afi.com/100Years/
320. Johnson, *Censored Screams: The British Ban on Hollywood Horror in the Thirties*, 86.
321. Andre Sennwald, "Murders in the Zoo," April 3, 1933, accessed October 25, 2015, http://www.nytimes.com/movie/review?res=9403E1D7173BEF3ABC4B53DFB2668388629EDE
322. John Balderston, "Dracula's Daughter—Treatment," January 1934, in Philip J. Riley, Ed., *James Whale's Dracula's Daughter* (Albany, GA: BearManor Media, 2009), 19.
323. Advert reproduced in Senn, *Golden Horrors: An Illustrated Critical Filmography of Terror Cinema, 1931–1939*, 186.
324. F.D. Langton, "Synopsis of Final Script," undated, Paramount Pictures Scripts, *Murders in the Zoo* (Paramount Pictures, 1933).
325. Philip Wylie and Seton I. Miller, "Treatment," undated, Paramount Pictures Scripts, *Murders in the Zoo* (Paramount Pictures, 1933).
326. Philip Wylie and Seton I. Miller, "First Draft Script," December 22, 1932, Paramount Pictures Scripts, *Murders in the Zoo* (Paramount Pictures, 1933).
327. *What Shocked the Censors! A Complete Record of Cuts in Motion Picture Films Ordered by the New York State Censors from January, 1932 to March 1933*, 60.
328. Letter, Breen to Hammell, September 18, 1933, PCA file, *Murders in the Zoo* (Paramount Pictures, 1933).
329. Cited in Johnson, *Censored Screams: The British Ban on Hollywood Horror in the Thirties*, 88.
330. "Murders in the Zoo," *Motion Picture Herald*, March 11, 1933, 19.
331. "Murders in the Zoo," *Hollywood Reporter*, May 1, 1933, 3.
332. See for example advert, *The Motion Picture Herald*, February 25, 1933, 19–26.
333. "Sideshow Ballyhoo in Lobby of Para." *Hollywood Reporter*, April 4, 1933, 4.
334. "New York Reviews," *Hollywood Reporter*, April 5, 1933, 2.
335. "What the Picture Did for Me," *Motion Picture Herald*, June 17, 1933, 48.
336. "What the Picture Did for Me," *Motion Picture Herald*, August 19, 1933, 54.
337. "What the Picture Did for Me," *Motion Picture Herald*, August 26, 1933, 92.
338. "Gabriel—Zoo Tops in London," *Hollywood Reporter*, June 17, 1933, 1.
339. Johnson, *Censored Screams: The British Ban on Hollywood Horror in the Thirties*, 88.
340. "Murders in the Zoo," *British Board of Film Classification*, accessed October 25, 2015, http://www.bbfc.co.uk/releases/murders-zoo-1970.
341. *Today's Cinema*, May 17, 1933, cited in Johnson, *Censored Screams: The British Ban on Hollywood Horror in the Thirties*, 88.
342. "Censors Reports," PCA file, *Murders in the Zoo* (Paramount Pictures, 1933).
343. Everson, *Classics of the Horror Film*, 113.
344. "New Administration Welcomed by Leaders in the Film Industry," *Film Daily*, March 4, 1933, 1, 6.
345. "Incoming Administration Viewed as Favorable by Film Chiefs," *Film Daily*, March 4, 1933, 1.
346. Balio, *The American Film Industry*, 260–261.
347. *The Black Cat*, budget, Universal Studio Collection, USC.
348. "The Return of Frankenstein," Budget and shooting schedule, Universal Studio Collection, USC.
349. "Dust Off Your Goose Pimples," *Universal Weekly*, March 31, 1934, 2–3.
350. Edwards, *Corporate Fictions: Film Adaptation and Authorship in the Classical Hollywood Era*, 226.
351. Weaver, Brunas and Brunas, *Universal Horrors: The Studio's Classic Horror Films, 1931–1946*, 88–89.
352. Peter Bogdanovich, "Edgar G. Ulmer interview," *Film Culture*, 1974, Issue 58–60, 190–205.
353. Scott Allen Nollen, *Boris Karloff: A Critical Account of His Screen, Stage, Television, Radio and Recording Work* (Jefferson, NC: McFarland & Co, 1991), 96.
354. Mank, *Bela Lugosi and Boris Karloff, the Expanded Story of a Haunting Collaboration*, 160.
355. "Laemmle, Jr., Cuts Short Foreign Route," *Variety*, January 9, 1934, 3.

356. Mank, *Bela Lugosi and Boris Karloff, the Expanded Story of a Haunting Collaboration*, 164.
357. "Biography Cycle," *Variety*, February 13, 1934, 25.
358. Reproduced in Johnson, *Censored Screams: The British Ban on Hollywood Horror in the Thirties*, 99.
359. Weaver, Brunas and Brunas, *Universal Horrors: The Studio's Classic Horror Films, 1931–1946*, 95.
360. Ibid.
361. Schatz, *The Genius of the System: Hollywood Film-Making in the Studio Era*, 167.
362. Letter, Hays to Wingate, March 8, 1933, MPPDA Digital Archive, Flinders University Library Special Collections (collection referred to hereafter as MPPDA Digital Archive), accessed October 27, 2015, http://mppda.flinders.edu.au/records/885.
363. Letter, Hays to Beetson, March 8, 1933, MPPDA Digital Archive, accessed October 27, 2015, http://mppda.flinders.edu.au/records/884.
364. Letter, Breen to Zehner, February 26, 1934, PCA file, *The Black Cat* (Universal, 1934).
365. Letter, Russell to Breen, February 28, 1934, PCA file, *The Black Cat* (Universal, 1934).
366. Islin Auster, "Memo," February 28, 1934, PCA file, *The Black Cat* (Universal, 1934).
367. Prince, *Classical Film Violence: Designing and Regulating Brutality in Hollywood Cinema, 1930–1968*, 77.
368. *The Black Cat*, budget, Universal Studio Collection, USC.
369. Mank, *Bela Lugosi and Boris Karloff, the Expanded Story of a Haunting Collaboration*, 192.
370. "Dust Off Your Goose Pimples," *Universal Weekly*, March 31, 1934, 2–3.
371. Letter, Breen to Zehner, April 2, 1934, PCA file, *The Black Cat* (Universal, 1934).
372. Letter, Zehner to Breen, April 6, 1934, PCA file, *The Black Cat* (Universal, 1934).
373. Vieira, *Hollywood Horror: From Gothic to Cosmic*, 68.
374. Letter, Breen to Hays, April 10, 1934, PCA file, *The Black Cat* (Universal, 1934).
375. MPAA certificate letter, May 27, 1938, PCA file, *The Black Cat* (Universal, 1934).
376. Vieira, *Hollywood Horror: From Gothic to Cosmic*, 68.
377. "The Black Cat," *Time*, May 28, 1934, accessed October 28, 1934 http://content.time.com/time/magazine/article/0,9171,754157,00.html.
378. "The Black Cat," *Variety*, May 22, 1934, 15, 29.
379. Anthony Aldgate and James C. Robertson, *Censorship in Theatre and Cinema* (Edinburgh: Edinburgh University Press, 2005) 157–158.
380. "Censor Reports," PCA file, *The Black Cat* (Universal, 1934).
381. Schatz, *The Genius of the System: Hollywood Film-Making in the Studio Era*, 203.
382. Gary D. Rhodes, "'Tremonstrous' Hopes and 'Oke' Results: The 1934 Reception of 'The Black Cat,'" in Gary D. Rhodes (ed.), *Edgar G. Ulmer: Detour on Poverty Row* (Lanham, MD: Lexington Books, 2008), 315.
383. "The Black Cat," *IMDB*, accessed October 28, 2015, http://www.imdb.com/title/tt0024894/business?ref_=tt_dt_bus.
384. "A Little from 'Lots,'" *Film Daily*, March 10, 1934, 3.

385. See Rhodes, "'Tremonstrous' Hopes and 'Oke' Results: The 1934 Reception of 'The Black Cat,'" 319.
386. "The Black Cat, *Film Daily*, May 19, 1934, 3.
387. "The Black Cat," *The Billboard*, May 26, 1934, cited in Rhodes, "'Tremonstrous' Hopes and 'Oke' Results: The 1934 Reception of 'The Black Cat,'" 309.
388. "The Black Cat," *Photoplay*, August 1934, 8.
389. Edwards, *Corporate Fictions: Film Adaptation and Authorship in the Classical Hollywood Era*, 236, 229.
390. Cited in Senn, *Golden Horrors: An Illustrated Critical Filmography of Terror Cinema, 1931–1939*, 239.
391. Cited in Mank, *Bela Lugosi and Boris Karloff, the Expanded Story of a Haunting Collaboration*, 190.
392. "No Rift Forecast in Laemmle Trek on European Biz," *Variety*, January 9, 1934, 5; Curtis, *James Whale: A New World of Gods and Monsters*, 223, 233–234.
393. Brian Taves, *Robert Florey: The French Expressionist* (Duncan Ok: Bear Manor Media, 2014), 146.
394. *Hollywood Reporter*, 15 November 1933, cited in Curtis, *James Whale: A New World of Gods and Monsters*, 218.
395. Quoted by R.C. Sherriff, in Philip J. Riley (ed.), *Boris Karloff as the Invisible Man* (Albany, GA: Bear Manor Media, 2011), 13.
396. L.G. Blochman, "Outline Treatment for the 'Return of Frankenstein,'" in Philip J. Riley (ed.), *The Return of Frankenstein* (Duncan, OK: Bear Manor Media, 2012), 54–68.
397. Philip McDonald, "'The Return of Frankenstein'—An Original Story By," in Philip J. Riley (ed.), *The Return of Frankenstein* (Duncan, OK: Bear Manor Media, 2012), 53.
398. *Universal Weekly*, December 30, 1933, cited in Curtis, *James Whale: A New World of Gods and Monsters*, 235.
399. Curtis, *James Whale: A New World of Gods and Monsters*, 236.
400. Finlay McDermid, "Inter-Office Memo," March 28, 1935, reproduced in Philip J. Riley (ed.), *The Return of Frankenstein* (Duncan, OK: Bear Manor Media, 2012), 202.
401. Ibid., 236.
402. Letter, Breen to Zehner, December 5, 1934, PCA file, *The Bride of Frankenstein* (Universal, 1935).
403. John Balderston, "First Rough Draft," June 9, 1934, revised June 19, 1934, reproduced in Philip J. Riley (ed.), *The Return of Frankenstein* (Duncan, OK: Bear Manor Media, 2012), 105.
404. "James Whale Tells All," *Universal Weekly*, March 23, 1935, cited in Curtis, *James Whale: A New World of Gods and Monsters*, 236.
405. "The Return of Frankenstein," no author, undated, Universal Studio Collection, USC.
406. Page Cook, "Franz Waxman," *Films in Review*, Vol.19, no. 7, August—September 1968, 416.
407. Will H. Hays, "Press Release," July 1, 1934, *MPPDA Digital Archive*, accessed November 11, 2015, http://mppda.flinders.edu.au/records/2410.
408. Letter, Russell to Breen, December 6, 1934, PCA file, *The Bride of Frankenstein* (Universal, 1935).
409. Letter, Breen to Zehner, December 7, 1934, PCA file, *The Bride of Frankenstein* (Universal, 1935).
410. Letter, Whale to Breen, December 7, 1934, PCA file, *The Bride of Frankenstein* (Universal, 1935).

411. Geoffrey Shurlock, "Memorandum," February 9, 1935, PCA file, *The Bride of Frankenstein* (Universal, 1935).
412. Prince, *Classical Film Violence: Designing and Regulating Brutality in Hollywood Cinema, 1930-1968*, 78.
413. Letter, Breen to Zehner, March 23, 1935, PCA file, *The Bride of Frankenstein* (Universal, 1935).
414. Letter, Whale to Breen, December 7, 1934, PCA file, *The Bride of Frankenstein* (Universal, 1935).
415. Thomas Doherty, "Hollywood and the Production Code," accessed November 6, 2015, http://microformguides.gale.com/Data/Introductions/32730FM.htm.
416. Letter, Breen to Zehner, March 23, 1935, PCA file, *The Bride of Frankenstein* (Universal, 1935).
417. Prince, *Classical Film Violence: Designing and Regulating Brutality in Hollywood Cinema, 1930-1968*, 79.
418. Joseph I. Breen, "Memo for Files," March 25, 1935, PCA file, *The Bride of Frankenstein* (Universal, 1935).
419. Prince, *Classical Film Violence: Designing and Regulating Brutality in Hollywood Cinema, 1930-1968*, 80.
420. Islin Auster, "Memorandum for the Files," April 8, 1935, PCA file, *The Bride of Frankenstein* (Universal, 1935).
421. Letter, Breen to Zehner, April 15, 1935, April 8, 1935, PCA file, *The Bride of Frankenstein* (Universal, 1935).
422. Letter, Zehner to Breen, April 19, 1935, April 8, 1935, PCA file, *The Bride of Frankenstein* (Universal, 1935).
423. Cited in Senn, *Golden Horrors: An Illustrated Critical Filmography of Terror Cinema, 1931-1939*, 287.
424. "Bride of Frankenstein," *Hollywood Reporter*, April 8, 1935, clipping, PCA file, *The Bride of Frankenstein* (Universal, 1935).
425. Curtis, *James Whale: A New World of Gods and Monsters*, 250.
426. "Censor Reports—'The Bride of Frankenstein,'" Universal Studios Collection, USC
427. Letter, Krieger to Singerman, May 7, 1935, PCA file, *The Bride of Frankenstein* (Universal, 1935).
428. Letter, Breen to Hays, May 8, 1935, PCA file, *The Bride of Frankenstein* (Universal, 1935).
429. "Eliminations Ordered by Ohio Board of Censors on 'The Bride of Frankenstein,'" May 4, 1935, PCA file, *The Bride of Frankenstein* (Universal, 1935).
430. Letter, Zehner to Breen, May 21, 1935, PCA file, *The Bride of Frankenstein* (Universal, 1935).
431. Letter, Breen to Hays, May 8, 1935, PCA file, *The Bride of Frankenstein* (Universal, 1935).
432. Senn, *Golden Horrors: An Illustrated Critical Filmography of Terror Cinema, 1931-1939*, 489-494.
433. "National Film Preservation Board—Complete Nation Film Registry Listing," *Library of Congress*, accessed November 11, 2015, http://www.loc.gov/programs/national-film-preservation-board/film-registry/complete-national-film-registry-listing/
434. "Universal on Unit System: Bergerman Resigns," *The Film Daily*, April 25, 1935, 1, 12.
435. "'U' Increases Budget for New Season: 78 Shorts on Program," *The Film Daily*, June 8, 1934, 1, 4.
436. "Poe Tales Combined," *Motion Picture Daily*, June 12, 1934, 7.
437. Weaver, Brunas and Brunas, *Universal Horrors: The Studio's Classic Horror Films, 1931-1946*, 142.
438. "A Little from 'Lots,'" *The Film Daily*, November 26, 1934, 6.
439. "The Raven—Note," The Jim Tully Papers 1883-1952 (Box 951575), UCLA Library Special Collections, Charles E. Young Research Library, UCLA.
440. Mank, *Bela Lugosi and Boris Karloff, the Expanded Story of a Haunting Collaboration*, 242-243.
441. "Friedlander on 'Raven,'" *Motion Picture Daily*, March 7, 1935, 2.
442. Edwards, *Corporate Fictions: Film Adaptation and Authorship in the Classical Hollywood Era*, 244.
443. Letter, Breen to Zehner, March 11, 1935, PCA file, *The Raven* (Universal, 1935).
444. Letter, Breen to Hart, February 21, 1935, MPPDA Digital Archive, accessed November 13, 2015, http://mppda.flinders.edu.au/records/1130.
445. Letter, Breen to Zehner, March 14, 1935, PCA file, *The Raven* (Universal, 1935).
446. Islin Auster, "Resume," March 16, 1934, PCA file, *The Raven* (Universal, 1935).
447. Mank, *Bela Lugosi and Boris Karloff, the Expanded Story of a Haunting Collaboration*, 256.
448. Letter, Breen to Zehner, March 20, 1935, PCA file, *The Raven* (Universal, 1935).
449. Letter, Breen to Zehner, March 26, 1935, PCA file, *The Raven* (Universal, 1935).
450. Mank, *Bela Lugosi and Boris Karloff, the Expanded Story of a Haunting Collaboration*, 260-261.
451. Ibid., 247, 254, 260.
452. "The Raven," *The Film Daily*, June 4, 1935, 6.
453. "'Love Me' $100,019 High at Music Hall," *Motion Picture Daily*, July 6, 1935, 3.
454. "Cleveland in Summer Slump Grosses Poor," *Motion Picture Daily*, July 31, 1935, 5; "'Farmer' Buffalo's Leader at $12,500," *Motion Picture Daily*, August 20, 8; "Shirley Nabs Another Top; It's in Cincy," *Motion Picture Daily*, August 21, 1935, 13.
455. "Censors Reports—The Raven ," Universal Studios Collection, USC.
456. "The Film Censor's 'Never More': Stricter Watch on Horror Films: 'Raven' Passed Before Warning," *The London Daily Telegraph*, August 2, 1935, press clipping, accessed November 15, 2015, http://mppda.flinders.edu.au/records/2570.
457. "The London Times," August 4, 1935, reproduced in Johnson, *Censored Screams: The British Ban on Hollywood Horror in the Thirties*, 117.
458. "The Daily Express," August 4, 1935, reproduced in Johnson, *Censored Screams: The British Ban on Hollywood Horror in the Thirties*, 117.
459. "Censor Boards on Vivisection Spree, Crack Down on Four Horror Operas," *Variety*, September 4, 1935, 2.
460. "Wave of Remakes Sweeping Studios," *The Film Daily*, December 21, 1938, 5.
461. Weaver, Brunas and Brunas, *Universal Horrors: The Studio's Classic Horror Films, 1931-1946*, 147.
462. Ibid., 585.
463. Steve Haberman, DVD commentary, *Mad Love*, Turner Entertainment/Warner Brothers, 2006.
464. Mank, *Hollywood Cauldron: Thirteen Horror Films from the Genre's Golden Age*, 122.
465. "Censor Boards on Vivisection Spree, Crack Down on Four Horror Operas," *Variety*, September 4, 1935, 2.

466. *Hollywood Reporter*, February 4, 1935, cited in Mank, *Hollywood Cauldron: Thirteen Horror Films from the Genre's Golden Age*, 124.
467. Mank, *Hollywood Cauldron: Thirteen Horror Films from the Genre's Golden Age*, 125.
468. "Karl Freund for M-G-M," *The Film Daily*, April 3, 1935, 2.
469. "Outline by Guy Endore," February 22, 1935, Turner/MGM Scripts, *Mad Love* (MGM, 1935).
470. "Treatment by Karl Freund and Guy Endore, March 13, 1935, Turner/MGM Scripts, *Mad Love* (Mgm, 1935).
471. "Temporary Complete Screenplay by P.J. Wolfson," April 6, 1935, Turner/MGM Scripts, *Mad Love* (MGM, 1935).
472. "Temporary Complete Screenplay by P.J. Wolfson," April 8, 1935, Turner/MGM Scripts, *Mad Love* (MGM, 1935).
473. "Conference Notes from John W. Considine and P.J. Wolfson," April 9, 1935, Turner/MGM Scripts, *Mad Love* (MGM, 1935).
474. "Temporary Complete Screenplay by P.J. Wolfson," April 18, 1935; April 22, 1935, Turner/MGM Scripts, *Mad Love* (MGM, 1935).
475. "Changes by Leon Gordon, John Balderston and T.F Maclaughlin," April 25—May 4, 1935, Turner/MGM Scripts, *Mad Love* (MGM, 1935).
476. Letter, Breen to Mayer, April 22, 1935, PCA file, *Mad Love* (MGM, 1935).
477. "Changes by Leon Gordon, John Balderston and T.F Maclaughlin," April 25—May 4, 1935, Turner/MGM Scripts, *Mad Love* (MGM, 1935).
478. Inter-Office Communication, Balderston to Breen, May 1, 1935, PCA file, *Mad Love* (MGM, 1935).
479. Mank, *Hollywood Cauldron: Thirteen Horror Films from the Genre's Golden Age*, 147.
480. "Mad Love Reviews," clippings, PCA file, *Mad Love* (MGM, 1935).
481. Mank, *Hollywood Cauldron: Thirteen Horror Films from the Genre's Golden Age*, 136–138.
482. *Ibid.*, 132–147.
483. "Mad Love," *Independent Exhibitors Film Bulletin*, July 31, 1935, 8.
484. "What the Picture Did for Me," *Motion Picture Herald*, November 16, 1935, 68.
485. "Mad Love," *Motion Picture Herald*, July 6, 1935, 74, 76.
486. "Censor Boards on Vivisection Spree, Crack Down on Four Horror Operas," *Variety*, September 4, 1935, 2.
487. Johnson, *Censored Screams: The British Ban on Hollywood Horror in the Thirties*, 119.
488. James C. Robertson, *The British Board of Film Censors: Film Censorship in Britain, 1896–1950*, 183.
489. Steve Haberman, DVD commentary, *Mad Love*.
490. "The Film Censor's 'Never More': Stricter Watch on Horror Films: 'Raven' Passed Before Warning," *The London Daily Telegraph*, August 2, 1935.
491. Mank, *Hollywood Cauldron: Thirteen Horror Films from the Genre's Golden Age*, 149–150, 153–154.
492. "Peter Lorre Talks About Real and Unreal Horror," *Film Weekly*, December 14, 1935, 10.
493. John Balderston, "Treatment," January, 1934, Reproduced in Riley, Philip J. (ed.), *James Whale's Dracula's Daughter* (Albany, GA: Bear Manor Media, 2009), 19–28.
494. Skal, *The Monster Show*, 195–196.
495. Balderston, "Treatment," 23.
496. Mank, *Bela Lugosi and Boris Karloff, the Expanded Story of a Haunting Collaboration*, 304.
497. "Universal Names 27 of Its New Titles," *The Film Daily*, June 7, 1935, 8.
498. Curtis, *James Whale: A New World of Gods and Monsters*, 254–255.
499. "Sherriff in with Script," *Variety*, October 2, 1935, 2.
500. *Ibid.*
501. BBFC Collection, Scenario Reports 1935, *Dracula's Daughter*, Item 1-4-448, August 28, 1935, BFI Reuben Library, Special Collections, Southbank.
502. *Ibid.*
503. R.C. Sherriff, "First Draft Script," Undated, Reproduced in Riley (ed.), *James Whale's Dracula's Daughter*, 49.
504. *Ibid.*, 42.
505. Robertson, *The Hidden Cinema: British Film Censorship in Action, 1913- 1975*, 66.
506. "Memorandum for Files," Sept 13, 1935, PCA file, *Dracula's Daughter* (Universal, 1936).
507. Letter, Breen to Hays, October, 1935, PCA file, *Dracula's Daughter* (Universal, 1936).
508. "Purely Personal," *Motion Picture Daily*, September 27, 1935, 2.
509. Letter, Breen to Zehner, October 23, 1935, PCA file, *Dracula's Daughter* (Universal, 1936).
510. Letter, Zehner to Breen, October 31, 1935, PCA file, *Dracula's Daughter* (Universal, 1936).
511. Letter, Breen to Hays, November 1, 1935, PCA file, *Dracula's Daughter* (Universal, 1936).
512. "Howard Spurns 'Dracula,'" *Variety*, November 13, 1935, 7.
513. "Dracula's Troubles," *Variety*, November 20, 1935, 4.
514. *Ibid.*
515. "Out Hollywood Way," *Motion Picture Daily*, December 6, 1935, 4.
516. "U Drops 30 in Prod. Slow Up," *Variety*, January 8, 1935, 5.
517. *Ibid.*
518. "'Dracula's Dotter' on Universal Sked Again," *Variety*, January 15, 1936, 7.
519. Letter, Asher to Breen, January 14, 1936, PCA file, *Dracula's Daughter* (Universal, 1936).
520. Naylor, ' "A Horror Picture at This Time Is a Very Hazardous Undertaking': Did British or American Censorship End the 1930s Horror Cycle?" *The Irish Journal of Gothic and Horror Studies*.
521. Letter, Breen to Asher, January 15, 1936, PCA file, *Dracula's Daughter* (Universal, 1936).
522. Mank, *Bela Lugosi and Boris Karloff, the Expanded Story of a Haunting Collaboration*, 305.
523. "The Cutting Room," *Motion Picture Herald*, March 21, 1936, 34.
524. "The Show Window," *Movie Classic*, July 1936, 60.
525. "Lady Vampire," *The National Board of Review Magazine, 1936-1938*, 12.
526. "Horror Films Taken Off U. Sked," *Variety*, May 6, 1936, 7.
527. Naylor, ' "A Horror Picture at This Time Is a Very

Hazardous Undertaking': Did British or American Censorship End the 1930s Horror Cycle?" *The Irish Journal of Gothic and Horror Studies*.

528. Schatz, *The Genius of the System: Hollywood Film-Making in the Studio Era*, 198.

529. Mank, *Bela Lugosi and Boris Karloff, the Expanded Story of a Haunting Collaboration*, 328–329.

Chapter 3

1. Edwards, "Morals, Markets and 'Horror Pictures,'" 26.

2. Naylor, ' "A Horror Picture at This Time Is a Very Hazardous Undertaking': Did British or American Censorship End the 1930s Horror Cycle?" *The Irish Journal of Gothic and Horror Studies*.

3. Doherty, *Pre-Code Hollywood: Sex, Immorality, and Insurrection in American Cinema, 1930-1934*, 19.

4. See Balio, *The American Film Industry*, 267–268; "1929-1932: Creating the Production Code," MPPDA Digital Archive, accessed December 14, 2015, http://mppda.flinders.edu.au/history/mppda-history/1929-1932-creating-the-production-code.

5. Ruth A. Inglis, "Self-Regulation in Action," in Balio, *The American Film Industry*, 378–383.

6. "Transcription MPPDA 2304: General Principles to Cover the Preparation of a Revised Code of Ethics for Talking Pictures, February 10, 1930," MPPDA Digital Archive, accessed December 14, 2015, http://mppda.flinders.edu.au/records/2304.

7. Prince, *Classical Film Violence: Designing and Regulating Brutality in Hollywood Cinema, 1930-1968*, 52.

8. Quoted in Maltby, "More Sinned Against than Sinning: The Fabrications of 'Pre-Code Cinema,'" *Senses of Cinema*.

9. "Code Report and Story Synopsis," January 14, 1931, PCA file, *Dracula* (Universal, 1931).

10. "Trailer Synopsis and Report," January 28, 1931, PCA file, *Dracula* (Universal, 1931).

11. "Comments of Previewers on 'Dracula,'" undated, PCA file, *Dracula* (Universal, 1931).

12. "1929-1932: Creating the Production Code," MPPDA Digital Archive.

13. Letter, Joy to Laemmle, August 18, 1931, PCA file, *Frankenstein* (Universal, 1931).

14. Edwards, "Morals, Markets and 'Horror Pictures,'" 29.

15. Letter, Beetson to Laemmle, November 2, 1931, PCA file, *Frankenstein* (Universal, 1931).

16. "Resume," December 4, 1931, PCA file, *Frankenstein* (Universal, 1931).

17. Letter, Joy to Hays, December 5, 1931, PCA file, *Frankenstein* (Universal, 1931).

18. Letter, Joy to Schulberg, December 1, 1931, PCA file, *Dr. Jekyll and Mr. Hyde* (Paramount, 1931).

19. *Ibid.*

20. Letter, Beetson to Laemmle, October 13, 1931, PCA file, *Murders in the Rue Morgue* (Universal, 1931).

21. Letter, Fithian to Joy, December 10, 1931, PCA file, *Frankenstein* (Universal, 1931).

22. Prince, *Classical Film Violence: Designing and Regulating Brutality in Hollywood Cinema, 1930-1968*, 59.

23. "Censor Report—Kansas State Censor Board," December 11, 1931, PCA file, *Frankenstein* (Universal, 1931).

24. Prince, *Classical Film Violence: Designing and Regulating Brutality in Hollywood Cinema, 1930-1968*, 63.

25. "Warning Is Issued by Lightman Against Too Many Horror Films," *The Film Daily*, December 28, 1931, 1, 8.

26. Letter, Joy to Cooper, February 21, 1931, PCA file, *Little Caesar* (Warner Bros/ First National, 1931).

27. Letter, Joy to Hays, January 11, 1931, PCA file, *Frankenstein* (Universal, 1931).

28. "Memo—Payne Fund Studies," August 5, 1931, MPPDA Digital Archive, accessed December 16, 2015, http://mppda.flinders.edu.au/records/753.

29. Herbert Blumer, *Movies and Conduct* (New York: The McMillan Company, 1933), 79.

30. "Record of Conference," May 29, 1931, MPPDA Digital Archive, accessed December 16, 2015, http://mppda.flinders.edu.au/records/754.

31. "Censor Report—Kansas State Censor Board," December 11, 1931, PCA file, *Frankenstein* (Universal, 1931).

32. Prince, *Classical Film Violence: Designing and Regulating Brutality in Hollywood Cinema, 1930-1968*, 68.

33. Letter, Joy to Laemmle, January 8, 1932, PCA file, *Murders in the Rue Morgue* (Universal, 1931).

34. "Censor Reports," PCA file, *Murders in the Rue Morgue* (Universal, 1931).

35. Letter, Skinner to Joy, February 20, 1932, PCA file, *Murders in the Rue Morgue* (Universal, 1931).

36. Memo, Pettijohn to Hart and Joy, February 26, 1932, PCA file, *Murders in the Rue Morgue* (Universal, 1931).

37. Edwards, "Morals, Markets and 'Horror Pictures,'" 34.

38. Letter, Joy to Singerman, June 27, 1932, PCA file, *The Old Dark House* (Universal, 1932).

39. "Report," Joy to Hays, undated, PCA file, *Island of Lost Souls* (Paramount, 1932).

40. Letter, Trotti to Warner, May 16, 1932, PCA file, *Dr. X* (Warner Bros./First National, 1932).

41. Letter, Joy to Zanuck, March 21, 1932, PCA file, *Dr. X* (Warner Bros./First National, 1932).

42. Letter, Trotti to Selznick, May 9, 1932, PCA file, *The Most Dangerous Game* (RKO, 1932).

43. Letter, Joy to Selznick, July 22, 1932, PCA file, *The Most Dangerous Game* (RKO, 1932).

44. Letter, Trotti to Laemmle, April 16, 1932, PCA file, *The Invisible Man* (Universal, 1933).

45. Letter, Wingate to Laemmle, January 5, 1933, PCA file, *The Invisible Man* (Universal, 1933).

46. Letter, Wingate to Zehner, June 15, 1933, PCA file, *The Invisible Man* (Universal, 1933).

47. Letter, Joy to Laemmle, July 28, 1932, PCA file, *The Mummy* (Universal, 1932).

48. Letter, Joy to Zanuck, September 27, 1932, PCA file, *Mystery of the Wax Museum* (Warner Bros./First National, 1932).

49. Prince, *Classical Film Violence: Designing and Regulating Brutality in Hollywood Cinema, 1930-1968*, 73.

50. "1932-1934: Hays, Breen and the PCA," MPPDA Digital Archive, accessed December 28, 2015, http://mppda.flinders.edu.au/history/mppda-history/1932-1934-hays-breen-and-the-pca/

51. Letter, Wingate to Hurley, December 8, 1932, PCA file, *Island of Lost Souls* (Paramount, 1932).
52. Letter, Wingate to Zanuck, December 28, 1932, PCA file, *Mystery of the Wax Museum* (Warner Bros/First National, 1932).
53. Letter, Wingate to Hays, December 30, 1932, PCA file, *Mystery of the Wax Museum* (Warner Bros/First National, 1932).
54. "Review by V.G. Hart," February 6, 1933, PCA file, *Mystery of the Wax Museum* (Warner Bros/First National, 1933).
55. "Chronology of Events and Mppda and Ampp Decisions," June 22, 1934, MPPDA Digital Archive, accessed December 28, 2015, http://mppda.flinders.edu.au/records/1048.
56. Maltby, "More Sinned Against than Sinning: The Fabrications of 'Pre-Code Cinema,'" *Senses of Cinema*.
57. Letter, Hays to Beetson, March 8, 1933, MPPDA Digital Archive, accessed December 28, 2015, http://mppda.flinders.edu.au/records/884.
58. "Chronology of Events and Mppda and Ampp Decisions," June 22, 1934, MPPDA Digital Archive, accessed December 28, 2015, http://mppda.flinders.edu.au/records/1048.
59. Balio, *The American Film Industry*, 270–271.
60. Doherty, *Pre-Code Hollywood: Sex, Immorality, and Insurrection in American Cinema, 1930–1934*, 120.
61. Letter, Breen to Hart, March 13, 1934, MPPDA Digital Archive, accessed December 28, 2015, http://mppda.flinders.edu.au/records/1033.
62. "1932–1934: Hays, Breen and the PCA," MPPDA Digital Archive.
63. Schatz, *The Genius of the System: Hollywood Film-Making in the Studio Era*, 203.
64. "Press Release," July 1, 1934, MPPDA Digital Archive, accessed December 28, 2015, http://mppda.flinders.edu.au/records/2410.
65. Letter, Breen to Kent, September 5, 1934, MPPDA Digital Archive, accessed December 28, 2015, http://mppda.flinders.edu.au/records/1078.
66. Letter, Breen to Hays, February 20th, 1935, MPPDA Digital Archive, accessed December 28, 2015, http://mppda.flinders.edu.au/records/2665.
67. Letter, Breen to Hart, August 13, 1934, MPPDA Digital Archive, accessed December 28, 2015, http://mppda.flinders.edu.au/records/1104.
68. Letter, Breen to Hart, February 21, 1935, MPPDA Digital Archive, accessed December 28, 2015, http://mppda.flinders.edu.au/records/1130.
69. Naylor, '"A Horror Picture at This Time Is a Very Hazardous Undertaking': Did British or American Censorship End the 1930s Horror Cycle?" *The Irish Journal of Gothic and Horror Studies*.
70. Letter, Breen to Hart, February 21, 1935.
71. Letter, Breen to Wingate, April 6, 1935, PCA file, *The Bride of Frankenstein* (Universal, 1935).
72. "Inter-Office Memo," Breen to Hays, September 5, 1935, MPPDA Digital Archive, accessed January 1, 2016, http://mppda.flinders.edu.au/records/1122.
73. Letter, Breen to Zehner, March 26, 1935, PCA file, *The Raven* (Universal, 1935).
74. Letter, Breen to Zehner, April 15, 1935, PCA file, *The Bride of Frankenstein* (Universal, 1935).
75. Letter, Breen to Cohn, March 27, 1935, PCA file, *The Black Room* (Columbia Pictures, 1935).
76. Letter, Breen to Mayer, December 18, 1934, PCA file, *Mark of the Vampire* (MGM, 1935).
77. Letter, Breen to Mayer, March 27, 1935, PCA file, *Mark of the Vampire* (MGM, 1935).
78. Letter, Halperin to Breen, January 21, 1936, PCA file, *Revolt of the Zombies* (Academy Pictures Distributing Company, 1936).
79. Naylor, '"A Horror Picture at This Time Is a Very Hazardous Undertaking': Did British or American Censorship End the 1930s Horror Cycle?" *The Irish Journal of Gothic and Horror Studies*.
80. Letter, Breen to Warner, September 26, 1935, PCA file, *The Walking Dead* (Warner Bros/First National, 1936).
81. Letter, Breen to Hays, September 4, 1935, MPPDA Digital Archive, accessed January 1, 2016, http://mppda.flinders.edu.au/records/2568.
82. Naylor, '"A Horror Picture at This Time Is a Very Hazardous Undertaking': Did British or American Censorship End the 1930s Horror Cycle?" *The Irish Journal of Gothic and Horror Studies*.
83. Letter, Breen to Mayer, September 13, 1935, PCA file, *The Devil Doll* (MGM, 1936).
84. Telegram, Blum to Marx, November 11, 1935, PCA file, *The Devil Doll* (MGM, 1936).
85. Cited in Naylor, '"A Horror Picture at This Time Is a Very Hazardous Undertaking': Did British or American Censorship End the 1930s Horror Cycle?" *The Irish Journal of Gothic and Horror Studies*.
86. Letter, Breen to Mayer, April 7, 1936, PCA file, *The Devil Doll* (MGM, 1936).
87. Letter, Breen to Zehner, March 22, 1938, PCA file, *The Invisible Man Returns* (Universal, 1940).
88. Prince, *Classical Film Violence: Designing and Regulating Brutality in Hollywood Cinema, 1930–1968*, 84–85.
89. Letter, Hays to Milliken, January 5, 1935, MPPDA Digital Archive, accessed January 1, 2016, http://mppda.flinders.edu.au/records/2691.
90. *Ibid.*
91. Letter, Breen to Hays, June 21, 1935, PCA file, *Dr. Jekyll and Mr. Hyde* (Paramount, 1931).
92. Letter, Breen to Hammell, June 22, 1935, PCA file, *Dr. Jekyll and Mr. Hyde* (Paramount, 1931).
93. Letter, Breen to Hammell, September 18, 1935, PCA file, *Murders in the Zoo* (Paramount, 1933).
94. Letter, Hart to Krellberg, June 4, 1936, PCA file, *White Zombie* (United Artists, 1932).
95. Letter, Breen to Zehner, October 2, 1936, PCA file, *Murders in the Rue Morgue* (Universal, 1931).
96. "The Production Code in Operation," MPPDA Digital Archive, accessed December 14, 2015, http://mppda.flinders.edu.au/history/mppda-history/1934–1939-the-production-code-in-operation/
97. Letter, Breen to Zehner, June 9, 1937, PCA file, *Frankenstein* (Universal, 1931).
98. Scott MacQueen DVD commentary, *Bride of Frankenstein*, 2008, Universal Studios.
99. Letter, Breen to Harmon, March 9, 1938, PCA file, *Dracula* (Universal, 1931).
100. Letter, Harmon to Miller, March 17, 1938, PCA file, *Dracula* (Universal, 1931).

101. Rhodes, *Tod Browning's Dracula*, 307.
102. Letter, Hart to Breen, August 25, 1937, PCA file, *Dr. X* (Warner Bros/First National, 1932).
103. "Reviewer Notes—Reissue," undated, PCA file, *Island of Lost Souls* (Paramount, 1933).
104. Letter, Breen to Vandervoort, November 26, 1938, PCA file, *Dracula* (Universal, 1931).

Chapter 4

1. Prince, *Classical Film Violence: Designing and Regulating Brutality in Hollywood Cinema, 1930–1968*, 73.
2. *Ibid.*, 85.
3. *Dracula* Pressbook, Universal Studio Collection, USC.
4. Stein, "Tod Browning," *Cinema: A Critical Dictionary*, 159.
5. Quoted in Curtis, *James Whale: A New World of Gods and Monsters*, 154–155.
6. Balderston, "Treatment," in Riley, *James Whale's Dracula's Daughter*, 19.
7. Thomas R. Atkins, "Dr. Jekyll and Mr. Hyde—An Interview with Rouben Mamoulian," The Film Journal, Vol. 2, no. 2 (January-March, 1973): 40.
8. *Ibid.*, 38.
9. *Ibid.*, 39.
10. Herbert Schwab, "On the Graveyards of Europe: The Horror of Modernism in 'The Black Cat,'" in Bernd Herzogenrath (ed.), *The Films of Edgar G. Ulmer* (Lanham, MD: The Scarecrow, 2009), 39.
11. Taves, *Robert Florey: The French Expressionist*, 141–146.
12. *Ibid.*, 124.
13. *Ibid.*, 67.
14. Richard J. Hand and Michael Wilson, *Grand-Guignol: The French Theatre of Horror* (Exeter: University of Exeter Press, 2015), 5.
15. *Ibid.*; 5–6; see also, Mel Gordon, *Grand Guignol: Theatre of Fear and Terror* (New York: Perseus Book Group, 1997).
16. Hand and Wilson, *Grand-Guignol: The French Theatre of Horror*, 3.
17. Agnès Pierron, "House of Horrors," *Grand Street Magazine*, 57 (Summer 1996), 98.
18. Richard J. Hand and Michael Wilson, "The Grand-Guignol: Aspects of Theory and Practice," *Theatre Research International*, Vol. 25, no. 3 (Autumn, 2000), accessed on-line, January 19, 2016, http://www.grandguignol.com/tri_5.htm.
19. Richard J. Hand and Michael Wilson, *London's Grand Guignol and the Theatre of Horror* (Exeter: University of Exeter Press, 2007), 4.
20. Curtis, *James Whale: A New World of Gods and Monsters*, 47–48.
21. Hand and Wilson, "The Grand-Guignol: Aspects of Theory and Practice," accessed January 19, 2016, http://www.grandguignol.com/tri_2.htm.
22. *Ibid.*, accessed January 20, 2016, http://www.grandguignol.com/tri_3.htm.
23. Quoted in František Deák, "Théâtre Du Grand Guignol." *The Drama Review*, Vol. 18, no. 1 (March 1974), 38.
24. Hand and Wilson, "The Grand-Guignol: Aspects of Theory and Practice," accessed January 19, 2016, http://www.grandguignol.com/tri_3.htm.
25. *Ibid.*, accessed January 19, 2016, http://www.grandguignol.com/tri_4.htm.
26. Taves, *Robert Florey: The French Expressionist*, 13.
27. Agnès Pierron, "House of Horrors," *Grand Street Magazine*, 57 (Summer 1996), 97.
28. Hand and Wilson, "The Grand-Guignol: Aspects of Theory and Practice," accessed January 19, 2016, http://www.grandguignol.com/tri_3.htm.
29. Rhodes, *Tod Browning's Dracula*, 319.
30. Ivan Butler, *The Horror Film* (London: The Tantivy Press, 1967), 40.
31. Hand and Wilson, "The Grand-Guignol: Aspects of Theory and Practice," accessed January 19, 2016, http://www.grandguignol.com/tri_2.htm.
32. Prince, *Classical Film Violence: Designing and Regulating Brutality in Hollywood Cinema, 1930–1968*, 57.
33. For a more detailed analysis of this scene, see my essay, "'An Abomination on the Silver Sheet': In Defence of Tod Browning's Skill as a Director in the Sound Era (On 'Freaks')," *Bright Lights Film Journal*, http://brightlightsfilm.com/tod-browning-director-in-the-sound-era-analysis-of-the-opening-of-freaks/
34. "Talkers to Develop Own School, Is Contention," *The Film Daily*, August 26, 1928, 11.
35. "Censor Report—Kansas State Censor Board," December 11, 1931, PCA file, *Frankenstein* (Universal, 1931).
36. Edwards, *Corporate Fictions: Film Adaptation and Authorship in the Classical Hollywood Era*, 214.
37. *Ibid.*, 248.
38. Prince, *Classical Film Violence: Designing and Regulating Brutality in Hollywood Cinema, 1930–1968*, 230.
39. *Ibid.*, 76.
40. *Ibid.*, 74.
41. Letter, Beetson to Laemmle, October 13, 1931, PCA file, *Murders in the Rue Morgue* (Universal, 1932).
42. Letter, Breen to Zehner, February 26, 1934, PCA file, *The Black Cat* (Universal, 1934).
43. Letter, Breen to Zehner, January 15, 1935, PCA file, *Werewolf of London* (Universal, 1935).
44. Letter, Wingate to Hays, October 28, 1932, PCA file, *Mask of Fu Manchu* (MGM, 1932).
45. Letter, Breen to Zehner, January 15, 1935, PCA file, *Werewolf of London* (Universal, 1935).
46. "Memorandum," February 7, 1935, PCA file, *Werewolf of London* (Universal, 1935).
47. Angela M. Smith, *Hideous Progeny: Disability, Eugenics and Classic Horror Cinema* (New York: Columbia University Press, 2012), 3.
48. Prince, *Classical Film Violence: Designing and Regulating Brutality in Hollywood Cinema, 1930–1968*, 54.
49. George Ochoa, *Deformed and Destructive Beings: The Purpose of Horror Films* (Jefferson, N.C: McFarland and Company, 2011), 1.
50. "Memorandum," March 14, 1935, PCA file, *The Raven* (Universal, 1935).
51. Islin Auster, "Resume," March 16, 1935, PCA file, *The Raven* (Universal, 1935).
52. "Memorandum," March 14, 1935, PCA file, *The Raven* (Universal, 1935).
53. Tudor, *Monsters and Mad Scientists: A Cultural History of the Horror Film*, 33.

54. Hand and Wilson, "The Grand-Guignol: Aspects of Theory and Practice," accessed January 19, 2016, http://www.grandguignol.com/tri_4.htm.
55. Tudor, *Monsters and Mad Scientists: A Cultural History of the Horror Film*, 188–189.
56. Ibid., 189.
57. "Sadism," *Oxford Dictionaries*, accessed January 31, 2016, http://www.oxforddictionaries.com/definition/english/sadism.
58. Lindsay Anne Hallam, *Screening the Marquis De Sade: Pleasure, Pain and the Transgressive Body in Film* (Jefferson, N.C: McFarland and Company, 2012), 63.
59. Ibid., 1.

Chapter 5

1. Tudor, *Monsters and Mad Scientists: A Cultural History of the Horror Film*, 28.
2. Pinedo, *Recreational Terror: Women and the Pleasures of Horror Film Viewing*, 29.
3. Wood, "The American Nightmare: Horror in the 70s," *Hollywood from Vietnam to Reagan ... And Beyond*, 78.
4. See for example, Doherty, *Pre-Code Hollywood: Sex, Immorality, and Insurrection in American Cinema, 1930–1934*, 295–318; Matthews Jnr., *Fear Itself: Horror on Screen and in Reality During the Depression and World War 2*, 75–94.
5. See Colin Campbell, "On Intellectual Life, Politics and Psychoanalysis: A Conversation with Gad Horowitz," Ctheory.Net, accessed October 8, 2012 http://www.ctheory.net/articles.aspx?id=397.
6. See also Denis Gifford, *A Pictorial History of Horror Movies* (London: Hamlyn, 1973).
7. Alfred Hitchcock, "Why 'Thrillers' Thrive," *Picturegoer*, January 18, 1936, 15.
8. See Richard Maltby, *Hollywood Cinema: An Introduction* (Cambridge: Blackwell, 1995), 418.
9. David Flint, *Sheer Filth: Bizarre Cinema, Weird Literature, Strange Music, Extreme Art* (Godalming: Fab Press, 2014), 4–5.
10. Butler, *The Horror Film*, 11.
11. Ibid., 12–13.
12. Ibid., 50.
13. Ibid., 43.
14. Ibid., 17.
15. Everson, *Classics of the Horror Film*, 2.
16. Ibid., 3.
17. Ibid., 5–6.
18. Ibid., 5.
19. Ibid., 74–76.
20. Ibid., 98–103.
21. Ibid., 106.
22. Ibid., 95.
23. Ibid., 85.
24. Ibid., 123.
25. Ibid., 131.
26. Ibid., 115.
27. Ibid., 219.
28. Maltby, *Hollywood Cinema: An Introduction*, 422.
29. Wood, "The American Nightmare: Horror in the 70s," *Hollywood from Vietnam to Reagan ... And Beyond*, 68.
30. Wood, "Horror in the 80s," *Hollywood from Vietnam to Reagan ... And Beyond*, 170.
31. Wood, "The American Nightmare: Horror in the 70s," *Hollywood from Vietnam to Reagan ... And Beyond*, 78.
32. Tudor, *Monsters and Mad Scientists: A Cultural History of the Horror Film*, 214.
33. Ibid., 103.
34. Ibid., 223.
35. Ibid., 219.
36. Tom Milne, "Children of the Night: Ghouls, Vampires, Werewolves, Monsters and Mutants," *the Movie: The Illustrated History of the Cinema*, Vol. 1, no. 6, 1979, 105.
37. Peter Hutchings, *The Horror Film* (Harlow: Pearson, 2004), 176.
38. Pinedo, *Recreational Terror: Women and the Pleasures of Horror Film Viewing*, 22.
39. Ibid., 14.
40. Harry M. Benshoff and Sean Griffin, *America on Film: Representing Race, Class, Gender, and Sexuality at the Movies* (Oxford: Blackwell, 2004), 30–31.
41. Ibid., 39.
42. Angela Ndalianis, *The Horror Film Sensorium* (Jefferson, N.C: McFarland, 2012), 16–17.
43. Jean-Louis Comolli and Jean Narboni, "Cinema/Criticism," in Bill Nichols (ed.), *Movies and Methods: Vol 1* (Berkeley: University of California Press, 1976), 24.
44. Ibid., 25.
45. Ibid., 27.
46. Robin Wood, "Ideology, Genre, Auteur," in Barry Keith Grant (ed.), Film *Reader II* (Austin: University of Texas Press, 1995), 63.
47. Barbara Klinger, "'Cinema/Ideology/Criticism' Revisited: The Progressive Text," in *Screen*, 25 (1), 1984, 33.
48. Ibid., 42–43.
49. Ibid., 35–36.
50. Ibid., 37.
51. Ibid., 38–39.
52. Ibid., 44.
53. See Tag Gallagher, "Shoot-Out at the Genre Corral: Problems in the Evolution of the Western," in Barry Keith Grant (ed.), Film *Reader IV* (Austin: University of Texas Press, 2012), 298–312.
54. Maltby, *Hollywood Cinema: An Introduction*, 446.
55. Doherty, *Pre-Code Hollywood: Sex, Immorality, and Insurrection in American Cinema, 1930–1934*, 295–318.
56. Ibid., 17–19.
57. Ibid., 296–297.
58. Prince, *Classical Film Violence: Designing and Regulating Brutality in Hollywood Cinema, 1930–1968*, 85.
59. Hutchings, *The Horror Film*, 176.
60. Ibid., 177.
61. Phillips, *Projected Fears: Horror Films and American Culture*, 32.
62. Hutchings, *The Horror Film*, 178.
63. Linda Williams, "When the Woman Looks," in Barry Keith Grant (ed.), *The Dread of Difference: Gender and the Horror Film* (Austin: University of Texas Press, 2015), 23.
64. Berenstein, *Attack of the Leading Ladies: Gender, Sexuality, and Spectatorship in Classic Horror Cinema*, 58.

65. *Ibid.*, 5.
66. *Ibid.*, 31.
67. Reynold Humphries, *The Hollywood Horror Film, 1931–1941: Madness in a Social Landscape* (Lanham: Maryland, 2006), xiv.
68. *Ibid.*, 63.
69. *Ibid.*, 91–92.
70. Hand and Wilson, "The Grand-Guignol: Aspects of Theory and Practice," accessed January 19, 2016, http://www.grandguignol.com/tri_4.htm.
71. Humphries, *The Hollywood Horror Film, 1931–1941: Madness in a Social Landscape,* 262.

Bibliography

Aldgate, Anthony, and James C. Robertson. *Censorship in Theatre and Cinema*. Edinburgh: Edinburgh University Press, 2005.

Atkins, Thomas R. "Dr. Jekyll and Mr. Hyde: An Interview with Rouben Mamoulian." *The Film Journal*, Vol. 2, no. 2 (January–March 1973), 36–44.

Balderston, John, and Garrett Fort. *Frankenstein: A Play*. Albany, GA: Bear Manor Media, 2010.

Balio, Tino. *The American Film Industry*, rev. ed. Madison: University of Wisconsin Press, 1985.

Benshoff, Harry M., and Sean Griffin. *America on Film: Representing Race, Class, Gender, and Sexuality at the Movies*. Oxford: Blackwell, 2004.

Berenstein, Rhona J. *Attack of the Leading Ladies: Gender, Sexuality, and Spectatorship in Classic Horror Cinema*. New York: Columbia University Press, 1996.

Black, Gregory D. *Hollywood Censored: Morality Codes, Catholics, and the Movies*. Cambridge: Cambridge University Press, 1996.

Blumer, Herbert. *Movies and Conduct*. New York: Macmillan, 1933.

Bogdanovich, Peter. "Edgar G. Ulmer Interview." *Film Culture*, 58–60 (1974), 190–205.

Bordwell, David. *The Classical Hollywood Cinema: Film Style & Mode of Production to 1960*. London: Routledge, 1985.

Butler, Ivan. *The Horror Film*. London: The Tantivy Press, 1967.

Campbell, Colin. "On Intellectual Life, Politics, and Psychoanalysis: A Conversation with Gad Horowitz." *Ctheory.Net*. Accessed October 8, 2012, http://www.ctheory.net/articles.aspx?id=397

"A Chat with Laemmle Jr." *New York Times*, April 3, 1932. Accessed January 29, 2015, http://timesmachine.nytimes.com/timesmachine/1932/04/03/100708691.html.

Clarens, Carlos. *Horror Movies: An Illustrated Survey*. London: Panther Books, 1971.

Comolli, Jean-Louis, and Jean Narboni. "Cinema/Ideology/Criticism." In Bill Nichols, ed., *Movies and Methods: Vol. 1*, 22–30. Berkeley: University of California Press, 1976.

Cook, Page. "Franz Waxman." *Films in Review*, Vol. 19, no. 7 (August-September 1968), 414–419.

Curtis, James. *James Whale: A New World of Gods and Monsters*. London: Faber, 1998.

Deák, František. "Théâtre Du Grand Guignol." *The Drama Review*, Vol. 18, no. 1 (March 1974), 34–43.

Doherty, Thomas. "Hollywood and the Production Code." Accessed November 6, 2015, http://microformguides.gale.com/Data/Introductions/32730FM.htm

_____. *Pre-Code Hollywood: Sex, Immorality, and Insurrection in American Cinema, 1930-1934*. New York: Columbia University Press, 1999.

Edwards, Kyle. *Corporate Fictions: Film Adaptation and Authorship in the Classical Hollywood Era*. University of Texas, 2006, Ph.D. dissertation.

_____. "Morals, Markets, and 'Horror Pictures': The Rise of Universal Pictures and the Hollywood Production Code." *Film & History: An Interdisciplinary Journal* 42, no. 2 (Fall 2012), 23–37.

_____. "'House of Horrors': Corporate Strategy at Universal Pictures in the 1930s." In Richard Nowell, ed., *Merchants of Menace: The Business of Horror Cinema*, 13–29. London: Bloomsbury, 2014.

Everson, William K. *Classics of the Horror Film*. Secaucus, NJ: Citadel Press, 1974.

Flint, David. *Sheer Filth: Bizarre Cinema, Weird Literature, Strange Music, Extreme Art*. Godalming: Fab Press, 2014.

Flynn, John L. *Cinematic Vampires: The Living Dead on Film and Television, from the Devil's Castle (1896) to Bram Stoker's Dracula*. Jefferson, NC: McFarland, 1992.

Gallagher, Tag. "Shoot-Out at the Genre Corral: Problems in the Evolution of the Western." In Barry Keith Grant, ed., *Film Reader IV*, 298–312. Austin: University of Texas Press, 2012.

Garside, W.R. *British Unemployment 1919-1939: A Study in Public Policy*. Cambridge: Cambridge University Press, 1990.

Gasten, David. "*Freaks* Script Synopsis and Footnotes." *Olga Baclanova: The Ultimate Cinemantrap*. Accessed September 8, 2015, http://www.olgabaclanova.com/freaks_script_synopsis.htm.

Gifford, Denis. *A Pictorial History of Horror Movies*. London: Hamlyn, 1973.

Gomery, Douglas. *The Hollywood Studio System: A History*. London: British Film Institute, 2005.

Gordon, Mel. *Grand Guignol: Theatre of Fear and Terror*. New York: Perseus Book Group, 1997.

Hallam, Lindsay Anne. *Screening the Marquis De Sade:*

Pleasure, Pain and the Transgressive Body in Film. Jefferson, NC: McFarland, 2012.

Hand, Richard J., and Michael Wilson. "The Grand-Guignol: Aspects of Theory and Practice." *Theatre Research International*, Vol. 25, no. 3 (Autumn 2000), 266–275.

_____. *Grand-Guignol: The French Theatre of Horror*. Exeter: University of Exeter Press, 2015.

_____. *London's Grand Guignol and the Theatre of Horror*. Exeter: University of Exeter Press, 2007.

Hantke, Steffen. "Capitalist Horrors." *Other Voices: The Ejournal of Cultural Criticism*, Vol. 3, No.1 (May 2007). Accessed November 22, 2014, http://www.othervoices.org/3.1/shantke/index.php.

Harris, Robert A. "RAH on King Kong." *The Digital Bits: Celebrating Film in the Digital Age*, October 25, 2005. Accessed October 22, 2015, http://www.thedigitalbits.com/site_archive/articles/robertharris/harris102505.html.

Humphries, Reynold. *The Hollywood Horror Film, 1931–1941: Madness in a Social Landscape*. Lanham, MD: Scarecrow, 2006.

Hunter, Russ. "Gothic Horror." In Philip Kemp, ed., *Cinema: The Whole Story*, 90–91. London: Thames and Hudson, 2011

Hutchings, Peter. *The Horror Film*. Harlow: Pearson, 2004.

Jacobs, Stephen. *Boris Karloff: More Than a Monster—The Authorised Biography*. Sheffield: Tomahawk Press, 2010.

Jancovich, Mark "'Hot Profits Out of Cold Shivers!': Horror, the First-run Market, and the Hollywood Studios, 1938 to 1942." In Richard Nowell, ed., *Merchants of Menace: The Business of Horror Cinema*, 163–185. New York: Bloomsbury, 2014.

Johnson, Tom. *Censored Screams: The British Ban on Hollywood Horror in the Thirties*. Jefferson, NC: McFarland, 1997.

Kirby, David A. "The Devil in Our DNA: A Brief History of Eugenics in Science Fiction Films." *Literature and Medicine*, Vol. 26, no. 1 (Spring 2007), 83–108.

Klinger, Barbara. "'Cinema/Ideology/Criticism' Revisited: The Progressive Text." *Screen*, Vol. 25, no. 1 (1984), 33–44.

Koszarski, Richard, ed. *Mystery of the Wax Museum*. Madison: University of Wisconsin Press, 1979.

Kuhn, Annette. "History of the Cinema: American Film Industry." In Pam Cook, ed., *The Cinema Book*, 3–24. London: British Film Institute, 1985.

Lennig, Arthur. *The Immortal Count: The Life and Films of Bela Lugosi*. Lexington: University Press of Kentucky, 2003.

MacDowell, James. *Happy Endings in Hollywood Cinema: Cliché, Convention and the Final Couple*. Edinburgh: Edinburgh University Press, 2013.

MacQueen, Scott. "The Mystery of the Wax Museum." *American Cinematographer*, Vol. 71, no. 4 (April 1990), 42–50.

Maddrey, Joseph. *Nightmares in Red, White and Blue: The Evolution of the American Horror Film*. Jefferson, NC: McFarland, 2004.

Maltby, Richard. *Hollywood Cinema: An Introduction*. Cambridge: Blackwell, 1995.

_____. "More Sinned Against than Sinning: The Fabrications of 'Pre-Code Cinema.'" *Senses of Cinema*, Issue 29 (December 2003). Accessed October, 22, 2014, http://sensesofcinema.com/2003/feature-articles/pre_code_cinema/

Mank, Gregory William. *Bela Lugosi and Boris Karloff: The Expanded Story of a Haunting Collaboration*. Jefferson, NC: McFarland, 2009.

_____. *Hollywood Cauldron: Thirteen Horror Films from the Genre's Golden Age*. Jefferson, NC: McFarland, 1994.

Marx, Samuel. "Screenwriters: The Hacks, Wordsmiths, and Literary Giants Who Invaded the New Soundstages of Hollywood." *The Movie: The Illustrated History of the Cinema*, Vol. 1, No.8 (1979), 156–159.

Matthews, Melvin E., Jr. *Fear Itself: Horror on Screen and in Reality During the Depression and World War II*. Jefferson, NC: McFarland, 2009.

McElwee, John. "Pre-Code Horror—Mystery of the Wax Museum." *Greenbriar Picture Shows*, April 12, 2008. Accessed October 9, 2015, http://greenbriarpictureshows.blogspot.co.uk/2008/04/pre-code-horror-mystery-of-wax-museum.html

Miller, John M. "Murders in the Zoo." *Turner Classic Movies*. Accessed 18 August, 2015.http://www.tcm.com/this-month/article/253085%7C0/Murders-in-the-Zoo.html.

Milne, Tom. "Children of the Night: Ghouls, Vampires, Werewolves, Monsters, and Mutants." *The Movie: The Illustrated History of the Cinema*, Vol. 1, no. 6 (1979), 103–108.

_____. *Rouben Mamoulian* [Cinema One series]. London: BFI/Thames and Hudson, 1969.

Naylor, Alex. "'A Horror Picture at This Time Is a Very Hazardous Undertaking': Did British or American Censorship End the 1930s Horror Cycle?" *The Irish Journal of Gothic and Horror Studies*, Issue 9 (February 2011). Accessed November, 20, 2013, http://irishgothichorrorjournal.homestead.com/1930shorrorbanprinter.html.

Ndalianis, Angela. *The Horror Sensorium: Media and the Senses*. Jefferson, NC: McFarland, 2012.

Nollen, Scott Allen. *Boris Karloff: A Critical Account of His Screen, Stage, Television, Radio and Recording Work*. Jefferson, NC: McFarland, 1991.

Ochoa, George. *Deformed and Destructive Beings: The Purpose of Horror Films*. Jefferson, NC: McFarland, 2011.

Phillips, Kendall R. *Projected Fears: Horror Films and American Culture*. Westport, CT: Praeger, 2005.

Pierron, Agnès. "House of Horrors," *Grand Street Magazine*, 57 (Summer 1996): 95–99.

Pinedo, Isabel Cristina. *Recreational Terror: Women and the Pleasures of Horror Film Viewing*. Albany: State University of New York, 1997.

Prince, Stephen. *Classical Film Violence: Designing and Regulating Brutality in Hollywood Cinema, 1930–1968*. New Brunswick: Rutgers University Press, 2003.

Rhodes, Gary D. *Lugosi: His Life in Films, on Stage, and in the Hearts of Horror Lovers.* Jefferson, N.C: McFarland, 1997.

_____. *Tod Browning's Dracula.* Sheffield: Tomahawk Press, 2014.

_____. "'Tremonstrous' Hopes and 'Oke' Results: The 1934 Reception of 'The Black Cat.'" In Gary D. Rhodes, ed., *Edgar G. Ulmer: Detour on Poverty Row,* 301–322. Lanham, MD: Lexington Books, 2008.

Riley, Philip J, ed. *Boris Karloff as the Invisible Man.* Albany, GA: Bear Manor Media, 2011.

_____. *Cagliostro: The Great Imposter.* Albany, G.A: Bear Manor Media, 2009.

_____. *Dracula: The Original 1931 Shooting Script.* Absecon, NJ: Magic Image, 1990.

_____. *James Whale's Dracula's Daughter: An Alternative History for Classic Film Monsters.* Albany, GA: Bear Manor Media, 2009.

_____. *The Return of Frankenstein.* Duncan, OK: Bear Manor Media, 2012.

_____. *Robert Florey's Frankenstein Starring Bela Lugosi.* Albany, GA: Bear Manor Media, 2010.

Robertson, James C. *The British Board of Film Censors: Film Censorship in Britain, 1896–1950.* London: Croom Helm, 1985.

_____. *The Hidden Cinema: British Film Censorship in Action, 1913- 1975.* London: Routledge, 1989, reprint 1993.

Robinson, David. "King Kong." *The Movie: The Illustrated History of the Cinema,* Vol. 1, no. 6 (1979), 114–5.

Savada, Elias. "The Making of Freaks." *Olga Baclanova: The Ultimate Cinemantrap.* Accessed November 30, 2014, http://www.olgabaclanova.com/the_making_of_freaks.htm

Schaefer, Eric. *Bold! Daring! Shocking! True! A History of Exploitation Films 1919–1959.* Durham: Duke University Press, 1999.

Schatz, Thomas. *The Genius of the System: Hollywood Film-Making in the Studio Era.* London: Faber, 1998.

Schwab, Herbert. "On the Graveyards of Europe: The Horror of Modernism in 'The Black Cat.'" In Bernd Herzogenrath (ed.), *The Films of Edgar G. Ulmer,* 39–52. Lanham, MD: Scarecrow, 2009.

Senn, Bryan. *Golden Horrors: An Illustrated Critical Filmography of Terror Cinema, 1931–1939.* Jefferson, NC: McFarland, 1996.

Skal, David J. *Hollywood Gothic: The Tangled Web of Dracula from Novel to Stage to Screen.* London: Andre Deutsch Ltd., 1992.

_____. *The Monster Show: A Cultural History of Horror.* London: Plexus, 1993.

Skal, David J., and Elias Savada. *Dark Carnival: The Secret World of Tod Browning, Hollywood's Master of the Macabre.* New York: Anchor Books, 1995.

Smith, Angela M. *Hideous Progeny: Disability, Eugenics and Classic Horror Cinema.* New York: Columbia University Press, 2012.

Stein, Elliot. "Tod Browning." In Richard Roud, ed., *Cinema: A Critical Dictionary,* 156–166. London: Secker & Warburg, 1980.

Taves, Brian. *Robert Florey: The French Expressionist.* Duncan, OK: Bear Manor Media, 2014.

Totaro, Donato. "Monsters, Mad Scientists, and Cultural Contexts of Horror." *Offscreen,* Vol. 17, 6–7 (July 2013). Accessed November, 20, 2013, http://offscreen.com/view/monsters_mad_scientists.

Towlson, Jon. "'An Abomination on the Silver Sheet': In Defence of Tod Browning's Skill as a Director in the Sound Era (On 'Freaks')." *Bright Lights Film Journal.* http://brightlightsfilm.com/tod-browning-director-in-the-sound-era-analysis-of-the-opening-of-freaks/.

Tudor, Andrew. *Monsters and Mad Scientists: A Cultural History of the Horror Film.* Oxford: Basil Blackwell, 1989.

Vieira, Mark A. *Hollywood Horror: From Gothic to Cosmic.* New York: Harry N. Abrams, 2003.

Weaver, Tom, Michael Brunas, and John Brunas. *Universal Horrors: The Studio's Classic Horror Films, 1931–1946,* 2d ed. Jefferson, NC: McFarland, 2007.

Williams, Linda. "When the Woman Looks." In Barry Keith Grant (ed.), *The Dread of Difference: Gender and the Horror Film,* 17–36. Austin: University of Texas Press, 2015.

Wood, Robin. *Hollywood from Vietnam to Reagan … and Beyond.* New York: Columbia University Press, 2003.

_____. "Ideology, Genre, Auteur." In Barry Keith Grant (ed.), *Film Reader II,* 59–73. Austin: University of Texas Press, 1995

Worland, Rick. *The Horror Film: An Introduction.* Oxford: Blackwell Publishing, 2007.

Wray, Fay. "King Kong's Girl." *The Movie: The Illustrated History of the Cinema,* Vol. 1, no. 6 (1979), 116.

Index

Numbers in **bold italics** refer to pages with photographs.

Abbott and Costello Meet Frankenstein (1948) 8
Academy of Motion Pictures Arts and Sciences 22, 86
Advertising Code 19, 152
Afraid to Talk aka *Merry-Go-Round* (1932) 80
After Dracula (book) 82
Airmail (1932) 83
The Airmail Mystery (film serial) 23
Alberta Censor Board 73, 117, 122
Alicoate, Jack 28
All Quiet of the Western Front (1930) 19, 21, 46
Almost Married (1932) 28, 34, 145
American Cinematographer (journal) 80
American Film Institute 97
"The American Nightmare" (Wood) 3, 15, 191
Anderson, Lindsay 180
Andrews, George Reid 23
Angkor (1937) 64
Antoine, André 167
Arbuckle, Roscoe 142
As You Desire Me (1932) 74
Asher, E.M. 42, 46, 47, 103, 104, 108, 137
Assembly Bill 22
Atkins, Thomas 166
Atlanta Constitution (newspaper) 26
Attack of the Leading Ladies (book) 3, 6, 199
Atwill, Lionel 34, 88, 89, *92*, 98, *98*, 99, 187
Au téléphone (play) 171
Auster, Islin 105, 112, 116, 120

Baby Face Nelson 23
Baby Faced Gangster (unproduced film) 23
Baily, Tom 84, 85, 152
Baker, Rick 180
Balderston, John L. 16, 46, 47, 49, 79, 80, 81, 98, 109, 110, 111, 125, 127, 129, 131, 132–133, 165, 166
Baldwin, Earl 65, 66
Balio, Tino 40
Banks, Leslie 71
Barrymore, John 50, 178
Barrymore, Lionel 180

Barton, Charles T. 8
Battling with Buffalo Bill (film serial) 23
Bauche, Henri 169
The Beast with Five Fingers (1946) 170
A Bedtime Story (1933) 84
Beery, Wallace 125
Beetson, Fred 49, 57, 151
Behind the Door (1919) *106*
Behlmer, Rudy 46
Belden, Charles 88, 89
Bennett, Constance 93
Benshoff, Harry M. 193
Berenstein, Rhona J. 3, 6, 197, 199, 200, 202, 204
Bergerman, Stanley 80, 103, 108, 118
Bern, Paul 74
Billboard (journal) 107
Billet, Phil 130
Binet, Alfred 168
The Birds (1963) 186
Birinski, Leo 56
The Black Cat (1934) (aka *House of Doom*) 1, 8, 9, *9*, 10, 12, 13, 16, 36, 37, 38, 83, 101–102, 118, 119, 122, 125, 167, 175, *177*, 181, 182, 189; and the Production Code 104–107; sadism in the screenplay 103–104; shadow-play 176–178; tag ending 13–14, 107–108
The Black Cat (1941) 8
The Black Cat (short story) 102, 103, 107
Blochman, L.G. 109, 110
Blondie Johnson (1933) 150, 178
Blum, Dave 157, 158
Blumer, Herbert 33, 146
Boehm, David 119, 120
Bogdanovich, Peter 103
Bordwell, David 13, 14
Borland, Carol *155*
Born Reckless (1930) 23
Bow, Clara 51
Brabin, Charles 74, 75
Breen, Joseph 2, 7, 10, 11, 18, 29, 37, 63, 64, 67, 73, 79, 86, 87, 100, 104, 105, 106, 110–118, 120–123, 127–133, 135–137, 139, 141–143, 145, 149–158, 160, 161–163, 176, 200; *see also* Production Code Administration

Brenon, Herbert 93
Bride of Frankenstein (1935) 12, 13, 36, 38, 39, 83, 105, 107, *112*, *113*, 108–110, 120, 130, 154, 155, 204; brutality in screenplay 111–114; and Production Code 114–116; revised "happy ending" 12–13, 116–118
Britannia Hospital (1982) 180
British Board of Film Classification (BBFC; previously known as British Board of Film Censors) 10, 67, 86, 96, 97, 101, 107, 123, 125, 130, 134, 135, 137, 139, 153, 156, 157, 158, 159, 187
Bromfield, Louis 42
Brooks, Louise 51
Brown, Herman J. 32
Browning, Tod 4, 6, 8, 13, 20, 41, 42–45, 50, 60, 61, 62, 74, 153, 157, 158, 164, 165, 170–175, 187, 199, 204
Bullet Proof (unproduced script) 24
Buñuel, Luis 52
Burke, Kathleen 36, 85, *98*, 100
Burn Witch Burn (novel) 157
Burnett, W.R. 24
Butler, Ivan 172, 185, 186, 187, 188, 189

The Cabinet of Dr. Caligari (1919) 167, 169, 189
The Cabinet of Dr. Caligari (play) 169
Caesar, Arthur 103
Cagliostro (unproduced film) 56, 79
Cahiers du Cinéma (journal) 190, 194
Cannes Film Festival 64
Čapek, Karel 30
Capone, Al 18
Carter, Leslie 103
Casson, Lewis 168
The Cat and the Canary (1927) 19
Cat People (1942) 124, 180
Censored Screams (book) 5, 15, 16
Chaney, Lon, Sr. 125
Chapin, Robert 157
Choisy, Camille 168
Churchill, Marguerite *157*
Clarens, Carlos 15

227

Clarke, Donald Henderson 23
Clarke, Mae 26
Classical Film Violence: Designing and Regulating Brutality in Hollywood Cinema, 1930-1968 (book) 53, 198
The Classical Hollywood Cinema (book) 13, 101, 188–190
Classics of the Horror Film (book) 15
Clive, Colin 12, 14, 26, 49, *112*, 125, 140
The Code of Ethics for the Production of Motion Pictures 142; *see also* Production Code
Cohn, Harry 155, 156
Columbia Pictures 18, 35, 147, 152, 155
Commission on Freedom of the Press 152
Comolli, Jean-Louis 190, 194–195
Comstock, Harry Warren 60
Congress (American) 17
Congressional Investigating Committee 87
Connell, Richard 60, 67
Considine, John W. 125, 127
Cooper, Jackie 22
Cooper, Merian C. 67, 80, 92, 93, 96, 97
Cowdin, Cheever J. 8
Creelman, James Ashmore 67, 68, 93, 94
Un Crime dans une Maison de Fous (play) 168
Criterion (film distributor) 87
Crowley, Aleister 103
Cunningham, Jack 103
Curtis, James 110, 117, 165
Curtiz, Michael 8, 10, 66, 88, 174

Dade, Frances *43*
The Daily Express (newspaper) 123
Danger Island (film serial) 23
Dark Carnival (book) 61
De Lorde, André 168
DeMille, Cecil B. 3, 16, 98, 132, 164, 181, 203
DeMille, Katherine *154*
Department of Research of the Association of Protestant Denominations 23
La Dernière Torture (play) 171
De Sade, Marquis 183, 202
Detective Story Hour (radio show) 2
Detroit Mirror (newspaper) 24
The Devil Doll (1936) 2, 3, 47, 141, 156, 157, *158*, 159, 170
Les Diaboliques (1954) 168
Diamond, David 119, 120, 121
Diggs, Richard 52
Ditcham, S.F. 135
Dr. Jekyll and Mr. Hyde (1931) 3, 7, 10, 24, 28, 31, 33, 40, 50, 60, 66, 83, 100, 124, 125, 142, 145, 146, 166, *166*, 167, 178–181, 189; and the Hays Code 52–54; off-screen space 172; reissue 160; sexual sadism in script 51–52; "transvection" scenes 178–179; truncation by studio 54–55; withdrawal from distribution 55
Dr. X (film) (*Doctor X*) 7, 32, 33, 40, 60, *66*, 87, 88, 124, 125, 148, 163, 176, 180, 181, 189; and Production Code 65–67; refusal of Production Code Seal of Approval for reissue 163
Doherty, Thomas 6, 7, 33, 34, 39, 63, 76, 79, 84, 92, 94, 114, 124, 142, 184, 197
Douaumont (French fort) 103
Dracula (1931) 2, 3, 5, 6, 8, 17, 19, *20*, 22, 23, 26, 27, 28, 31, 33, 40, *41*, 41–42, 46, 50, 51, 56, 59, 60, 80, 82, 93, 123, 131, 132, 133, 134, 139, 141, 142, 143, 144, 145, 147, 163, 165, 167, 187, 198; marketing campaign 20–21; and narrative closure 199; off-screen space 171–176; and preview-retake system 44–45; and Production Code 43–44; reissue 140, 162; use of sound 174
Dracula's Daughter (1936) 2, 3, 8, 10, 16, 131–133, *138*, 139–141, 156, 159, 165, 166, 198, 200, 204; BBFC censorship of screenplay 134; and Production Code 135–137
Dracula's Guest (short story) 131
Drake, Frances 14, *128*
Dreyer, Carl 81
Dupont, E.A. 81
Dvorak, Geraldine *42*

Earles, Harry 60
The Edgar Allan Poe Mystery Show! (TV show) 124
Edison Company 164
Edwards, Kyle 26, 56, 59, 102, 107, 119, 125, 141, 147, 175
Electrocuting an Elephant (1903) 164
Eliscu, Edward 68
Elizabeth and Mary (unproduced film) 103
Emery, Katherine 188
Endore, Guy 119, 125, 126, 127, 157
Erickson, Carl 89
Esper, Dwain 63, 64, 103
Eugenics 10, 85
Everson, William K. 15, 16, 101, 185–190, 202
Exhibitor's Herald-World (newspaper) 20

Factor, Max 181
Faithless (1932; aka *Tin Foil*) 74
Famous Monsters of Filmland (magazine) 55, 186
Faragoh, Francis Edward 48, 56
Fassbinder, Werner Rainer 14
Fast Workers (1933) 153
Federal Council of Churches of Christ in America 23, 24
Federal Trade Commission 17

The Film Daily (trade newspaper) 6, 21, 22, 24, 26, 27, 28, 31, 32, 34, 36, 37, 38, 66, 80, 86, 89, 91, 101, 102, 107, 119, 122, 125, 129, 174
Film Weekly (journal) 108, 131
First National Pictures 7, 32, 34, 35, 41, 65, 66, 87, 88, 92, 146, 150, 157; *see also* Warner Bros.
Fisher, James B. 52, 54
Fithian, Ted 29, 59, 72
Five Star Final (1931) 65
Flesh (1932) 125
Fletcher, Bramwell *78*, 82
Flint, David 186
Florey, Robert 47, 48, 55, 56, 108, 167, 169, 170, 176
Ford, John 23, 125, 195
Forde, Arthur 36
Fort, Garrett 42, 47, 48, 103, 137, 157
42nd Street (1933) 91
The Four Feathers (1929) 93
Foster, Preston *66*
Fox (studio) 17, 18, 23, 28, 34, 35, 83, 102, 125, 145, 152
Fox, Sidney 23, *30*
Francis, Arlene *58*, 59, *201*
Frankenstein (1931) 1, 2, 6, 7, 13, 21, 22, 23, 24, 27, *27*, 28, 29, 31, 32, 33, 37, 39, 41, 44, 45, *47*, 51, 55, 56, 57, 59, 60, 62, 64, 65, 79, 84, 86, 93, 111, 116, 117, 124, 125, 139, 142, 143, 146, 147, 163, 167, 169, 170, 172, 181, 187, 204; advertising campaign 26; gruesomeness and brutality in script 46–48; "happy ending" 12–13, 48–50; and Hays Code 144–145; reissue 140, 161–162; suture 172–174; use of sound 175
Frankenstein Meets the Wolf Man (1943) 159
Freaks (1932; aka *Nature's Mistakes, The Monster Show, Forbidden Love*) 1, 4, 7, 8, 12, 13, 26, 28, 30, 32, 36, 39, 40, 60–61, 65, *61*, 66, 74, 124, 125, 145, 150, 175, 189, 197, 204; "happy ending" 12–13, 62; suture 173; truncation 62–64
Frenzy (1972) 186
Freund, Karl 5, 79, 80, 81, 82, 83, 124, 125–131
Friedlander, Louis 119, 120, 121
The Front Page (1931) 65
Frye, Dwight *47*, 140

Gallagher, Ted 196
Galsworthy, John 109
Gasten, David 63
The Genius of the System (book) 5, 37, 46
The Ghoul (1933) 96
Gifford, Denis 185, 188
Gift of Gab (1934) 125
Go and Get It (1920) 146
The Gold Bug (short story) 119
Goldbeck, Willis 60, 61, 62
Golden Horrors (book) 75, 118
Gomery, Douglas 8

Index

Gordon, Leon 62, 74, 127
Gordon, Richard 82
The Gorilla (1927) 146
Grainger, James E. 108
Grand Guignol 1, 26, 89, 124, 125, 129, 171, 176, 178, 182, 185–189, 202, 203; *see also* Théâtre du Grand Guignol
The Grand-Guignol: Aspects of Theory and Practice (book) 169
The Great Depression 2, 6, 7, 8, 10, 12, 17, 18, 19, 32, 37, 39, 50, 60, 88, 142, 153, 184, 188, 193, 197, 203
Griffin, Sean 193
Gropper, Milton H. 99

Haberman, Steve 124, 131
Haggard, H. Rider 80
Hall, Mordaunt 26, 91
Hallam, Lindsay Anne 183
Halperin, Victor 156, 160
Hammell, John 85
Hammer 15, 168, 187, 189
Hand, Richard J. 168, 169, 171, 172, 202
The Hands of Orlac (novel) 125
The Hangover Murders (novel) 133
Hanna, John 134, 135
Hansen, Gunnar 1
Hantke, Steffen 17
Happy Endings and Hollywood Cinema (book) 64
Harmon, F.S. 64, 162, 163
Harrington, Curtis 73
Harrison's Reports (trade journal) 66
Hart, Vincent G. 67, 91, 147, 150, 151, 152, 153, 160, 163
Hart, William S., Jr. 61
The Hatchet Man (1932) 32
Hawks, Howard 195
Hays, Will 19, 22, 23, 24, 28, 31, 34, 37, 49, 65, 67, 76, 85, 90, 101, 104, 106, 118, 135, 136, 142, 144–147, 150, 151, 152, 154, 156, 160
Hays Code 16, 27, 52, 54, 71, 136, 141, 142, 184; *see also* Production Code
Hays Office 2, 3, 16, 18, 21–24, 27–29, 33, 39, 42, 48, 53, 63–66, 68, 71, 74, 76, 83, 85, 89–91, 94, 96, 105–107, 118, 135, 136, 141–163; *see also* Production Code Administration; Studio Relations Committee
Heath, Percy 51, 52, 55
Henigson, Henry 48, 108
Heroes of the Law (film serial) 23
Hersholt, Jean 75, 76
Hibbard, Enid 50
Hillyer, Lambert 137
Hinds, Samuel S. 11
Hitchcock, Alfred 185–187, 195
Hitler, Adolf 8, 9, 10, 109
Hix, John 23
Hobhouse, Alan 133
Hobson, Valerie 117
Hoffenstein, Samuel 52, 55

Holden, Gloria 137
Hollywood Cauldron (book) 74
Hollywood Cinema (book) 190
Hollywood Filmograph (trade magazine) 35, 36, 80, 93
The Hollywood Horror Film, 1931–1941: Madness in a Social Landscape (book) 200
Hollywood Reporter (trade newspaper) 57, 71, 79, 92, 93, 100, 101, 117, 129
The Homicide Squad (1931) 23
Hoover, Herbert 197
Hoover Doctrines 184
Hopkins, Miriam 51, **53** 189
Horowitz, Gad 185
The Horror Film (book) 3, 187, 198
Horror Movies: An Illustrated Survey (book) 15
Hostel (2005) 194
Houghton, Arthur 120
House of Dracula (1945) 159
House of Frankenstein (1944) 159
House of Representatives 87
House of Wax (1952) 88, 187
Howard, William K. 136
Hull, Henry 178, 179, **180**
Humphries, Reynold 197, 200, 202
The Hunchback of Notre Dame (1923) 19, 56
Hunter, Russ 51
Hurlbutt, William 109
Hurley, Harold 84, 85
Huston, John 56
Hutchings, Peter 3, 193, 197, 198, 199, 202, 204
Huxley, Sir Julian 85
Hyams, Leila 87

I'm No Angel (1933) 153
The Immortal Count (book) 43
Impatient Maiden (1931) 23, 147
Independent Exhibitors Film Bulletin (trade newspaper) 130
Ingagi (1931) 84
The International Photographer (newspaper) 88
The Invisible Man (1933) 38, 47, 56, 79, 96, 102, 107, 109, 110, 133, 139, 148, **149**, 159, 167
The Invisible Ray (1936) 137, 156
The Island of Dr. Moreau (novel) 35, 36, 60, 83
Island of Lost Men (1939) 87
Island of Lost Souls (1932) 8, 32, 35, 36, 125, 147, 150, **162**, 180, 181, 189, 197; and the BBFC 86; and the Production Code 83–86; reissue 86–87; **163**; *see also* Isle of Lost Souls
Isle of Lost Souls (script) 34, 60
Isle of the Dead (1945) 188

Jancovich, Mark 8
Janus Films 97
Jenson, Paul 80, 81, 82
Johnson, Noble **30**
Johnson, Tom 5, 15, 51, 70, 79, 96, 98, 101, 130

Jouvi, Jack 168
Joy, Jason 19, 20, 28, 29, 31, 33, 35, 36, 48, 49, 53, 54, 57–60, 65, 66, 68, 70, 71, 72, 73, 81, 83–86, 89, 142–151, 160
Joyce-Selznick Agency 136

Kansas State Board of Censors 29, 59, 73, 106, 117, 122, 145, 146, 147, 175
Karloff, Boris 9, **9**, **11**, 14, 16, 26, 38, **47**, 62, 73, 75, 76, **77**, **78**, 79, 81, **81**, **82**, 103, 104, 106, 107, 108, **112**, **113**, 119, 120, **121**, 122, 124, 125, 140, **154**, 156, **157**, **177**, 181
Keats, John 54
Kenton, Erle C. 8, 84
Kilpatrick, Tom 103
King Kong (1933) 2, 36, 37, 38, 59, 67, 84, 92–97, **95**, 118
The King of Kings (1927) 23
King of the Jungle (1932) 100, 101, 147
Kirby, David A. 85
Klinger, Barbara 195–197, 200
Kohner, Paul 136
Kongo (1932) 74, 147
Krellberg, S.S. 160
Krieger, Paul 117
Kuhn, Irene 74, 75

A Lady of Resource (unproduced film) 24
Laemmle, Carl, Jr. 7, 8, 19, 20–23, 26, 35, 41–50, 55–60, 71, 72, 79, 80, 82, 83, 88, 102–110, 115, 116, 118, 125, 133, 135–137, 144, 147, 148
Laemmle, Carl, Sr. 5, 8, 12, 21, 23, 26, 28, 29, 37, 41, 42, 45, 46, 49, 71, 79, 102, 105, 108, 133
Laemmle, Edward 35
L'Age d'Or (1930) 52
Lanchester, Elsa **113**, 115
Lang, Fritz 81, 188
Latham, Jack 165
Latham, Maude 36, 86
Laughton, Charles 87, 126, **162**, 163
Law and Order (1931) 57
Leavis, F.R. 190
Legion of Decency 18, 104, 107, 111, 152
Lennig, Arthur 43, 56
LeRoy, Mervyn 65
Levy, José 168, 169
Lewton, Val 191
Library of Congress 73, 118
Lightman, M. A. 21, 31, 145
Lischka, Karl 120
Little Caesar (1931) 18, 145
Little Caesar (novel) 24
The Little Theatre 168, 169
Loews Theaters 17, 18, 60, 63; *see also* MGM
London Daily Telegraph (newspaper) 123, 131
London Times (newspaper) 100, 123

Lord, Father Daniel 143
Lord Chamberlain's Office 107, 169
Lorre, Peter 14, 127, 129, 130, 131, **182**
Los Angeles Times (newspaper) 86
The Lost Squadron (1932) 93
Louis B. Mayer Productions 40
Loy, Myrna 75, 76, **77**, 78, 132
Lubitsch, Ernst 51
Lugosi, Bela 1, 9, **11**, 14, 16, 21, 23, **30**, 32, 38, **43**, 44, 45, 56, **58**, 65, 102, 103, 104, 105, 106, 107, 108, 119, 124, 125, 136, 137, **155**, 176, **177**, **201**
Lui (play) 168
Lunt, Lucille 105

M (1931) 188
MacDonald, Philip 109
MacDowell, James 64
MacLaughlin, T.F. 127
MacQueen, Scott 65, 67, 89, 162
Mad Love (1935) 1, 3, 10, 14, 18, 36, 37, 40, 81, 107, 123, **128**, 170, 180, 181, **182**, 189, 196, 200; as genre parody 124–125; and Production Code 127–131; sadism 182–183; screenplay development 125–127
Maddrey, Joseph 5, 6
Mademoiselle Fifi (play) 168
Mademoiselle Fifi (short story) 168
The Mail Goes Through (1932) 147
Majestic Pictures 36
Maltby, Richard 10, 144, 150, 151, 152, 161, 186, 190, 197
Mamoulian, Rouben 6, 30, 50, 51–53, 55, 145, 164, 166, 167, 172, 174, 178, 179
The Man Who Laughs (1927) 19
Manchester Guardian (newspaper) 82
Maniac (1934) 103
Mank, Gregory William 54, 73, 74, 75, 103, 105, 108, 121, 124, 125, 133, 139
Manners, David 13, 105, 108
Mannix, Eddie 62
Mansfield, Richard 178
March, Frederic **53**, 62, 125, **166**, 179
Marcuse, Herbert 190
Margaret Herrick Library 4, 127
Mark of the Vampire (1935) 123, 130, **155**, 156
Marks, Clarence 119
Marriage Interlude (1931) 23
Martin, Harry 67
Marx, Sam 158
The Mask of Fu Manchu (1932) 32, 73–75, **77**, 132, 147; and the Production Code 76; sensationalism 75–76; state censor cuts 77
Matthews, Lester 14
Maupassant, Guy de 168
Maurey, Max 168
Maxa, Paula 170
Mayer, Carl 157
Mayer, Louis B. 10, 40, 62, 127, 131, 155

McDermid, Finlay 110
Meehan, Leo 26, 50, 62, 64
Méténier, Oscar 167, 168
Metro-Goldwin-Mayer (MGM) 7, 8, 17, 18, 26, 28, 30, 32, 35, 40, 46, 55, 60, 61, 63, 64, 67, 73–78, 93, 102, 106, 121–125, 127–132, 155, 157, 158, 160, 182
Meyrinck, Gustav 103
Miller, Allen C. 60
Miller, Seton I. 99
Milliken, Carl 23, 67, 159
Milne, Tom 51, 55, 193
Miracles for Sale (1939) 61
Mirbeau, Octave 202
The Mirror (newspaper) 101
Moffitt, John C. 29
Monogram Pictures 7, 102
Monster Kid generation 3, 67
Monsters and Mad Scientists (book) 3, 191–193
Montagne, E.J. 56
Montgomery, Robert 74
Moore, Eva 71, **72**
Morley, Karen 75, 76
The Most Dangerous Game (1932) 32, 35, 67, 71, **69**, 124, 148, 176, 181; and the Production Code 68–70; trophy room scene 71
The Most Dangerous Game (short story) 60, 67
Motion Picture Daily (newspaper) 119, 122, 129, 136
Motion Picture Herald (newspaper) 3, 26, 29, 32, 34, 38, 50, 62, 66, 70, 86, 91, 93, 97, 100, 130, 137, **138**
Motion Picture News (journal) 44
Motion Picture Producers and Distributors of America (MPPDA) 23, 37, 49, 59, 64, 67, 71, 71, 83, 84, 102, 104, 106, 112, 117, 142, 150, 151, 156, 163; *see also* Hays Office; Production Code Administration; Studio Relations Committee
Motion Picture Research Council 21, 151
Motion Picture Theater Owners of America 21, 31, 145
Movie Classic (magazine) 38, 75, 137
Movies and Conduct (report) 33, 146
Mullaly, Don 89
The Mummy (1932) 32, 47, 75, **78**, 78–79, **81**, 124, 147, 148; issues of authorship 80–81; off-screen space 81–83
Murder by the Clock (1931) 24, 93
Murdered Alive (play) 32
Murders in the Rue Morgue (1932) 1, 6, 15, 16, 21–23, **25**, 26, 28, **30**, 31–33, 37, 44, 47, 55–56, 60, 79, 84, 124, 142, 145–147, 167, 170, 175, 177, 178, 181, 189, 201; reissue 161; retakes and re-editing 57; shadow-play 176; soundtrack 58–59; and state censors 59

Murders in the Zoo (1933) 15, 16, 37, **98**, 98–101, 142, 160; marketing 100–101; reissue 160; script development 99–100
Murnau, F.W. 81, 171
Murphy, Dudley 42
The Mysterious Fu Manchu (1929) 74
Mystery of the Wax Museum (1933) 3, 33, 34, 39, 40, 64, 67, 87–88, **92**, 124, 125, 148, 150, 176, 180, 187, 189; combining film cycle elements 89; "final couple" ending 90–91

Nagana (1932) 147
Narboni, Paul 190, 194–195
The Nation (newspaper) 39, 64
National Board of Review Magazine 139
The National Council on Freedom from Censorship 39
National Films Registry 118
National Industrial Recovery Act 17, 37, 151
Naylor, Alex 137, 139, 141, 153, 156, 159
Ndalianis, Angela 194
Neely Anti-Block Booking and Blind Bidding Bill 87
New Deal 8, 37, 38, 102
The New Movie Magazine 36
New York Board of Censors 28, 30, 59, 73, 77, 96, 97, 100, 106, 115, 117, 146
New York Daily News (newspaper) 82
New York Times (newspaper) 26, 31, 60, 77, 82, 86, 91, 98
Nice Women (1931) 23
Nichols, Dudley 80
Night of the Living Dead (1968) 189, 190
Night on Lonely Mountain (1935) 130
Nightmares in Red, White and Blue (book) 5
Nosferatu (1922) 171

O'Brien, Willis 93
Ochoa, George 181
Ode to a Nightingale (poem) 54
Office of the Censor (Universal Pictures) 112, 114
Ohio State Censor 33, 73, 91, 106, 115, 117, 118, 122, 147, 151
The Old Dark House (1932) 3, 32, 35, 40, **72**, 125, 142, 160; and the Production Code 71–73
The Omen (1976)
One More River (1934) 109, 111, 115
Orpheum (film theater) 31
Ottiano, Rafaela 170
Our Gang (1931) 22
Our Movie Made Children (report) 151

Pantages Theater 106
Paramount Pictures 7, 17, 18, 20,

24, 28, 30, 34–36, 50–55, 56, 60, 61, 74, 83–87, 89, 98–101, 102, 109, 132, 150, 152, 160, 162, 163, 166, 179, 181
Pasolini, Pier Paolo 167
Payne Fund Studies 21, 33, 146, 151
Pearson, Edmund 109
Peeping Tom (1960) 183
Peirse, Alison 79, 82
Pettijohn, CC. 59, 147
The Phantom of the Opera (1925) 19, 89, 125, 146, 176
The Phantom President (1932) 84
Phillips, Kendall 45, 199
Photoplay (magazine) 62, 107
Pichel, Irving 70
The Picture of Dorian Gray (novel) 51
Picturegoer (magazine) 185, 186
Pierce, Jack **81**, 120, 180, 181
Pierron, Agnès 168, 170
Pinedo, Isabel Cristina 3, 12, 184, 190–194
The Pit and the Pendulum (short story) 119
Plague of the Zombies (1966) 189
Poe, Edgar Allan 6, 56, 102, 103, 107, 118, 119, 123, 124, 189
Portrait of a Man with Red Hair (play) 169
"Poverty Row" 31, 102
Pre-Code Hollywood: Sex, Immorality, and Insurrection in American Cinema, 1930-1934 (book) 6, 33, 197
Prince, Stephen 6, 53, 57, 59, 83, 105, 114, 115, 116, 143, 145, 146, 149, 150, 159, 164, 173, 176, 177, 181, 198
Producers' Releasing Corporation 102
Production Code 1–3, 7, 10, 13, 14, 16, 18, 20, 21, 27, 28, 30, 38, 43–45, 51–54, 57, 63–68, 70–73, 79, 81–89, 92, 96, 100–106, 110–117, 120–123, 127–130, 133, 135, 136, 139, 152–153, 155–160, 162–164, 170–176, 198, 204; and "gruesomeness" loophole 141–143; and pre-Code horror films 143–151; the Reaffirmation 37, 151–152; *see also* Hays Code
Production Code Administration (PCA) 3, 7, 8, 10, 11, 24, 37–39, 54, 55, 63, 64, 67, 73, 79, 86, 96, 104–106, 108–112, 114–116, 118, 120–124, 127, 129, 130–133, 135, 137, 139, 140, 141–145, 149, 151-152, 175–179, 181–185, 187, 200, 204; and horror pictures 153–159; and reissues of horror pictures 159–163
Projected Fears: Horror Films and American Culture (book) 199
Psyche Revived by Cupid's Kiss (painting) 172
Psycho (1960) 1, 166, 168, 182, 183, 185, 186, 187, 191, 194
The Public Enemy (1931) 33, 145
Putnam, Nina Wilcox 79

Quigley, Martin 142, 152

Rains, Claude **149**
Rasputin and the Empress (1932) 75
The Raven (1935) 1, 10, 11, **11**, 12, 13, 14, 18, 37, 107, 118–120, 125, 130, 131, 155, 175, 181, 182, 189; and censorship backlash 122–124; and the Production Code 120–121; self-referential sadism 119; tag ending 14, 121–122
The Raven (poem) 119
RCA (sound system) 19
Recreational Terror (book) 3, 12
Red Dust (1932) 74, 75
Red-Headed Woman (1932) 74
Reed, Tom 56, 108, 110
Regal Distributing Corporation 160
Remember Last Night? (1935) 133
Renard, Maurice 125
Rennahan, Ray 88
Republic Pictures 7, 102
The Return of Frankenstein (unproduced scripts) 102, 107, 109, 110, 112, 113, 165
The Return of Fu Manchu (1930) 74
Revolt of the Zombies (1936) 156, 160
Rhodes, Gary D. 4, 22, 41, 42, 44, 45, 107
Riley, Philip J. 118
Ritz Theater 70
RKO Downtown Theater 24
RKO Studios 17, 18, 24, 34, 37, 41, 60, 67, 68, 70, 71, 80, 88, 92–97, 102, 124, 147, 148, 152
Robbins, Tod 60
Robert Florey: The French Expressionist (book) 167
Robertson, Arnot E. 68
Robertson, James C. 86, 130
Rogell, Albert S. 8
Rogers, Charles 8, 88, 123, 136, 139
Rohauer, Raymond 55
Rohmer, Sax 74
Roman Catholic Church 17, 24, 151, 152
Romantic Movie Stories (periodical) 119
Roosevelt, Franklin D. 8, 10, 17, 36, 37, 38, 87, 97, 101, 102, 151
Rope (1948) 186
Rose, Ruth 80, 93
Rosenberg, George 66
Roxy (film theater) 21, 122, 130
Ruggles, Charles 15, 99, 101
R.U.R (play) 30
Ruric, Peter 103, 104, 105, 106, 108
Russell, Lillian 114, 120

Salo, or the 120 Days of Sodom (1975) 167
Savada, Elias 32, 60, 61
Savini, Tom 181
Scarface (1932) 19, 20, 31, 33, 145
Schaefer, Eric 63, 64
Schary, Dore 121

Schatz, Thomas 5, 12, 37, 38, 40, 41, 46, 48, 90, 107, 139
Schayer, Richard 46, 47, 48, 49, 79, 80, 103, 157, 167, 170
Schenck, Nick 60, 62, 63
Schoedsack, Ernest B. 67, 70
Schulberg, B.P. 35, 36, 50, 51, 52, 53, 54, 83, 84, 145
Schwaab, Herbert 167
Screen Gems *Shock* 124
Screenland (magazine) 33
Seattle Censorship Board 59, 147
Selznick, David O. 41, 46, 67, 68, 70, 71, 93, 96, 97, 131–133, 136, 148
Selznick, Lewis J. 46
Senn, Bryan 57, 65, 75, 83, 118
Sennwald, Andre 98
A Serbian Film (2010) 167
70,000 Witnesses (1932) 88, 89, 99
The Shadow (radio show) 23
Shame of Temple Drake (1933) 100
She: A History of Adventure (book) 80
She Done Him Wrong (1933) 100
Sheldon, E. Lloyd 99
Shelley, Mary 47
Sherman, Lowell 103
Sherriff, R.C. 110, 132–136
Shock! Theater (TV) 3, 4, 73, 140, 186; *see also* Screen Gems *Shock*
Shortt, Edward 86
Shortt, Nora 134
Show Boat (1929) 19, 118
Show Boat (1936) 136
Shurlock, Geoffrey 85, 112, 114, 135
The Sign of the Cross (1932) 98, 100, 132
Simmons, Michael 119
Singerman, Sydney 73
Six Hours to Live (1932) 147
Skal David J. 7, 61, 80
Skinner, B.O. 33, 60, 91, 117, 118, 147, 151
Smith, Angela M. 180, 181
Smith, Dick 181
Snelson, Tim 8
Son of Frankenstein (1939) 11, 123, 139, 159
Song of Joy (unproduced film) 136
The Song of Songs (1933) 100
Spigelgass, Leonard 112
Spurs (short story) 60
Standard Capital Corporation 88, 123, 136
Starrett, Charles 76, **77**
Stein, Elliot 43, 165
Stevenson, Robert Louis 24, 35, 50, 51, 166
Stoker, Bram 41, 70, 131, 132, 133
Stone, Lewis 76
Strange as It Seems (film shorts series) 23
Strickling, Howard 74
Stuart, Gloria 71, **72**, 73
Stromberg, Hunt 74, 75, 77
Studio Relations Committee (SRC) 7, 20, 29, 35, 48, 52, 53, 56, 57–59, 71, 76, 84, 85, 104–106, 141–

152, 160, 163, 175, 176, 178, 179, 189, 198; see also Hays Office
The Suicide Club (novel) 24, 26, 35, 79, 107
Sullavan, Margaret 103
Susan Lennox (1931) 74
Sutherland, Edward 136, 137

Tarzan and His Mate (1934) 106
Tarzan, the Ape Man (1932) 26, 67, 92, 93
Tasker, Robert 65, 66
Taurog, Norman 84
Taves, Brian 167, 170
Technicolor 66, 67, 88, 91, 92, 150
Terrett, Courtenay 74, 75
The Texas Chain Saw Massacre (1974) 1
Thalberg, Irving 2, 8, 44, 57, 74, 76, 142, 143, 203; and *Freaks* 60–64; and preview-retake system 40–41
Thaw, Cornelia **42**
Théâtre du Grand Guignol 167–170, 172
Thesiger, Ernest **112**
Thorndike, Russell 168
Thorndike, Sybil 168
Three Came Unarmed (novel) 68
Time (magazine) 106
Today's Cinema (trade journal) 77
Totaro, Donato 10
Tracy, Lee 65
Tree, Dorothy **42**
Trotti, Lamar 66, 68, 144, 148
Tudor, Andrew 3, 12, 182–184, 191–193, 202
Tully, Dr. Jim 119
Tunberg, Karl Owen 50
Turner, George E. 70, 71
Turner Classic Movies 15, 101, 198
Turner-MGM Collection 127

Ulmer, Edgar G. 8, 9, 13, 14, 102–108, 164, 167, 178
The Unholy Three (1925) 60
United Artists 18, 34, 35
Universal Horrors (book) 82
Universal Pictures 1, 2, 5, 7, 8, 11, 12, 16–21, 23–26, 28, 29, 32, 35, 38, 40, 41–50, 56, 58–60, 63, 65, 72, 73, 75, 78, 79, 80, 82–84, 86–88, 97, 101–112, 116–125, 131–137, 139, 140, 144–147, 152, 153, 155, 156, 159, 160, 162, 163, 165, 167, 169, 170, 175, 176, 179, 180, 181, 186, 189, 193, 200, 204
Universal Weekly (magazine) 102, 105, 109, 111

The Vampire Bat (1933) 36, 96, 198
Vampires of Prague (screenplay) 155; see also *Mark of the Vampire*
Vampyr [1932] 96
Vandervoort, Katherine 163
Van Every, Dale 56, 103, 108
Van Sloan, Edward 50
Van Sternberg, Josef 51
Variety (trade journal) 17, 21, 24, 26, 27, 29, 30, 31, 32, 33, 35, 36, 37, 54, 55, 57, 60, 74, 77, 78, 87, 89, 91, 106, 119, 123, 125, 129, 130, 136, 137, 139, 141, 143, 144
Veidt, Conrad 125
Veiller, Bayard 74
Vidor, Charles 74, 75
Vieira, Mark 45, 80
Vitagraph 46
Vollmer, August 22
Von Stroheim, Erich 157

The Walking Dead (1936) 2, 141, 156, 157, 159
Wall Street Crash 142
Wallace, Edgar 93, 94, 97
Walpole, Hugh 168
Ware, Irene 14
Warner, Harry 101
Warner, Jack 65, 66, 148
Warner Bros. 7, 17, 18, 32, 33, 34, 35, 41, 60, 65–67, 87–92, 97, 101, 102, 147, 150, 151, 152, 156, 157, 163, 178; see also First National Pictures
The Wax Museum (play) 88, 89
The Wax Works (short story) 88
Waxman, Franz 112
Weaver, Tom 15, 16, 73, 82, 103, 104, 124
Webling, Peggy 46, 47
Wells, H.G. 35, 36, 56, 60, 83, 84
Wells, Jacqueline 13, 105, 175

Werewolf of London (1935) 120, 121, 123, 130, 155; "transvection scenes" 178–179
The Werewolf of Paris (novel) 119
West, Mae 153
West of Zanzibar (1928) 74
Westmore, Wally **85**, 86, 181
Westwick Village Theater 54
Whale, James 6, 7, 8, 12, 13, 48, 49, 55, 56, 59, 73, 82, 102, 108–118, 133, 136, 161, 165, 166, 170, 172–175, 204
White Zombie (1932) 32, 34, 35, 142, 160, 189
Wiene, Robert 125
Wilde, Oscar 51
Wilkinson Joseph Brooke 135
Willard, John 75
Williams, Linda 199
Wilson, John V. 52, 53
Wilson, Michael 168, 169, 171, 172, 202
Wingate, James 30, 35, 36, 76, 77, 85, 86, 89, 90, 150, 151, 154, 178
The Wolfman (1941) 180
Wolfson, P.J. 125
Wometco 138
Wood, Robin 3, 14, 15, 184, 185, 190–192, 193, 194, 195, 202
Woodring, Harry H. 29
Woolf, Edgar Allan 75
Worland, Rick 13, 14, 49
World-Telegram (newspaper) 101
World War I 9, 10, 165, 167, 169
World War II 7, 86, 168, 184
World Wide Pictures 35
Wrangell, Basil 62
Wray, Fay 37, 67, 94, **95**, 180
Wunder, Clinton 22
Wylie, Philip 84, 99

Les Yeux Sans Visage (1959) 168
Young, Waldemar 84

Zanuck, Darryl F. 33, 41, 65, 66, 89, 148, 150
Zehner, Harry 104, 105, 106, 110, 114–118, 120, 121, 135, 136, 160, 161
Zeidman, B.F. 119
Zukor, Adolph 24, 101

www.ingramcontent.com/pod-product-compliance
Ingram Content Group UK Ltd.
Pitfield, Milton Keynes, MK11 3LW, UK
UKHW050532150426
5217IPUK00026B/1906